THE
GRAIN
BRAIN
WHOLE LIFE
PLAN

THE
GRAIN
BRAIN
WHOLE LIFE
PLAN

Boost Brain Performance, Lose Weight,
and Achieve Optimal Health

BY DR DAVID PERLMUTTER

WITH KRISTIN LOBERG

yellow
kite

First published in Great Britain in 2016 by Yellow Kite
An imprint of Hodder & Stoughton
An Hachette UK company

First published in the USA in 2016 by Little, Brown and Company

A CIP catalogue record for this title is available from the British Library

Trade Paperback ISBN 978 1 473 64777 0
eBook ISBN 978 1 473 64778 7

Printed and bound by Clays Ltd, St Ives plc

Hodder & Stoughton policy is to use papers that are natural, renewable and recyclable products and made from wood grown in sustainable forests. The logging and manufacturing processes are expected to conform to the environmental regulations of the country of origin.

Yellow Kite
Hodder & Stoughton Ltd
Carmelite House
50 Victoria Embankment
London EC4Y 0DZ

www.yellowkitebooks.co.uk

This book is dedicated to my wife, Leize.
To be blessed by your love is the brightest light of my life.

Contents

INTRODUCTION   You've Come to This Book for a Reason   3

PART I
WELCOME TO THE GRAIN BRAIN WHOLE LIFE PLAN

CHAPTER 1   What Is the Grain Brain Whole Life Plan?   11

CHAPTER 2   The Chief Goals   19

CHAPTER 3   The Food Rules   42

PART II
THE GRAIN BRAIN WHOLE LIFE PLAN ESSENTIALS

CHAPTER 4   Getting Started: Assess Your Risk
             Factors, Know Your Numbers, and
             Prepare Your Mind   67

CHAPTER 5   Step 1—Edit Your Diet and Pill-Popping   87

CHAPTER 6   Step 2—Add Your Support Strategies   119

Contents

CHAPTER 7   Step 3—Plan Accordingly   165

CHAPTER 8   Troubleshooting   175

PART III
LET'S EAT!

CHAPTER 9   Final Reminders and Snack Ideas   191

CHAPTER 10   The 14-Day Meal Plan   200

CHAPTER 11   The Recipes   209

ACKNOWLEDGMENTS   263

SELECTED BIBLIOGRAPHY   265

INDEX   281

THE
GRAIN
BRAIN
WHOLE LIFE
PLAN

You've Come to This Book for a Reason

YOU CAN CHOOSE YOUR HEALTH destiny. Whether it's effortless weight loss. Freedom from neurological disorders and other chronic conditions. Boundless energy. A radiant appearance. Sound sleep. A happy belly. A robust immune system. Relief from depression and anxiety. A sharp, fast-thinking brain. A great sense of self-confidence and well-being. A super-high quality of life....

These are all terrific goals, and my bet is you're hoping to achieve them yourself soon enough. People who've followed my protocols in the past have indeed experienced these results. Seriously. But to be sure: Such monumental accomplishments don't come without hard work and sacrifices. You can't necessarily turn away from a standard Western diet— bread, fizzy drinks, OJ, sugar, cereal, muffins, bagels, processed foods—and embrace a totally gluten-free, low-carb lifestyle overnight. It takes commitment. It takes effort. But it's doable with this book in your personal library.

More than a million people around the world have improved their health—physical, mental, and cognitive—thanks to *Grain Brain*, a book that became an instant bestseller. The book was followed by *Brain Maker*, another instant bestseller that added to the conversation by highlighting the importance of the human microbiome—the trillions of microbes that inhabit the gut—to our health. Now the time has come to bring these two forces together in a highly practical, step-by-step holistic lifestyle program.

Welcome to *The Grain Brain Whole Life Plan*.

The main purpose of this book is to help you put my ideas into practice in the real world and to show you that living your best life is about much more than what you put in your mouth. It expands upon the core advice in my previous works and introduces exciting new information about the advantages of eating more fat and fiber, consuming fewer carbs and protein, evicting gluten forever, and catering to your intestinal flora. Included in the book are a bounty of delicious original recipes, tips for addressing unique challenges, a 14-day easy-to-follow meal plan, and advice about habits beyond the diet. From sleep hygiene to stress management, exercise, supplements, and more, *The Grain Brain Whole Life Plan* details how to live happily and healthily ever after.

Grain Brain and *Brain Maker* share the foundation of my general nutritional recommendations, complete with all the scientific evidence supporting them. I highly recommend you read these books if you haven't already before tackling this program. They tell you the WHY part of the story in rich detail. *The Grain Brain Whole Life Plan* offers the HOW. If you've read my previous works, you'll hear some echoes in these pages, but that's intentional. The reminders will reinforce your motivation to change, or to keep up the good work.

My ideas may have seemed out there when I began writing *Grain Brain* in 2012, but since then, not only have they been validated over and over again in the scientific literature, but also more extensive science has emerged, which I'll address in this work. Even the U.S. government has modified its dietary guidelines to reflect this research, backpedaling away from endorsing low-fat, low-cholesterol diets and moving closer to my way of eating.

Another new theme in this book that I haven't covered previously is weight loss. Although I didn't strongly promise weight loss before, I know from thousands of people who took the tenets of *Grain Brain* and *Brain Maker* to heart that weight loss is one of the most common, immediate outcomes of the program. And the weight loss can be huge. You won't feel like you're on a dreaded diet, you won't feel an insatiable hunger, but the pounds will melt away.

I was motivated to write this book from my own personal experience, too. I have tried my best to do everything possible to remain healthy. But now in my sixties, I've experienced my own health issues, and I have learned how to navigate through them successfully within the context of my own principles. I started to think about this book as an opportunity to get myself into the very best shape for the next forty years. Like anyone my age, I'm certainly at risk for all the common disorders. And, by virtue of my family history, I have a higher risk for Alzheimer's disease. But I know I am reducing my risk and stacking the deck in my favor by following the strategies presented in these pages. I want to show you what I have learned and what I do day in and day out.

Some of you are coming to this with the assumption that it is just another diet and lifestyle book that will test your willpower and resolve for a finite period. I'm delighted to disappoint you on that front. *The Grain Brain Whole Life Plan* gives you a jump-start to a healthy way of living that you will be able to sustain indefinitely.

Food is a central component of the program, but so are other key aspects to achieving the best results: the timing of *when* you eat, sleep, and exercise; skipping breakfast once or twice a week; knowing which supplements to take and which medications to potentially drop; reducing daily stress and even chemical exposures in your physical environment; nurturing relationships and your own self-care; addressing the challenges in life with grace and ease; routinely creating goals for your personal development; and finding time for the kinds of physical activities that power the brain while healing the body.

Part I explains the what, why, and how of the program. I'll detail the ground rules, present new data, and offer a 3-step framework that will help you execute my recommendations. You'll start, however, with a prelude to Step 1, during which you will perform a self-assessment to gauge your risk factors, undergo some laboratory tests, and prepare your mind. The main steps are as follows:

Step 1: **Edit** your diet and pill-popping.
Step 2: **Add** your support strategies.
Step 3: **Plan** accordingly.

Part II gives you all the information you need to follow my program, from which foods to eat to which supplements to take and how to leverage the power of sleep, physical movement, and other stress-reducing strategies that will enhance your success.

In Part III, you'll find final tips and reminders, a menu of snack ideas, a basic shopping list, the 14-day meal plan, and delicious recipes to enjoy on your journey. For ongoing support and additional resources, go to www.DrPerlmutter.com.

ON A PERSONAL NOTE

Before we jump into the science in the coming pages, I'd like to share something personal. A lot has happened to me since *Grain Brain* was first published in 2013. In 2015 I lost my dear father, once a brilliant neurosurgeon, to Alzheimer's disease. I also closed my medical practice and took to spreading my message through teaching, the media, and the lecture circuit. I've had the privilege of collaborating with the world's top experts in various fields of clinical medicine and biomedical research whose work further reinforces my recommendations (You'll be reading about some of these people in the book; for videos of my interviews with many of them, please visit www.DrPerlmutter.com/learn).

In early 2016, I came to grips with the sudden, tragic loss of a beloved friend. This was followed by a medical crisis of my own as I lay in the intensive care unit. You'll read about this event later in this book, but suffice it to say that it radically changed my perspective. It vividly taught me the perils of stress and the power of love. And it reinforced the notion that having a healthy mind and body goes far beyond what we eat and how much we exercise.

The day after I was discharged from the hospital, I went to a yoga class with my wife and her mother. At the end of the class, the instructor read a moving passage that struck me right away. It came from the book *How Yoga Works* and basically said that in order for us to reach our highest goals in life, we should try to maintain "...a constant, modest, joyful state of mind which is always looking for ways to protect others from harm—all day long, just in the little world we live in."

Although I am no longer directly involved in patient care on a daily basis, in moving forward, I believe my purpose will be to do just that—to continue to write, lecture, teach, learn, and do my best to protect you from harm. I will keep connecting with people, hearing their stories of transformation, and cheering them on. It's incredibly gratifying to know that I can change people's lives for the better—no surgery or prescription required. May you, too, be a changed person through the execution of a few practical strategies. By reading this book, you are already getting a head start on the path to a better, healthier future.

So no matter what brings you to this book, whether you are concerned for your own health or that of a loved one, rest assured that you have an amazing opportunity right in front of you. And despite your trepidations, this isn't that hard. You've done more difficult things in your life, for sure. Maybe you've given birth, raised a child, cared for someone with special needs, run a company, eulogized a loved one, or battled a serious illness such as cancer. Just getting through life's day-to-day battles is challenging enough. So pat yourself on the back because you've gotten this far, and know that what lies ahead can positively and profoundly change your life for the better.

All that I ask of you at this point is to accept the commitment. You will change your relationship with lots of things in your life, from food to people. You will create new habits and traditions. You will transform how you live your life and reap the ultimate rewards: reaching all those goals I listed earlier. You will not be counting down the days of my 14-day meal plan, waiting for it to end, or suddenly feel like you're force-feeding yourself foods you can't stand no matter how they are prepared. Much to the contrary, you will proceed at your own pace and learn a new way of life that's doable and sustainable *for you* by making a few adjustments to your daily habits.

Take it one day, one new habit, at a time. Be patient and kind with yourself. I have a friend who is also a doctor, and he likes to ask his patients this question: "Who is the most important person in the world?" If they don't answer with a resounding "I am," he teaches them that lesson. Because that's the truth: You are the most important person in the world. Admit that. Live up to that. You deserve it. Choose health. That's the first step to take on the path to radiant wellness.

Welcome to *The Grain Brain Whole Life Plan*. Now let's get going.

PART I

WELCOME TO THE GRAIN BRAIN WHOLE LIFE PLAN

I was given Grain Brain *and* Brain Maker *as birthday presents on January 22, 2016, when I reached age seventy-one, and started a gluten-free, sugar-free, high-fat diet on February 1. After twenty-five days, I have solved two of the three "neurological" health problems I had: left arm trembling while leaning [it] on the arm of a chair, loss of equilibrium, and memory deterioration. The first two are now gone, but for the memory recovery I cannot yet claim an improvement, but I am hopeful. Further, I would like to think that maybe I have improved my speech as well, since before the diet I was reaching the point where it was difficult to have a fluent conversation, because my brain and mouth simply could not speak to each other. I have also lost 3 kilograms [about 6½ pounds] of weight!* —Antonio L.

CHAPTER 1

What Is the Grain Brain Whole Life Plan?

IN THE NEXT EIGHTEEN MINUTES, *four Americans will die from the food they eat.* That's one person every four-and-a-half minutes, a fact that's almost impossible to comprehend. But it's heartbreakingly true. That statement was how celebrity chef Jamie Oliver opened his eighteen-minute TED talk a few years ago, stunning the audience and the millions of people who have since watched his video. Oliver has been leading a crusade against the use of processed foods in schools, and he is a staunch advocate for children's rights to wholesome, healthy fare that won't lead to a lifetime of chronic conditions, pain, and illness. It has been postulated that today's generation of children may not live to as ripe an old age as their parents, largely due to the downstream effects of obesity.

But it's not just about children. In developed Western nations, diet-related diseases kill more people than accidents, murder, terrorism, war, *and all other diseases (not diet-related) combined.* Overweight, obesity, type 2 diabetes, high blood pressure, heart disease, dental diseases, strokes, osteoporosis, dementia, and many types of cancer can all be linked somehow to diet. Some of these afflictions have been around for centuries, but not in such epidemic proportions.

I decided to be a neurologist – a doctor who specializes in brain disorders – more than thirty-five years ago. In the early years of my work, I practiced under the idea of "diagnose and adios" for the most part. In other words, once I made a diagnosis I often found that I couldn't offer much to my patients in terms of a treatment, much less a cure. There wasn't anything available at the time, and that was immensely disappointing both for me as a physician and them as patients. I am here to tell you, however, that a lot has changed since then. But it's not all positive. Let me first put a few more facts into perspective.

As you may be aware, over the past century science has made great progress in many areas of medicine. One hundred years ago, the top three causes of death came from infectious germs: pneumonia and flu, tuberculosis, and gastrointestinal infections. Today few of us die from contagions; the top causes of death are noncommunicable illnesses that are *largely preventable*: cerebrovascular disease, heart disease, and cancer. Sadly, while we've made some strides in reducing the rates of some of these chronic illnesses thanks to better prevention and pharmaceuticals, not much has revolutionized my field: averting and treating brain disorders. And these present some of the biggest challenges in medicine. Throughout my career, there have been so many times when I've had to tell patients that I have nothing left in my arsenal to treat them—they have a grave neurological disease that will likely shatter their life and the lives of those they love.

Despite billions of dollars of research, we've had no meaningful treatments or cures for conditions like Alzheimer's disease, Parkinson's disease, depression, ADHD, autism, multiple sclerosis, and so many others. Even chronic conditions like obesity and diabetes, which affect tens of millions today and which are indeed connected to brain disorders, don't have reliable therapies and remedies. A whopping one in five deaths in America is now attributed to obesity, which is among the biggest risk factors for brain-related ailments. You might be surprised to learn that obesity is really a form of malnutrition. As counterintuitive as it sounds, people are overfed and undernourished.

The United States is among the ten wealthiest Western nations where death from brain disease – most commonly dementia – has sky-rocketed over the past twenty years. In fact, it leads the way. Since 1979, deaths in America due to brain disease increased an astounding 66 percent in men and 92 percent in women. In America today, it's estimated that 5.4 million people are living with Alzheimer's disease, and that number is predicted to *double* by the year 2030! Someone in the United States develops the disease every 66 seconds; it kills more than breast and prostate cancer combined.

More than 26 percent of adults in the United States — that's about one in four people — suffer from a diagnosable mental illness, from anxiety and mood issues to psychotic disorders, bipolar disorder, and full-blown depression, which is now a leading cause of disability world-wide. One in four women in their prime takes an antidepressant, and may end up staying on that medication for the rest of her life.

When was the last time you had a headache? Yesterday? Right now? Headaches are among the most common brain ailments, and by some estimates they are the number one ailment. More people complain about headaches than any other medical problem. Although nearly everyone has a headache occasionally, one in twenty people has a headache every single day. And an incredible 10 percent of Americans suffer from debili-tating migraine headaches — more than diabetes and asthma combined.

Multiple sclerosis (MS), a debilitating autoimmune disease that dis-rupts the brain's and spinal cord's ability to communicate, affects an estimated 2.5 million people worldwide. Nearly half a million of those patients are in America. The average lifetime cost of treating someone with MS exceeds $1.2 million, and mainstream medicine tells us that there is no cure in sight. Aside from MS, autoimmune disorders in general have been on the rise. I find it interesting and quite telling that, according to people who study ancient diseases, or paleopathologists, humans did not suffer from many autoimmune disorders before the adoption of an agricultural way of life. Autoimmune disease was not nearly as pervasive in the population as it is today. Some autoimmune diseases are three times more common now than they were several decades ago—especially in developed countries like the United States. I love how Lierre Keith, author of *The Vegetarian Myth*, explains it: "That's because it's grains that can turn the body against itself. Agriculture has devoured us as surely as it has devoured the world."

Attention deficit hyperactivity disorder, also known simply as ADHD, has been diagnosed in more than 4 percent of American adults and well over 6 million American children, and an astounding two-thirds of these children are taking mind-altering medications, the long-term consequences of which have never been studied. In fact, 85 percent of the ADHD medicines used across the entire planet are used in America. This is certainly not something to be proud of. Are Americans genetically different from the rest of the world? Or is there something else going on that may be responsible for their overzealous use of drugs?

We also can't ignore the rising prevalence of autism. One in forty-five children age three through seventeen has been diagnosed with autism spectrum disorder (ASD). In boys, ASD is about 4.5 times more common than in girls. The surge in the number of diagnosed cases over the past fifteen years has led some experts to call it a modern-day epidemic. What is going on?

Why have we experienced such a disturbing spike in these afflictions over the past few decades? Why the lack of cures and better treatments? How can only one in one hundred of us get through life without a mental impairment, let alone a headache or two? With so many scientists and so much funding, why has there been so little progress? The answer may simply be that we have been looking in the wrong place. The solution to these challenging disorders may well lie *outside* the brain, and even *outside the body*:

It's in our food.

It's in our gut.

It's in how we live each day and deal with our commitments and responsibilities.

It's in how we move our bodies and stay active, strong, mobile, flexible, and agile.

It's in how we deal with setbacks, illness, injury, and pain.

It's in our relationships and social engagements.

It's in our outlook on life.

And it's in this book.

The Grain Brain Whole Life Plan gives you a way to take control of your mind, body, and spirit. It's a solution to these challenging health problems. It's a way of life. I should emphasize from the get-go that it doesn't just address brain disorders. As I've detailed in previous works, virtually every noncommunicable disease has a lot in common. So whether we're talking about asthma or Alzheimer's disease, diabetes or depression, you might be surprised to learn about the connections among them. You'll read about that soon.

Now, let me play devil's advocate for a moment. Despite our vast knowledge in medicine today, especially compared to what we knew a century ago, the development of disease within the context of the human body still remains puzzling—even to the most educated, brilliant individuals who stay on top of the scientific literature. There's a lot we've figured out: We've cracked the human genome code, our DNA; we've developed advanced diagnostic tools and revolutionized treatments; and we've produced vaccines, antibiotics, and other antidotes to combat known invaders. But in the face of all this, we can struggle mightily to understand why one person dies relatively young while another lives vigorously past ninety. Or why one individual looks 65 at the age of 85, and another appears to be in her 50s when she's really barely 40. We've all heard of the athlete with no documented risk factors for coronary artery disease who dies suddenly of a heart attack; the lung cancer victim who never smoked; and the slim health-nut who is diagnosed with diabetes or early onset dementia. What explains these phenomena?

We have to accept a certain mystery surrounding the body's functionality and whether or not it becomes sick and enfeebled. We also have to acknowledge that how we choose to live—and think—has a significant effect on our health and psychology. It's far easier, and cheaper, to prevent illness than to treat it once it's established. But there is no such thing as "spot prevention" targeting one specific area; we have to honor the body as a whole, complex unit. That is the main idea underlying this program.

Every day I meet people who've tried everything they can to achieve the health that they want and deserve. These individuals often fall victim to dubious, unproven health practices and poor nutrition, and they don't even know it. They complain of various symptoms that share common themes: low energy, difficulty losing weight, digestive disorders, insomnia, headaches, low libido, depression, anxiety, memory problems, burnout, sore joints, relentless allergies. *The Grain Brain Whole Life Plan* is a rallying cry for anyone who hasn't been able to discover true health and maintain that health indefinitely. All roads to perfect health—and ideal weight—begin with simple lifestyle choices.

As I always say, food is more than fuel for the body to survive. Food is information; what I mean by that is that it ultimately has the power to influence how your personal genome—your DNA—expresses itself. In biology this phenomenon is called epigenetics, a concept we'll be exploring shortly. Epigenetics has transformed the way we think about DNA, as well as about food. On a more basic level, food also helps generate the connection between your mind-set and how you *feel.* What you eat directly impacts how you experience life and nourish your body's needs. What you *do* — in your work, in your environment, in your routines, and in your efforts to reduce stress, manage chronic conditions, and address challenges — also affects your body and whether or not you put yourself in harm's way and at risk for serious health issues. And optimizing your body's innate requirements, my friends, is the essence of *The Grain Brain Whole Life Plan.*

The Grain Brain Whole Life Plan can help all of the following:

- ADHD

- asthma

- autism

- allergies and food sensitivities

- chronic fatigue

- chronic pain

- mood disorders, including depression and anxiety

- diabetes and irrepressible cravings for sugar and carbohydrates

- heartburn and gastroesophageal reflux disease, or GERD

- overweight and obesity, as well as weight-loss struggles

- memory problems and poor concentration

- headaches and migraines

- chronic constipation or diarrhoea

- frequent colds or infections

- intestinal disorders, including celiac disease, irritable bowel syndrome, ulcerative colitis, and Crohn's disease

---

- thyroid dysfunction
- multiple sclerosis
- fibromyalgia
- infertility
- insomnia
- joint pain and arthritis
- high blood pressure
- atherosclerosis
- chronic yeast problems
- skin problems such as acne, eczema, and psoriasis
- bad breath, gum disease, and dental problems
- Tourette's syndrome
- extreme menstrual and menopausal symptoms
- and many more

You don't have to be sick to reap enormous rewards from the plan. Even if you feel relatively good and healthy, you can benefit. So whether you're desperate for a better body and clearer mind or just want to know you're doing all you can to live a healthier, longer life, this program is for you.

Most of you should start to feel the effects of the program within a matter of days. But it will take a little longer for it to have a lasting impact on your body at both the cellular and metabolic levels. It will also take a while to reset your attitude so that you can effortlessly enjoy your new lifestyle. It doesn't matter how often you've failed to follow protocols in the past or how much doubt you have in the effectiveness of my recommendations. What matters is that you focus on your goals and have faith that health and happiness await you.

CHAPTER 2

The Chief Goals

IF YOU'RE LIKE MOST PEOPLE, you can't take time away from your busy life to check into a wellness retreat center or medical spa oasis for a month to concentrate squarely on good nutrition, stress relief, and twice-daily exercise classes worthy of a *Biggest Loser* episode. I've created this book to give you the tools you need to experience maximum results in the shortest period of time. I expect you to continue to go about your daily routine and do your best to make the modifications to your lifestyle that I describe. I will be asking you to start an exercise routine (see page 120) and to seriously consider all the advice I've outlined throughout the book. Some of the strategies will be easy to implement, such as drinking more water throughout the day and keeping a journal to practice gratitude. But some, such as being strict with your sleep schedule, establishing a strength-training routine, spending distraction-free time for self-reflection, and evicting gluten, grains, and sugar from your diet, will likely take time to master. And that's okay. I've included plenty of ideas to help make these strategies doable and practical in today's world.

Unfortunately, many of us live in a highly reactive rather than proactive prevention mode. We avoid taking proper care of ourselves as we chase everything else in life and tend to other responsibilities—and other people. Some of us don't slow down or change our ways until illness or injury strike, and then we are forced to take a detour, if we can find one. We perpetuate negative thinking or say self-sabotaging things to ourselves like "once I achieve X" or "when I make Y dollars, I'll be able to take better care of myself." But as you probably know, this rarely happens in the real world. By the time we're compelled to change, it can be very challenging to do so successfully. And well-meaning intentions to regain health when we could have avoided the problem in the first place don't usually work out the way we want. We can get so run-down and burned out that there's no motivation to do anything but await a serious diagnosis and then come to rely on pharmaceuticals forever. I encounter many people who reach midlife encumbered with chronic conditions or serious illnesses that are not easily treatable or reversible, if at all. Although they may finally have all the resources they need to access high-quality health care, it might be too late. My goal for you is to commence change today to prevent such a fate and relieve any health challenges you currently have so you can enjoy a higher quality of life from here on out. Wouldn't it be wonderful to rely less on drugs and more on your body's natural machinery?

It's amazing to me that in the wake of this epidemic of chronic illness and brain disorders, so few of us stop to think about how our daily lifestyle choices factor into our well-being. It's human nature to prefer the shortcut and ask for a prescription or seek a potion that we believe will make our problems disappear. Yes, there's work and effort involved in choosing to eat a certain way and avoiding the habits that get us into trouble, but it doesn't have to feel like a Herculean task. No sooner do you begin to feel better than you have more motivation to keep going.

So with that in mind, let's take a tour of the chief goals of the program:

- to reduce and control inflammation

- to turn your body into a fat-burning machine using fat

- to balance levels of beneficial bacteria in your belly

- to balance your hormones and increase leptin sensitivity

- to take control of your own genes

- to balance your life

Let's look at each of these goals in turn. I'll remind you of some of the fundamental science as we go.

REDUCE AND CONTROL INFLAMMATION

One of the most paradigm-shifting discoveries in Western science during my career has been that the cornerstone of most diseases and degenerative conditions, including being overweight and being at risk of brain dysfunction, is inflammation. And by now you probably have a rough idea of what "inflammation" means in terms of the body. It's the body's natural healing process whereby it temporarily amps up the immune system to deal with what it thinks is an insult or injury. Whether you're fighting a cold or dealing with a torn muscle, inflammation lies at the heart of your recovery.

The problem with inflammation is that it can become chronic. A water hose turned on momentarily to extinguish a small fire is one thing; but leave the hose on indefinitely, and you've got another problem on your hands. Millions of people are besieged by an inflammatory process that's always in the "on" mode. Their immune systems have been permanently keyed up, but they won't necessarily feel it as they would if they had a laceration or sore throat. This type of inflammation is systemic — it's a slow-boil full-body disturbance that is usually not confined to one particular area. The bloodstream allows it to spread to every part of the body; hence, we have the ability to detect this kind of pervasive inflammation through blood tests.

Many of the biological substances produced as a result of inflammation are injurious to cells, leading to cellular dysfunction and destruction. It's no wonder that the leading scientific research shows that chronic systemic inflammation is a fundamental cause of the morbidity and mortality associated with all manner of disease and virtually every chronic condition you can imagine. Even your mood is affected by inflammation. One of the first things I hear from people I put on my protocol is that it has more than a physiological impact; it has a tremendous psychological effect, too. And new science tells us that mood disorders as severe as depression are, in fact, rooted in inflammation — not necessarily in low or misbehaving brain chemicals.

The Grain Brain Whole Life Plan turns on the pathways in your body that help reduce and control inflammation. You'll be embracing an anti-inflammatory lifestyle and applying basic strategies to your everyday habits that are designed to lower inflammation. Natural substances like those you'll find on this diet (for example, turmeric) have been described in medical literature for more than two thousand years, but it is only in the past decade that we have begun to understand their intricate and eloquent biochemistry. And it's not just what you eat that can help you manage inflammation. You're going to learn about the latest studies on how exercise and sleep come into play, too.

TURN YOUR BODY INTO A FAT-BURNING MACHINE USING FAT

A central premise of *Grain Brain* is that fat — not carbohydrate — is our metabolism's preferred fuel and has been for all of human evolution. I made my case for choosing high-quality fats and not worrying about so-called "high cholesterol" foods. Nutritional therapist Nora Gedgaudas states it perfectly in her book *Primal Body, Primal Mind*: "99.99% of our genes were formed before the development of agriculture." As *Homo sapiens*, we are virtually identical to every human that has walked on the planet. And, as a species, we have been shaped by nature over thousands of generations.

Throughout human evolution, and for the greater part of the last 2.6 million years, our ancestors' diets consisted of wild game and seasonal fruits and vegetables. We sought fat as a calorie-dense food source. It kept us lean and served us well in our hunter-gatherer days. In fact, we consumed a diet estimated to contain as much as ten times more fat than our current intake. Today most people fear dietary fat, equating the idea of eating fat to *being* fat. The truth is quite different. Obesity and its metabolic repercussions have almost nothing to do with dietary fat consumption and everything to do with an addiction to carbs. People continue to gravitate toward "fat-free," "low-fat," "multigrain," and "whole grain" labels, foods that contain ingredients whose downstream effects assault the brain and body. Eating carbohydrates stimulates insulin production, which leads to fat production, fat retention, and a reduced ability to burn fat (much more on insulin shortly). Dietary fat does not do this. What's more, as we consume carbohydrates, we trigger an enzyme called lipoprotein lipase that tends to drive fat into the cell; the insulin secreted when we consume carbohydrates makes matters worse by triggering enzymes that promote fat storage.

> The human dietary requirement for carbohydrate is virtually *zero*.

When I tell people that we can survive — *thrive* — on zero dietary carbohydrates but lots of dietary fat, cholesterol included, I am sometimes met by bewildered faces. But these days, that's changing. Up until quite recently, we had been told that the brain needs glucose to survive and that we supply that nutrient through carbs. The science has finally prevailed, and now it's clear that, yes, the brain needs glucose, but our bodies can make glucose. I repeat: It is the sugar we consume that makes us fat — not the dietary fat.

The same is true of cholesterol: Eating foods high in cholesterol has no impact on our actual cholesterol levels, and the alleged correlation between higher cholesterol levels and higher cardiac risk is untrue. We have been consuming animal protein and saturated fat for the past 100,000 generations. Yet we've been told that saturated fat is dangerous. The fact that approximately 50 percent of the fat in human breast milk is saturated should go a long way to highlight the value and importance of saturated fat.

So what happens when you substantially reduce your carbohydrate intake and derive more of your calories from fat? You turn your body into a fat-burning machine. When you follow a diet low in carbohydrates, minimal in protein, and rich in healthy fats and plant-based fibers, you stimulate the body to use fat rather than glucose for fuel. More specifically, you force the body to turn to specialized substances called ketones for energy. In the absence of carbohydrates, ketones are produced by the liver using fatty acids from your food or body fat. These ketones are then released into the bloodstream, where they can travel to the brain and other organs to be used as fuel. A so-called ketogenic diet — one that derives 80 to 90 percent of calories from fat, and the rest from fibrous carbohydrates (e.g., whole fruits and vegetables) and high-quality protein—is the foundation of the Grain Brain Whole Life Plan.

There is nothing new or faddish about the ketogenic diet. Versions of the diet have been used for centuries, and it may even date back to biblical times. It has been successfully used to treat drug-resistant epilepsy in children since the 1920s. New evidence is emerging from animal research and clinical trials to show that ketogenic diets help treat an array of neurological disorders, from headaches and sleep disorders to bipolar disorder, autism, brain cancer, and other diseases.

Your body is in a state of ketosis when it's creating ketones for fuel instead of relying on glucose. A mild state of ketosis is healthy. We are mildly ketotic when we first wake up in the morning, as our liver is mobilizing body fat to feed our hungry organs. Both the heart and the brain run more efficiently, by as much as 25 percent, on ketones than on blood sugar. The brain's energy needs account for 20 percent of total energy expenditure, and healthy, normal brain cells thrive when fueled by ketones.

Neurological diseases may all have their distinct characteristics and underlying causes, but one feature they share in common is deficient energy production. When the body uses ketones to maintain normal brain cell metabolism, some of those ketones are a more efficient fuel than glucose, as ketones provide more energy per unit of oxygen used. Being in ketosis also amplifies the number of mitochondria in brain cells, the cells' energy factories. Studies have documented that ketosis shores up the hippocampus, the brain's main center for learning and memory. In age-related brain diseases, hippocampus cells often degenerate, leading to cognitive dysfunction and memory loss. But with greater energy reserves, the neurons are better buffered against disease stressors.

I should add that despite entering ketosis, the body's blood glucose levels remain physiologically normal. You won't experience the ills of low blood sugar because the body can derive glucose from certain amino acids and the breakdown of fatty acids. (And, as we'll see in Part II, there's one ketone in particular that serves as an excellent alternative fuel source that also has the power to prevent the body from breaking down muscle tissue to generate glucose.)

The diet protocol outlined in Part II honors the main ketogenic principles of significantly reducing carbohydrates to the point that the body is pushed to burn fat, while dietary fat and other nutrients turn on the body's powerful "pro-health" technology. The key, of course, is to eat the right kind of fat. I'll explain more shortly.

BALANCE LEVELS OF BENEFICIAL BACTERIA IN YOUR BELLY

During my public talks, I like to refer to "Slick Willie" Sutton, one of the most infamous and prolific bank robbers of the 20th century, who was once asked why he robbed banks. His answer: "Because that's where the money is." Likewise, you'd think that if you wanted to understand problems with the brain, that's where you'd need to look, right? But here's where the story gets interesting. Recent research has shown that the root of many brain-related disorders could be not within the brain but rather within the body, especially within the gut. Let me repeat: What's taking place in your intestines today plays a critical role in determining your risk for any number of brain conditions. Which is why optimizing intestinal health and maintaining the structure and function of the gut barrier—the wall that separates the interior of your gut and your bloodstream—is paramount.

First, a quick anatomy lesson. The gut is, at a very basic level, a biological "pipeline" that goes from the mouth to the anus. Anything you consume that isn't digested will pass through you and go out the other end. One of the most crucial functions of the gut is to prevent foreign substances from entering your bloodstream and reaching vulnerable organs and tissues, including the brain.

The gut and the brain are, in fact, intricately connected. The gut has an impact on the brain's function in the moment as well as in the long term; it influences your risk of developing a neurodegenerative condition, like Alzheimer's or Parkinson's disease. *Brain Maker* covered the science of the microbiome in depth, especially as it relates to brain health, and since its publication newer studies have continued to confirm the facts. For example, in 2015 a landmark European study found a powerful relationship between an unhealthy intestinal microbiome, often referred to as gut dysbiosis, and the development of Parkinson's disease. Some are even calling the intestinal microbiota, or gut flora, the brain's "peacekeeper."

Just what exactly makes up the human microbiome? It consists of a large and extended family of more than 100 trillion organisms — mostly bacteria living within the gut — that outnumber your own cells ten to one. These organisms' metabolic products and genetic material are also considered to be part of the microbiome. Amazingly, a full 99 percent of the genetic material in your body is housed by your microbiome! It supports and nurtures every aspect of your physiology, including what goes on in the brain.

We now know that our lifestyle choices help shape and sustain our microbiome. We also know that the health of the microbiome factors into immune system function, inflammation levels, and risk for illnesses as diverse as depression, obesity, bowel disorders, multiple sclerosis, asthma, and even cancer. Indeed, the National Cancer Institute has recently revealed that certain gut bacteria regulate and "educate" the immune system in such a way that they can help reduce the growth of tumors; what's more, gut bacteria help control the efficacy of certain well-established anticancer therapies. They also do a lot of work on behalf of our physiology: They manufacture neurotransmitters and vitamins that we couldn't otherwise make, promote normal gastrointestinal function, provide protection from infection, regulate metabolism and the absorption of food, and help control blood sugar balance. They even affect whether we are overweight or lean, hungry or satiated.

New science is emerging that demonstrates that microbes not only influence the activity of our DNA, moment to moment, but also have become part of our own DNA throughout evolution. In other words, microbes have inserted their genes into our own genetic code to help us evolve and flourish. Isn't that astonishing? In the words of one prominent team of researchers at Stanford and the University of California, San Francisco: "Recent discoveries make clear that our microbiota is more like an organ than an accessory: These microbes are not just key contributors to human health but a fundamental component of human physiology." The National Institute of Health is investing more than $190 million over a five-year period to look at how the human microbiome influences gene expression. And in May 2016, the US government launched a $500 million project called the Unified Microbiome Initiative to study the microbial communities on Earth. This will be a coordinated collaboration among numerous federal agencies, universities, philanthropic organizations, and industry.

In neurology, a field that has essentially been devoid of real cures and treatments, this burgeoning new area of study is finally giving us revolutionary approaches to relieve suffering. My recommendations in Part II leverage the power of this dazzling new science, showing you how you can take advantage of it for your own health. Best of all, you can reap the rewards within a matter of *days*.

Microbiomes exist throughout the world. In addition to the human microbiome, the oceans, soil, deserts, forests, and atmospheres each have their own microbiomes that support life. Microbiomes have captivated the scientific world, fueling multimillion-dollar research projects globally. A nifty fact: Microbes in our oceans produce 50 percent of the oxygen we breathe while absorbing carbon dioxide. Methane-ingesting microbes that inhabit the deep sea also act as a powerful incinerator for that notorious greenhouse gas. It's important to recognize that the health of the planet depends on its microbial communities.

One of the key areas that intestinal bacteria help control is gut permeability. When we are talking about permeability issues in the gut, or so-called "leaky gut," we are referring to problems in the competency of the tight junctions — the small connections between the cells that line the gut and control the passage of nutrients from the gut into the body via your circulation. If the junctions are somehow compromised, they fail to appropriately police what should be allowed in (nutrients) or kept out (potential threats). As the gatekeepers, these junctions determine, to a large extent, your body's set point of inflammation — your baseline level of inflammation at any given time.

The term "leaky gut" used to be dismissed by conventional researchers and doctors, especially as it relates to autoimmunity. But now an impressive number of well-designed studies have repeatedly shown that when your intestinal barrier is damaged, which can result in having an unhealthy gut flora that cannot protect the intestinal lining, you are susceptible — through increased inflammation and an activated immune response — to a whole spectrum of health challenges, including rheumatoid arthritis, food allergies, asthma, eczema, psoriasis, inflammatory bowel disease, celiac disease, type 1 and type 2 diabetes, and even cancer, autism, Alzheimer's, and Parkinson's.

According to this new science, the intestinal wall has everything to do with whether we tolerate or adversely react to substances we ingest. A break in that intestinal wall can cause food toxins such as gluten and pathogens to pass through and agitate the immune system. This breach affects not only the gut, but also other organs and tissues, such as bones, skin, kidneys, the pancreas, liver, and brain.

What can cause an unhealthy intestinal microbiome?

- diets high in refined carbohydrates, sugar, and processed foods

- diets low in fiber, especially the kind that feeds the flora

- dietary toxins, such as gluten and processed vegetable oils

- chronic stress

- chronic infections

- antibiotics and other medications like nonsteroidal anti-inflammatories (NSAIDs) and acid-reflux drugs (proton pump inhibitors or PPIs); see page 114

When researchers at Stanford University, led by Dr. Justin Sonnenberg, explored the mucus layer that lines the gut, they found that it is home to several groups of bacteria that are vital for regulating immunity and inflammation. The mucus layer, which renews itself every hour, is critical in maintaining the integrity of the gut lining and reducing leaky gut. It's becoming clear that the bacteria in this layer depend on dietary fiber to thrive, which is why the carbohydrates we do consume should be in the form of fiber-rich fruits and vegetables. These complex carbohydrates are broken down by our gut bacteria. That's right: The gut's beneficial bacteria use the fiber we eat as fuel to promote their own growth.

Prebiotics are a specialized form of dietary fiber that our bodies cannot digest but that gut bacteria love to consume, and they are an important part of the Grain Brain Whole Life Plan. Prebiotics are often categorized as carbohydrates because they are found in many fruits and vegetables. Prebiotics act like a fertilizer; it has been estimated that for every 100 grams of prebiotics consumed, a full 30 grams of bacteria are produced. As our gut bacteria metabolize this fiber, they produce substances called short-chain fatty acids (SCFAs), which help us stay healthy. Butyric acid, for example, is an SCFA that improves the health of the intestinal lining. In addition, these fatty acids help regulate sodium and water absorption and enhance our ability to take in important minerals and calcium. They effectively lower the pH in the gut, which inhibits the growth of potential pathogens and damaging bacteria. They enhance immune function and even help explain why some people have trouble losing weight, even though they cut back on calories. The production of these SCFAs effectively activates a signaling pathway that tells the brain that the body has gotten enough food. This messaging in turn triggers food in the gut to move more quickly, so there is less absorption of calories. On the other hand, when SCFAs are low, the body believes it's not getting enough food, and so food moves more slowly, allowing the body to extract more calories.

The typical Western diet supplies plenty of calories but little or no prebiotic fiber. So despite our huge caloric intake, our digestive system believes we are starving! The body reacts to this misguided sensation of starvation by doing what it can to extract as many calories as possible from our food. This may well represent one of the primary issues underlying obesity. The average American consumes a scant 5 grams of prebiotic fiber daily, while estimates reveal that their slender hunter-gatherer forebears may have consumed as much as 120 grams each day. I'll show you how to stock up on prebiotic fiber so your body doesn't believe it's in starvation mode and doesn't have to forage as many calories from the food you eat.

New research also reveals that gut bacteria play an important role in maintaining the blood-brain barrier, which protects the brain from potentially harmful substances. The blood-brain barrier ensures homeostasis of the central nervous system, too. In fact, there are many newly discovered similarities between the blood-brain barrier and the gut's lining. It was recently demonstrated, for instance, that gliadin, a protein found in gluten, may lead to increased permeability of the blood-brain barrier, just as it leads to increased permeability of the gut. This could further explain the relationship between gluten-containing foods and neurological problems. So if you thought having a leaky gut was bad, just imagine what might happen with a leaky brain! As a matter of fact, problems with the blood-brain barrier have been associated with Alzheimer's disease, stroke, brain tumors, multiple sclerosis, meningitis, rabies, seizures, and even autism.

In the fall of 2014, I had the opportunity to speak at Harvard Medical School on the role of the microbiome in brain health and disease. Just before it was my turn to speak, I had a chat with my friend and colleague Dr. Alessio Fasano, one of the world's leading authorities on gluten and health, who was also presenting. Dr. Fasano, who heads the Center for Celiac Research at Harvard's Massachusetts General Hospital, made it clear that, in his opinion, the number one factor shaping the microbiome is diet. And we have control over our diet.

Dr. Lawrence David, another Harvard researcher, has addressed the question of how long it takes for the human microbiome to change once the diet has changed. His study, published in January 2014, assessed changes in the gut bacteria that occurred in six men and four women between the ages of twenty-one and thirty-three when they consumed either an animal-based diet or a plant-based diet. Although it was a small study involving only a handful of people, it nonetheless spurred further research. Dr. David documented fairly dramatic changes in the genetic signature of the gut bacteria in as little as *three days*. In another, collaborative study involving a consortium of researchers from Germany, Italy, Sweden, Finland, and the United Kingdom, it was found that "A key factor in determining gut microbiota composition is diet...Western diets result in significantly different microbiota compositions than traditional diets." Their investigations have also found that the way the gut bacteria function can vary greatly depending on diet. And they noted differences in gene expression of the bacteria, too.

My bet is that the science will increasingly highlight the power of "traditional diets," high in healthy fats and low in carbohydrates, and the perils of the Western diet, high in carbs and low in healthy fats.

It may have been bold to write a whole chapter in *Brain Maker* about the connection between gut health and risk for autism, but the science continues to confirm this link. A pattern of gastrointestinal disorders, likely brought on by leaky gut and gut dysbiosis, are routinely documented in children with autism. One theory currently making waves supposes that distinctive microbes associated with autism spectrum disorder create by-products in the microbes' metabolism that in turn affect human brain function. So powerful is the science that the FDA has approved a study at Arizona State University in which doctors will perform a fecal microbial transplant (FMT) in a group of twenty children aged seven to seventeen years with autism who also have severe gastrointestinal problems. FMT is the most aggressive therapy available to reset and recolonize a sick microbiome. In the procedure, filtered good bacteria is transplanted from a healthy person into the colon of another person.

The incredible role of the microbiome in keeping you healthy is captivating researchers around the globe. You'll be learning more throughout the book, including what you can do starting today to balance your gut's microbial community and avoid gut dysbiosis. For now, however, let's briefly turn to another chief goal of this program.

BALANCE YOUR HORMONES, REDUCE INSULIN SURGES, AND INCREASE LEPTIN SENSITIVITY

Your endocrine system, which manages and controls your body's hormones, holds the remote control to much of what you feel—moody, tired, hungry, sexual, sick, healthy, hot, or cold. It lords over development, growth, reproduction, and behavior through an intricate system of hormones, the body's chemical messengers. These messengers are manufactured in different parts of the body (for example, the thyroid, adrenal, or pituitary gland or gonads) and then travel through the bloodstream to reach target organs and tissues. Once there, they act on receptors to elicit a biological response—usually with the goal of effecting change that allows your body to run smoothly and maintain balance. They serve a vital role in every bodily system, including your reproductive, nervous, respiratory, cardiovascular, skeletal, muscular, immune, urinary, and digestive systems. To keep the body balanced, the forces of one particular hormone are usually counterbalanced by those of another hormone.

Hormone imbalances can lead to serious health issues—metabolic and thyroid disorders, infertility, cancer, hair loss, fatigue, depression, a loss of libido, chronic pain, and more. Hormonal chaos can happen quite naturally during stressful periods or as a result of your age or various health conditions that disrupt the harmony. Women experience decreases in oestrogen and fluctuations in thyroid hormones during and after menopause, while men have a drop in their testosterone levels by 1 to 2 percent every year after age thirty (part of this drop, however, can be attributed to lifestyle factors—typically weight gain—rather than aging alone). As we've just seen, a misbehaving microbiome can certainly come into play as well. And hormone levels can be affected by certain toxins.

The good news is that hormonal dysfunction can often be addressed through diet...and through the plan of action outlined in this book. One key factor is probiotics ("for life"), live bacteria you can ingest through foods and supplements. Remarkable new studies have emerged that show just how powerful probiotics can be in balancing insulin, the body's master hormone, as well as other hormones related to appetite and metabolism; they can help reduce and even eliminate insulin resistance and diabetes.

Let me give you a quick primer on insulin and some of the other important hormones related to metabolism. Insulin, as you likely already know, is one of the body's most important hormones. A carrier protein produced by the pancreas, insulin is best known for helping us transport carbohydrate-based energy in the form of glucose from food into cells for their use. Insulin circulates in your bloodstream, where it picks up glucose and moves it into cells throughout the body, where it can then be used as fuel. Extra glucose that the cells don't need is stored in the liver as glycogen or deposited in fat cells.

Normal, healthy cells have no problem responding to insulin. But when cells are relentlessly exposed to high levels of insulin as a result of persistent spikes in glucose—again, typically caused by consuming too many modern carbohydrates—our cells adapt and become "resistant" to the hormone. This triggers the pancreas to pump out more, so now higher levels of insulin are required for glucose to enter cells. But these higher levels also cause blood sugar to plummet to dangerously low levels, resulting in physical discomfort and brain-based panic.

As I detailed in *Grain Brain*, the connections among high blood sugar, insulin resistance, diabetes, obesity, and risk for brain disorders are irrefutable. Studies show not only that high body fat correlates with a smaller hippocampus, the brain's memory center, but also that the metabolic consequences of diabetes and obesity have far-reaching effects on the brain. After 1994, when the American Diabetes Association recommended that Americans should consume 60 to 70 percent of their calories from carbohydrates, the rate of diabetes exploded. And so did the rate of brain disorders. People with diabetes have twice the risk of Alzheimer's disease.

The exact nature of that relationship was just recently brought to light. For starters, if you're a diabetic, by definition you have high blood sugar because your body cannot transport critical glucose into cells. And if that glucose remains in the blood, it will inflict a lot of damage. It will attach to proteins in the body in a process called glycation, which then triggers inflammation as well as the production of free radicals. All of these—glycation, inflammation, and free radical production—are implicated in Alzheimer's, Parkinson's, and multiple sclerosis. Even being prediabetic, when blood sugar issues are just starting to arise, is associated with a decline in brain function and a risk factor for full-blown Alzheimer's disease.

In 2016, Melissa Schilling, a professor of management and organizations at New York University, added to our understanding of how diabetes and Alzheimer's disease are related when she uncovered a pathway between these two diseases. Integrating decades of research on molecular chemistry, diabetes, and Alzheimer's, she found a commonality: insulin and the enzymes that break down this important hormone. The same enzymes that break down insulin also break down amyloid-beta, the protein that forms tangles and plaques in the brains of people with Alzheimer's. When people secrete too much insulin due to a poor diet, obesity, and diabetes (a condition called hyperinsulinemia), the enzymes are too busy breaking down insulin to break down amyloid-beta, causing amyloid-beta to accumulate. Schilling's work has led to a stunning new fact: Almost half of all Alzheimer's disease cases in the United States are likely due to hyperinsulinemia. Fortunately, hyperinsulinemia is preventable and treatable using this very protocol. (I recently had the opportunity to interview Professor Schilling for *The Empowering Neurologist* online program, and you can watch this compelling video on my website, www.DrPerlmutter.com.)

There are two other important hormones related to metabolism that share a relationship with insulin: leptin and ghrelin. The biochemistry of all three hormones in the body is intricately complex and a highly regulated affair, but I'm going to distill it down for you so you understand why it's so important to keep these critical hormones balanced.

Leptin and ghrelin are your two chief appetite hormones. Whereas insulin controls energy use and storage upon the intake of food, leptin and ghrelin control whether you feel hungry or full—they orchestrate the stop and go of our eating patterns. Leptin, from the Greek word for "thin," is involved in dozens of bodily processes, including helping to coordinate the body's inflammatory responses, but it is best known for its role in appetite suppression. It reduces the urge to eat by acting on specific centers of the brain. As nutritional therapist Nora Gedgaudas is fond of saying, leptin tells your brain that "the hunting is good." It's what allows you to put that fork down and stop eating. Here's how it works in a nutshell: When fat cells start to fill up and expand, they secrete leptin. Once the fat cells begin to shrink as their contents are burned for energy, the tap is slowly turned off and less leptin gets released. Eventually you're able to feel hunger again, thanks to the release of ghrelin, and the cycle starts all over.

Ghrelin, the "hunger hormone," is triggered by an empty stomach and increases your appetite. As the stomach fills with food and expands, signals to your brain tell the ghrelin tap to turn off. As you can imagine, a disruption in the balance between leptin and ghrélin will wage war on your cravings, sense of fullness, and waistline. People who are leptin resistant don't feel full (and can't stop eating). Gedgaudas calls leptin resistance the Holy Grail of obesity. In the same way that too much insulin pushes you toward insulin resistance (and diabetes), too much leptin, triggered by an overload of dietary carbs and sugar, leads to leptin resistance. And high levels of insulin render the brain less sensitive to leptin.

Due to the prevalence of insulin resistance today, most people — regardless of their weight — release twice as much insulin as people did just 30 years ago for the same amount of glucose. And that high insulin is responsible for perhaps 75 to 80 percent of all obesity.

Obviously, the goal is to not only achieve optimal blood sugar control through healthy insulin levels, but also to balance the relationship between leptin and ghrelin, and, in particular, to increase your body's sensitivity to leptin. I'm going to show you how to do that not just through diet but also through sleep and exercise. Sleep deprivation reduces leptin, so your brain gets the message to seek out more calories; exercise improves leptin signaling (as well as insulin sensitivity).

TAKE CONTROL OF YOUR OWN GENES

When you think of your DNA, your inherited genetic code, you probably think about what kinds of characteristics and risk factors your biological parents bestowed on you through their own DNA. Did they give you blue eyes, an athletic build, and a propensity to have heart trouble later in life? We used to think that DNA was like a permanent marker in your body's chromosomes. You couldn't change it. But now we know that even though genes encoded by DNA are essentially static (barring the occurrence of mutation), the *expression* of those genes can be highly dynamic.

I mentioned one of the hottest areas of research earlier: epigenetics, the study of sections of your DNA (called "marks" or "markers") that influence how your genes act and behave. Put simply, these epigenetic markers have a say in your health and your longevity, as well as the health and longevity of your own children. Indeed, the forces acting on the activity of your DNA today—for good or bad—can be passed on to your future biological children. Epigenetic activity may even change your *grandchildren's* risks for certain diseases and disorders. By the same token, these markers can be changed to affect your DNA's expression differently, making it fully possible to change your underlying risk for certain diseases.

Epigenetic forces can affect us from our days in utero to the day we die. There are many windows during our lifetime when we are extra sensitive to environmental influences that can change our biology and have downstream effects such as dementia and brain cancer.

There's one important molecule I'd like to highlight that has everything to do with your ability to control your own genes' expression: Nrf2. When the body experiences high oxidative stress, which is another way of saying there's an imbalance between the production of free radicals and the ability of the body's ability to counteract their harmful effects, it sounds the alarm by activating Nrf2, a specific protein found within every cell. This protein remains dormant, unable to move or operate, until it is released by an Nrf2 activator. Once activated, it then migrates into the cell nucleus and bonds to the DNA at a specific spot, which then opens the door for the production of a vast array of important antioxidants as well as detoxification enzymes. The result is both the elimination of harmful toxins and the reduction of inflammation.

The Nrf2 pathway's chief role is to protect cells against external stresses such as toxins and carcinogens. It is an ancient circuit. As described in a 2014 paper by researchers at the University of Colorado, the Nrf2 pathway has been referred to as the "master regulator of antioxidant, detoxification, and cell defense gene expression." For these reasons, a great deal of research has been carried out on the role of this life-sustaining pathway, especially in disorders such as Alzheimer's disease, Parkinson's disease, multiple sclerosis, and even autism.

But you don't need to wait until the body sounds its own alarm to activate the Nrf2 pathway. You can turn it on through the consumption of certain ingredients in the diet and through calorie restriction. The healthy omega-3 fat DHA, found in many fish, acts directly upon the Nrf2 pathway, as do compounds found in broccoli, turmeric, green tea extract, and coffee. You'll find these ingredients recommended in the dietary protocol. And calorie restriction will happen quite naturally due to the nature of the protocol's low-carb approach as well as the occasional fast (more on this soon).

In the past couple of years, scientists have discovered that lactobacilli—good bacteria that are very much a part of the gut's community and can be found in probiotics—stimulate the Nrf2 pathway. In experimental studies, these good bacteria allow animals to respond to stress by turning on their protective genes through the Nrf2 pathway. This illustrates the true power of our friendly gut bacteria. Not only are they participating in creating vital substances we need to survive, but they also are creating an environment that influences the expression of our genes for the better.

I've never included a discussion about telomeres in my books before, but the science is finally giving us clues to how important they are, as well as to what can adversely affect them. Telomeres are the caps on the ends of the chromosomes. Because they protect our genes and make it possible for cells to divide, they are critical to our health and are believed to hold secrets on how we age and develop disease. In terms of brain disease, for example, it has recently been shown by researchers at the Karolinska Institute in Sweden that "telomeres are involved in the actual active mechanism behind the development of [Alzheimer's] disease...."

Oxidative stress, brought on by psychological stress or too much sugar and carbs, has been shown to shorten telomeres and, thus, life. The shorter the telomeres, the faster we age. Smoking, exposure to pollutants, and obesity also cause oxidative stress, thereby shortening telomeres. On the other hand, we can protect our telomeres with aerobic exercise, reduced sugar, more dietary fiber, and added DHA. This protocol will help you do just that.

BALANCE YOUR LIFE

We all want it: more balance in our lives. More harmony between work and play, and more strength to overcome difficulties, especially when they are unexpected. We all have things that can derail us, whether physical challenges or mental ones. I trust that once you implement the strategies in this book, you'll enjoy an all-around better, more balanced life. Now let's get to the rules.

CHAPTER 3

The Food Rules

YOUR BODY IS AN INCREDIBLY dynamic, self-controlled machine. It has built-in systems of checks and balances to keep it on an even keel. Just because you pig out and shun exercise one day, for example, doesn't mean you'll gain ten pounds overnight. The body doesn't work like that. Cellular transactions are happening every second, without your even knowing it, that help to maintain your body's overall balance and preferred settings — what we call homeostasis. Consider your personality as an analogy. It remains relatively constant even though you have good days and bad days, times when your mood dips and others when you feel elated.

The body changes day by day based on your experiences and how you treat it, yet it tends to have a general baseline — a state of being where hormones and other biomolecules are flowing as they should, neurons are firing properly, and your immune system is working for you, not against you. Trouble, however, can arise from overriding the body's systems that maintain that homeostasis. Suddenly we can find ourselves vulnerable to illness, disorder, and disease. Nowhere is it easier to open the door to dysfunction than through the assaults we inflict on our body from our daily dietary choices.

I recommend that you keep a daily journal to record what is happening in your life as you move forward. You can write down not only your reasons for pursuing this new way of life, but also your thoughts, goals, and the events that are most affecting you and how you make decisions. See if you can maintain an ongoing record of your feelings and emotions, especially those around food and eating. Catch yourself when you eat mindlessly because you're tired or stressed out. Find patterns between your emotional well-being and the choices you make in daily life. Your attitude and perspective have a big impact on your daily decisions and overall health, and you can learn to use contentment as well as frustration or disappointment as a motivator on your path to success. On the bad days, which are inevitable, aim to be extra vigilant about how the challenging moments affect those behavioral patterns that prevent you from engaging in healthy activities. Such self-awareness will help you to make positive changes and avoid getting derailed by a vending machine or pushy coworker who brings in a box of jelly doughnuts.

My wish for you is that you learn to live in a way that you can sustain for the long term. At this juncture, all I ask is that you make the most of my recommendations and tune in to how your body is feeling and changing. You are recalibrating one day, one meal, one thought at a time and will see the results build up over time. So take a deep breath, relax, and get ready to discover a whole new you.

Now let's get to the training grounds. Time to learn the dietary rules:

- Evict gluten (even if you don't think you have a problem with it)

- Go low-carb, higher fat and fiber

- Abandon sugar (real, processed, and artificial)

- Avoid GMO foods

- Watch out for too much protein

- Embrace the incredible egg

EVICT GLUTEN (EVEN IF YOU DON'T THINK YOU HAVE A PROBLEM WITH IT)

I wrote extensively about gluten in *Grain Brain*, calling the "sticky" protein found in wheat, barley, and rye among the most inflammatory ingredients of the modern era. I argued that while a small percentage of the population is highly sensitive to gluten and suffers from celiac disease, it's possible for virtually *everyone* to have a negative, albeit undetected, reaction to gluten. And now my position has been validated by many fine research groups, including a consortium of scientists from Harvard University, Johns Hopkins, the Naval Medical Center, and the University of Maryland, who published their findings in 2015. My position may have seemed bold, aggressive, and seemingly outrageous and controversial at the time, but it has been confirmed over and over again in the scientific literature since then. Let me give you more details and provide updated evidence.

Gluten sensitivity—with or without the presence of celiac—drives the production of inflammatory cytokines, which are pivotal players in neurodegenerative conditions. The brain is among the organs most susceptible to the deleterious effects of inflammation. And the downstream inflammatory effects of gluten reach the brain via a leaky gut that fails to prevent the toxic ingredient from igniting an immune response. Gluten is a silent poison because it can inflict lasting damage without your knowing it. Those who experience symptoms of gluten sensitivity complain primarily of abdominal pain, nausea, diarrhoea, constipation, and intestinal distress. They also can suffer neurological symptoms such as headaches, brain fog, feeling unusually tired after a gluten-containing meal, dizziness, and a general feeling of being off balance. Most people, however, have no obvious symptoms yet could be experiencing a silent attack somewhere in the body; for example, in the nervous system. While gluten's effects might start with unexplained headaches, chronic fatigue, and anxiety, they can worsen to more dire disorders, such as depression and dementia. It's important to understand that you don't have to experience gastrointestinal symptoms to have a leaky gut. As I explained in Chapter 2, this condition can manifest as an autoimmune disorder, skin problems such as eczema or psoriasis, heart disease, and the spectrum of brain-based challenges.

Although there used to be a debate about whether someone without celiac disease could be sensitive to gluten, science has spoken. Non-celiac gluten sensitivity (NCGS) is finally a diagnosis in mainstream medicine. In one of the most stunning papers of late, published in *Clinical Gastroenterology and Hepatology*, a group of Italian researchers performed a rigorous study (i.e., randomized, double-blind, placebo-controlled) to determine the effects of giving low doses of gluten to people with suspected NCGS. Participants were randomly assigned to consume a little over 4 grams of either a gluten-containing product (approximately the amount in two slices of wheat bread) or a non-gluten-containing product (rice starch), which acted as the placebo, for one week. During that week, participants didn't know whether they were getting gluten or not. They were then put on a gluten-free diet for one week, and after that, participants switched groups. The researchers found a clear relationship between gluten and intestinal symptoms, irritation around the mouth, and, notably, foggy mind and depression; that is, non-intestinal symptoms. They reported: "We found that the overall symptom score was significantly higher while ingesting gluten in comparison with placebo."

Gluten is everywhere today, despite the gluten-free movement taking hold among food manufacturers. It lurks in everything from wheat products to ice cream to hand cream. It's even used as an additive in seemingly "healthy" wheat-free products. I hear about the effects of gluten every day from people I encounter. Regardless of what ails them, whether chronic headaches, anxiety, or a host of neurological symptoms with no definite diagnosis, one of the first things I do is suggest the total elimination of gluten from their diets. And I continue to be astounded by the results. I don't even recommend gluten sensitivity tests anymore. **You must operate from a place of assuming that you are sensitive to gluten and avoid it entirely.**

It's crucial to understand that gluten is made up of two main groups of proteins, the *glutenins* and the *gliadins*. You can be sensitive to either of these proteins or to one of the twelve smaller units that make up gliadin. A reaction to any of these can lead to inflammation. Gliadin in particular has been implicated in new studies showing the protein's damaging effects on the gut lining, inducing permeability. In the words of Harvard's Dr. Alessio Fasano, "... gliadin exposure induces an increase in intestinal permeability in all individuals, regardless of whether or not they have celiac disease."

In 2015 Dr. Fasano published a landmark paper showing how gliadin can wreak so much havoc and even be the culprit behind autoimmune disorders and cancer. Briefly, gliadin triggers production of another protein called zonulin, which breaks down the gut lining and increases permeability. Once the lining is compromised, as you already know, substances that are supposed to stay in the gut leak into the bloodstream and incite inflammation. The discovery of zonulin's effects on the body inspired researchers to look for illnesses characterized by intestinal permeability. And lo and behold, this led to the finding that most autoimmune disorders, including celiac disease, rheumatoid arthritis, multiple sclerosis, type 1 diabetes, and inflammatory bowel disease, are distinguished by abnormally high levels of zonulin and a leaky gut. So powerful is zonulin that when scientists expose animals to the toxin, the animals develop type 1 diabetes almost immediately; the toxin induces a leaky gut, and the animals start making antibodies to islet cells. These are the cells responsible for making insulin.

For those of you trying to lose weight, gluten can prevent your body from doing so. Overweight and obesity, after all, are also rooted in inflammation. And it's a two-way street: Inflammation promotes weight gain, and weight gain promotes inflammation. First, elevated inflammatory cytokines in the bloodstream, the hallmarks of inflammation, cause insulin resistance. This explains why people with other inflammatory conditions are at a higher risk of developing type 2 diabetes. Second, inflammation rages in the fat cells themselves upon the development of obesity. To be sure, body fat does serve a purpose; nobody can be totally fat-free. Fat alone is not an inflammatory tissue, but copious amounts of it beyond what's healthy for the body are problematic and trigger a self-perpetuating cycle of inflammation. This intracellular inflammation in fat tissue further promotes insulin resistance and weight gain.

Inflammation that takes place in the brain and gut exacerbates matters. Recall that leptin controls appetite and metabolism. When inflammation reaches the brain, specifically the hypothalamus, leptin resistance results, which then impairs glucose and fat metabolism. A similar scenario can happen in the gut: Inflammation of the gut causes leptin and insulin resistance, largely due to the exposure of toxins from the gut leaking into the bloodstream. One toxin in particular, lipopolysaccharide (LPS), is produced in the gut, where it belongs, by certain bacteria. Once LPS sneaks through the gut lining, however, it causes not only inflammation, but also insulin resistance in the liver and weight gain.

There are other connections between inflammation and

overweight/obesity. But the point I want to make is that gluten leads to a leaky gut, which then opens the door to the chronic inflammation that makes weight loss virtually impossible. I can't tell you how many people who have ditched gluten share stories of significant weight loss. As I've mentioned, this was not something I expected when I wrote my previous books.

In 2015 and 2016, newer research surfaced about the damaging effects of gluten on the microbiome as well. Indeed, it's quite possible that the entire cascade of adverse effects that takes place when the body is exposed to gluten starts with a change in the microbiome — ground zero. It goes without saying: You're going to evict this ingredient from your life. I'll show you how to do that in Part II.

GO LOW-CARB, HIGHER FAT AND FIBER

What's better for you, a low-carb or low-fat diet? Let's turn to the best medical literature available. In a Tulane University study, published in 2014 in the prestigious *Annals of Internal Medicine,* of 148 obese men and women who did not have cardiovascular disease or diabetes, half were placed on a low-fat diet and the other half on a low-carb diet. They were then followed for one year. The results were compelling: "The low-carbohydrate diet was more effective for weight loss and cardiovascular risk factor reduction than the low-fat diet. Restricting carbohydrate may be an option for persons seeking to lose weight and reduce cardiovascular risk factors." The people on the low-carb diet lost more weight, shrunk their waistlines to a greater extent, improved their cholesterol profiles (more good cholesterol, less bad), and enjoyed a dramatic drop in triglycerides, which are a strong risk factor for cardiovascular disease (CVD).

Now, why in a book about brain health would I address heart health? For starters, more than one-third of American adults have at least one form of CVD, and one-third of total deaths are due to CVD. The annual cost of caring for Americans with CVD is in the hundreds of billions and is projected to increase to approximately $1.48 trillion by 2030. Cardiovascular disease is one of the most important public health challenges in the United States. Second, both CVD and obesity are well-documented risk factors for brain disease. The common denominator is, of course, inflammation. In fact, in the low-carb vs. low-fat study, those on the low-carb diet experienced a drop in their levels of C-reactive protein, a blood marker for inflammation. Those on the low-fat diet, however, showed a *hike* in their C-reactive protein levels.

To me, these facts are staggering. Over the past sixty-odd years, we've learned over and over again that fat is fattening, and that avoiding traditional fats (such as olive oil, coconut oil, animal fats, nuts, avocados, and eggs) in favor of processed, manufactured fat substitutes is better for us and our waistlines. This led people to turn to a high-carb diet filled with sugars and synthetic fats, and the results have been disastrous.

The publication of a flawed study decades ago ignited the campaign against fat. In the 1950s, the University of Minnesota's Dr. Ancel Keys was determined to prove a correlation between the consumption of certain fats, particularly saturated fat and cholesterol, and cardiovascular disease. He charted the incidence of heart disease in various countries. Seeking to find a linear relationship, he removed some of the data points on his graph until he could see a clear pattern between fat consumption and heart disease. He left out countries that showed a paradox — countries like Holland and Norway where people eat a lot of fat but have little heart disease, and places like Chile where heart disease rates are high despite low-fat diets. What became known as the Seven Countries Study was not one that employed the rigors of the scientific method. But his contrived ideas stuck, and cholesterol became the villain.

Let me say a few quick things about this so-called villain. Cholesterol serves a critical role as a brain nutrient essential to the function of neurons. It is also crucial in building cellular membranes. Moreover, cholesterol acts as an antioxidant and a precursor to important brain-supporting molecules like vitamin D, as well as the steroid-related hormones (for example, sex hormones such as testosterone and estrogen). The brain demands high amounts of cholesterol as a source of fuel. All of the latest science shows that when cholesterol levels are low, the brain simply doesn't work well. People with low cholesterol are at much greater risk for neurological problems from depression to dementia.

But the food industry would have you thinking otherwise. When cholesterol became the bad guy, corporate food executives got to work to make and distribute hydrogenated butter-like substances, processed vegetable oils, and food products made with these horrible ingredients. They started labeling these products, which are teeming with dangerous trans fats, as "low in cholesterol" or "cholesterol-free." In the aftermath of this move from real food to manufactured food, we have suffered rising rates of chronic diseases rooted in inflammation, many of which are the very maladies we were hoping to prevent, such as diabetes and heart disease.

The idea that we should restrict our saturated fat is not supported by the latest dietary guidelines. In fact, when the new 2015 federal guidelines were published, most people — health "experts" included — were shocked to see that they had removed recommendations to limit the consumption of cholesterol-rich foods and added a nod to coffee as potentially being part of a healthy diet. Imagine that! The greatest risk to our health and to weight gain comes from replacing saturated fat with pro-inflammatory carbohydrates and sugars. We've got to welcome saturated fat back to the table. We've also got to embrace more natural fats in general, and not be afraid of a fat-driven diet. And we have to simultaneously lower our carb intake. High-fat and high-carb diets filled with gluten are the worst; not only do they wreak havoc on the metabolism and drive inflammation, but they also do a number on our gut bacteria. Study after study shows that the only way the high-fat diet works is when it is accompanied by low carbs; and the more fiber, the better. Remember, it's the fiber that feeds those gut bugs and contributes to intestinal health.

In Part II, I ask you to add more olive oil to your diet, especially in light of results from the recent PREDIMED (Prevención con Dieta Mediterránean) studies. They were conducted in Spain, and published in the American Medical Association's journal in 2015, to evaluate the effect of the Mediterranean diet vs. the effect of the low-fat diet recommended for people with breast cancer. Incidence of breast cancer has increased by more than 20 percent worldwide since 2008.

The Mediterranean diet is nutrient dense and low in sugars, and it welcomes an abundance of fat to the table. The studies, on more than 4,200 women aged sixty to eighty years, covered a six-year period. The women were split into three different groups: One group was placed on a Mediterranean diet with added mixed nuts. A second group was also on a Mediterranean diet, but with added olive oil. And the third group followed a low-fat diet. After 4.8 years, there were a total of thirty-five confirmed cases of breast cancer across all three groups. Breast cancer risk in the Mediterranean diet group with the added mixed nuts was 34 percent lower compared to risk in the low-fat diet group, while the risk for breast cancer in the Mediterranean diet group with added olive oil was an incredible 55 percent lower compared to the low-fat diet group.

If, through diet, you can guard against a disease as grave as cancer, a disease rooted in inflammation, imagine what else you can guard against. Other studies have echoed the PREDIMED project and arrived at the same conclusion. One in particular, published in the same journal in 2015, found that "a Mediterranean diet supplemented with olive oil or nuts is associated with improved cognitive function."

It's clear to me that the U-turn in our dietary choices over the past century is at fault for many of our modern scourges. As we went from eating a high-fat, high-fiber, low-carb diet to a low-fat, low-fiber, high-carb one, we concomitantly began to suffer from chronic conditions, many of which affect the brain. So get ready to eat like a hunter-gatherer. You will no longer fear dietary fat, even the saturated kind that's high in cholesterol. You will cut the carbs, and amp up the fat and fiber.

ABANDON SUGAR (REAL, PROCESSED, AND ARTIFICIAL)

Sugar is in almost every packaged food. It may be labeled differently—cane sugar, barley malt, crystalline fructose, evaporated cane juice, caramel, high-fructose corn syrup, maltodextrin—but it's all sugar (there are more than sixty names for sugar). Americans consume 22 teaspoons of sugar per day and more than 130 pounds (59kg) of sugar each year. In the past hundred years, there's been a fivefold increase in the consumption of fructose, found naturally in fruits but mostly consumed through highly processed foods containing high-fructose corn syrup. Fructose is implicated in the development of nonalcoholic fatty liver disease, a condition in which fat accumulates in the liver and triggers inflammation; it can also lead to scarring and cirrhosis. Consuming fructose, in fact, is associated with insulin resistance, high blood fats, and high blood pressure (hypertension). It is seven times more likely than glucose to result in sticky, caramel-like protein/carbohydrate aggregates called glycation end products, which cause oxidative stress and inflammation. Fructose does not prompt the production of insulin and leptin, the two key hormones that regulate metabolism, which is partly why diets high in fructose can lead to obesity and its metabolic consequences that indeed reach the brain and cause dysfunction. In fact, sugar causes adverse changes in our cellular membranes, our arteries, our hormones, our immune systems, our intestines, and our entire neurological system.

Oust the OJ: Would you drink a can of fizzy drink for breakfast? Probably not (though some do). When I ask audiences this question, I follow it with: What's the better choice, OJ or a can of regular Coke or Pepsi? They assume the former, but the truth is a 350ml glass of OJ contains 36 grams of carbohydrate, or 9 teaspoons of pure sugar, about the same as in a can of regular cola. But what about the vitamin C? Sorry, folks. The vitamin C in no way offsets the damaging effects of all that sugar. And if you think homemade is better, know that juicing in general is a bad idea. When fruits and vegetables are in their whole state, with all their fiber, the sugar is released slowly into your bloodstream, so your insulin response is tempered. In the juicing process, the fiber — the pulp — is strained out.

While we like to think we're doing ourselves a favor by replacing refined sugar with seminatural products like Truvia and Splenda (which are marketed as "made from nature"), these are processed chemicals in disguise. What about artificial sweeteners? The human body cannot digest these, which is why they have no calories. But they must still pass through the gastrointestinal tract. For a long time, we assumed that artificial sweeteners were, for the most part, inert ingredients that didn't affect our physiology. Far from it. In 2014 a watershed paper, which has since been widely referenced, was published in *Nature* proving that artificial sweeteners affect gut bacteria in ways that lead to metabolic dysfunction, such as insulin resistance and diabetes, contributing to the same overweight and obesity epidemic they were marketed to provide a solution for.

Be On the Lookout: Examples of Popular Sugars and Sweeteners

evaporated cane juice

corn syrup

high-fructose corn syrup

crystalline fructose

fructose

sucrose

malt

maltose

maltodextrin

dextrose

beet sugar

turbinado sugar

invert sugar

aspartame

cyclamate

saccharin

sucralose

AVOID GMO FOODS

A lot of research is currently under way to study the effects of genetically modified organisms (GMO) on our health and on the environment. GMOs are plants or animals that have been genetically engineered with DNA from other living things, including bacteria, viruses, plants, and animals. The genetic combinations that result do not happen naturally in the wild or in traditional crossbreeding. GMO foods are commonly created to fight louses and viruses that can destroy crops, or to cultivate crops with certain desired characteristics. In the 1990s, for example, the ringspot virus decimated nearly half the crop of Hawaiian papaya in the state. In 1998, scientists developed a genetically engineered version of the papaya called the Rainbow papaya, which is resistant to the virus. Now more than 70 percent of the papayas grown in Hawaii are GMO.

Corn and soy are the top two GMO crops in the United States, and it's estimated that GMOs are in as much as 80 percent of conventional processed foods. Restrictions or complete bans have been placed on the production and sale of GMOs in more than sixty countries worldwide, including Australia, Japan, and all of the countries in the European Union. But in the United States, the government approves them. The problem: Many of the studies showing GMOs to be safe have been performed by the same corporations that created and now profit from them. People are rallying around the country for better food labeling so they can choose to opt out of what some call "the experiment."

There are a variety of genetically modified or engineered foods that the GMO industry features when trying to convince us of the merits of this technology. There is a sweet potato grown across Africa that has been engineered to be resistant to a particular virus. Rice has been engineered to increase its vitamin and iron content. Plants are genetically modified to be more resistant to various extremes of weather. There are fruit and nut trees that are engineered to yield crops years earlier than they would normally. Bananas are even genetically modified to produce human vaccines against diseases like hepatitis B. This all sounds promising, especially in light of issues of food scarcity in developing countries. But the story is not yet complete. While it's true that not all genetically modified organisms are inherently bad, the methods used to create and farm GMOs can entail practices with far-reaching consequences, many of which we don't understand yet.

We've been told, for example, that the new AquAdvantage salmon (made by AquaBounty Technologies) is safe for human consumption. But the FDA has only looked at the effect of this genetically modified fish on the environment. No studies have been performed to examine its effects on humans. We know that gene modification changes specific proteins, and that proteins we consume affect our own gene expression. You will not find any study on how the consumption of this fish changes gene expression in humans who eat them. According to Jaydee Hanson, senior policy analyst at the Center for Food Safety, "The modus operandi at FDA is to rubber stamp AquaBounty's studies and then call its review process science-based." Hanson goes on to say, "FDA's inadequate risk assessment is at odds with reality, with science and with the public, which has long called on the agency to put consumers' health and environmental safety ahead of the corporate interests of the biotechnology industry."

In a scathing review of GMOs by Consumer Reports, Robert Gould, MD, president of the board of Physicians for Social Responsibility, was quoted as stating: "The contention that GMOs pose no risks to human health can't be supported by studies that have measured a time frame that is too short to determine the effects of exposure over a lifetime." He then goes on to call for more studies to assess GMOs' long-term effects, especially given the fact that animal studies show they might cause damage to the immune system, liver, and kidneys. He also points out that a lack of labeling prevents researchers from even tracking the potential health effects of GMOs.

In addition to concerns about the effects of altered genetics in GMOs on human health, one of the most problematic—and contentious—aspects of GMOs has to do with current farming practices to grow GMO foods. No longer do farmers yank weeds from their fields by hand or machinery. They now spray a weed-killing chemical, glyphosate (the active ingredient in the common herbicide Roundup), on their crops. And they apply even more of this chemical just before the harvest to obtain a bigger yield and as a drying agent to prime the soil for a new crop. U.S. farm workers have sprayed 1.8 million tons of glyphosate since Roundup came on the market in 1974. Globally, 9.4 million tons of the chemical have been sprayed onto fields. It's estimated that by 2017 American farmers will apply an astounding 1.35 million metric tons of glyphosate to their crops. That's just under 3 billion pounds.

In order to protect crops from the herbicide, the seeds are genetically modified to be resistant to the herbicide's effects. In the world of agriculture, these seeds are known as "Roundup-ready". The use of Roundup-ready GMO seeds has allowed farmers to use huge amounts of this herbicide. Which means GMO foods—and foods conventionally farmed—are invariably contaminated with glyphosate, the "tobacco" of the 21st century that wreaks havoc on human health. Farmers who grow organic foods fear contamination in their fields as well. Glyphosate is a poison like no other, toxic to the gut all the way up to the brain.

Many of glyphosate's adverse effects are found at very low doses, challenging the notion that there is such a thing as a safe threshold of exposure. An entire book could be written about the politics and the biological effects of glyphosate. But for now, let me point out the main concerns as they relate to human health.

Glyphosate:

- acts as a powerful antibiotic, slaughtering beneficial bacteria in your gut and thereby disrupting the healthy balance of your microbiome

- mimics hormones like oestrogen, driving or stimulating the formation of hormone-sensitive cancers

- impairs the function of vitamin D, an important player in human physiology

- depletes key compounds like iron, cobalt, molybdenum, and copper

- compromises your ability to detoxify toxins

- impairs the synthesis of tryptophan and tyrosine, important amino acids in protein and neurotransmitter production

It wouldn't surprise me in the least if it were soon revealed that the obesity epidemic could partly be blamed on the widespread use of glyphosate and consumption of GMOs due to the chemical's effects on gut health and the microbiome. The importance of avoiding foods that have come into contact with glyphosate cannot be overemphasized. It can be found in unlikely places. In 2015, for instance, it was detected in PediaSure Enteral formula, which is widely used by hospitals in the United States for children in intensive care in need of nutrition. It is used in the wine industry. It has even been found in sanitary products because it is used by the cotton industry.

We must stand up in protest against this unacceptable experiment. Until glyphosate is banned, you'll need to focus on organic produce, pastured animal foods, and non-GMO verified products.

There is now a urinary test to measure glyphosate. This is one of the tests you might consider taking (see page 72 for more).

WATCH OUT FOR TOO MUCH PROTEIN

Picture yourself at a dinner party with friends. That morning, a headline in the media reported on the health risks surrounding red meat. This particular report spread like wildfire in the media because it came from Harvard's School of Public Health. According to the study, for every extra serving of unprocessed red meat consumed daily beyond an acceptable single serving (about the size of a deck of cards), the risk of dying prematurely went up by 13 percent; one daily serving of processed red meat, such as one hot dog, two slices of bacon, or one slice of cold cuts, increased the risk by 20 percent. You love your steak, but a dinner mate across the table—a vegetarian—decides to debate you and it gets a little heated. Who is right?

I am frequently asked about meat consumption. The Harvard study I just referenced was no small study, and to date it has been the largest, longest study on the alleged link between red meat and life span. It included data from two studies of more than 37,000 men and 83,600 women. These volunteers were followed for an average of twenty-four years, during which a combined 23,926 of them died— 5,910 from cardiovascular disease and 9,464 from cancer. Every four years, they submitted information about their diets. Generally speaking, those who ate the most red meat had higher death rates compared to those who ate the least. In particular, in those who ate one serving of red meat per day or more, the corresponding increases in risk for both men and women were 18 percent and 21 percent for cardiovascular death, and 10 percent and 16 percent for cancer death. These analyses factored chronic disease risk factors into the equation, including age, family medical history for heart disease and cancer, body mass index, and amount of physical activity. While the findings have merit, they do not tell the whole story. These are statistical links, after all.

If eating red meat hiked your risk of dying prematurely by as much as 21 percent, that might encourage you to learn to love tofu and tempeh instead of steak and bacon. But we're talking about the *relative* risk of eating more red meat versus less. It behooves us to consider the *absolute* risk, which brings those percentages down considerably—to single digits. Complicating this already complex story is the fact that big red meat eaters often have other risk factors for serious, life-shortening diseases. While seemingly stereotypical, data shows that people who eat too much red meat also tend to avoid exercise, drink alcohol excessively, and smoke. The researchers tried to compensate for the effects of unhealthy lifestyles in their study, finding that mortality and meat consumption remained associated, but with so many variables, it's hard to tease out hard numbers that are meaningful. And it's harder still to apply those statistics to everyone. The effects of unhealthy choices are relative to where you start—how old you are, how long you've been engaging in certain habits, and what your underlying risk factors are from a genetic standpoint. This muddies the waters even further.

An important conclusion in the study was that the higher death rate could have been mitigated had meat consumption been limited to less than half a serving per day. That's less than three-and-a-half servings per week. Moderation wins. Meat is not necessarily bad, particularly when it's not processed. And therein lies the key to enjoying red meat: Choose high-quality meat that has not been treated with antibiotics or force-fed genetically modified grains sprayed with glyphosate. I bet if a study were done comparing people who eat conventional meat to those who eat grass-fed organic meat, you'd see a difference in their health risks, despite how much meat they are consuming! High-quality meats come with high-quality fats, too.

Let me touch upon that other misconception I often hear. Contrary to what you might think, going low-carb does not mean going high-protein. You will not be eating meat every day. A lot of people think they need upward of 100 grams of protein a day, but in fact we only need about half that (see next page). Vegetarians often ask me if they should worry about getting enough protein, and I reassure them that they consume plenty from plant sources, legumes, eggs, nuts, and seeds. You probably eat more than enough protein each day, but you could be consuming too much. Protein is an essential component of any diet, but more doesn't mean better or healthier. Extra protein will not help you burn more fat, build more muscle, or render you stronger. If you consume too much of it, you'll eat more calories than your body requires, store more fat, and put yourself at risk for an earlier death.

A 2014 study conducted at multiple centers around the world demonstrated the value in reducing protein consumption for longevity. Those individuals with the highest protein intake during the eighteen-year study had a fourfold increased risk of dying from cancer and a fivefold increased risk of dying from diabetes (note that some of this increased risk could be attributed to too much animal protein in particular). But here's what they also found: The increased risk of cancer death was identified in people aged fifty to sixty-five years old who were consuming a high amount of protein. In people over the age of sixty-five, the trend reversed: These people had a *reduced* cancer risk (but still the same fivefold increased risk of diabetes mortality). So what do we make of this? The study concluded: "These results suggest that low protein intake during middle age followed by moderate to high protein consumption in old adults may optimize health span and longevity."

According to the Centers for Disease Control and Prevention, we only need to get 10 to 35 percent of our day's calories from protein foods; this translates to about 46 grams of protein for women and 56 grams of protein for men. It's easy to get your daily requirement when you consider the following: A 75g piece of meat has about 21 grams of protein (if you eat a 225g piece of meat, it could contain more than 50 grams).

More Isn't Better: You Need Less Protein Than You Realize

Low-carb does not mean high-protein. The Grain Brain Whole Life Plan calls for a limited daily intake of protein—no more than about 46 grams for women and 56 grams for men.

On the Grain Brain Whole Life Plan, you're going to rejoice in the delicious proteins you get to enjoy, and you won't feel deprived. To ensure you get just the right blend of different proteins and their amino acid makeup, you'll be mixing up the types of protein you eat. And one source of high-quality protein that you'll love as much as I do is the incredible egg.

EMBRACE THE INCREDIBLE EGG

Eggs are a staple in my diet. I panic when I run out of eggs. I don't panic at the thought that they are a high-cholesterol food. Remember, the idea that dietary cholesterol, such as that in saturated fat from beef, converts directly into blood cholesterol is totally false. Science has never been able to connect dietary animal fats and dietary cholesterol to levels of blood cholesterol or risk of coronary heart disease. And when scientists try to track a relationship between blood cholesterol and egg consumption, they continually document that cholesterol levels in people who eat few or no eggs are identical to people who consume lots of eggs. More than 80 percent of the cholesterol in your blood is produced by your own liver, and, contrary to what you might think, consuming cholesterol has been shown to actually *reduce* your body's production of cholesterol.

Eggs—yolks included—are an unrivaled food. They are versatile, and cost-effective, nutritional gold mines. I invite you to check out my online video about eggs when you have a moment at www.DrPerlmutter.com. Whole eggs contain all of the essential amino acids we need to survive, vitamins and minerals, and antioxidants known to protect our eyes. And they can have far-reaching positive effects on our physiology. Not only do they keep us feeling full and satisfied, but they also help us control blood sugar and, in turn, a whole panoply of risk factors for illnesses as diverse as heart disease, cancer, and brain-related disorders.

You'll see that I recommend lots of eggs in the plan. I find they are a perfect way to start the day; they give you the ideal combination of fat and protein to set your body's biological "tone" for the day. Please don't be afraid of them, especially the "high-cholesterol" yolks. But, as with other sources of proteins, choose your eggs carefully. Pastured eggs, which come from chickens that are allowed to roam free and eat what they normally would in the wild (plants and insects, not processed grains), are best. They taste better, too! There are so many things you can do with eggs. Whether you scramble, fry, poach, boil, or use them in dishes, eggs are indeed among the most multipurpose ingredients.

IT'S MORE THAN JUST FOOD

I highlighted a lot of "rules" in this chapter that cover nutrition. But as you'll see coming up, it goes far beyond that. Nobody changes his or her health for the better solely through food. Although implementing the ideas in this section will set you free in a lot of ways, there's much more to consider in terms of what factors into your health and risk for brain disease: how you reduce the stress in your life, how well you sleep at night, the drugs you reach for because you think you need them, and whether or not you think highly of yourself and the people around you. I'll be giving you the practical tools and strategies to address every angle of your lifestyle. Now let's get to Part II.

PART II

THE GRAIN BRAIN WHOLE LIFE PLAN ESSENTIALS

It's been fifteen months since I made a forever change to my diet and lifestyle by converting to a low-carb, gluten-free, high-fat diet. From a starting point of a fleshy 225 pounds, I am now down to 198 pounds and loving it! I started small, by eliminating all sugars, carbohydrates, and gluten for thirty days. I lost 3 pounds per week, even with no change to my gym schedule, which was sporadic at best. My jeans that were once tight were falling off my butt and I had to wash them in hot water and shrink them. For the first time in a long time, I was happy to look at myself in the mirror after a shower—heck, at forty-eight years young, I look better than I did when I went to the gym two hours a day when I was twenty! —Pat L.

Getting Started: Assess Your Risk Factors, Know Your Numbers, and Prepare Your Mind

TIME TO TURN THE SCIENCE into success. I've given you a great deal of information up to this point. You've learned a lot about the biology of health in the 21st century, some of which may have turned what you believed as conventional wisdom on its head. If you haven't already begun to change a few things in your life based on what you've read, now is your chance. In Part II, you'll learn how to shift your lifestyle and bring your body—and brain—back to optimal well-being. You'll feel energetic and vibrant, suffering less from chronic conditions.

Making lifestyle changes, even small ones, can seem overwhelming at first. How will you be able to resist your usual habits? Will you feel deprived and hungry? Will you find it impossible to keep up this new lifestyle forever? Is this program doable, given the time and commitments you have? Can you reach the point where following these guidelines is automatic, like second nature?

Take a deep breath. You will soon have even more knowledge and inspiration to help you stay on a healthy path for the rest of your life.

The closer you stick to my guidelines, the faster you will see results (and maintain them!). Bear in mind that this program has many benefits beyond the obvious physical ones. Ending fears of cognitive decline might be first and foremost on your mind, but the rewards don't stop there. You will see change in every area of your life. You will feel more confident and have more self-esteem. You'll feel younger and more in control of your life and future. You'll be able to navigate through stressful times with ease, have the motivation to stay active and engage with others, and feel more accomplished at work and at home. In short, you will feel and *be* more productive and fulfilled.

And your success will propagate more success. When your life becomes better, fuller, and more energized, you won't want to go back to your old, unhealthy lifestyle. I know you can do this. You must, for yourself and your loved ones. The payoffs are huge.

Let's get started with a quick rundown of the entire program:

Prelude: *Assess* Your Risk Factors, Know Your Numbers, and Prepare Your Mind

- Assess your risk factors using the quiz on page 70

- Have lab tests performed using the guide on page 72

- Turn off your autopilot (see page 76) and consider fasting for a day

Step 1: *Edit* Your Diet and Pill-Popping

- Learn how to nix the villains in your diet (see page 88) and welcome in the heroes (see page 93) that will help support the structure and function of your body

- Know which supplements you should consider adding to your daily regimen (see page 102) and the medications you should try to dump if possible (see page 113)

Step 2: *Add* Your Support Strategies

- Establish an exercise routine you can sustain (see page 120)

- Pay attention to pain, especially in your back and knees (see page 132)

- Make room for sleep (see page 136)

- Reduce stress and find calm in four simple ways (see page 142)

- Detoxify your physical environment (see page 159)

Step 3: *Plan* Accordingly

- Know when to eat (see page 166), sleep (see page 170), and exercise (see page 168). Train yourself to plan your days so that you achieve your daily goals given your time constraints and responsibilities. Be ruthless with your schedule and your realities

Now, on to the prelude, which will gear you up for Step 1

ASSESS YOUR RISK FACTORS

The quiz below will arm you with some personal data that can help provide a sense of your risk factors for brain disorders and disease, which can manifest in migraines, seizures, mood and movement disorders, sexual dysfunction, and ADHD, as well as serious mental decline in the future.

Remember, the organs and systems of the body are highly interconnected and intertwined. If this quiz determines that you're at higher risk for brain disease, then it also means you're at greater risk for a medley of other illnesses that are not, in and of themselves, brain related.

Respond to these statements as honestly as possible (Y means yes; N means no). If you don't know the answer to a question, skip over it.

1. Do you suffer from depression or chronic anxiety?   Y/N

2. Were you born via C-section?   Y/N

3. Are you more than twenty pounds (9kg) overweight?   Y/N

4. Have you taken antibiotics at least once
   in the past year?   Y/N

5. Do you avoid exercise?   Y/N

6. Do you consume artificial sweeteners at least once
   a week (found in diet fizzy drinks, sugar-free gum, and
   other foods or products labeled "sugar-free")?   Y/N

7. Are you on a low-fat diet?   Y/N

8. Have you been diagnosed with a sleep disorder or
   do you suffer from insomnia?   Y/N

9. Do you take proton pump inhibitors (Prilosec,
   Nexium, Prevacid) once in a while for heartburn or
   acid reflux?   Y/N

10. Do you eat GMO foods such as nonorganic
    corn and soy?   Y/N

11. Do you feel like you don't handle stress well?   Y/N

12. Do you have a blood relative who has been diagnosed
    with Alzheimer's disease or coronary artery disease?   Y/N

13. Is your fasting blood sugar 100 mg/dL or greater?   Y/N

14. Have you been diagnosed with an autoimmune
    disorder (for example, Hashimoto's thyroiditis,
    Crohn's disease, rheumatoid arthritis, lupus,
    inflammatory bowel disease, multiple sclerosis,
    type 1 diabetes, psoriasis, Graves' disease)?   Y/N

15. Do you sometimes take laxatives?   Y/N

16. Do you take a nonsteroidal anti-inflammatory (for
    example, ibuprofen, naproxen) at least once a week?   Y/N

17. Do you have type 2 diabetes?   Y/N

18. Are you extra sensitive to chemicals often found
    in everyday products?   Y/N

19. Do you have food allergies or are you gluten
    sensitive?   Y/N

20. Do you eat bread, pasta, and cereal?   Y/N

Don't be alarmed if you find yourself answering "yes" to most of these questions. The more yeses you have, the higher your risk for having dysfunctional physiology that might be impacting your health. But you are not doomed. The whole point of this book is to empower you to take charge of your health like never before.

KNOW YOUR NUMBERS: BASELINE BLOOD WORK

I recommend that you schedule the following lab tests, or as many of them as you can, as soon as possible. You can certainly start this program today while you wait for your appointment with a clinician and get the results, but knowing your numbers will not only motivate you to move forward but will also help you set target goals for each test result. You'll know where your biological weaknesses are, so you'll be able to pay attention to improving those numbers.

I've included healthy target levels where appropriate. Note that some of these tests are not normally performed by traditional doctors, so you may need to seek additional help from a functional medicine practitioner to complete these tests (see my website, www.DrPerlmutter.com, for details).

Fasting insulin: If you get only one test on this list, make it this one. It is critically important, and any health-care provider can perform it. Long before blood sugar begins to climb as a person becomes diabetic, the fasting insulin level will rise, indicating that the pancreas is working overtime to deal with the excess of dietary carbohydrates. It is a very effective early warning system for getting ahead of the diabetes curve, and so has tremendous relevance for preventing brain disease. You want this number to be below 8 uIU/ml (ideally, below 3).

Fasting blood glucose: A commonly used diagnostic tool to check for prediabetes and diabetes, this test measures the amount of sugar (glucose) in your blood after you have not eaten for at least eight hours. A level between 70 and 100 mg/dL is considered normal, but don't be fooled. A blood sugar pushing 100 is anything but normal. At that level, you're showing signs of insulin resistance and diabetes, and you have a heightened risk for brain disease. Ideally, you want to have a fasting blood glucose of less than 95 mg/dL.

Hemoglobin A1C: Unlike the fasting blood glucose test, this test reveals an "average" blood sugar over a ninety-day period and provides a far better indication of overall blood sugar control. Specifically, it measures the amount of *glycation* that the protein hemoglobin has undergone. Glycation, as I defined earlier, simply means that sugar has become bonded to a protein, in this case hemoglobin. This is a relatively slow process, but glycated hemoglobin is a powerful predictor of risk for Alzheimer's disease, as well as being one of the greatest predictors of brain shrinkage. A good A1C value is between 4.8 and 5.4 percent. Note that it can take time to see this number improve, which is why it's typically only measured every three to four months.

Fructosamine: Similar to the hemoglobin A1C test, a fructosamine test is used to measure an average blood sugar level but over a shorter time period—two to three weeks. Your fructosamine level should be between 188 and 223 μmol/L. It's possible to see positive changes in this test within two to three weeks.

Glyphosate urine test: Glyphosate, you'll recall, is the active ingredient in the popular weed killer Roundup that's used extensively in conventional farming today. We finally have a way to test for this man-made chemical in the body through a new urine test. You want to test negative for detectable levels of glyphosate in your urine, measured as ug/L.

C-reactive protein: This is a marker of inflammation in the body. You want to see 0.00 to 3.0 mg/L (ideally, less than 1.0 mg/L). CRP may take several months to improve, but you may well see positive changes even after one month following my protocol.

Homocysteine: Higher levels of this amino acid, produced by the body, are associated with many conditions, including atherosclerosis (narrowing and hardening of the arteries), heart disease, stroke, and dementia. It is now generally regarded as being quite toxic to the brain. Having a homocysteine level of just 14—a value exceeded by many of my patients when first examined—was described in the *New England Journal of Medicine* as being associated with a *doubling* of the risk for Alzheimer's disease (an "elevated" homocysteine level is anything above 10 µmol/L in the blood). High levels of homocysteine have also been shown to triple the rate of telomere shortening (remember that telomeres are those caps on the ends of your chromosomes that protect your genes and whose lengths are a biological indication of how fast you are aging). Homocysteine levels are almost always easy to improve (see below). Your level should be 8µmol/L or less. Both vitamin D and omega-3 fats can lengthen telomeres by increasing the activity of telomerase, the enzyme involved in lengthening telomeres. Many drugs can inhibit the B vitamins and raise homocysteine (see the list at www.DrPerl mutter.com under Resources), but most people can immediately correct their level just by supplementing with some B vitamins and folic acid. Typically, I ask patients with a poor homocysteine test to take 50 milligrams of vitamin B_6, 800 micrograms of folic acid, and 500 micrograms of vitamin B_{12} daily and retest after about three months.

Vitamin D: This is now recognized as a critical brain hormone (remember, it's not actually a vitamin; see page 106 for more details). Interestingly, higher levels of vitamin D are also associated with longer telomeres, a good thing. Your vitamin D level will probably be low (normal is between 30 and 100 ng/ mL, but you ideally want to be around 80 ng/mL). The majority of Americans are deficient in this critical nutrient due to indoor living and the use of sunscreen; those living in northern latitudes are most at risk for being deficient.

Because it can take time for the body to shore up its levels of vitamin D upon supplementation, you'll start with 5,000 international units (IU) of vitamin D once a day, and test your level after two months. If after two months your level is 50 nanograms per milliliter (ng/mL) or under, you'll take an additional 5,000 IU daily and retest in two months. It's the level maintained in your body that matters, not the dosage. Ask your health-care practitioner to help you adjust your dosage to achieve an optimal level. Once you do, a daily dose of 2,000 IU will usually suffice to maintain a healthy level, but ask your doctor for specific recommendations.

Once you've been following my protocol for a couple of months, it's a good idea to have these laboratory studies repeated to measure improvements. It can take time to see dramatic changes in some of these parameters, but if you follow the plan to a T, you should nonetheless begin to feel positive changes within a few weeks, and that will inspire you to keep going.

PREPARE YOUR MIND

I realize that some of you might be a little worried at this juncture. Given the self-assessments and lab work you've hopefully completed (or soon will), maybe you think that the cards are stacked against you. And the thought of cutting carbs is adding more unwanted stress. I'm here for you, which is why we're going to consider three things to prepare your mind to go forward with resolve and the understanding that you have control and can change those cards so they are stacked in your favor.

Turn Off Your Autopilot

Rituals. Traditions. Habits. Ruts. We all have them. Some of them are good and help us stay healthy and fit. But some of them keep us running in the other direction and getting stuck. Do you find yourself rising in the morning in a semi-fog, inhaling a carb-filled breakfast without much thought, rushing throughout your day drinking fizzy drinks and calorie-laden coffee drinks, coming home exhausted and wishing you had energy to exercise, eating dinner mindlessly in front of the television, and then falling into bed? Is your life automated so much that one day seamlessly and monotonously becomes another?

If so, don't feel bad. You're reading this book to get out of your rut—that comfort zone that in the long run won't be so comfortable. You don't want to look at yourself in the mirror five or ten years from now and be twenty pounds heavier, a hundred times more miserable, and on the road to experiencing serious health issues, if you don't have them already. My guess is you have your staples — your favorite foods, restaurants, routines, and shortcuts in every aspect of life. Now is the time to awaken to a new *whole life*.

It's important that we learn how to turn off our autopilot. I'm going to help you do that with the strategies in the rest of the book. The moment you begin to 1) edit your diet and pill-popping; 2) add your support strategies; and 3) plan accordingly, you'll start to avoid autopilot and turn instead to a much more fulfilling, energizing life. Turning off your autopilot will also happen automatically once you flip a few switches in your body by jump-starting the program with a fast and then cutting carbs cold turkey.

Fast and Furious (Should You Jump-Start with a Fast?)

If you've gone on diets before, then at one point you were probably told to eat five or six small, healthy meals during the day to keep your metabolism in gear. You were persuaded to believe that eating this way supported calorie burning, and that any sensation of hunger triggered alarms in the body to store fat and slow down metabolism.

We might have come a long way in our technological advancement, but from an evolutionary standpoint, our DNA isn't much different from the DNA of our hunter-gatherer ancestors. And contrary to what you may have been told, our ancestors didn't eat six times a day. For them, it was feast or famine. They needed to be able to endure long periods of time without food.

Plato was right when he said, "I fast for greater physical and mental efficiency." And so was Mark Twain when he declared, "A little starvation can really do more for the average sick man than can the best medicines and the best doctors." Many religions encourage the practice of fasting as a spiritual practice. There's the Islamic fast of Ramadan, the Jewish fast of Yom Kippur, and a variety of centuries-old fasting practices in Christianity, Buddhism, Hinduism, and Taoism. Although there are many different types of fasting, in general all fasts share one thing: They call for a willing abstinence from or a reduction of food, drink, or both for a period of time.

Fasting is a long-established way of physically rebooting the metabolism, promoting weight loss, and even increasing mental clarity and insight. (This latter fact makes sense from an evolutionary standpoint: When food was scarce, we needed to think quickly and smartly to find our next meal!) The scientific evidence for its benefits has been accumulating. In the early part of the twentieth century, doctors began recommending it to treat various disorders such as diabetes, obesity, and epilepsy. Today we have an impressive body of research to show that intermittent fasting, which includes everything from seasonal fasts lasting a few days to merely skipping a meal or two routinely on certain days of the week, can increase longevity and delay the onset of diseases that tend to cut life short, including dementia and cancer. And despite popular wisdom that says fasting slows down the metabolism and forces the body to hold onto fat in the face of what it perceives as starvation mode, it actually provides the body with benefits that can accelerate and enhance weight loss.

Typically, our daily food consumption supplies the brain with glucose for fuel. Between meals, the brain receives a steady stream of glucose made from glycogen, stored mostly in the liver and muscles. But glycogen reserves can provide only so much glucose. Once they are depleted, our metabolism shifts and we create new molecules of glucose from amino acids taken from the protein primarily found in muscle. On the plus side, we get more glucose; on the minus side, it comes at the expense of our muscles. And muscle breakdown is not a good thing.

Luckily, our physiology offers one more pathway to power the brain. When quick sources of energy like glucose are no longer available to fuel the body's energy needs, the liver begins to use body fat to create ketones, specialized molecules I described in Part I. One ketone in particular plays a starring role: beta-hydroxybutyrate (beta-HBA). Beta-HBA serves as an exceptional fuel source for the brain. This alternative fuel source allows us to function cognitively for extended periods during food scarcity. It helps reduce our dependence on gluconeogenesis and, therefore, preserves our muscle mass. Gluconeogenesis is the process by which the body creates new glucose by converting non-carbohydrate sources, such as amino acids from muscles, into glucose. If we can avoid the breakdown of muscle mass for fuel and instead utilize our fat stores with the help of ketones like beta-HBA, that's a good thing. And fasting is a way to achieve this goal.

Fasting also powers up the Nrf2 pathway I discussed in Chapter 2, leading to enhanced detoxification, reduction of inflammation, and increased production of brain-protecting antioxidants.

Despite all the benefits of fasting I just described, perhaps one of the best outcomes of the practice, especially during the prelude period of this program, is that it can help you mentally prepare for the dietary protocol. If you're worried about what it will be like to drastically reduce your carbohydrate consumption overnight, then I can't think of a better way to equip your mind—and body—for that achievement than to fast for a twenty-four-hour period before commencing the program. I also recommend that regardless of your medical status and history, you check with your doctor first before fasting for any length of time. If you take any medication, for example, ask about continuing to do so during your fast.

So unless you have a medical condition that prevents you from fasting, make it a goal to try the following:

Fast for one full day: Before you commence my 14-day meal plan (see page 200), set the foundation mentally and physically by drinking filtered water only for the twenty-four-hour period leading up to that first meal. For many, it helps to do the fast on a Saturday (last meal is dinner Friday night), and then begin the diet program on a Sunday morning. A twenty-four-hour fast is also a great way to jump back into this way of life if you fall off the proverbial wagon.

Skip breakfast once in a while: The body wakes up in mild ketosis. If you skip breakfast, you can keep this state going for a few hours before eating lunch at midday. Try skipping breakfast once or twice a week. I'll be asking you to do that during the 14-day meal plan. If the days I ask you to skip breakfast are not ideal for you, then choose one or two other days during the week when it works for you.

Fast for a full seventy-two hours: Four times a year, go on a prolonged fast of seventy-two hours, during which you only drink filtered water. This type of fast is more intense, as you can imagine, so be sure that you've tried a few twenty-four-hour fasts before attempting this one. Fasting during the seasonal changes (the last week of September, December, March, and June) is an excellent practice to maintain.

Go Cold Turkey (Cutting Off the Carbs)

Okay, you're almost ready for Step 1. I know what you're thinking. The thought of going cold turkey on cutting carbs is terrifying. Let me share Jen Z.'s story and then offer some advice.

My name is Jen, I am fifty-four years old, and for quite a number of years I had been dealing with some very questionable illnesses. I was overweight with no success in getting my weight down, was chronically tired, had trouble concentrating, and had developed an autoimmune skin disorder called vitiligo, where the skin no longer produces pigment. A couple of years into these problems, I was diagnosed with metastatic melanoma and went through surgery and very aggressive immunotherapy as well as radiation. The treatment for the cancer left me with very damaged nerves, damaged skin, no energy at all, arthritis and joint pains so bad I could hardly walk sometimes, and the brain power of a pea. I could not remember things that I had known all my life, nor could I concentrate on anything.

With all my research trying to figure out how long this would last, I was led to the conclusion that this would be my new normal and I would just have to deal with it. I am an avid horsewoman, and this left me feeling that everything I had worked toward was being taken away.

Then one day about seven months ago, a friend shared with me an article about a doctor who was diagnosed with untreatable stage 4 brain cancer. In his quest to fight for his life, he discovered the low-carb lifestyle. I say lifestyle because it is not a diet to be jumped on and off of but a new way of life. At this point, I was searching for a way to regain some of my health and try to avoid any need for cancer treatments, so I thought I would give it a try. The cancer version of this new lifestyle is quite extreme, but it has been so worth it! The first two weeks were pretty rough with food cravings and my body adjusting to the change in diet, but I could feel changes happening and they felt good. I went cold turkey, all in! About four weeks in, my body no longer hurt from arthritis pain, joint swelling was gone, and my weight was dropping without me doing anything but changing the way I eat. Jumping ahead seven months now, I have been very faithful to the program! Only a handful of times have I put food in my body that does not belong and it was not but a few bites. Does not take much and you know that it was not a smart choice!

Anyway, I feel better now than I have in probably twenty years or longer. My brain function is back better than before, nerves are regenerating that were destroyed by radiation, the skin disorder that I was told would get progressively worse is actually reversing, my energy level is crazy good, and I am back training horses again. Best of all, I am three years cancer-free, my weight is almost what it should be, and I feel great. I will be the first to say it was not simple getting started, but once you get it figured out (there are lots of food labels to read), it gets easier by the day.

The vast majority of you will have no trouble going cold turkey on cutting carbs. But it may be difficult for some, especially if carbs have been a large part of your diet. If you experience mood swings, crashing energy levels, and intense cravings during the first couple of days on the program, have patience. These effects are temporary and will go away within the first week. Your mind will clear, your energy levels will soar, and you'll realize how important this decision has been.

You'll never want to go back. Here are some additional thoughts to consider while facing the task of nixing those addictive carbs.

Leverage your motivation: Sugar and drugs have a lot in common. Cravings for both act on the same neurochemical pathways, which is why weaning yourself off either drugs or sugar in the form of processed carbs can involve unwanted withdrawal effects (though withdrawing from sugar is easier than withdrawing from most drugs). As I just mentioned, many people don't have a hard time cutting carbohydrates, but you might experience a short-lived "thirst" for sugar, crankiness, headaches, low energy, maybe some aches and pains. This is normal. When you understand that the discomfort is merely a side effect of your body's natural withdrawal from an addictive substance, you can use the knowledge to allay your fears and frustrations, turning that knowledge into a source of motivation and resolve. Remind yourself that these effects are temporary and won't last long. When you don't feel great and have the urge to eat a carbohydrate-rich food that is calling to you like a best friend, talk yourself out of it. You will not let carbs control you like a drug. Think about how much better you'll feel when you expel them from your diet.

Arm yourself with alternatives: Let's be honest. Going from a carb-rich diet to a carb-less diet overnight can be a significant lifestyle change. Recognize that. Acknowledge that this way of eating can take a little while to get used to, and that's okay. During the first few days of your transition, arm yourself with the supplies for a counterattack when cravings hit by always having high-quality snacks on hand, such as raw nuts and nut butters, beef jerky, tasty cheeses, hard-boiled eggs, and raw veggies with a delicious dip (see page 198 for more snack ideas). Don't worry about counting calories or eating too many snacks. Just do it to get through the transition and I promise that you will emerge healthier, happier, and a whole lot lighter—and the cravings will soon vanish.

Avoid temptations: Say goodbye to some of your favorite restaurants. The hardest part of this carb-conscious transition is the beginning. Don't sabotage yourself or make it any harder by patronizing restaurants and food courts where you know that you'll be tempted and will have a difficult time finding something to eat that satisfies this lifestyle. Set yourself up for success at the start by avoiding unnecessary temptations. Of course, all within reason. You have commitments to fulfill and places to go, including events at your children's school, your work, and occasions in your personal, social world. Life does go on around you, so be mindful of that. Engineer the start of your new way of living when you know you can make a real go of this. If you have a work-related breakfast function on Friday morning that you know will involve a buffet filled with pancakes, doughnuts, and waffles, get past that and plan to start the protocol on Saturday. During the 14-day meal plan, bring lunch to work so you're in control and you're not stuck deciding between unhealthy options.

Take the challenge: Make the commitment today that you'll stick with the low-carb lifestyle forever. This is quite possibly the best thing you'll ever do for your health. But the benefits won't last if you revert back to your old ways. If you stray, so will your body—it will go back to its prior state after about two months (about the same amount of time it takes a fully fit body to go from physical greatness to being totally out of shape). So before you execute the steps, ask yourself why you want to change. Be honest and write those reasons down. Then go ahead and take a selfie—the "before" picture of yourself. Mark on the calendar the day you will begin. That is the day you accept the challenge, knowing that you are making a real commitment to your health. This is not a short-term diet. This is a *whole life* change. And your body—and future—will love it.

Believe in yourself, even when others don't: You will encounter people who support your new lifestyle and others who will try to sabotage it. Some individuals will express curiosity at your new dietary choices and some will mock you or tell you that you're ill-informed, stupid, or downright crazy. They may even include your best friends and family members. Be prepared to face these challenging, often embarrassing, encounters. When you turn down your cousin's homemade pie at Christmas, let alone all the other things on the dinner table, know what you're going to say: "I've been on this new diet and feel too fantastic to divert; unfortunately, certain ingredients are not allowed. Do you want to hear more about it?" With discourse and information comes understanding. Though you will face some people who will remain skeptics, don't let them bring you down. They may act appalled that you choose not to have a slice of pizza or a sandwich with them for lunch, but stay strong and comfortable in your decision. Your goal is to be the healthiest you can be. People will always judge. I bet that once you get used to fending off the naysayers and explaining yourself, soon they will follow in your footsteps.

Remember, it's a good idea to check with your doctor about beginning this new protocol, especially if you have any health issues for which you take prescribed medication. This is important if you're going to opt for the twenty-four-hour fast at the start. As you commence this new lifestyle, you will achieve the following important goals:

- Introduce a new way of nourishing your body, including your microbiome and brain, through the foods you eat

- Support the structure and function of your whole body through the right blend of supplements, probiotics included

- Add complementary strategies to the plan by focusing on more physical movement, restful sleep, attention to your emotional self and self-care, and cleaning up your physical environment

You know the rules. You know your goals. And you know the data that supports both. Now you are ready. Let's get to Step 1.

CHAPTER 5

Step 1—Edit Your Diet and Pill-Popping

WHAT EXACTLY IS ALLOWED ON this diet? The menu plan and recipes in Part III will help you follow the protocol, but let me give you a cheat sheet to guide you in shopping for and planning your meals. I'll also give you guidance on how to choose the right supplements to complement the diet and how to avoid certain medications if possible.

THE YES/NO KITCHEN CLEAN-OUT

The Grain Brain Whole Life Plan calls for the main dish to be mostly fibrous, colorful, nutrient-dense whole fruits and vegetables that grow above ground, with protein as a side dish. I cannot stress this enough: A low-carb diet is not all about eating copious amounts of meat and other sources of protein. To the contrary, a low-carb plate features a sizeable portion of vegetables (three-quarters of your plate) and just 3 to 4 ounces (about 100g) of protein (and no more than 8 ounces – 225g – of protein total in a day). You'll get your fats from those found naturally in protein, from ingredients used to prepare your meals such as butter and olive oil, and from nuts and seeds. The beauty of this diet is that you don't have to worry about portion control. If you follow these guidelines, your natural appetite-control systems kick into gear and you eat the right amount for your body and energy needs.

The Villains ("NO")

As you prepare for this new way of eating, one of the first things to do is eliminate items that you'll no longer be consuming. Start by removing the following:

All sources of gluten, including whole-grain and whole-wheat forms of bread, noodles, pastas, pastries, baked goods, and cereals. The following ingredients can also hide gluten and should be banished from your kitchen (and check labels to make sure other products don't contain these):

Avena sativa (a form of oats)

baked beans (canned)

barley

beer

blue cheeses

breaded foods

brown rice syrup

broths/stocks (commercially prepared)

bulgur

caramel color (frequently made from barley)

cereals

chocolate milk (commercially prepared)

cold cuts

couscous

cyclodextrin

dextrin

egg substitute

energy bars (unless
   certified gluten-free)

farina

fermented grain
   extract

flavored coffees and teas

french fries (often dusted
   with flour before
   freezing)

fried vegetables/tempura

fruit fillings and puddings

gravy

hot dogs

hydrolysate

hydrolyzed malt
   extract

ice cream

imitation crabmeat,
   bacon, etc.

instant hot drinks

kamut

ketchup

malt/malt flavoring

malt vinegar

maltodextrin

marinades

matzo

mayonnaise (unless
   certified gluten-free)

meatballs, meat loaf

modified food starch

natural flavoring

nondairy creamer

oat bran (unless certified
   gluten-free)

oats (unless certified
   gluten-free)

phytosphingosine extract

processed cheese (e.g.,
   Kraft cheese slices)

roasted nuts

root beer

rye

salad dressings

sausage

seitan

semolina

soups

soy protein

soy sauces and teriyaki sauces

spelt

tabbouleh

trail mix

triticale

Triticum aestivum (a form of wheat)

Triticum vulgare (a form of wheat)

vegetable protein (hydrolyzed vegetable protein and textured vegetable protein)

veggie burgers

vodka

wheat

wheat germ

wine coolers

yeast extract

Be extra cautious of foods labeled "gluten-free," "free of gluten," "no gluten," or "GF certified." Although the FDA issued a regulation in August 2013 to define the term "gluten" for food labeling (the gluten limit for foods that carry any gluten-free label has to be less than 20 parts per million in America), it's the responsibility of the manufacturers to comply and be accountable for using the claim truthfully. Some of the foods listed above, such as energy bars and mayonnaise, do come certified gluten-free and quality brands exist today. Do your homework, though. A gluten-free energy bar, for example, may contain lots of sugars and artificial ingredients that you want to avoid. Just because a food is labeled "gluten-free" and "organic" doesn't mean it lives up to my guidelines. And such products can derail your best efforts to put my protocol into practice and reap the health benefits.

Many foods marketed as being gluten-free never contained gluten to begin with (such as water, fruits, vegetables, eggs). But the term "gluten-free" does not indicate that a food is organic, low-carb, or healthy. In fact, food manufacturers use this term on products that have been processed so that their gluten has been replaced by another ingredient such as cornstarch, cornmeal, rice starch, potato starch, or tapioca starch, any of which can be equally as offensive. These processed starches can be allergenic and pro-inflammatory.

All forms of processed carbs, sugar, and starch:

agave	honey
cakes	jams/jellies/preserves
candy	juices
chips	maple syrup
cookies	muffins
corn syrup	pastries
crackers	pizza dough
doughnuts	soft drinks
dried fruit	sports drinks
energy bars	sugar (white and brown)
fried foods	sugary snacks
frozen yogurt/sherbet	

Most starchy vegetables and those that grow below the ground:

beetroot	sweet potatoes
peas	sweetcorn
potatoes	yams

Packaged foods labeled "fat-free" or "low-fat": unless they are authentically fat-free or low-fat and within the protocol, such as water, mustard, and balsamic vinegar.

Margarine, vegetable shortening, trans fats (hydrogenated and partially hydrogenated oils), any commercial brand of cooking oil (soybean, corn, cottonseed, rapeseed, groundnut, safflower, grape seed, sunflower, rice bran, and wheat germ oils): even if they are organic. People often mistake vegetable oils as being derived from vegetables. They are not. The term is incredibly misleading, a relic from the days when food manufacturers needed to distinguish these fats from animal fats. These oils typically come from grains such as corn, seeds, or other plants such as soybeans. And they have been highly refined and chemically altered. The majority of Americans today get their fat from these oils, which are high in pro-inflammatory omega-6 fats as opposed to anti-inflammatory omega-3 fats. Do not consume them.

Non-fermented soy (e.g., tofu and soy milk) and processed foods made with soy: Look for "soy protein isolate" in the list of ingredients; avoid soy cheese, soy burgers, soy hot dogs, soy nuggets, soy ice cream, soy yogurt. Note: Although some naturally brewed soy sauces are technically gluten-free, many commercial brands have trace amounts of gluten. If you need to use soy sauce in your cooking, use tamari soy sauce made with 100 percent soybeans and no wheat.

The Heroes ("YES")

First things first: Remember to choose organic wherever possible and non-GMO foods, which will help you steer clear of gut-busting, fattening glyphosate. Choose antibiotic-free, grass-fed, 100 percent organic beef and poultry. This is key, because "grass-fed" doesn't necessarily mean "organic." When buying poultry, seek pastured meats that are also certified organic. This means the poultry is raised right on top of living grasses where they can eat all the various grasses, plants, insects, and so on that they can find in addition to their feed. When buying fish, choose wild, which often have lower levels of toxins than farmed.

Beware of the term "natural." The FDA has not fully defined the word, other than to say that it can be used on foods that do not contain added color, artificial flavors, or synthetic substances. But note that "natural" does not mean "organic," and it doesn't necessarily mean a food is healthy. It could still be loaded with sugar, for example. When you see this term, make sure to read the ingredient list.

Vegetables:

alfalfa sprouts	broccoli
artichoke	brussels sprouts
asparagus	cabbage
bok choy	cauliflower

celery

chard

fennel

garlic

ginger

green beans

jicama

kale

leafy greens and lettuces

leeks

mushrooms

onions

parsley

radishes

shallots

spinach

spring onions

turnips

water chestnuts

watercress

Low-sugar fruits:

aubergines

avocados

bell peppers

courgettes

cucumbers

lemons

limes

pumpkin

squash

tomatoes

Fermented foods:

fermented meat, fish, and eggs

kefir

kimchi

live-cultured yogurt

pickled fruits and vegetables

sauerkraut

Healthy fats:

almond milk

avocado oil

cheese (except for blue
  cheeses)

coconut oil (see note below)

coconuts

extra-virgin olive oil

ghee

grass-fed tallow and organic
  or pasture-fed butter

medium-chain triglyceride
  (MCT) oil (usually
  derived from coconut
  and palm kernel oils)

nuts and nut butters

olives

seeds (flaxseed, sunflower
  seeds, pumpkin seeds,
  sesame seeds, chia seeds)

sesame oil

A note about coconut oil: This superfuel for the brain also reduces inflammation. It's known in the scientific literature as helping to prevent and treat neurodegenerative disease. Use more of it when preparing meals. Coconut oil is heat-stable, so if you are cooking at high temperatures, use this instead of olive oil. (And if you don't like cooking with it, then you can take a teaspoon or two straight, as if it were a supplement — see page 105.) Coconut oil is also a great source of medium-chain triglycerides (MCT), an excellent form of saturated fatty acid. You can also add it to coffee and tea.

Proteins:

grass-fed meat, fowl, poultry, and pork (beef, lamb, liver, bison,
  chicken, turkey, duck, ostrich, veal)

shellfish and mollusks (shrimp, crab, lobster, mussels, clams,
  oysters)

whole eggs

wild fish (salmon, black cod, mahimahi, grouper, herring, trout, sardines)

wild game

Herbs, seasonings, and condiments:

cultured condiments (lacto-fermented mayonnaise, mustard, horseradish, hot sauce, relish, salsa, guacamole, salad dressing, and fruit chutney)

horseradish

mustard

salsas, if they are free of gluten, wheat, soy, and sugar

tapenade

Note: Sour cream, while technically a fermented dairy product, tends to lose its probiotic power during processing. Some manufacturers, however, add live cultures at the end of the process; look for brands that indicate this on the label ("with added live cultures").

Other foods that can be consumed occasionally (small amounts once a day or, ideally, just a couple times a week):

carrots

cow's milk and cream: Use sparingly in recipes, coffee, and tea

legumes (beans, lentils, peas): With the exception that chickpeas and hummus are fine, as long as they are organic. Watch out for commercially made hummus that's loaded with additives and inorganic ingredients. Classic hummus is simply chickpeas, tahini, olive oil, lemon juice, garlic, salt, and pepper

non-gluten grains:
    amaranth
    buckwheat
    millet
    quinoa
    rice (brown, white, wild)
    sorghum
    teff
parsnips

A note about oats: Make sure any oats you buy are truly gluten-free; some come from plants that process wheat products, causing contamination. I generally recommend limiting non-gluten grains because when processed for human consumption (such as milling whole oats and preparing rice for packaging), their physical structure can change, and this may increase the risk of an inflammatory reaction.

Sweeteners: natural stevia and chocolate (at least 75 percent cacao)
Whole sweet fruit: Berries are best; be extra cautious of sugary fruits such as apricots, mangos, melons, papayas, plums (or prunes), and pineapples

Label Lookout

Organic certification means that a food was produced without synthetic pesticides, genetically modified organisms (GMOs), or fertilizers made from petroleum. When it comes to organic meats and dairy products, it also means that they are from animals fed organic, vegetarian feed, are not treated with antibiotics or hormones, and are provided access to the outdoors. If the product was made with 100 percent organic ingredients, then it can say "100% organic." Just the word "organic" means the food was made with at least 95 percent organic ingredients.

"Made with organic ingredients" signifies that the product was made with a minimum of 70 percent organic ingredients, with restrictions on the remaining 30 percent, including no GMOs. As with the term "natural," "organic" doesn't imply healthy. Many organic junk foods line the shelves in supermarkets today, including candy and baked goods that are anything but healthy. When in doubt, scrutinize the ingredient list. It's the best way to know.

A note about buying produce: There's nothing more frustrating than splurging on fresh produce that wilts and begins to mold the moment you get home. Plan which fruits and vegetables you intend to use in the coming days based on the meal plan and purchase them on an as-needed basis, unless you're going to stock up on flash-frozen varieties. Flash-frozen fruits and vegetables are fine to buy as long as you choose organic or non-GMO verified. Three more tips:

- Avoid damaged, discolored, dull-looking fruits and vegetables. Ask your grocer what just came in and what's local. Stick with what's in season if you're buying fresh produce. If you crave berries, but the "fresh" ones have been shipped from thousands of miles away, opt for organic flash-frozen ones instead. These will have been picked during the peak of their ripeness, thus retaining their nutrients.

- Brighter means better: The brighter the colors you see, the more nutrients the fruit or vegetable contains. When you have choices in color, such as in bell peppers or onions, choose an array. Different colors impart different nutrients.

- High-risk crops for GMO: Papaya, courgettes, and yellow summer squash are often genetically modified foods, so look for non-GMO verified when buying these.

What to Drink?

The number one drink to have on hand at all times is filtered water, which is free of chemicals that can assault your microbiome. I urge you to buy a household water filter for all of your drinking and cooking purposes. There are a variety of water treatment technologies available today, from simple filtration pitchers you fill manually to under-the-sink contraptions or units designed to filter the water coming into your home from its source. I'm a big fan of the systems that employ reverse osmosis and carbon filters, so check those out if possible. It's up to you to decide which system best suits your circumstances and budget. Make sure the filter you buy removes fluoride, chlorine, and other potential contaminants. It's important that, with whichever filter you choose, you follow the manufacturer's directions to maintain it so that it continues to perform. As contaminants build up, a filter will become less effective, and it can then start to release chemicals back into your filtered water.

Other beverages that are allowable include coffee, tea, and wine (preferably red) in moderation. These drinks contain compounds that support gut and brain health. Just be sure not to overdo it. Coffee and tea contain caffeine, which can interfere with your sleep (unless you choose decaffeinated). In addition to green tea, which contains compounds known to fire up that Nrf2 pathway we discussed, I highly recommend trying kombucha tea. This is a form of fermented black or green tea that has been used for centuries. Fizzy and often served chilled, it's believed to help increase energy, and it may even help you lose weight. Note that wine should be limited to one glass for women and two for men per day.

Build and Maintain a Herb and Spice Collection

There's no better way to liven up meals than to add a dash of spice or a pinch of fresh herbs. Culinary herbs and spices can transform a dish from drab to fab. Although some do get expensive, you don't have to run out and spend a fortune in one fell swoop to create a spice rack worthy of a cooking magazine. Build it up over time. Here's a list of items you'll want to start collecting and experimenting with in your dishes. Choose garden-fresh organic herbs and non-irradiated herbs and spices wherever possible. You can start by purchasing 25g of each of the herbs and spices you want to try; for items you buy dried, store them in their original containers or transfer them to glass bottles that you can label. For fresh varieties, store them in the refrigerator and use them quickly.

- allspice
- basil
- bay leaves
- black pepper
- cayenne pepper
- chilli powder
- chives
- cilantro (coriander)
- cinnamon

- cloves
- cumin
- curry powder (red and yellow)
- dill
- garlic (powder and fresh cloves)
- ground ginger (and gingerroot)
- mint
- mustard seeds (black and yellow)
- nutmeg
- oregano
- paprika
- parsley
- red chilli flakes
- rosemary
- saffron
- sage
- savory
- sea salt
- tarragon
- thyme
- turmeric
- vanilla pods

Restock Your Pantry

If you followed the kitchen clean-out lists, chances are your pantry might be feeling lonely. You likely had to dump a lot of villains. So what goes in there now, besides your oils and vinegars?

- almond flour

- broth (beef, chicken, and vegetable)

- canned fish (salmon, tuna, anchovies)

- canned tomatoes (including paste)

- canned vegetables

- cocoa powder (at least 75 percent cacao)

- dill pickles

- hot sauces

- nuts and seeds

Now that you've edited your kitchen, it's time to edit your medicine cabinet.

PILLS TO POP — OR NOT

Every week it seems that we hear something in the media regarding the use of supplements. One day it's reported that certain vitamins are good for us and will extend our life; the next, we read that some can increase our risk for certain diseases, including dementia. While it's true that vitamins and supplements should never be used as an insurance policy against lapses in our diet, there's a time and place for certain products. And there's a difference between megadosing on multivitamins and adding natural supplements of nutrients that the body won't otherwise obtain easily from the diet.

There are many manufacturers of supplements today, and two formulas created for the same effect can have a different combination of ingredients as well as different dosages. Do your homework to find the best, highest-quality supplements that don't contain fillers, whether you're buying general supplements or probiotics. A good way to know which brands are best is to speak with the supervisor of the supplement and probiotic section at your health food store or retailer. These people tend to be knowledgeable about the top products and are not representatives of any particular company, so their advice is not biased. Supplements, probiotics included, are not regulated by the FDA like pharmaceuticals are, so you don't want to end up with a brand whose claims don't match the actual ingredients.

If a package of "high-potency" probiotic supplements with ten probiotic strains, for example, is marketed as delivering "50 billion live cultures per capsule," by the time you purchase the product, you may not be consuming that amount. The freshness and viability of packaged probiotic strains decline over time, even under ideal storage conditions. This is why it's important to know what you're getting and to ask for the superior brand with a reputable track record. Purchase your probiotics in smaller quantities and buy more frequently rather than buying the supersize value packs.

Note: If you currently take any prescription medication, it's important that you talk with your physician before starting any supplement program. You can take most of these supplements whenever it's convenient for you. Most do not have to be taken with food. The two exceptions: Probiotics should be taken on an empty stomach, and acacia gum, a prebiotic fiber I highly recommend that's now widely available in health food stores around the country, should be taken before an evening meal (more details follow).

It's usually best to take the supplements at the same time every day so you don't forget, which for many people is in the morning, before leaving home. Only one of my suggested supplements, turmeric, should be taken twice daily; have one dose in the morning and another in the evening. On page 112, I've created a cheat sheet for you to use that lists all the supplements and probiotics and their recommended dosages.

Following are my recommendations.

General Supplements to Consider

DHA: Docosahexaenoic acid (DHA) is a hero in the supplement kingdom and one of the most well-documented darlings in protecting the brain. DHA is an omega-3 fatty acid that makes up more than 90 percent of the omega-3 fats in the brain. Fifty percent of the weight of a neuron's membrane is composed of DHA, and it's a key component in heart tissue. DHA deficiency is seen in several disorders, including dementia and anxiety. The richest source of DHA in nature is human breast milk, which explains why breast-feeding is continually touted as important for neurologic health. DHA is also now added to formula as well as to hundreds of food products. Take 1,000 mg daily. It's fine to buy DHA that comes in combination with EPA (eicosapentaenoic acid), and it doesn't matter whether it's derived from fish oil or algae.

Coconut oil: As mentioned on page 95, if you don't cook often with this oil or use it in coffee and tea, enjoy its benefits by consuming a teaspoon or two once a day.

Turmeric: A member of the ginger family, turmeric is the seasoning that gives curry powder its yellow color. It's long been known for its anti-inflammatory, antioxidant, and anti-apoptotic properties — it reduces cell suicide or apoptosis. Turmeric is being studied today for its potential applications in neurology. Research shows that it can enhance the growth of new brain cells, as well as increase DHA levels in the brain. In some people, turmeric can even rival the antidepressant effects of Prozac. It's been used for thousands of years in Chinese and Indian medicine as a natural remedy for a variety of ailments. Curcumin, the most active constituent of turmeric, activates genes to produce a vast array of antioxidants that serve to protect our precious mitochondria. It also improves glucose metabolism, which helps maintain a healthy balance of gut bacteria. If you're not eating a lot of curry dishes, I recommend a supplement of 500 mg twice daily.

Alpha-lipoic acid: This fatty acid is found inside every cell in the body, where it's needed to produce energy for the body's functions. It crosses the blood-brain barrier and acts as a powerful antioxidant in the brain. Scientists are now studying it as a potential treatment for strokes and other brain conditions, such as dementia, that involve free-radical damage. Although the body can produce adequate supplies of this fatty acid, it's best to supplement to ensure you're getting enough. Aim for 300 to 500 mg daily.

Coffee fruit extract: This is one of the most exciting additions to my supplement regimen. This extract, which contains very little caffeine, has recently been shown to increase blood levels of a protein called "brain-derived neurotrophic factor," or BDNF. I can't emphasize enough how important BDNF is, not only to keeping the brain healthy and maintaining its resistance to damage, but also to triggering the growth of new brain cells and increasing the connections between them. Study after study shows a relationship between levels of BDNF and risk for developing Alzheimer's disease. In a seminal 2014 study published in the prestigious *Journal of the American Medical Association,* researchers at Boston University found that in a group of more than 2,100 elderly people followed for ten years, 140 of them developed dementia. Those with the highest levels of BDNF in their blood had less than half the risk for dementia as compared to those who had the lowest levels of BDNF. Low levels of BDNF are documented in people with Alzheimer's as well as in people with obesity and depression. Look for whole coffee fruit concentrate, and take 100 mg daily. A single dosage of whole coffee fruit extract has been shown to *double* blood levels of BDNF during the first hour after consumption.

Vitamin D: This is technically a hormone, not a vitamin. By definition, vitamins cannot be produced by the body. But vitamin D is produced in the skin upon exposure to ultraviolet (UV) radiation from the sun. Although most people associate it with bone health and calcium levels, vitamin D has far-reaching effects on the body and especially on the brain. We know there are receptors for vitamin D throughout the entire central nervous system; in fact, researchers have identified approximately 3,000 binding sites on the human genome for vitamin D. We also know that vitamin D helps regulate the enzymes in the brain and cerebrospinal fluid that are involved in manufacturing neurotransmitters and stimulating nerve growth. Both animal and human studies have indicated that vitamin D protects neurons from the damaging effects of free radicals and reduces inflammation. As previously noted, vitamin D is also associated with longer telomeres. And here's a most important fact: Vitamin D performs all of these tasks through its relationship with the gut bacteria. In 2010 we found out that gut bacteria interact with our vitamin D receptors, controlling them to either increase their activity or turn it down.

As mentioned on page 75, I encourage you to get your vitamin D levels tested and have your doctor help you find your optimal dose. For adults, I generally recommend starting with 5,000 IU of vitamin D daily. Some people need more and others less. It's important to have your doctor track your vitamin D levels until you land on a dosage that will keep you in the upper range of normal on the blood test.

Supplements to Support Gut Health

The two secrets to improving the composition and function of your gut bacteria are prebiotics and probiotics.

Prebiotics

Prebiotics, the ingredients that gut bacteria love to eat to fuel their growth and activity, can easily be ingested through certain foods. To qualify as prebiotics, they must have three characteristics. First and foremost, they must be nondigestible, meaning they pass through the stomach without being broken down by either gastric acids or enzymes. Second, they have to be able to be fermented or metabolized by the intestinal bacteria. And third, this activity has to confer health benefits. Prebiotic dietary fiber, for example, meets all these requirements, and its effects on the growth of healthy bacteria in the gut may well be the reason it's anticancer, anti-diabetes, anti-dementia, and pro-weight loss.

By and large, we don't get anywhere near enough prebiotics. I recommend aiming for at least 12 grams daily, from either real foods, a supplement, or a combination thereof. Again, this is one of the most important steps you can take to nurture the health and function of your good gut bacteria and open the door for a healthy future for yourself. Below is the list of top food sources of natural prebiotics.

- acacia gum (or gum arabic)

- asparagus

- chicory root

- dandelion greens

- garlic

- leeks

- onions

- sunchokes (Jerusalem artichokes)

While some of these may be a bit unfamiliar, my menu plan will show you how to make use of them and get plenty of prebiotic fiber into your diet every day. Health food stores now also carry powdered prebiotic fiber products that you can simply mix with water. These products, which are often derived from acacia gum, provide a convenient source of concentrated prebiotic fiber that will nurture your gut bacteria. Acacia gum has been extensively studied. It has been found to have a significant impact on weight loss. One recent study showed a dramatic reduction in both body mass index and body fat percentage among healthy adult women taking acacia gum as a nutritional supplement. The FDA considers acacia gum one of the safest, best-tolerated dietary fibers; it doesn't increase the risk of bloating, abdominal cramps, or diarrhea.

So if you are looking for a prebiotic fiber supplement, look for acacia gum. All you need is a level tablespoon or two a day in any beverage—fifteen to thirty minutes before the evening meal is ideal. While 12 grams of prebiotic fiber a day is a great target, it may take a week or two to be able to tolerate that much—you may experience some gas. You can start with just 1 tablespoon of acacia fiber daily and build up to 2 tablespoons daily.

When choosing a prebiotic supplement, look for:

- certified organic, Non-GMO Project verified, vegan, gluten-free labeling

- products that are free of psyllium, soy, and sugar

- no artificial colors, sweeteners, or flavors

Probiotics

As with prebiotics, you can get your probiotics through food and supplements. In terms of food, I recommend keeping the following in your kitchen:

- Live-cultured yogurt. The dairy section has gotten crowded. There are lots of options today when it comes to yogurt, but you have to be careful about what you are buying. Many yogurts—both Greek-style and regular—are loaded with added sugar, artificial sweeteners, and artificial flavors. Read the labels. If you are sensitive to dairy, try coconut milk yogurt. It is an excellent way to get plenty of gut-promoting enzymes and probiotics into your diet.

- Kefir. This fermented milk product is similar to yogurt. It's a unique combination of kefir grains (a symbiotic culture of yeast and bacteria) and goat's milk that's high in lactobacilli and bifidobacteria, two of the most studied probiotics in the gut. Kefir is also rich in antioxidants. If you are sensitive to dairy or are lactose-intolerant, coconut milk kefir is equally delicious and beneficial.

- Sauerkraut. This fermented cabbage fuels healthy gut bacteria and provides choline, a chemical needed for the proper transmission of nerve impulses from the brain through the central nervous system.

- Pickles. I believe pregnant women crave pickles for a reason. Pickles are one of the most basic and beloved natural probiotics. For many, pickles can be your gateway food to other, more exotic fermented foods.

- Pickled fruits and vegetables. Pickling fruits and veggies, such as carrot sticks and green beans, transforms the ordinary into the extraordinary. Whether you do this yourself or buy pickled produce, keep in mind that only unpasteurized foods pickled in brine, not vinegar, have probiotic benefits.

- Cultured condiments. You can buy or make your own lacto-fermented mayonnaise, mustard, horseradish, hot sauce, relish, salsa, guacamole, salad dressing, and fruit chutney. Remember to look for sour cream with added live cultures.

- Fermented meat, fish, and eggs. See my website, www.DrPerlmutter.com, for brand ideas and recipes for these. It's best to make these on your own rather than buying commercially made products, which are often processed with other ingredients you don't want.

The number of probiotic supplements available today can be overwhelming. Thousands of different species of bacteria make up the human microbiome, but I have a few gems to recommend:

Lactobacillus plantarum
Lactobacillus acidophilus
Lactobacillus brevis
Bifidobacterium lactis
Bifidobacterium longum

Most probiotic products contain several strains, and I encourage you to seek a probiotic supplement that contains at least ten different strains, with as many of the above-mentioned species as possible. Different strains provide different benefits, but these are the ones that will best support brain health by:

- fortifying the intestinal lining and reducing gut permeability

- reducing LPS, the inflammatory molecule that can be dangerous if it reaches the bloodstream

- increasing BDNF (brain-derived neurotrophic factor), which is fondly known as the brain's "growth hormone"

- sustaining an overall balance of bacteria to crowd out any potentially rogue colonies

If you're wanting to lose weight, I suggest looking for the following species in addition to those above:

Lactobacillus gasseri
Lactobacillus rhamnosus

For those with mood issues, including depression, look for:

Lactobacillus helveticus
Bifidobacterium longum

Remember, plan to take your probiotics on an empty stomach, and aim to take them at least thirty minutes before a meal.

THE SUPPLEMENT CHEAT SHEET

Name	Amount	Frequency
DHA	1,000 mg	daily
Coconut oil	1–2 teaspoons	daily (if not using in cooking/coffee/tea)
Turmeric	500 mg	twice daily
ALA	300–500 mg	daily
Coffee fruit extract	100 mg	daily
Vitamin D	5,000 IU	daily
Prebiotic fiber	12 g	daily (15–30 minutes before dinner)
Probiotics	1 multi-strain capsule	daily (at least 30 minutes before a meal)

Pills that Should Give You Pause Before Popping

The vast majority of Americans take a medication of some sort daily, whether it's prescribed or over the counter. Nearly three in five American adults take a prescription drug; in 2015, the *Journal of the American Medical Association* published findings that the prevalence of prescription drug use among people twenty and older had risen to 59 percent in 2012 from 51 percent just a dozen years earlier. And the percentage of people taking five or more prescription drugs nearly doubled during the same time period. It went from 8 percent to 15 percent.

Among the most commonly used drugs are the ones that increase the risk of brain ailments: statins. I've made my case about statins in the past and I briefly outline my main lesson below. But statins aren't the only problem. I highly recommend that you take inventory of your medicine cabinet and aim to reduce the number of drugs you take unless they are absolutely necessary to treat a condition. (Obviously, speak with your doctor should you consider stopping any medication specifically prescribed for you.) Following are the worst offenders:

Statins: Cholesterol-lowering statins are now being sold as a way to reduce overall levels of inflammation. But new research reveals that these powerful chemicals may decrease brain function and increase risk for diabetes, heart disease, impaired cognitive function, and depression. The reason is simple: The body, and especially the brain, needs cholesterol to thrive. What's more, cholesterol is involved in cell membrane structure and support, hormone synthesis, and vitamin D production. Reams of scientific data show time and time again that extremely low cholesterol levels are linked to depression, memory loss, and even violence to oneself and others.

Acid-reflux drugs (proton pump inhibitors): An estimated 15 million Americans use proton pump inhibitors (PPIs) for gastroesophageal reflux disease, or GERD. These drugs are sold by prescription and over the counter under a variety of brand names, including Nexium, Prilosec, Protonix, and Prevacid. They block the production of stomach acid, something your body needs for normal digestion. In the past two years, the negative effects of these drugs have been shown in widely reported studies. Not only do they leave people vulnerable to nutritional deficiencies and infections, some of which can be life-threatening, but they also put people at greater risk of heart disease and chronic kidney failure. And they do a number on your gut bacteria. When researchers examined the diversity of microbes in stool samples of those taking two daily doses of proton pump inhibitors, they documented dramatic changes after just one week of treatment. These drugs can effectively ruin the integrity of your digestive system by dramatically changing your gut bacteria.

Acetaminophen: Nearly a quarter of American adults (about 52 million people) use a medicine containing acetaminophen (brand name Tylenol) each week for aches, pains, and fever. It's also the most common drug ingredient in the United States, found in more than 600 medicines. But it's not as benign as we've been led to believe. It's now been shown to be ineffective for osteoarthritis pain, the very condition for which it's heavily marketed. What's more, new research shows that it compromises brain function, increasing the risk of making cognitive mistakes. Although early research had shown that acetaminophen not only affects physical pain, but also psychological pain, we now know the true nature of its effects thanks to a 2015 Ohio State University study revealing that acetaminophen blunts emotions, positive and negative. Participants who took acetaminophen felt less strong emotions when they were shown both pleasant and disturbing photos as compared to the controls who were given placebos.

Acetaminophen is also known to deplete one of the body's most vital antioxidants, glutathione, which helps to control oxidative damage and inflammation in the body and especially in the brain. And in another 2015 study, Danish scientists found that women who took acetaminophen during pregnancy were more likely to have children medicated for ADHD by age seven. Tylenol is often "prescribed" to pregnant women and regarded as "safe." I hope that thinking changes soon.

Nonsteroidal anti-inflammatories: Think ibuprofen (Advil) and naproxen (Aleve). Like Tylenol, these are hugely popular pain relievers and fever reducers—on any given day about 17 million people take them. These drugs work by reducing the amount of prostaglandins in the body, a family of chemicals produced by the cells that have several important functions. Prostaglandins promote the kind of short-term inflammation necessary for healing; they support the blood clotting function of platelets; and they protect the lining of the stomach from the damaging effects of acid. Because of these last two functions, NSAIDs can compromise that intestinal lining; their number one side effect is stomach bleeding, ulcers, and stomach upset. Research shows that they damage the small intestine and indeed harm the gut lining, thereby setting the stage for the very problem they are intended to address: inflammation.

Antibiotics: This one should be obvious. Antibiotics are anti-life. They kill bacteria, both the good guys and the bad. Almost all of us need to take a round of antibiotics at some point in our lives. The effects of exposure to antibiotics on gut bacteria can persist for months after treatment, and new research has concluded that even one course of antibiotics can change the microbiome for the rest of a person's life. Such changes can have far-reaching effects on the body if the balance of healthy bacteria is not restored.

This new knowledge follows mounting evidence that they also drive adverse changes in insulin sensitivity, glucose tolerance, and fat accumulation due to how they alter the gut bacteria. The drugs also tinker with our own physiology, changing how we metabolize carbohydrates and how the liver metabolizes fat and cholesterol. Dr. Brian S. Schwartz of the Johns Hopkins Bloomberg School of Public Health, who has studied these connections, has gone so far as to say, "Your BMI may be forever altered by the antibiotics you take as a child."

Scientists have been tracking the strong correlation between exposure to antibiotics and risk for weight gain and type 2 diabetes. Take a look at the following two maps. On the left we see antibiotic prescriptions per 1,000 people, and on the right we see rates of obesity listed by state. These two maps look strikingly similar.

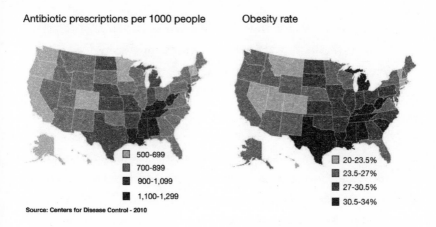

Antibiotic prescriptions per 1000 people

Obesity rate

500-699
700-899
900-1,099
1,100-1,299

20-23.5%
23.5-27%
27-30.5%
30.5-34%

Source: Centers for Disease Control - 2010

This next graphic shows antibiotics prescriptions per 1,000 people and prevalence of adult diabetes. Again we see a correlation. Also, remember that there is a notable relationship between obesity as well as adult diabetes and the risk for dementia. I think you can see the point I'm trying to reiterate: Our overuse of antibiotics is not only fueling our obesity and diabetes epidemics but also our increasing rates of dementia.

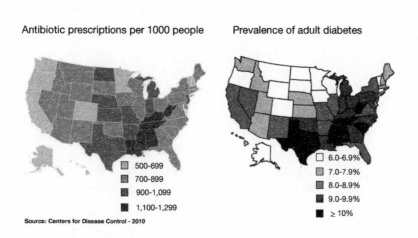

Antibiotic prescriptions per 1000 people

Prevalence of adult diabetes

500-699
700-899
900-1,099
1,100-1,299

6.0-6.9%
7.0-7.9%
8.0-8.9%
9.0-9.9%
≥ 10%

Source: Centers for Disease Control - 2010

The bottom line: You should be cautious about taking antibiotics. And parents should be wary of asking their pediatricians for antibiotics for their children at the slightest sign of a sniffle. In Part III, I'll give you some guidelines for when antibiotics might be necessary for you and your family.

No doubt there is a time and place for medications, be they over-the-counter or prescribed. But we live in a world where we are too quick to medicate, self-prescribe, and depend upon pills. The national conversation about pain and pain relief in particular has sparked a lot of debate over painkiller abuse. In 2014 alone, more than 14,000 Americans died of overdoses involving prescription opioids, and each day more than 1,000 people enter emergency rooms for misusing those drugs. May we see the day when we can minimize medications and maximize our body's innate ability to heal itself. If you rely on medications, I encourage you to work with your health-care provider to find alternative methods for treating and managing your conditions. I do trust that if you follow this program you will experience a lessening of your symptoms, whether you need to continue treatment with drugs or not.

CHAPTER 6

Step 2—Add Your Support Strategies

IN STUDIES OF POPULATIONS AROUND the world where the inhabitants live unusually long, healthy, productive lives well into their nineties and have less than half the rate of cancer as Americans, very little depression, and almost no dementia, there are a few common denominators. In these "Blue Zones," people maintain a positive outlook on life, have strong family and personal relationships, and feel part of a close-knit community. They are physically mobile in everyday life, consume fresh, local ingredients, and don't eat processed food. In the Blue Zone of Ikaria, Greece, fat accounts for more than 50 percent of Ikarians' daily calories, and more than half of their fat energy comes from olive oil. In Sardinia, Italy, where there's a community of mostly sheepherders, people spend their days walking, enjoying the company of others, and drinking local red wine with their meals. The famous Okinawan residents of Japan, many of whom live for about 110 years, base their diet on vegetables, drink mugwort sake, and remain physically active as they age. They also honor and celebrate their elders. The only Blue Zone in the United States is tucked just east of downtown Los Angeles, a city notoriously known for its smog and dense population. The community of Seventh-day Adventists in Loma Linda, California, near the big city, defies the belief that you have to live in a pristine, remote area to enjoy a long, disease-free life.

All of these people have mastered the tenets of healthy living without trying that hard or even knowing it. Self-care beyond the diet is sorely neglected in our society, yet factors like regular exercise, more sleep, and distraction-free time for self-reflection can make a huge difference in our health. The fast-paced world in which we live causes us to feel time-deprived and anxious, and during stress we turn to unhealthy habits that push us in the wrong direction and leave us ever more tired, uncreative, drug- and stimulant-dependent, and unsatisfied. Stress adds tremendous pressure on our biological systems, from the gut all the way up to the brain.

With that in mind, let me give you some non-diet-related strategies to boost overall health and prevent brain disease:

- Establish an exercise routine you can sustain

- Pay attention to pain, especially in your back and knees

- Make room for sleep

- Reduce stress and find calm in four simple ways

- Detoxify your physical environment

ESTABLISH AN EXERCISE ROUTINE YOU CAN SUSTAIN

Did you know that you can physically bulk up your brain with exercise and slash your risk for Alzheimer's disease in half?

The evidence is no longer anecdotal. Every week a new study emerges showing the neuroprotective benefits of exercise. Sedentarism appears to cause the brain to atrophy while simultaneously increasing the risk for Alzheimer's disease and other types of dementia. Being sedentary has even been shown to be twice as deadly as being obese.

In February 2016, a Finnish study found that being out of shape in middle age is linked to smaller brain volume down the road in later life. Gray matter is where all of your neurons are, so its volume can reflect brain health. Soon after, another study, conducted by researchers at four major research institutions in the United States, found that people with Alzheimer's disease or mild cognitive impairment (MCI, a precursor to Alzheimer's disease) experienced less gray matter shrinkage the more calories they burned through their exercise regimen. In other words, more physical activity meant more retained brain volume and less risk of disease. The researchers followed 876 adults over a thirty-year period and kept careful records of the amount and type of exercise that each participant reported. In addition, each of the individuals underwent a rigorous examination to determine brain function. Further, all of the participants had brain imaging done with a sophisticated MRI scanner. Those at the highest level of exercise activity experienced an incredible reduction of risk for Alzheimer's of 50 percent when compared to those who were more sedentary.

We live in a time when we have been fairly well trained to expect "magic bullets" to resolve our ailments. When it comes to Alzheimer's, none exists. Yet look at how you can safeguard your brain just by lacing up your sneakers and moving.

In addition to protecting the brain, exercise improves digestion, metabolism, elimination, immunity, complexion, body tone and strength, bone density, and circulation and heart health, and it helps us normalize weight. Just a twenty-five minute walk can cut your risk of dying prematurely by 30 percent; a brisk walk for the same time can add seven years to life. Physical movement is also an emotionally positive experience. It can increase self-worth and confidence and bring us greater energy. It can turn on our "smart genes," make us feel younger, stave off depression, and generally help us make healthier lifestyle choices, including what we're eating for dinner.

Regular aerobic exercise:

lowers the risk of death from all causes

lowers the risk of brain disorders

lowers the risk of depression (and can be used as a treatment for depression)

increases the quantity of BDNF, the brain's "growth hormone"

increases stamina, strength, flexibility, and coordination

increases blood circulation, oxygen supply to cells and tissues, and heart health

decreases food cravings, blood sugar levels, and risk for diabetes

decreases inflammation and risk for age-related disease, including cancer

increases sense of well-being and happiness

The last time you tried to get into shape, what happened? Did you succeed? Or did you keep up a routine for a few weeks, maybe right after New Year's, and then suddenly it was Memorial Day weekend and you didn't want to be seen in a bathing suit? Maybe you don't even remember when you fell off the wagon, but it happened.

The problem for anyone trying to get active is not so much the starting part as it is the *sustaining* part. The key is to figure out what it is that you love to do and that achieves the following: 1) stretches and strengthens your muscles, and 2) gets your blood flowing physically, increases your heart rate, and puts healthy demands on your cardio-vascular system.

Check with your doctor before starting an exercise program if you have any personal conditions and/or use medication that might be a factor in this endeavor.

Stretching and strengthening is important because far too many people focus solely on cardio and skip the stretching and weight-bearing exercises. If you don't stretch and strengthen your muscles, you not only impair bone health and muscle mass, but you also run the risk of injury, which will prevent you from staying active. Starting on page 129, I've created a very basic strength-training routine you can do at home. I also invite you to go to www.DrPerlmutter.com, where I provide video clips of these exercises that I encourage you to do in addition to a cardio routine of your choice. These clips cover all the major muscle groups—arms and shoulders, chest, back, abdominals, and legs. Perform these exercises three or four times a week, and have a rest day in between each session.

Ideally, aim for a **minimum of twenty minutes of cardio work six days a week**. You'll want to get your heart rate up at least 50 percent above your resting baseline for a least fifteen of those twenty minutes. There are lots of different kinds of heart-rate monitors on the market; and various types of gym equipment, such as stationary bikes, elliptical machines, and treadmills, now include heart-rate monitors, too. Online calculators can also help you find your maximum and target heart rates so you know when you're in the zone, as well as when you're pushing the limits. At first you may not be able to hit any reasonable target heart rate or, if you can, you may not be able to sustain it for long. But you can build up to that target. I've often said to my patients, "If you can't run five miles, then at least walk to the mailbox." You have to start somewhere, and if walking to the mailbox represents your first steps toward improving your health, then so be it. Even people who are confined to a wheelchair can and absolutely should engage in aerobic exercise.

Golfing doesn't count: One frequent response I get when asking patients about their exercise program, likely because I live in South Florida, goes something like this: Well, Doctor, I play eighteen holes of golf three times a week." I have nothing against golf, but this doesn't constitute aerobic exercise—even if you're walking the course, which is painfully rare these days.

Create a realistic plan that you can maintain. For some, that might mean participating in group classes at a local gym; for others, spending more time gardening, taking up yoga and swimming, joining a competitive sports team in your community, power walking around the mall, or following a workout routine online or on TV. I have been a long-distance runner since high school, and recently I have been using the elliptical machine as well as a stationary bike and road bike for aerobics. I go hard on some days and easier on others. I suggest you do the same: Mix up the days you work out at a high intensity for shorter periods of time and then have those days when you go at a moderate pace for a longer time. The twenty-minute rule should be your minimum. You should be able to add more minutes as you gain strength and physical fitness. Build up to more intense workouts, too. Intensity can be increased through speed (e.g., running or pedaling faster), resistance (e.g., steeper climbs, heavier barbells), duration (e.g., longer intervals of giving it your all to the point you're out of breath), and range of motion (e.g., deeper lunges, lower bends).

The optimal amount of exercise time, in fact, to gain the most benefits is close to 450 minutes per week. That averages out to a little more than an hour a day, which may seem like a lot, but it's not when you consider that this amount reflects *cumulative* minutes of exercise. You don't have to max out your heart rate for an entire hour, either, but you do need to be moving your body physically for at least that amount of time in total on most days of the week. It's easier than you think. You might do a twenty-minute jog in the morning, run errands at lunch during which you walk briskly for another twenty minutes, and then spend twenty minutes before dinner tending to household chores that are physically demanding. If you skimp on exercise one day, that just means you go longer the next. It doesn't really matter how you allocate those 450 minutes over the course of the week. Try to be as consistent as possible with when you plan your formal exercise daily (e.g., twenty minutes of cardio every morning before taking a shower), but don't beat yourself up if you're not perfect every single day. There will be days when you'll need to move the timing of your usual routine and days when fitting in formal exercise isn't possible. Strive for progress, not perfection.

And you don't have to get too techy, despite the number of devices available to track physical parameters like heart rate. Just as pain can be your guide to let you know when you've overdone it (more on this coming up), how you feel in the moment can be as good as any high-tech gadgetry. Pay attention to your breathing and level of sweating. Does your breath get deep and rapid during your formal workouts? Do you break a sweat? Do your muscles start to burn a little during weight-bearing exercises and feel a tad sore the next day while resting? There is a difference between running and leisurely mowing the lawn, as well as between using 3-pound versus 8-pound weights.

We all think in pictures, and studies show that imagining yourself in the physical shape you want to be in can help you reach your fitness goals. Try to keep a vivid, realistic image in your mind. This will motivate you every step of the way as you work toward your personal picture of health. Think about what it means for you to have a fit, toned body. You'll be able to participate in life to its fullest and not be constrained by low energy and no strength. Visualize yourself engaged in various fun activities you want to try, including adventures and vacations that make physical demands on you. Consider activities done alone, with a group, or with your family.

Concentrate also on what you'll gain in terms of vigor, balance, coordination, flexibility, and mental sharpness (and mental toughness!). You're sleeping better, managing stress more easily, enjoying a faster metabolism, being more productive overall, and spending less time sick in bed with a cold or other illness. You know that you're doing the best you can to ward off disease. If you are dealing with any chronic conditions, you're managing them superbly and they are having less impact on you. You're feeling more accomplished both at work and at home—because you are! And you're experiencing stronger, more intimate relationships with your loved ones.

How to Create Your Own Gym for Strength Training (No Trainer Required!)

You don't need much in the way of equipment to get a great strength-training workout. In fact, you don't even have to belong to a traditional gym, hire a trainer, or spend money on machines and fancy gadgetry to generate resistance against your body. There's a lot you can do using your own body weight. Classic push-ups and sit-ups, for example, don't require anything but you and a floor. But to get a full-body strength-training workout, I suggest you obtain a couple of inexpensive free weights. You can buy them online or at a local sporting goods store. Choose weights that are comfortable to grip. Start on the light side (3- or 5-pound – 1 or 2kg – weights) and add more weight as you gain strength and want to challenge yourself further.

Although there are many muscles and muscle groups in the body to work on a regular basis, it helps to think in terms of upper body, lower body, and core:

- Upper body: shoulders, triceps, biceps, chest, and lats (latissimi dorsi muscles of the back)

- Lower body: thighs/quads and calves

- Core: midsection and abdominals

On the days you choose to do your strength training—again, which you should do three or four times a week—perform exercises from each of the three main areas. While it would be optimal to hit every muscle group during your sessions, if you're short on time, you can split up the areas you focus on. So, for instance, if you exercise your triceps, biceps, calves, and core on Monday, you can turn to your shoulders, chest, thighs, and more core on Wednesday. Some people like to include strength training in their daily exercise routine, which is also okay as long as you don't repeat the same muscle groups two days in a row. Give those muscles at least a day or two of rest in between.

I encourage you to include a little bit of core work in each strength-training session. Powering up your core muscles and maintaining their strength is fundamental to health—more so than having toned arms. Your core is largely responsible for keeping you active and able to perform everyday tasks—from getting out of bed to sitting on the toilet, dressing, standing, and walking—as well as for playing sports and engaging in activities like biking, tennis, and dancing. Having a strong core prevents back pain, provides stability and balance, propels your endurance, and supports good posture. You don't have to aim for ripped, washboard abs. Far from it. You just need to work your midsection and abdominals routinely to prevent weak and inflexible core muscles. In fact, a weak or inflexible core can hinder how well your legs and arms function, draining energy from your movement and impairing everyday activities.

There are dozens of different exercises that will work your upper body, your lower body, and your core. And many exercises will engage the core even though you're focusing on another body part. Following are some basic exercises for a strength-training workout. Most of these require free weights. Because many cardio routines also place heavy demands on various muscle groups, you'll find that some of your muscles will be quicker to tone and strengthen because they are getting more of a workout (e.g., taking a spin class will also work your quads and calves in ways that are equivalent to weight-bearing exercises; swimming will work your upper body and back).

Remember to go to my website, www.DrPerlmutter.com, where you can watch me demonstrate these very exercises. You may want to venture out and test other methods of resistance training, either by using formal gym equipment or by taking a group fitness class that is centered on strength training (e.g., Pilates, many forms of yoga, and gym classes geared specifically toward building muscle mass and strength). I usually go to the gym for strength training because I can access a wider array of tools.

Shoulders: Basic Lifts

Stand up straight with your feet hip distance apart, arms by your side. Hold one weight in each hand, keeping your shoulders down and chest open, and maintain good posture. Lift the weights out to the side to shoulder height (as if you're making a letter "T" with your body). As you lift, with palms facing down, squeeze your shoulder blades together, and then lower the weights. Complete three sets of twelve repetitions (lift and lower twelve times).

Try a variation: Instead of lifting your arms out to the side, lift them up in front of you with straight arms, palms facing down.

Triceps: The Triceps Extension

Hold a free weight with both hands overhead. Try to use a weight that's at least 5 pounds (2kg). Draw your shoulders down and back, and engage your core. While keeping your elbows pointed forward, bend the elbows and allow the weight to lower down behind your head. Then bring the weight back up and overhead by extending your arms. Keep your core and glutes engaged the entire time. Complete three sets of twenty repetitions.

Biceps: Basic Bicep Curl

Stand up straight with your feet hip distance apart, gripping a free weight in each hand. Your starting position is to have your hands down by your sides, palms facing forward. While keeping your elbows close to your torso and your upper arms stationary, lift your forearms up, curling the weights up while contracting your biceps. Complete three sets of twenty repetitions.

Chest: Classic Push-Ups

Lying face down on the floor, place your hands under your shoulders and tuck your toes underneath you. Push up into a plank. Hold for five seconds, then slowly lower down toward the floor, trying to achieve about a 90-degree bend in the elbows. Try not to collapse onto the floor, and repeat the push-up again into the plank position. Complete three sets of twelve push-ups.

Lats: The Wide Row

The best exercise to work these back muscles is to do pull-ups to a raised bar. But another way, using your free weights, is the following. Stand straight, chest up and back flat, while holding a pair of free weights in each hand in front of your thighs with a palms-down grip. Now, slightly bend your knees and lean forward, hinging at the waist. Continue to lean forward until your upper body is almost parallel to the floor. Let the weights hang straight down in front of your shins. With your head in a neutral position and your eyes focused on the floor in front of you, lift both weights straight up, bending at the elbows. This is a rowing-like motion but you're in a semi-squat. Don't alter the angles at your knees and hips and lower the weights back after a short pause. Complete three sets of twelve repetitions.

Thighs/Quads: Lunges

Stand up straight with your feet hip distance apart, and have a slight bend in your knees. Hold the free weights down at your sides. This is your starting position. Now, step forward with your right leg while maintaining your balance and squat down through your hips. Keep your torso straight and your head up. Don't let your knee extend out over your toes. Using your heel to drive you, push yourself back to the starting position. Repeat this motion with your left leg to complete the full rep. Do three sets of twelve repetitions.

Calves: Tippy-Toes

Stand up straight with your feet hip distance apart. Hold a free weight in each hand, with each weight hanging by your sides. Push up onto your tippy-toes, and hold there for five seconds. Return to the start. Complete three sets of twelve repetitions.

Core: The Classic Sit-Up

Sit on the floor with your knees bent and your heels touching the floor. Cross your arms on your chest, making an "X." Make sure to keep your shoulders dropped and relaxed to avoid tension in the neck. With your feet firmly on the ground, lay back as far as you're able before rising back up. Maybe you can get all the way to the floor, maybe not. Continue doing sit-ups for one minute, then take a thirty-second break. Repeat for five rounds.

Core: Bicycle Crunch

Begin in the same starting position as the sit-up (see above). Twisting gently, bring your left knee and right elbow toward one another. Return to the starting position. Complete the movement with the right knee and left elbow. Continue for two minutes, then take a thirty-second break. Repeat for five rounds.

* * *

Take the time to write down your reasons for making these important fitness changes in your life. Rather than stating, "I want a flatter stomach and toned arms," go for more meaningful, purposeful goals like "I want to spend more quality time with my family rather than constantly dealing with my chronic pain," "I want to feel stronger and live longer," or "I want to do everything I can to prevent the Alzheimer's disease that my mother has." Think big picture and be bold and brave with your goals.

PAY ATTENTION TO PAIN, ESPECIALLY IN YOUR BACK AND KNEES

I cannot emphasize enough the importance of not neglecting two parts of your body that are critical to staying mobile and therefore reducing your risk of disease: your lower back and knees. Let's cover the lower back first.

The numbers are staggering. After colds and influenza, back pain is the second most common reason Americans see their doctor, and it's the most common cause of job-related disability. Back pain is the second most common neurological ailment in the United States — only headaches are more common. And it's the third most common reason for emergency room visits. At some point, more than 90 percent of American adults will experience severe lower back pain that adversely affects their quality of life. It's estimated that lower back pain costs the American economy $50 to $100 billion annually.

In my thirty-odd years of practice I saw lower back pain routinely. Early on in my practice, many of these patients would be referred to neurosurgeons because in those days, it was believed that most lower back pain was caused by "ruptured disks." We now know that this was completely off base and that, by and large, lower back pain is only rarely caused by disk problems. It is almost always caused by damage in the soft tissues — meaning muscles, tendons, and ligaments.

Although many things can cause back pain, from strained muscles to cancer, I do want to highlight one condition in particular that is extremely common but under-recognized: piriformis syndrome. Your piriformis (from the Latin word meaning "pear-shaped") is a narrow muscle deep in each buttock. These muscles lie close to the sciatic nerve, so when the piriformis muscle spasms or is irritated, it can aggravate the sciatic nerve and trigger pain to shoot right down the leg from the buttock, as if it were coming from a ruptured disk. Patients are told that they have "disk disease" because of pain going down the leg, called sciatica. They may also experience numbness and tingling along the back of the leg and into the foot due to the irritated sciatic nerve.

It's hard to imagine how many patients have undergone lower back surgery unnecessarily for what seems to be a disk problem, when the problem was piriformis syndrome all along. Recently, I found myself in a car showroom looking to buy a new car. The showroom manager was clearly in terrible pain. He was hunched over and was extremely reluctant to bear weight on his left leg. I couldn't help myself. I asked him to follow me to his private office, whereupon I proceeded to have him lie on his back on the floor. Keep in mind that he had no clue that I was a neurologist or even a physician for that matter. He followed my instructions while all of the curious sales staff watched through the glass wall of his office.

I asked him to bend his left knee while turning his chin to the left. I gently stretched his piriformis muscle by pushing the bent knee across his body to the right. It was extremely stiff and even slightly painful when I began the piriformis stretch technique, but after a few moments, the spasmodic piriformis began to release. I then had the manager get up and walk around. His pain had completely abated. This was quite a moment at the car dealership.

I can tell you from personal experience that spasm of the piriformis muscle can be incapacitating. It can keep you from working, exercising, and at times can make it difficult to even get out of a chair. Use the exercises on my website to stretch and work the muscle. It's the surest way to keep you moving.

Knee pain is also an extremely common cause of disability. It is the number two cause of chronic pain; more than one-third of Americans report being affected by knee pain. That's more than 100 million people. In the United States alone, more than 600,000 knee replacements are performed annually. By 2030, demand for total knee replacement surgery is expected to exceed $3 million, largely due to older folks staying in the workforce longer and rising obesity rates. There is a time and place for knee replacement, but so often after this procedure is performed, people regret that they consented to it. Surgery should be reserved for the small handful of patients who qualify and who are likely to benefit from it. Most people, however, would do well to avoid it—and all of its risks—and instead focus on strengthening the knees and surrounding muscles.

Lots of people who engage in athletics experience knee pain from something called patellofemoral syndrome. The main sign of this syndrome is pain in front of the knee when sitting, jumping, squatting, or using a staircase—especially going down stairs. Knee buckling, in which the knee suddenly does not support your body weight, is also common. Or you might have a popping or grinding sensation when you are walking or moving your knee. This is usually due to overuse, injury, excess weight, a kneecap that is out of alignment, or structural changes under the kneecap.

So often at the gym, I see people wearing knee braces of various sorts designed to keep the patella in line and alleviate this symptom. Ultimately, though, this tends to make the situation worse. Exercises that can keep the quadriceps and hamstring muscles strong will keep the kneecap where it needs to be, unless there is a significant alignment issue with the legs. Orthotics, corrective inserts in your shoes, may also be helpful.

I myself have had patellofemoral syndrome on both sides, and it is incredible how painful this can be. I once was unable to climb the twenty stairs in my house to get to the bedroom. My orthopedist wanted to inject me with steroids, but I chose to see a physical therapist first, who put me on the path back to health with basic exercises to strengthen my quads. I went from being unable to climb a single staircase to climbing 3,200 feet four months later in just under three-and-a-half hours while traveling in New Zealand.

If you're experiencing pain anywhere in your body, you need to pay attention to that. That is your signal that something is wrong. It may indicate that you're simply overexerting yourself during your exercise — whether cardio or weight-bearing — and not letting the body recover enough between sessions. It may be that you haven't fully stretched for a specific exercise and have strained a muscle, ligament, or tendon. And it could mean that there is an alignment issue that calls for orthotics. If you're engaging in an exercise and it's causing pain, stop, and reassess. Take care of pain when it strikes by modifying your exercise routine as needed, resting sore muscles, and mixing up your routine to make sure you're using different muscles.

When in doubt about the source of pain, get some help from a physical therapist or, even better, a physiatrist. Physiatrists are physicians who treat a wide variety of medical conditions that affect the brain, spinal cord, nerves, bones, joints, ligaments, muscles, and tendons. Go online to learn more about this specialty and find a practitioner in your area.

MAKE ROOM FOR SLEEP

When was the last time you had a good night's sleep? If it wasn't last night, then you're not alone. One in five of us has difficulty sleeping. I've written a lot about sleep in the past, as sleep disorders directly affect the brain, levels of inflammation, and risk for brain issues. The quality and amount of sleep you get have an astonishing impact on virtually every system in your body. Just a generation ago, we didn't think much about the value of sleep other than to refresh the body somehow, like recharging batteries. Today, however, the study of sleep constitutes an entire field of medicine, which has revealed some breathtaking findings about sleep's significance in human health.

Sleep can be described as a "diet of the mind." It repairs and refreshes the brain and body on so many levels; it's no wonder we spend roughly one-third of our life sleeping. Our pituitary gland, for instance, cannot begin to pump out growth hormone until we're asleep. Natural anti-aging growth hormone does more than just stimulate cellular growth and proliferation; it also rejuvenates the immune system and lowers risk factors for heart attack, stroke, and osteoporosis. It even aids our ability to maintain an ideal weight, helping us to burn fat for fuel.

Indeed, getting quality sleep is a requirement for optimum well-being. The better you sleep on a regular basis, the lower your risk for all kinds of health problems. And, conversely, low-quality sleep has far-reaching adverse effects on the body and its functionality. Studies have convincingly shown that our sleep habits impact how much we eat, how fat (or thin) we get, how strong our immune systems are (and whether we can sail through the cold season), how creative and insightful we can be, how well we cope with stress, how fast we can think, and how well we remember things. Prolonged poor sleep habits are a factor in brain fog and memory loss, diabetes and obesity, cardiovascular disease, cancer, depression, and Alzheimer's disease.

In fact, while much has been written about the fact that sleep disturbances are common in patients with Alzheimer's, it was thought that the sleep issues were a consequence of the disease. Newer research, however, indicates that it may be the other way around: Disturbances of sleep may in fact enhance the way the brain makes beta-amyloid protein, a hallmark of Alzheimer's disease. As the authors of a 2015 study state, paying attention to sleep issues and intervening when sleep is not fully restorative may be a way of modifying a risk factor for the future development of the disease.

Here are a few strategies to make the most out of sleep:

Prioritize and protect your sleep time. Just as you would schedule important meetings, schedule your sleep and be brutal about protecting that time period for sleep only. Because the body metabolizes a lot of waste products after 10 p.m. and the immune system revitalizes itself between 11 p.m. and 2 a.m., it's important to be asleep during these hours. So figure out what your bedtime and wake-time should be (e.g., 10 p.m. and 6 a.m.), and don't let anything disturb that pocket of time (see page 171 for more about how to figure out the number of sleep hours you need).

365 *days a year.* Don't let weekends and holidays derail your sleep routine. Do your best to keep a rigid sleeping schedule every day of the year, no matter what. Your body—and brain—will thank you for it.

Have a sleep study performed on you. The medical term for this study is "polysomnogram." This is a painless, noninvasive procedure that has you spending a night or two in a sleep facility. As you sleep, a sleep technologist records multiple biological functions to determine if you have any disorders like sleep apnea (see next page) or restless leg syndrome. You can find reputable sleep clinics and specialists online.

Watch what you consume. Avoid caffeine late in the day and be mindful of medications you take that might infringe on sleep. Drugs that can undermine sleep include pseudoephedrine (e.g., Sudafed), headache medicines with caffeine (e.g., Excedrin), nicotine, drugs to treat high blood pressure and congestive heart failure, SSRI antidepressants, corticosteroids, and statins.

Cultivate a peaceful, clean sleeping environment. No electronics in the bedroom. Keep it tidy, neat, and at a comfortable temperature for sleeping, which is 65 to 70 degrees Fahrenheit (20°c).

Prepare for sleep. Take time before bed to unwind, disconnect from stimulating activities, and cue the body that it's time for rest. Avoid screens (computers, tablets, and the like) for at least an hour before bedtime. Try a warm bath, listening to soothing music, light reading, or coloring in an adult coloring book. Before lying down, try some deep-breathing exercises (see page 155 for a quick lesson). For some people, physical exercise can bring on restful sleep, but for many, exercising too close to bedtime can be stimulating, preventing you from feeling tired enough to sleep. If you're that type, schedule your regular exercise routine earlier in the day, at least four hours prior to bedtime.

Gear up. Wear loose clothing to bed that's appropriate for the room temperature so you're not too hot or cold.

Try melatonin. If your circadian rhythm is off, which can happen from time to time if you travel across time zones or force your body out of its preferred sleep-wake cycle (maybe you stayed up too late or had a long nap in the afternoon), you might want to try a melatonin supplement. You can also try melatonin if you have unexplained trouble sleeping for many days in a row, as this may be a sign that your body's rhythm is off. Melatonin is our body's natural sleep hormone. But it helps control our twenty-four-hour rhythm as well. Released after the sun sets, it slows body function and lowers blood pressure and core body temperature so that we're prepared to sleep. You can purchase melatonin as an over-the-counter supplement. A proper dosage would be 1 to 3 mg at bedtime.

Rule out sleep apnea. As mentioned above, a sleep study can help you determine if you suffer from this increasingly common disorder that robs millions of restful sleep. Sleep apnea can be more serious than previously thought. It causes the airway to collapse during sleep. Your breathing gets cut off multiple times and your sleep becomes fragmented. Loud snoring and dreamless sleep are often signs of sleep apnea (see box). In 2015, an alarming new study published in *Neurology* found that sleep apnea may be a factor in earlier onset of mild cognitive impairment (MCI) and Alzheimer's disease. MCI often precedes dementia. The researchers of the study found that people with sleep apnea developed mild cognitive impairment nearly ten years sooner than those who didn't suffer from breathing problems during sleep. The time span for developing Alzheimer's also seemed to speed up: Those with sleep apnea developed the disease, on average, five years sooner than the sound sleepers. Researchers theorize that the adverse effects of oxygen restriction on the brain may have something to do with this connection, as well as the fact that sleep drives a slew of physiological events that help the brain "freshen up," do some housecleaning, and clear out proteins that can otherwise gunk up nerve cells.

Signs of sleep apnea:

- frequent fatigue and lack of energy

- excessive daytime sleepiness

- frequent nocturnal urination

- nighttime gasping, choking, or coughing

- irregular breathing during sleep (e.g., snoring)

- morning headaches

- gastroesophageal reflux

- depression

Scientists have documented abnormal brain changes in people who suffer from sleep apnea. The good news is these changes can be reversed through treatment. Studies show that white matter irregularities, for example, can improve immensely when sleep apnea is treated. This is usually achieved through the help of a CPAP device. CPAP stands for "continuous positive airway pressure"; the device, which you wear while sleeping, uses mild air pressure to keep the airways open. The benefits can be felt immediately, and research has shown that within a matter of months, those brain changes go back to normal and there's a vast improvement in cognitive function as well as in mood, alertness, and quality of life. Obesity can also trigger sleep apnea, through the extra weight and fat around the neck. People who lose weight often find relief and no longer need the CPAP machine.

People tend to underestimate the value of sleep. It's arguably more important than what we do during the day. Arianna Huffington wrote an entire book about this subject. I encourage you to read *The Sleep Revolution* if you want to learn more about sleep and how to achieve the best kind. She writes: "It's one of humanity's great unifiers. It binds us to one another, to our ancestors, to our past, and to the future. No matter who we are or where we are in the world and in our lives, we share a common need for sleep."

I should note that your newfound dietary choices will work in sync with your newfound sleep habits. As you clean up your diet and reduce inflammation, you'll be increasing your chances for sound, restful sleep. Check out A. K.'s story of transformation:

As someone who watched a bedridden mother die of Alzheimer's, I have a deep personal interest in preventing this disease in my family. I am always alert for leading-edge information on how to prevent this terrible illness.

Before my diet, I had been consuming lots of processed junk food, including diet colas, crackers and chips, and the daily oatmeal my doctor told me to eat. I was on a dangerous path. Once information about a low-carb, high-fat, gluten-free lifestyle was put before me, I instantly realized this was the information I had been waiting for.

I went to an olive oil store and bought a bottle, started eating grass-fed beef, eliminated grains, switched to green tea, and bought some stevia for (occasional) sweetening. I've also begun to eat more organic greens (daily, in fact).

Previously, I also suffered from arthritis in my joints, especially at night, when the pain would wake me up several times. If a change in sleep pattern is any evidence that this diet is working, then it is worth it to me for that reason only. It has only been six weeks, and the change is already AMAZING!!!

REDUCE STRESS AND FIND CALM IN FOUR SIMPLE WAYS

In my book *Power Up Your Brain: The Neuroscience of Enlightenment*, Dr. Alberto Villoldo and I told the story of how science has come to understand the gift of neurogenesis in humans. Although scientists have long proven neurogenesis in various other animals, it wasn't until the 1990s that the focus turned to humans. In 1998, the journal *Nature Medicine* published a report by Swedish neurologist Peter Eriksson in which he claimed that neural stem cells exist within the brain that are continually replenished and can develop into brain neurons.

And indeed, he was right: We experience brain "stem cell therapy" every minute of our lives. We're not stuck with a finite number of brain cells; conversely, the brain is pliable and can continually make new cells and connections. This is known as neuroplasticity. It explains how stroke victims can learn to speak again.

In September 2014, I was fortunate to serve as conference chair for an international symposium exploring the latest research in brain health. Dr. Michael Merzenich, a professor emeritus neuroscientist at the University of California, San Francisco, and one of the leading pioneers in brain plasticity research, explained that lifestyle factors — some of which might surprise you — can indeed affect the ability of the brain to make new connections.

I've already discussed the ways in which we can positively affect the brain, such as physical exercise, getting restful sleep, following a ketogenic diet, and adding certain nutrients like curcumin and the omega-3 fat DHA. These techniques also have the added effect of reducing the stress our brains and bodies endure daily. Stress will always be a part of our lives; the key is to keep unnecessary stress at bay to preserve and promote those neural connections. And there are other means to positively impact the brain and its connections that have nothing to do with what you eat, how much you exercise, and how well you sleep. When we take a moment to change how we view the world around us, and to act in particular ways that further reduce the stress on our bodies, we are actually changing the physical and functional structure of the brain for the better. To this end, let me outline the four additional ways that can help support this outcome.

- Flex your gratitude muscle

- Maintain strong social networks — mostly offline

- Plan personal downtime

- Get out into nature as much as possible

Flex Your Gratitude Muscle

The science has spoken: The more grateful we feel, the more resilient the brain becomes, physically and even emotionally and spiritually.

Let me explain by way of example how I've incorporated the notion of seeking gratitude in the face of adversity into my life. Several months ago, I received an e-mail that linked to a magazine article about me. The article was anything but positive. The author had published the article—a litany of accusatory and derogatory statements about me—just as he was about to launch a new book, so it was clear he was seeking attention for himself and his book. My first response, coming from my more primitive brain center, was one of anger, outrage, and a strong sense of needing to retaliate.

Over the next several hours, I received more e-mails from concerned friends wondering how I would "respond." I vividly recall being on the phone with my literary agent and publisher, and being asked, "What do you plan to do?" My response to them: "God bless him." Though I was initially angry that someone could have attacked me like this, I realized that I owed the author of this highly disparaging article a great deal of gratitude, as it allowed me the opportunity to truly experience the fact that I do not let others define me. This experience was quite positive, as it did nothing more than strengthen my sense of self.

Gratitude has been studied in the laboratory. In 2015 researchers at Indiana University looked at two groups of people who were being treated for depression and/or anxiety. One group was asked to participate in a gratitude writing exercise, while the other group, which acted as the control, was not. The people in the gratitude writing group spent twenty minutes during the first three sessions of their weekly counseling writing thank-you letters to people in their lives. Three months after the counseling ended, the individuals in both groups underwent a clever experiment using a brain scanner.

The participants were placed in a specific type of functional MRI brain scanner and were gifted various amounts of pretend money by imaginary benefactors. To add realism, the benefactors' names and photos appeared onscreen for the participants to see. The researchers told the participants the following: If they wanted to communicate their gratitude for the money, they could donate all or some of the money to a named third party or to a charity. This may seem like an odd experiment because it's so contrived, but the researchers collected real data by telling the participants that someone would receive real cash minus any amount pledged to another party or charity.

What the researchers found was that, on average, the stronger the thankful feelings a person reported, and the more money a person gave away, the more activity they showed in their brain scans, particularly in areas that are not normally associated with emotions. Which means gratitude is a unique emotion that affects the brain in a unique way. Moreover, the researchers discovered that the gratitude exercise had both short- and long-term effects. Not only did the gratitude writing individuals report feeling more gratefulness two weeks after the exercise, as compared to the controls, but their brain scans showed more activity related to gratitude months later. They were still wired to feel extra thankful.

The takeaway here is that gratitude works mainly because it feeds further cycles of gratitude. It is self-perpetuating. As you practice gratitude, you become more attuned to it, which then allows you to enjoy more of its psychological benefits. In the words of the study's authors: "…you could even think of your brain as having a sort of gratitude 'muscle' that can be exercised and strengthened (not so different from various other qualities that can be cultivated through practice, of course). If this is right, the more of an effort you make to feel gratitude one day, the more the feeling will come to you spontaneously in the future."

One of the easiest ways to practice gratitude is to keep a journal designated for this very exercise. Spend two minutes daily, maybe right before bedtime, writing down a few things for which you feel thankful. These can be little things that occurred during your day or larger experiences or notes of thanks for named people who have had a positive impact on you. Try writing a letter to someone thanking him or her for being in your life, and send it!

Maintain Strong Social Networks — Mostly Offline

One of my favorite quotes is from the 1948 song "Nature Boy" by Nat King Cole. He sings about love being the most important thing one can ever learn — loving others and being loved. I once read that people who work with the dying in hospice care facilities often hear similar questions: Am I loved? And did I love well? These people are at a point in their lives when all the trivial sources of stress are gone and all that's left to ponder is their legacy of love. Love is, after all, everything. I am continually reminded of the power of compassion and love — of the social bonds we maintain, whether they are ones that endure for a long time or are brief but nonetheless impactful. Let me share a real-life story that illustrates what I mean.

Thirty years ago, when I had finally completed my residency training, I was offered a job with an established group of neurologists in Naples, Florida. Soon after I began work, I met Mike McDonnell, an attorney who had an office one floor above us. Mike was a well-known personality in South Florida, and we soon became very close friends. We began sharing evenings together, playing guitar, and singing with other friends. Mike became such an important part of our lives that my future wife and I asked him to perform at our wedding ceremony, and in fact, he and his wife, Nina, joined us on our honeymoon. Mike became the godfather of our daughter Reisha.

Mike turned to me for all things medical, and I in turn relied upon him for his incredible legal acumen. In early February 2016, I was unprepared for the text message that I received from his wife. It simply stated, "Need you, Mike is dying." I rushed to our local hospital and found my friend on a breathing machine with his wife and three of his five children at his bedside. I knew at that moment that I had to assume the role of neurologist and immediately examined him. After reviewing his brain scans, I knew Mike had sustained a massive stroke and had essentially no brain function.

I explained the gravity of the situation to Mike's family and friends. We made arrangements to transfer Mike to the intensive care unit. There, his situation remained fairly stable while on life support. Fortunately, this allowed all of his children to make their way to the hospital and share in Mike's last moments of life.

At 11:14 p.m., Mike left us.

I thought about Mike pretty much the entire next day and later that evening. As fate would have it, one of Mike's close friends, and ours as well, was playing piano at a local restaurant. During his performance, he mentioned how we had lost a close friend the day before. After dinner that night, we spent time with friends talking about Mike and his passing. When we got home, I became violently ill, with shaking chills and nausea. I finally fell asleep about 2 a.m., and when I woke up the next day, I knew something wasn't right.

Plans were made to have a celebration of Mike's life the following day, and we all gathered up our photographs for a retrospective. As it turned out, not only did we have lots of photographs, but we also had a DVD of a performance that our musical group had given at a fund-raiser many years before. After watching the video with my wife and daughter, I felt I needed to lie down on the couch. I wasn't sure what was going on with me, but I was certainly lightheaded and my heart was racing. I then began to lose my vision. I called for my wife and let her know how I was feeling, and she called 911. Prior to the ambulance arriving, fire rescue was in my living room. A young man asked me how I was feeling, and I explained how my heart was racing. He then asked if I was under any stress or had experienced a stressful event, at which point I burst into tears and explained the loss of my friend. The firefighter believed my symptoms were anxiety related, and he encouraged me to take deep breaths and try to relax. My medical mind, while accepting the fact that I was certainly in an anxious state, nevertheless told me that there was something more going on, especially when I took my own pulse and found that it was not only rapid but irregular.

When the ambulance arrived, it was clear that my heart was beating erratically, with a heart rate as high as 170. I was taken to a local hospital, where medicine was administered intravenously to slow my heart, but it failed, twice. At that point, I was transferred to the intensive care unit. The medicine to slow my heart rate was progressively increased, but my heart rate remained dangerously elevated. Finally, Bob, the intensive care nurse, explained that I had reached the maximum dosage of the medication and that a second medication needed to be added. I knew if the medications failed that I would be looking at having a cardioversion procedure done, which is a nice way of saying I'd have my heart shocked back into a normal rhythm.

As evening arrived, I began having a conversation with Bob. He explained that he had worked as a nurse in the trauma unit of an emergency room and described some of his experiences there. As I listened to his stories, I was so taken by his compassion toward me and his wish for me to get better. He carefully adjusted my medications while continuing to tell me about some of the most meaningful events in his life.

As he continued, I closed my eyes and suddenly felt a wave of intense gratitude, not only for my friendship with Mike, but also for my newfound bond with Bob, who was providing care and sharing his life story with me. I can only describe this feeling as one of love. And it was at that moment, as my body was flooded with this emotion, that my heart rhythm suddenly converted back to normal.

As you can imagine, sleeping in an intensive care unit is difficult. I was in and out of sleep throughout the night, and every time I awakened, I checked the cardiac monitor that was behind my bed to make sure that my heart rhythm remained normal. A little after 4 a.m. I woke up again, but this time there was no pulse on the screen. It was flatlined. I thought I was dreaming, but I was awake. I reached down and found that one of my heart monitor leads had become dislodged. I quickly reconnected it, which immediately restored my normal heart tracing to the monitor.

By the time the cardiologist arrived the next morning, I had been out of bed doing yoga. My heart and all my vital signs were deemed normal, and I was discharged with no medication except the recommendation of aspirin.

So many times over the years, I've been asked the question, "What was it that got you into integrative medicine?" I've always said that there was no single epiphany. But I can truly state that the experience in the hospital—first with Mike and then with Bob—has been a major and pivotal event in my life. I left the hospital a changed man. While over the years I have lectured and written about the detrimental effects of stress, those events certainly made a believer out of me. But far more important, they brought me to a place of fully understanding the meaning of love. While we have love for our families and friends, having love and gratitude for others—even strangers—is something that was, at least for me, unexpected but is now fully welcomed in my life. And this was Mike's final gift to me. He actually passed within the same year my father did. My dad was a dedicated physician who throughout his life emphasized to everyone around him the fundamental importance of compassion toward others.

When you are loved and you love well, every cell in your body is allowed to work at its maximum capacity. If love is the single most important ingredient for health and wellness, then I know of no better way of staying on the path of continual healing than to love as much as you can and enjoy its returns. And you do that by maintaining strong social networks. Be open to unexpected newcomers into your life like Bob, and nourish the bonds that have been with you for a long time. You never know when you might need to call on those people when you face serious challenges or have to endure a tragedy in your life.

Social relationships no doubt also change our physiology and sense of well-being. You'd be surprised by how the nature of our health hinges on the nature of our relationships, from the ones we have with others to those we have with ourselves. We are, after all, very social creatures. Recent research has even shown that the bonds we keep with others can enhance longevity. In 2015 a team of researchers at the University of North Carolina at Chapel Hill sought to understand how social relationships affect health. In particular, they were interested in how social relationships "get under the skin" to influence physiological well-being as people age. Among the questions they wanted to answer: When do these effects emerge in life? What do they entail? Do they change as a person ages? How long do they last?

By synthesizing data from four large surveys of Americans ranging from adolescents as young as twelve to seniors as old as eighty-five — a total of more than 14,600 people — the researchers looked at several parameters. In terms of social bonds, they considered social integration, social support, and social strain. To analyze the biological side to the experiment, they considered four common measurements of health: body mass index (a factor of height and weight), waist circumference, blood pressure, and C-reactive protein to assess systemic inflammation. These biomarkers are associated with risk for many diseases, including heart disease, stroke, dementia, and cancer. The results were not surprising on some levels, but they were astonishing on others. We already knew from previous research that older individuals who had a larger social network tended to live longer than those who didn't. But this was the first time a study showed that social bonds lowered health risks in *everyone* — from the young to the old. Among the more surprising findings: social isolation in teenagers contributes equally to bad inflammation as does physical inactivity, and having a strong social network may protect against obesity; social isolation in seniors can be a bigger factor than diabetes in the development and management of high blood pressure; and in middle-aged people, the quality of one's social bonds is more important than the quantity.

There is a lot we can take away from this comprehensive, innovative study, regardless of which stage of life we are in. The relationships we maintain matter to our health, and quality trumps quantity. How well do you relate to other people? Do you have a trusted set of friends? Is your marriage enriching or a source of hardship and stress? Does bad news or a bully in your circle of friends, colleagues, or acquaintances affect you in a way that severely lowers your quality of life? Do you like *yourself*?

Cultivating healthy relationships starts with establishing a healthy relationship with yourself first. This will then allow you to extend that inner love to others and all that surrounds you. And the happier you are in your relationships, the easier it will be to make excellent decisions in all that you do.

Even though there are more gadgets and apps to connect with others than ever, there are also more lonely people who harbor feelings of disconnectedness. It seems as though the more artificial connections we make through social media, the less time we spend with one another in person. To this end, try to nourish your relationships in authentic, intimate ways. Plan more time with the people who inspire, encourage, and de-stress you. And don't rely on social media. Social media platforms have their place in the world, but you can't substitute them for real, face-to-face interactions. Get out there and do things with others. Try new hobbies together. Some ideas:

- Designate a date night (e.g., movie and dinner) with a spouse or best friend at least once a week or twice a month. This doesn't mean you have to go out. Cook the meal together at home and have movie night on the couch.

- Have weekly dinner parties with close friends. Make it a potluck and tell people what to bring.

- Establish a hiking or power-walking group with friends that meets weekly on a designated morning.

- Pick up the phone on weekends and call at least one good friend who lives far away. Catch up.

- Keep a daily ritual with the person closest to you — a spouse, best friend, maybe a child old enough to engage in this exercise. The ritual can be any of a number of things, from simply talking about your day and what's on your mind to sharing a passage from a book of quotes or proverbs. Each morning, my wife and I share a quotation or passage. For us, it serves to remind us of what is important and meaningful in life. It also helps us to bond. We find that our morning reading stays with us through the day. I often revisit our quote during the course of the day.

- Have a few non-negotiable habits in your life, such as leaving work by 5:30 p.m. so that you can be home to have dinner with the kids. Savor Sundays with family by ditching all electronic devices and focusing on those in-person relationships. Have at least one device-free day a week.

Strengthening those personal connections in real life can be as powerful as any other strategy to support health and well-being.

Plan Personal Downtime

Do you ever try to power through feelings of illness, pain, anger, frustration, exhaustion, being overwhelmed, and the yearning to take a break? Do you have personal downtime on a regular basis? It sounds cliché to say "relax" because it will "reduce stress," but it's all the more important today because we seem to value busy-ness so much. Technologies provide opportunities to be endlessly entertained and engaged, but also distracted and spent. A few neuroscientific studies are starting to emerge, for example, showing that we may be impairing our reflective abilities by relying too much on electronic devices. We use our phones more than we think: In a 2015 paper in the journal *PLOS One*, it was found that people sorely underestimate their smartphone use.

You might think you use your phone an average of thirty-seven times throughout the day, which is what the study's participants believed, but that number is closer to eighty-five! And the total amount of time you spend on your phone daily is probably a little over five hours.

More than a quarter of our days are now spent immersed in information overload. Some of that information is valuable, but some of it is the equivalent of junk food for the brain. The massive digital input could be preventing us from learning and remembering information or from being creative. Some of us don't even take advantage of paid vacation time anymore. But it's essential that we plan personal downtime to let our bodies recover from stress, renew themselves, and gather more strength and energy. Get into the habit of having insightful, distraction-free conversations with yourself during that downtime. Make sure that inner dialogue helps you to stay positive, upbeat, and present.

Scientists at the University of California, San Francisco, have documented that when rats experience something novel, such as encountering a new area, their brains show new patterns of activity. That fresh experience, however, cannot become a solid memory in the rats' brains if they don't take a break from their exploration. The researchers reckon that the findings also apply to how we learn as humans. Downtime allows the brain to take a break and solidify experiences it's had, turning them into permanent long-term memories. If the brain is constantly stimulated, this process could be hampered.

Self-care begins with self-discovery. It's important that we stop to collect our thoughts and check in on our goals regularly. This should be done daily, weekly, monthly, and annually. Some ideas:

- On a daily basis, set a time during which you turn off your cell phone and don't respond to non-emergency calls, e-mails, or

text messages so you can practice some deep breathing. This
will calm your mind and body and help you evaluate how you
feel and what you're thinking. Here's how to do that: Sit
comfortably in a chair or on the floor. Close your eyes and
make sure your body is relaxed, releasing all tension in your
neck, arms, legs, and back. Inhale through your nose for as long
as you can, feeling your diaphragm and abdomen rise as your
stomach moves outward. Sip in a little more air when you
think you've reached the top of your lungs. Slowly exhale,
pushing every breath of air from your lungs. Continue for at
least five rounds of deep breaths. Then open your eyes and ask
yourself whether or not your body feels good and energetic in
general. For some, first thing in the morning upon getting out
of bed — before looking at any digital device — is an ideal time
for deep breathing. Or set the alarm on your phone for 3 p.m.
every afternoon. Make it part of your daily routine. Another
idea is to end your deep-breathing session with an inspirational
quotation. See the box on page 156 for examples.

- On a weekly or monthly basis, tune into broader questions
about yourself, such as whether or not you're feeling content,
how you're feeling physically, and the status of your
relationships. Is there someone you should spend more time
with? Anyone you'd be better off excluding from your life?
What in life is causing you a great deal of stress and anxiety?
How can you begin to remedy that?

- On an annual basis, set new goals and address any challenges.
Consider the big goals, such as anything you might want to
accomplish that may require long-term planning. What would you
like to do in the next year or the next decade? Find a new job?

Perfect a skill? Try a new hobby? Start a business? Climb Mount Kilimanjaro? Travel around Europe? Volunteer more? Enrol in an art workshop? Go on a weekend retreat? Write a memoir?

As mentioned earlier, recording your thoughts, goals, feelings, anxieties, and the events most affecting you in a journal can be helpful. It allows you to review later, can help assuage those worries, and gives you accountability (for a list of the journals to maintain, see page 172).

Reading a short but meaningful quotation is a great way to cap a deep-breathing session. Here are thirty suggestions to get you started:

1. If you do not change direction, you may end up where you are heading. — Lao Tzu

2. If not now, when? — Rabbi Hillel

3. The best and most beautiful things in the world cannot be seen or even touched — they must be felt with the heart. — Helen Keller

4. We must let go of the life we have planned, so as to accept the one that is waiting for us. — Joseph Campbell

5. Our greatest weakness lies in giving up. The most certain way to succeed is always to try just one more time. — Thomas A. Edison

6. Consult not your fears but your hopes and your dreams. Think not about your frustrations, but about your unfulfilled potential. Concern yourself not with what you tried and failed in, but with what it is still possible for you to do. — Pope John XXIII

7. If you want others to be happy, practice compassion. If you want to be happy, practice compassion. — Dalai Lama

8. Perseverance is not a long race; it is many short races one after the other. — Walter Elliot

9. Patience and perseverance have a magical effect before which difficulties disappear and obstacles vanish.—John Quincy Adams

10. As we express our gratitude, we must never forget that the highest appreciation is not to utter words, but to live by them.—John F. Kennedy

11. True success is overcoming the fear of being unsuccessful.—Paul Sweeney

12. Peace is not absence of conflict; it is the ability to handle conflict by peaceful means.—Ronald Reagan

13. Once we accept our limits, we go beyond them.—Albert Einstein

14. God grant me the serenity to accept the things I cannot change, the courage to change the things I can, and the wisdom to know the difference.—The Serenity Prayer

15. The only real security is not in owning or possessing, not in demanding or expecting, not in hoping, even. Security in a relationship lies neither in looking back to what it was, nor forward to what it might be, but living in the present and accepting it as it is now.—Anne Morrow Lindbergh

16. Never give up, and be confident in what you do. There may be tough times, but the difficulties which you face will make you more determined to achieve your objectives and to win against all the odds.—Marta Vieira da Silva

17. The friend in my adversity I shall always cherish most. I can better trust those who helped to relieve the gloom of my dark hours than those who are so ready to enjoy with me the sunshine of my prosperity.—Ulysses S. Grant

18. Faith is the bird that feels the light when the dawn is still dark.—Rabindranath Tagore

19. There are two great days in a person's life—the day we are born and the day we discover why.—William Barclay

20. There is no end to education. It is not that you read a book, pass an examination, and finish with education. The whole of life, from the moment you are born to the moment you die, is a process of learning. — Jiddu Krishnamurti

21. Your task is not to seek for love, but merely to seek and find all the barriers within yourself that you have built against it. — Jalal Al-Din Rumi

22. Let the one among you who is without sin be the first to cast a stone. — Jesus Christ

23. You can search throughout the entire universe for someone who is more deserving of your love and affection than you are yourself, and that person is not to be found anywhere. You yourself, as much as anybody in the entire universe, deserve your love and affection. — Buddha

24. We ourselves feel that what we are doing is just a drop in the ocean. But the ocean would be less because of that missing drop. — Mother Teresa

25. We must welcome the future, remembering that soon it will be the past; and we must respect the past, remembering that it was once all that was humanly possible. — George Santayana

26. Despite everything, I believe that people are really good at heart. — Anne Frank

27. The only thing worse than being blind is having sight but no vision. — Helen Keller

28. In the end, it's not the years in your life that count. It's the life in your years. — Abraham Lincoln

29. It does not matter how slowly you go as long as you do not stop. — Confucius

30. Accept the challenges so that you can feel the exhilaration of victory. — George S. Patton

Get Out into Nature as Much as Possible

Our ancestors used to work and live mostly in the outdoors, but few of us do that anymore. We live and work indoors, usually tethered to electronics, chairs, couches, meetings, and chores. There is a biological reason why going for walks and hikes, for example, or doing anything in the open air can be so invigorating. Being outside and among plants and other living things enhances feelings of well-being through a variety of biochemical reactions, including a real calming effect on your mind and nervous system.

Get out in nature as much as possible during the day, whether you live in a big city or a rural area. Find a park to take a daily walk after lunch. Try to sit near a window with a view when at work, or place a chair in front of the window with the best view from your home. Notice the movement of trees in the wind, the nearby birds and other creatures. Plan your workouts outside when the weather is agreeable. Take in the air and scenery along natural bodies of water or mountainous regions. Enjoy the first light of the day at dawn and the sunsets at night. On clear nights, go stargazing. And don't forget to bring the outdoors inside. Decorate your rooms and office with living plants (see the next section for ideas). They will keep your air clean and bring Mother Nature closer to you. And as you're about to read, they will help you to detoxify your physical environment.

DETOXIFY YOUR PHYSICAL ENVIRONMENT

Let me state the obvious. We live in a sea of chemicals. Scientists who measure the so-called body burden, or levels of toxicants in tissues of the human body, tell us that virtually every resident in the United

States, regardless of location or age, harbors measurable levels of synthetic chemicals, many of which are fat-soluble and therefore stored in fatty tissue indefinitely. I wish there were more focus on policing these chemicals than on monitoring them. Unfortunately, it takes years—sometimes decades—for studies to gather enough evidence for the government to justify writing new standards or regulations, and even to take dangerous products off the market. In 2014, a meta-analysis published in the *Journal of Hazardous Materials* reviewed 143,000 peer-reviewed papers to track the patterns of emergence and decline of toxic chemicals. The study exposed the sad truth: It takes an average of fourteen years for appropriate action to take place. We need to take matters into our own hands.

The good news is the Grain Brain Whole Life Plan helps you do just that. Don't wait until something is officially labeled as being dangerous to eliminate it from your life; when in doubt, take it out of your life.

I've already made my case against glyphosate, the main ingredient in Roundup. Here are some additional ideas to support a cleaner way of life:

- When buying canned foods, be sure the cans are not lined with BPA. Look for "BPA-free lining" language on the can.

- Avoid using nonstick pans and other cookware. Teflon-coated wares contain perfluorooctanoic acid, or PFOA, which the EPA has labeled a likely carcinogen. Cast-iron cookware, ceramic, uncoated stainless steel, or glass are your best bet.

- Minimize the use of the microwave. Never place plastic—including plastic wrap—in a microwave. Don't put hot foods in plastic, which can release nasty chemicals that are absorbed by the food.

- Avoid plastic water bottles, or at least avoid plastics marked with "PC," for polycarbonate, or the recycling labels 3, 6, or 7 on the little triangle. Buy reusable bottles made of food-grade stainless steel or glass.

- When it comes to toiletries, deodorants, soaps, cosmetics, and general beauty products, switch brands when you restock. Remember, your skin is a major entry point to your body, and what you slather on may make its way inside to inflict harm. Look for organic certification and choose products that are safer alternatives. Use the Environmental Working Group's (EWG) user-friendly website (www.ewg.org) and I Read Labels For You (www.ireadlabelsforyou.com) to find the safest products. Endocrine-disrupting chemicals, or EDCs, have been shown to disrupt normal metabolism and even trigger weight gain. The most insidious ones are:

  ○ aluminium chlorohydrate (in deodorants)

  ○ diethyl phthalate (in perfumes, lotions, and other personal care products)

  ○ formaldehyde and formalin (in nail products)

  ○ "fragrance" and "parfum" (in perfumes, lotions, and other personal care products)

  ○ parabens [methyl-, propyl-, isopropyl-, butyl-, and isobutyl-] (in cosmetics, lotions, and other personal care products)

  ○ PEG/ceteareth/polyethylene glycol (in skin care products)

- sodium lauryl sulfate (SLS), sodium laureth sulfate (SLES), and ammonium lauryl sulfate (ALS) (in a variety of products: shampoos, body washes and cleansers, liquid hand soaps, laundry detergents, hair color and bleaching agents, toothpastes, makeup foundations, and bath oils/bath salts)

- TEA (triethanolamine) (in skin care products)

- toluene and dibutyl phthalate (DBP) (in nail polishes)

- triclosan and triclocarban (in antibacterial hand soaps and some toothpastes)

- Select household cleaners, detergents, disinfectants, bleaches, stain removers, and so on that are free of synthetic chemicals (look for brands that use natural, nontoxic ingredients; again the www.ewg.org site can be helpful here). Or make your own: Simple, inexpensive, and effective cleaning products can be made from borax, baking soda, vinegar, and water (see the box on page 163).

- Indoor air is notoriously more toxic than outdoor air due to all the particulate matter that comes from furniture, electronics, and household goods. Ventilate your home well and install HEPA air filters if possible. Change your air-conditioning and heating filters every three to six months. Get the ducts cleaned yearly. Avoid air deodorizers and plug-in room fresheners. Reduce toxic dust and residues on surfaces by using a vacuum cleaner with a HEPA filter. Naturally ventilate your house by opening the windows.

- Request that people take off their shoes upon entry.

- Plants — such as spider plants, aloe vera, chrysanthemums, gerbera daisies, Boston ferns, English ivies, and philodendrons — naturally detoxify the environment. Keep as many in your home as possible.

- When purchasing clothes, fabrics, upholstered furniture, or mattresses, choose items that are made of natural fabrics with no flame-retardant, stain-resistant, or water-resistant coatings. (Some states mandate a certain level of flame retardants on products, but do your best to find the most natural products possible.)

- Wet-mop floors and wipe down windowsills weekly.

- Speak with your local garden store or nursery personnel for recommendations on pesticide- and herbicide-free products you can use in your garden to control pests.

THREE HOMEMADE CLEANING PRODUCTS

All-purpose cleaner and deodorizer:

115g bicarbonate of soda

2 liters warm water

Combine the ingredients and store in a spray bottle.

Glass and window cleaner:

1 liter water

250ml white vinegar

125ml 70% rubbing alcohol

2 to 4 drops essential oil (optional, for aroma)

Combine the ingredients and store in a spray bottle.

Disinfectant:

2 teaspoons borax

4 tablespoons white vinegar

750ml hot water

Combine the ingredients and store in a spray bottle.

While it may seem like an overwhelming task to clear out your house of questionable products and replace them with alternatives, it needn't be stressful and you needn't do it all in one day. Go one room or one product at a time. The goal is to do the best you can based on what you can afford and what you're willing to change. As part of your daily checklist during the 14-day menu plan, I'll ask you to do one thing that helps you to detoxify your physical environment.

But before we get to that, there's one more step to take that will help you pull all these ideas together: Plan accordingly.

CHAPTER 7

Step 3 — Plan Accordingly

THE BODY LOVES AND CRAVES consistency and predictability. So much so, in fact, that it will rebel in subtle ways if you force it to be out of sync with its natural rhythms. This is partly why traveling across multiple time zones and temporarily abandoning your usual routine can feel so difficult and uncomfortable. Your smart body will do everything it can to get you back on track quickly. One of the easiest ways of reducing unnecessary stress on your body and maintaining a balanced, homeostatic state is to keep a steady daily routine year-round to the best of your ability, including weekends and holidays. This demands that you plan your days well in advance.

Work obligations, social demands, and unexpected events have us all breaking this rule occasionally, but see if you can regulate at least the three aspects of your life that will have the biggest impact on your health: when you eat, when you exercise, and when you sleep. If you do, you will notice a difference in how you feel. It may also help you to stick to a routine and be better prepared for unforeseen challenges that can derail your new way of life under the Grain Brain Whole Life Plan.

So to that end, let me give you some guidance.

WHEN TO EAT

Calories cannot tell time, but the body can, and it will receive calories differently depending on a variety of factors, including—you guessed it—the time of day.

Each us has an internal system of biological clocks that help the body manage and control its circadian rhythm—your body's sense of day and night. This rhythm is defined by the patterns of repeated activity that correlate with the twenty-four-hour solar day and include your sleep-wake cycle, the rise and fall of hormones, and changes in body temperature. Just recently we've discovered that when these clocks are not "on time"— when they're not functioning properly—disordered eating and weight problems can result. It's well documented, for example, that obese people often have disrupted circadian rhythms, triggering them to eat frequently and at irregular times, especially late at night. Obese people also often suffer from sleep apnea, which further disturbs their sleep rhythm. And, as you already know, sleep deprivation can impact the balance of those appetite hormones leptin and ghrelin, further exacerbating problems.

In Chapter 4, I gave you some parameters for intermittent fasting, suggesting that you skip breakfast once or twice a week and fast for seventy-two hours four times throughout the year. As an additional tip, I recommend that you *eat more of your daily sum of calories before 3 p.m.* and avoid eating a bounty of food at night. In fact, *avoid eating anything within four hours of bedtime.* (You can drink water and caffeine-free tea, but try not to drink anything within a half an hour of bedtime. Otherwise, you might have to get up in the middle of the night to use the bathroom.)

The power of eating lunch before 3 p.m., for example, was recently highlighted by researchers at Harvard's Brigham and Women's Hospital, Tufts University, and Spain's University of Murcia, who conducted their study in the Spanish seaside town of Murcia. Spaniards make lunch their main meal of the day. To the researchers' surprise, all things being equal, such as total calories eaten daily, levels of activity, and sleep quantity, those who ate lunch later in the day struggled more with weight loss. All of the participants — a total of 420 individuals — in the study were either overweight or obese. And all of them were put on the same five-month weight-loss program. But they didn't eat lunch at the same time, and they didn't experience the same weight loss. Half of them ate lunch before 3 p.m., and the other half ate after 3 p.m. Over the course of the twenty weeks, the early lunchers lost an average of twenty-two pounds (10kg), while the later lunchers shed only seventeen (7.5kg) and at a slower clip.

We intuitively know that overeating toward the end of the day is not a good idea. That's when we're likely to be tired. Even our brains are tired of making decisions, so we cave in to a mindless feast at the dinner table with multiple portions of unhealthy food choices and dessert. This is especially the case when we've had a busy day, skipped lunch entirely, and grazed on nutrient-poor snacks and food products. And if it has been a very long time since we've eaten, and we haven't taken in enough calories earlier in the day, it's far too easy to gorge at dinner because the body will want to make up for those lost calories. It's a biological and metabolic assault. I recommend the following to avoid this scenario and maximize your body's energy needs:

- Over the weekend, plan your upcoming week's eating schedule and meals based on what's on your calendar in terms of work and personal responsibilities. Use a journal for this planning (see page 172). Choose the one or two days you'll skip breakfast. On those days, be sure to have a nutrient-dense lunch between 11:30 a.m. and 1:30 p.m.

- Create your grocery list based on the meals you plan to prepare. Don't forget to include snacks. Take care of that shopping before the week begins. You don't want to wake up Monday morning and be scrambling to find food to eat for breakfast or to pack for a lunch.

- Identify which meals and snacks you can take with you for lunch when you're away from home.

The more you plan your eating habits, from *when* you eat to *what* you eat, the more you can have effortless control over sticking with the plan and reaping its health rewards. The same is true when it comes to exercise.

WHEN TO EXERCISE

The body might be physically stronger in the late afternoon and early evening due to a peak in body temperature and certain hormones like testosterone, but that doesn't mean you have to engage in physical activity at that time. You should schedule your exercise when it works best for you. It's far more important to do the exercise than to worry about the "best" time of day for your body to be active. Some people enjoy an early morning jog, while others prefer to end their day with exercise.

Keep in mind, though, that an hour daily spent working out hard won't erase the effects of sitting down for the rest of the day. A growing body of research is revealing that it's entirely possible to get plenty of physical activity and still suffer increased risk of disease and death—just like smoking harms no matter how much you engage in other, healthier lifestyle habits. So many of us barely move an inch to go from home to car to office chair, and back again to sit on the couch and watch TV. It behooves all of us to work more movement into our day, no matter what kind of job we have. Get creative with turning to-do's that could be done without much effort into tasks that require physical movement. Take the stairs. Park far away from the building you plan to enter. Use a headset to walk and talk on your phone so you're getting up from your desk. Take a twenty-minute walk during your lunch break. Build more opportunities to be active during your day. Some additional tips:

- When you map out your upcoming meals for the week, plan your exercise time as well. Also plan what kind of exercise you will do, using a journal for this planning (see page 172). Remember, the minimum is twenty minutes of cardio six days a week with weight-bearing exercises three or four times a week. Build in extra time for stretching, too. Decide which days you'll engage in vigorous exercise and which will be less intense (see the sample plan on the following page). On that seventh day of "rest" (which doesn't need to be a Sunday), plan to do something low-key, like going for a walk with a friend or taking a meditative yoga class. A day of rest doesn't mean you stay totally inactive on your derriere all day.

- If you suffer from sleep disorders or have a hard time falling asleep at night, try to break a sweat outdoors in the early morning hours. Exposure to daylight (say, during a morning bike ride, jog, or drive to an exercise class) soon after waking effectively reboots your circadian rhythm. Morning exercise has also been shown to reduce blood pressure throughout the day and cause an additional 25 percent dip at night, which further correlates with better sleep.

Here is a sample exercise plan for someone who already has a base-line level of fitness and is hoping to gain more strength and fitness with higher-intensity workouts and longer stretches of moderate activity throughout the week. Note that Sunday doesn't have to be the "off" day of rest—here, it's Wednesday. Plan those longer workouts on days when you have more time, which for many is over the weekend.

Monday: Midday brisk walk (twenty to thirty minutes); weight training and stretching at the gym after work (twenty minutes)

Tuesday: fifty-minute indoor cycling class in the morning, plus ten minutes of stretching

Wednesday: Crazy busy day – thirty minutes of brisk walking anytime during the day, and fifteen minutes of weight-bearing exercises and light stretching while dinner is cooking

Thursday: Elliptical machine (thirty minutes) in the morning, plus ten minutes of stretching

Friday: Vinyasa flow yoga class at 6 p.m.

Saturday: Weekend Warrior Power Walking Group at 9:30 a.m. (ninety minutes)

Sunday: Elliptical machine (forty minutes), plus weight-bearing exercises and stretching (twenty minutes)

The more specific you are with your formal exercise plan during the week, the more likely you are to stick to it.

WHEN TO SLEEP

Remember, the body—and especially the brain—revitalizes itself during sleep. While we used to think that there was a magic number of hours the body needed to sleep, new science has overturned that myth. Everyone has different sleep needs. How much do *you* require to function optimally? Find out:

- Determine an ideal wake-up time given your morning duties

- Set your morning alarm for that time every day

- Go to bed eight to nine hours prior to that time until you wake up *before* your alarm. The number of hours of sleep you get that night is your ideal number

Some additional reminders:

- Use the strategies I outlined in Chapter 6 to prepare for sleep and make the most of it

- Be strict about going to bed and getting up at the same time every day, 365 days a year. Don't shift your sleep habits on weekends or holidays or while on vacation

Aim to be asleep before 11 p.m. The hours between 11 p.m. and 2 a.m. are critical for health. This is when your body's powers of rejuvenation are at their peak.

A DAY IN THE LIFE

I've been mentioning the use of journals throughout the book. I can't think of a better way to plan and track your daily life than to keep a few journals for various purposes. This automatically holds you accountable to your intentions and goals. Here's a summary of the three main journals I recommend:

- Food journal: This is where you keep a running tab of not only what you eat, but also what you *plan* to eat—your meals and snacks throughout the week. On the weekend, look ahead at the upcoming week and map out your daily menu, then write down exactly what you eat each day and see how close you come to living up to your plans. Note which foods and ingredients you like or dislike, writing down your favorite meals and recipes. Add details like which foods make you feel extra good and which others may be problematic for your unique physiology. If you tweak a recipe to your liking, record that.

- Exercise journal: This is where you maintain your plans for exercise and record what you do in fact accomplish each day. Track your minutes of cardio, strength training, and stretching. List which muscle groups you work and what type of cardio workout you do. If you experience any pain or soreness, jot that down. See if you can find patterns in the exercises you choose and how your body feels, as this can help you tailor the right exercise regimen for your body. Over the course of a week, make sure you're mixing up your routines, going hard on some days and lighter on others.

- General journal: This is where you document your thoughts, feelings, ideas, wishes, goals, and notes of gratitude. Don't hesitate to record your worries and anxieties, as writing those down can have the effect of reducing their psychological impact on you.

It doesn't matter what type of books you use for journaling. You can buy inexpensive spiral-bound notebooks for your food and exercise journals and splurge on a leather-bound diary for your general journal. Keep a journal by your bedside for early morning and evening writing, and take small, convenient notebooks with you wherever you go to jot down notes throughout the day. Do what works for you and keeps you on track.

Below is a daily checklist followed by a sample daily schedule.

Your Daily Checklist

- ❑ Get up and go to bed at the same time daily.

- ❑ Take your supplements, including your prebiotics and probiotics. See page 112 for your cheat sheet about which supplements to take, how much, and when.

- ❑ Unless you're skipping breakfast, which I encourage you to do at least once a week, make sure you're getting a little protein in the morning. Remember that eggs are a perfect way to start the day.

- ❑ Do cardio exercise for a minimum of twenty minutes, with stretching before and after. Every other day, do weight-bearing exercises (see www.DrPerlmutter.com for videos). See page 168 for information about timing your exercise.

- ❑ Do one small thing to clean up your physical environment (see page 159).

- ❑ Eat lunch before 3 p.m.

- ❑ Drink water throughout the day.

- ❑ Take a ten-minute distraction-free timeout in the a.m. and p.m. to check in with yourself, maybe do some deep breathing (see page 155), write in a journal, or read an inspiring quote or passage from a book. If you'd like to try meditation, go to www.how-to-meditate.org/breathing-meditations.

❏ Plan dinner so that it's not within four hours of bedtime.

❏ Try to be in bed with the lights out before 11 p.m.

Sample Daily Schedule

6:30 a.m.	Wake up!
6:30–6:45 a.m.	Morning deep-breathing exercise and journal writing
7:00–7:45 a.m.	Exercise (e.g., stationary bike, weight training, and stretching)
7:45–8:15 a.m.	Bathing and grooming
8:15 a.m.	Prepare breakfast and bagged lunch
8:45 a.m.	Out the door for work
12:30 p.m.	Lunch and 20-minute walk
4:00–4:15 p.m.	Snack and a few minutes of self-reflection
5:30 p.m.	Leave work
6:30 p.m.	Supper with kids
7:30–8:00 p.m.	Personal downtime
9:30 p.m.	Cutoff time for electronics, prepare for bed
10:30 p.m.	Lights out!

While there are plenty of apps out there to help you map out your day and send reminders to your phone through texts, there is nothing wrong with using an old-fashioned daily planner. Do what works for you. Get as detailed as you like, but understand that everything in your life should revolve around your eating, exercising, and sleeping patterns. Be consistent, even selfish, with those routines, and your whole body will reap tremendous health benefits. I hate to be cliché, but it's true: Timing is everything.

CHAPTER 8

Troubleshooting

EVERY MINUTE OF EVERY DAY we get to choose. Like I always say, life is an endless series of choices. Right or left? Yes or no? Fish or french fries? The whole point of this book has been to help you learn to make better decisions that will ultimately allow you to participate in life at its fullest. Even though you will be faced with difficult decisions, I know you can do this. You know the value of being healthy and mentally sharp. You know what sudden illness and chronic disease can do. Your health should be the most important thing in your life. Because what would you do without it?

Christopher E. posted the following story to my website:

I didn't start out unhealthy, but I had let myself get run down through a combination of work stress, physical stress, and poor nutrition. I'm not an old guy and I've always been able to get away with whatever I wanted to do, so why not work eighty hours a week, train to climb a mountain, and knock out the Bataan Death March all in a six-month period, all while getting four hours of sleep a night and supplementing with lots of coffee! Shockingly, I started feeling super-fatigued every day a few weeks after the mountain climb, and then, to my surprise, my hair started falling out. Seriously, patches of hair started falling out! Being an Army officer, I keep my hair short, but one day one of my sergeants said, "Sir, what's going on with the back of your head?" I checked it out and sure enough, I had a bald patch.

Over the months, it kept getting worse, and the dermatologist said it was alopecia and that we might be able to treat the patches with steroid injections. Without that, Doc said they may get better or worse, but he also said the best thing I could do was limit stress. Yeah, right. I got orders to change duty stations, and my wife told me that we were pregnant all in the same month. The patches kept getting worse, and being a leader in the military who also happens to work in health care, it certainly didn't help my leadership presence or put patients at ease to see my patchy head.

Fast forward eight months or so after moving, and I picked up a copy of Grain Brain. Intrigued by the assertion that some nutritional supplements (gasp) were being touted by a neurologist as being neuroprotective and restorative, along with the idea that the gut microbiome could impact not only the brain but also just about every system in your body, I quickly read the book.

Feeling and looking terrible, I went ahead and gave the ketogenic diet a shot and I began six of the seven supplements suggested in the book (minus the resveratrol). We had the baby the next month (September 2015), so my stress level and sleep got worse, but the patches magically started filling in. By January they were all gone, and I no longer feel like I'm lifting a piano every time I get out of bed. I've also lost twenty pounds.

The success has inspired and empowered me, and now I'm tackling my stress and sleep. I recently began a daily meditation period (not sure if it's doing anything but I'm hopeful), writing a gratitude list, and I'm trying to get seven hours of sleep every night.

I seriously used to think this approach to health was laughable (I was actually taught that it was garbage), but after my own personal case study, I'm starting to come around.

There will no doubt be challenges as you proceed. And there will be times when you will have to address these challenges one by one. That's life. Following are some troubleshooting tips for those moments that threaten to derail you. By all means this is not an exhaustive list, but it will help you handle those inevitable times when you have to make hard choices.

"HOW DO I FOLLOW THE PLAN WHILE EATING OUT OR AWAY FROM HOME?"

I recommend that you avoid eating out during the first couple of weeks on the program so that you can focus on getting the dietary protocol down using my 14-day meal plan. This will prepare you for the day you do venture away from your kitchen and have to make good decisions about what to order from someone else's kitchen.

Most of us eat out several times a week, especially while we're at work. It's virtually impossible to plan and prepare every single meal and snack we consume, so you'll need to learn to navigate other menus. See if you can order from the menu at your favorite restaurants. Don't be shy about asking for substitutions (e.g., a side of more steamed veggies instead of potatoes; extra-virgin olive oil instead of their commercially produced vinaigrette). If you find it too challenging, then you may want to try new restaurants that can cater to your needs. It's not that hard to make any menu work as long as you're savvy about your decisions. Look for healthy sources of organic, GMO-free vegetables. Then add some fat—a drizzle of olive oil or half an avocado—and a little bit of protein and you'll be fine. Watch out for elaborate dishes that contain multiple ingredients. When in doubt, ask the waiter or chef about the dishes.

Rather than eating lunch out while you're at work, consider packing meals. Having precooked foods—such as roasted or grilled chicken, hard-boiled eggs, poached salmon, or strips of grilled sirloin steak or roast beef—in your refrigerator ready to go is helpful. Fill a container with salad greens and chopped raw veggies and add your protein and dressing of choice before eating. I travel with avocados and cans of sockeye salmon. Canned foods can be excellent sources of good, portable nutrition, as long as you're careful about which products you buy and that the cans are labeled BPA-free.

Keep snacks on hand, too, especially at the beginning of this new way of life when you're cutting carbs. There are plenty of snack and "on-the-go" ideas listed in Part III, many of which are portable and nonperishable.

And when you're faced with temptation (the box of muffins at work or a friend's birthday cake), remind yourself that you'll pay for the indulgence somehow. Be willing to accept those consequences if you cannot say no. But keep in mind that a grain-brain-free way of life is, in my humble opinion, the most fulfilling and gratifying way of life there is. Enjoy it.

"OH, NO! I'VE STRAYED FROM THE PROTOCOL. NOW WHAT?"

Maari C.'s story says a lot about what can happen when you revert to your old ways of eating, or suddenly reintroduce wheat after evicting it from your diet. Even though Maari intentionally strayed from the protocol for a couple of days, the effects were so massive that it's worth learning from her experience:

> Several years ago, I started suffering from panic attacks and anxiety, and I quickly began researching holistic alternatives to the pharmacy medications doctors wanted to put me on. After three months of these attacks, my health was repaired within a month.
>
> Fast forward seven years, and after my second pregnancy I started breaking out in hives all over my body, on top of having an underactive thyroid (a big surprise, as I had an overactive thyroid). I was forced to take Synthroid.
>
> A few months ago, my skin rashes came back. On top of that, I was exhausted and depressed. After stumbling across some literature, I adopted a wheat-free diet. As a result, I feel amazing. In two weeks of stopping wheat, my skin cleared up from a rash I've had for seven years! My energy soared through the roof. I didn't get hungry or cranky (amazing, since I was eating 1,200 calories a day on this cleanse). I found myself so excited to drink my green juice for lunch because it made me feel like a million bucks!
>
> The other thing that amazed me was that I was no longer dizzy. I was two weeks into "wheat-free" while on the swings with my daughter, and for the first time I wasn't dizzy or nauseous on the swings. It has been amazing!
>
> I have been amazed at how my brain feels after this. It feels clearer and I'm more articulate. I did go back on wheat for two days to see how it affected me, however, and within thirty minutes of eating a slice of bread, I felt lightheaded. Later, I had some pizza and was miserable that night. Within the day, I had a cold sore and an eye infection, things I haven't had since college.

As with so many things in life, discovering and establishing a new habit is a balancing act. Even once you've shifted your eating and exercise behaviors and changed the way you buy, cook, and order food, you'll still have moments when old habits emerge. (And of course I don't endorse intentionally experimenting with old habits again as Maari did. That will derail you physically and emotionally.) I don't expect you to never eat a slice of crusty pizza or drink a beer again, but I do hope that you stay mindful of your body's true needs and live according to these principles as best you can.

Aim to stick to the 90-10 rule: Follow these guidelines 90 percent of the time, leaving 10 percent wiggle room. There is always an excuse for not taking better care of yourself. We have parties and weddings to attend. We have work to address that leaves us high on stress and low on energy, time, and the mental bandwidth to make good food, exercise, and sleep choices. Hit reboot whenever you feel like you've fallen too far off the wagon. You can do this by fasting for a day and recommitting to the protocol. Take a Friday or Monday off from work to enjoy a three-day weekend during which you get out of town to focus on yourself or enjoy a staycation. Maybe try a yoga retreat or visit a friend you haven't seen in a long time. The point is to shake things up a bit, get out of that health-depleting rut, and refresh your resolve to succeed.

"I'M HAVING SERIOUS HEADACHES AND OTHER SIDE EFFECTS FROM THE DIET"

No sooner do you begin this dietary protocol than your body goes into high gear, detoxifying itself and shedding excess poundage. Headaches can be a common response to a sudden shift in your diet, especially if you've been eating poorly. But they're actually a sign that the diet is working, and they will go away within days. If you feel the need to use an over-the-counter pain reliever, try aspirin. Unlike other NSAIDs, which can disrupt the microbiome and blunt emotions, aspirin can relieve pain and also have some anti-inflammatory effects. As noted in Chapter 4, you might also crave carbs and feel a bit moody and irritable at first when you go cold turkey on the carbs. Remember, gluten and sugar can act much like drugs, leaving those quitting them going through a period of withdrawal. This is normal as your body adjusts and goes through the transition away from the processed, packaged (or otherwise low-quality) foods you may have been eating. Your mood will adjust as you go along, but how can you handle the cravings? What can you do to overcome them?

Be assured that cravings will not last long. Many readers of *Grain Brain* have told me that once they went cold turkey and dove right into my protocol, they never again experienced a craving like they had back when carbs were a staple in their diet. It takes some willpower for the first week and then it gets easier. As one of my fans wrote to me, "It is like feeding the dog from the table — if you keep eating even a little bit of the bad stuff your system will keep begging for it."

But if you do experience a gravitational force toward a bread basket, a chocolate chip cookie, or a bowl of steaming hot pasta, try to distract yourself by engaging in a new activity. Shift gears. Go outside for a 20-minute walk. If it's not too close to bedtime, do some formal exercise (e.g., download an exercise video you can follow at home). Take fifteen minutes to write in a journal or perform some deep-breathing exercises. Listen to uplifting music. Tackle a project you've been meaning to do, such as cleaning out a desk drawer or closet. Or simply find something else to eat. Have a snack on hand to settle those cravings: a handful of nuts, or half an avocado drizzled with some olive oil and balsamic vinegar. Try to keep a meal prepared and ready to go in the fridge all the time, so that if you're super hungry or out of energy you don't go for take-out. Remind yourself that the carbs and sugary foods are just filler foods—made to fill you up with inflammation and pain in the long run. Tell yourself that you'd rather fill up with good-quality foods that do your body and mind good. Remind yourself that you are worth it.

"HELP, I'M GOING TO BED HUNGRY"

If you're having a hard time blocking out that four-hour time period after dinner during which you don't eat anything, here's what you can do. Make sure you're getting enough satiating fat at dinner. Add more olive oil to your vegetables or have a small portion (8 tablespoons) of a rich non-gluten grain such as quinoa with a drizzle of olive oil at dinner.

Rather than heading to the refrigerator when you feel hungry toward bedtime, distract yourself. Try drinking some chamomile tea or other warm herbal tea while reading a good book or magazine article. Call a friend (see page 195 about finding a partner for your journey). Take an evening stroll around the neighborhood. Write in one of your journals. If you have young children, play with them or read books to them. The goal is to distract yourself from thinking about food. If you find yourself lying in bed unable to go to sleep, focus on your breathing and keep your thoughts fixated on the health benefits that are happening at that moment.

"I'M VEGAN. WHAT SHOULD I DO?"

A vegan diet can be wonderfully healthy as long as you're getting good sources of vitamins D and B_{12}, and the omega-3 DHA, as well as minerals like zinc, copper, and magnesium. DHA is available as a supplement derived from marine algae, a vegetarian source. Although people sometimes worry that vegans don't get enough protein, they can get plenty from vegetables, legumes, and non-gluten grains. What I worry about most with vegans is that they don't get enough fat due to the exclusion of all animal products, including eggs and fish. So added olive oil and coconut oil will help bring this dietary choice into balance.

ATTENTION PREGNANT WOMEN AND NEW MOMS

You can indeed build a better baby through the strategies outlined in this book. When expectant and new moms ask me for advice, I offer four important tips:

1. Take prenatal vitamins and probiotics.

2. Supplement with 900–1,000 mg DHA, one of the most important fatty acids for brain development.

3. Cut back on fish consumption to once or twice a week. Moms-to-be are often told to boost their fish consumption due to the high content of fatty acids. But it's hard to know today where your fish are coming from, and they could have high levels of mercury, PCBs, and other toxins.

4. Breast-feed if you can, as no manufactured formula can match the nutrients found in breast milk. For example, breast milk contains substances that protect a baby from diseases and infections and nurture proper growth and

development—substances that formulas don't have because they cannot be artificially synthesized. Breast-feeding has other benefits, too, such as the bonding it provides through physical contact.

A note about C-sections: C-sections do save lives, and they are medically necessary under certain situations. But only a fraction of deliveries need to be done surgically. The advantages of being born through a bacteria-filled vagina that physically baptizes the baby with life-sustaining microbes rather than a sterilized abdomen are truly stunning. Babies born via C-section face a lifetime higher risk of allergies, ADHD, autism, obesity, type 1 diabetes, and dementia later in life.

If, for whatever reason, you undergo a C-section, speak with your doctor about using the so-called gauze technique. New York University's Dr. Maria Gloria Dominguez-Bello has presented research suggesting that using gauze to collect a mother's birth canal bacteria and then rubbing the gauze over the baby's mouth and nose does help the baby grow a healthy bacterial population. It's not as good as a vaginal delivery, but it's better than a sterile C-section.

Dr. Dominguez-Bello also recommends taking probiotics and breast-feeding. She writes: "The synergy of the probiotic and prebiotic components of human breast milk provides breast-fed infants a stable and relatively uniform gut microbiome compared to formula-fed babies."

"I'VE BEEN TOLD TO TAKE ANTIBIOTICS. IS THAT OKAY?"

At some point, most of us will have to take a course of antibiotics to treat an infection. Take antibiotics only if they're absolutely necessary and recommended by your physician. Understand that antibiotics do not treat viral illnesses. Colds, the flu, and the typical sore throats that people experience are caused by viruses, and antibiotics are entirely useless.

When an antibiotic is necessary, rather than getting a "broad-spectrum" antibiotic that will kill many different bacterial species, ask your doctor for a "narrow-spectrum" medication that uniquely targets the organism that is causing the illness. And be an advocate for your children if the pediatrician wants to write a prescription for an antibiotic. Question the doctor to make sure the antibiotic is truly necessary. Antibiotics account for one-quarter of all medications for children, yet it's been shown that up to one-third of these prescriptions are not necessary.

It's important to follow your doctor's prescription exactly (i.e., do not stop taking the drug even if you feel better, as this can spur new strains of bacteria that could potentially make the situation worse). Continue to take your probiotics, but do so "on the half time," meaning take them halfway between dosages of the antibiotics. For example, if you're instructed to take the antibiotics twice daily, then take the drug once in the morning and once at night, and take your probiotics at lunchtime. And be sure to get some *L. brevis* into the mix, which is especially helpful in maintaining a healthy microbiome while taking antibiotics.

"I FEEL SO MUCH BETTER. CAN I STOP TAKING MY MEDS?"

Many people write to me to express their joy at feeling so much better after they start following my protocol. And many begin to rethink medications they are taking, wondering if they don't need them any-more. This is especially true when it comes to psychiatric drugs to treat anxiety and depression. Consider, for example, Linda T.'s experience:

> I am fifty-two years old and am currently taking Cymbalta, 30 mg, for depression. I have been seriously depressed for too long along with severe anxiety. Only one month after becoming gluten-free and reducing my carbohydrate and sugar intake, I am a totally dif-ferent person. Honestly, it is like night and day. My anxiety has disappeared; I am calm. I'm not depressed. Instead, I'm feeling good and content. I used to think that I would be on antidepres-sants forever, but now I feel like there's hope that one day I won't need them anymore.

It's important that you speak with your treating physician before stopping any prescribed medication. You may indeed be able to wean yourself from certain drugs, but this should be done under the supervi-sion of your doctor. Like Linda, have hope that you can one day say goodbye to your medication, but be smart about how you come off any meds that were prescribed to you for a reason.

A FINAL NOTE ABOUT CHILDREN

Stories of children getting their health and their future back are truly uplifting. Here is Jen W.'s story:

> My eleven-year-old son suffered tremendously. It's no stretch to say there were days he just didn't want to wake up. He was diagnosed

with depression, anxiety, OCD, daily nausea, severe eczema, joint pain, psychotic episodes, and unexplained weight gain. Beyond that, he was obese: 65 pounds heavier than his brother, who is thirteen months younger than him. Diets didn't work, antidepressants did nothing, and neither did the countless therapists he saw. Nothing helped, but I kept searching.

The best day of our families' lives came two years ago when a new doctor told us to eliminate sugar, gluten, dairy, processed foods, and legumes from his diet, and to go organic. By day two, all his symptoms were gone and I mean gone!!!!!! It was unreal. I am constantly telling people and doctors about my son's success! I am so so so thankful for your new book, and that there is a real movement and plan that can change people's lives.

I am routinely asked whether children can follow this protocol. You bet. In fact, children stand to gain even greater lifelong benefits, since they are still developing. I can't tell you how many parents write to me about the turnarounds they witness in their children, some of whom have been battling serious brain-related disorders, from epilepsy and ADHD to autism.

While mainstream medicine seems reluctant to embrace dietary intervention as a true medical therapy, I talk to parents all the time who report positive effects of dietary changes in their children. I would encourage any parent of a child exhibiting gastrointestinal and/or behavioral problems to try the strategies outlined in this book. The child's plate should look like yours—lots of colorful, fibrous veggies, some fruit and protein, and healthy fats.

> The protocol in this book will help the vast majority of people. I'm confident that at least 80 percent of you will relieve your suffering, and all of you will be investing in your future health. Some of you, however, might need further intervention. If, after three months on this program, you do not see the results you'd hoped for, it's likely time to seek help from a practitioner trained in functional or integrative medicine. There may be deeper imbalances to address that are affecting your health and that require the support of a professional for complete healing. Don't be afraid to ask for help if you need it.

You don't need to do much to reinforce the body's instinctive proclivity toward health and optimal wellness. You are an incredibly self-regulating machine. So take a moment to appreciate—and perhaps marvel at—that wondrous reality. And then open yourself to the possibilities that await you.

PART III

LET'S EAT!

I'm a thirty-eight-year-old female and I have epilepsy. I have focal motor seizures that mimic dystonia. I suffer from night seizures and occasional daytime seizures, presenting themselves as cramping in my right arm and leg, lasting one to ten seconds. For most of my years, I believed this was a life sentence. However, I've remained mainly seizure-free on a gluten-free diet and haven't taken daily medication for years. I take muscle relaxants when I have seizures. Further, although I have remained mainly seizure-free over the last few years, I have been a terrible sleeper . . . very restless and wakeful. But I have had great success on my new diet and supplement regimen. I have never slept so good! I'm sleeping through the night and I feel so well rested in the morning.

—Anonymous from Wicklow, Ireland

CHAPTER 9

Final Reminders and Snack Ideas

CONGRATULATIONS. YOU ARE ON THE road to a better, healthier you. I'm excited for you in this next chapter of your life—one filled with a vibrancy that you might not have thought was possible before. With every meal, minute of physical movement, night of good sleep, deep exhalation of stress, and time you focus on yourself, your body is shifting in a big way and will continue to do so. All of the strategies you've learned and will eventually master will have monumental biological effects in the long term.

I predict that within the first week you'll be feeling the payoff of this protocol. You'll have fewer symptoms of a chronic condition if you currently have one, less brain fog, better sleep, and improved energy. Although you won't necessarily feel it, you'll also have a heightened protection against future illness. You'll feel stronger and more resilient. Over time, your clothes will loosen as the unwanted weight falls off, and those laboratory tests will show vast improvements in many areas of your biochemistry. For added inspiration, read Gabrielle H.'s story:

I started 2015 by adopting a gluten-free, low-carb lifestyle. I had suffered from anxiety since the age of six, and added chronic stress to that when I was in my thirties. Many other symptoms would come up later, including irritable bowel syndrome in 2005, severe joint pain/muscle aches, lack of sleep, lack of concentration, depression, and finally, a breakdown in 2009. Conventional medicine only scratched the surface. I was grasping at straws last year by trying to exclude different foods from my diet, suffering acid reflux all the while. I would fall asleep to be awakened by a dead arm and, in panic, try to get the circulation back.

This regimen has saved my life. Within five days, I started to sleep. Within twelve, I broke free from depressive moods. I have no joint pain or muscle aches now, no acid reflux at all. My gut feels like it's been repaired. I do not eat any carbs and do eat a high-fat diet with extra-virgin olive oil, coconut, butter, and the like. I feel energetic and feel that my brain is functioning again. I am sixty-three now and am looking forward to getting even better. Last week, I started eating fermented foods including kimchi, red cabbage, and cauliflower. In a week or so, I know I will find even more improvement in my overall health.

In this chapter, I'm going to set you even more firmly on your path by giving you some final reminders, a basic shopping list, and snack ideas. In the next chapter, you will find the 14-day meal plan, followed by the recipes in Chapter 11.

FINAL REMINDERS

Drink Water Throughout the Day

At a minimum, drink half of your body weight in ounces of purified water daily. If you weigh 150 pounds (68kg), drink at least 75 ounces

(2 liters) of water per day. Keep a stainless steel bottle of water with you all day. In addition, you can drink tea or coffee, and have a glass of wine with dinner. Be careful, however, about caffeine late in the day or an extra glass of wine, which will interfere with your sleep.

Avoid juicing. I realize that juice bars are all the rage today, but when you juice whole fruits and vegetables, you substantially reduce if not totally eliminate the fiber content and wind up with a sugary beverage that can rival regular soda. Don't be fooled by juice bars that advertise that juices will "cleanse" and "detoxify" your body. The same goes for sugar-filled smoothies, coconut water, and 100 percent pure watermelon water for "clean, natural hydration." Even with no added sugar, a cup of watermelon juice contains 12 grams of sugar and no fiber. If you're going to drink yourself clean, stick with filtered water.

Be Generous with Olive Oil

You are free to use olive oil liberally (extra-virgin and organic), though I trust you're not going to dump a whole cup of it onto a plate in one sitting. Note that in many cases, you can substitute coconut oil for olive oil in your recipes.

Get Used to It

For those who think "everything in moderation" makes sense, think again: "Everything in moderation" diet advice may lead to poor metabolic health. It's not the "moderation" part that's the problem; it's the "everything" part—eating every type of food available to you rather than sticking to a few choice, healthy staples.

In the 2015 Multi-Ethnic Study of Atherosclerosis, researchers looked at data from 6,814 U.S. participants—whites, blacks,

Hispanic-Americans, and Chinese-Americans. They measured diet diversity and examined how diet quality affected metabolic health. Turns out that the more diverse your diet (meaning you're eating from a very wide range of foods), the more likely you are to eat poorly and suffer metabolic consequences. In describing these results, lead researcher Dariush Mozaffarian, MD, DrPH, stated: "Americans with the healthiest diets actually eat a relatively small range of healthy foods.... These results suggest that in modern diets, eating 'everything in moderation' is actually worse than eating a smaller number of healthy foods."

In my experience, the healthiest people I know eat the same thing most days of the week. They have their trusty breakfasts, lunches, and dinners and don't stray from those blueprints. They generally use the same shopping lists every week. Once you've established a lineup of breakfast, lunch, and dinner ideas using my guidelines, you'll want to keep up your new patterns.

Don't Cheat

No one likes to be a cheater, but in today's world, cheating in the diet arena is practically a given. We are bombarded by choices and seductive advertising everywhere we look. Even the FDA isn't up to speed on what a "healthy" food is. In 2016 it announced plans to update its policies, recommendations, and definitions, but this will take years to execute. Believe it or not, for a long time the FDA has considered fortified cereals loaded with sugar "healthy," while it deemed avocados, salmon, and nuts "unhealthy"! It's truly ridiculous when you think about it.

Our innate survival skills might not know the difference between a slice of pizza and a slice of frittata. We have to become extremely adept at talking ourselves out of thinking one croissant won't hurt us, or that a bowl of organic mac and cheese with the kids will be okay.

This means honing a special set of survival skills, such as being hyper-aware of your brain telling you one thing ("Eat this!") while your body really needs another ("Don't eat this!"). Plan your defense when faced with temptation and obstacles to success. When a friend, for example, invites you to lunch at a restaurant where you know there's not much on the menu for you to eat, politely suggest another restaurant where you know you can live up to the principles of the Grain Brain Whole Life Plan. Don't get discouraged or let your guard down. The faster you move past these speed bumps, the healthier you'll be.

If, after following my protocol for a few weeks, you don't feel like you're getting the results you want or expect, you must ask yourself: *Am I living up to the principles of the program? Have I let things sneak into my diet through mindless nibbling or eating? Have I unwittingly caved in to the pressures of my friends offering me foods I shouldn't be eating?* This is why it's important to track your diet and record what you eat on a daily basis, especially at the start. It's also critical to make a habit of meticulously reading labels. In fact, see if you can avoid reading labels altogether by eating only foods that don't come with them!

Find a Partner

The vast majority of people who pay personal trainers do so because it buys them an accountability partner. You are somewhat forced to show up and do the work with a trainer because you've paid for that person to be there. For the same reason, it helps to have at least one other person with you on this new path. Pick someone—a friend or a family member—who wants to follow the Grain Brain Whole Life Plan with you. Work together toward your goals. Plan meals, shop, cook, and exercise as a team. Come up with new recipes and meal ideas. Share your frustrations as well as your successes along the way. After all, life is a team sport.

Make Vegetables Your Centerpiece

Stop thinking about food pyramids. Think in terms of how we eat: using a plate. A full three-quarters of your plate should be filled with fibrous, colorful, nutrient-dense whole vegetables that grow above ground. That will be your main entrée. I bet you're used to seeing your protein as the centerpiece. Now it becomes a side dish of 3 to 4 ounces (100g). Aim to consume no more than 8 ounces (225g) of protein total in a day. You'll get your fats from those found naturally in protein; from ingredients such as the butter, coconut oil, and olive oil used to prepare your meals; and from nuts and seeds (see page 198 for snack ideas).

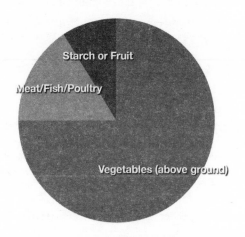

The Basic Shopping List:

almond butter

almond milk

almonds

avocado oil

avocados

balsamic vinegar

bell peppers

berries

black pepper

broccoli

coconut milk

coconut oil

dark chocolate

dark leafy greens, including
kale and spinach

feta cheese

free-range chicken

free-range turkey

fresh guacamole

fresh salsa or pico de gallo

garlic

goat cheese

grass-fed beef

Greek-style yogurt (plain
and coconut milk, 2%)

lemons

macadamia nuts

mixed greens

mozzarella

mushrooms

olive oil

olives

onions

pastured eggs

sea salt

shredded coconut

vine-ripened tomatoes

walnuts

whole fresh seasonal fruit

wild salmon

SNACKS

Better blood sugar control means you are not likely to feel super hungry in between meals. You won't be crashing an hour after that bagel breakfast because bagels are not on the program. Two 70-calorie eggs, for instance, can get you through an entire morning. So even though you might not need to snack, it's nice to know you can whenever you want to on this diet. I recommend keeping some of the less perishable snack options on hand as "emergency food" when you're on the go or at work. Keep a stash of nuts and jerky in your car, purse, or desk at work, just in case. That way, you won't get stuck running behind schedule when it's time for lunch and be tempted by the nearest fast-food restaurant or food truck. Here are some healthy snack ideas:

- a handful of raw nuts, olives, and/or seeds (no peanuts)

- a few squares of dark chocolate (anything above 70 percent cacao)

- chopped raw vegetables (e.g., bell peppers, broccoli, cucumbers, radishes) dipped into guacamole, tapenade, hummus, tahini, baba ganoush, soft goat cheese, or nut butter

- slices of cold roasted turkey, roast beef, or chicken dipped into mustard and Grain Brain Mayonnaise (page 227). [Note: Be wary of traditional deli meats, especially those that are packaged. They can be contaminated with gluten depending on how they are processed. Always ask at the deli counter for fresh, unprocessed meats that they can slice right there.]

- half an avocado drizzled with olive oil, lemon, salt, and pepper

- two hard-boiled eggs

- caprese salad: 1 sliced tomato topped with sliced fresh mozzarella cheese, drizzled with olive oil and sprinkled with basil, salt, and pepper

- Tomato-Basil Tower with Kefir Dressing, Bacon, and Fresh Dill (page 231)

- cold peeled prawns with lemon and dill

- smoked salmon (Optional: Try dipping smoked salmon in Grain Brain Mayonnaise or spreading goat cheese on top)

- one piece or serving of whole, low-sugar fruit (e.g., grapefruit, orange, apple, berries, melon, pear, cherries, grapes, kiwi, plum, peach, nectarine)

- grass-fed beef, turkey, or salmon jerky

- lacto-fermented vegetables (Try my Mixed Vegetable Kraut on page 243)

- protein bars (See my recipe online at www.DrPerlmutter.com)

Remember, this type of diet is self-regulating: You won't be victimized by blood sugar chaos brought on by too many carbohydrates stimulating irrepressible hunger and cravings. Much to the contrary, you'll feel satisfied quickly and for several hours by the fat and protein in your meals. So say goodbye to feeling foggy, sluggish, hungry, and tired throughout the day. And say hello to a whole new vibrant you. Here comes 14 days of deliciousness.

CHAPTER 10

The 14-Day Meal Plan

WELCOME TO THE MEAL PLAN, a 14-day sample menu that will serve as a model for planning your meals in the future. You'll find the recipes in Chapter 11. Although I have added nutritional data to the recipes for your information, I don't expect you to count calories and fat grams or obsess over your daily total intake. I trust you know the difference between a supersized plate of food and a reasonable portion. Vegetables that grow above ground—broccoli, asparagus, spring greens, kale, spinach, dandelion greens, cabbage, brussels sprouts, mushrooms, lettuces, leeks, radishes, bean sprouts, and cauliflower—are pretty much unlimited. You'll minimize your protein to the size of a deck of cards or the palm of your hand.

You might find it helpful to keep a food journal as you press forward. Make notes about recipes you like and foods that you don't or that could be giving you trouble (e.g., you experience symptoms such as stomach upset or headaches every time you eat sesame seeds; or you can't stand feta cheese). You can always find substitutes. Pay attention to the foods that make your body sing. You do not have to follow this menu plan strictly as written. If you love what you ate for breakfast on

Day 1, for example, feel free to repeat that again on Day 2. Don't hesitate to substitute any suggested meal for another.

Many of the dishes require that you plan (and cook) ahead. I suggest that you take a good look at these next 14 days and decide which meals you'd like to prepare. The recipes that call for fermentation time, such as the Asian-Scented Greens (page 245) and Mixed Vegetable Kraut (page 243), will need to be prepared days in advance. I purposefully didn't include them in the menu plan until the second week, so aim to make those in the first few days.

Most of these recipes serve more than one person, so think about that in your planning; you could be feeding your whole family or using leftovers the next day. In fact, on many occasions you'll simply use leftovers from the evening before to cover your lunch to make it easy and quick. And feel free to double up on recipes for a greater yield to feed more people or to have more leftovers for yourself.

Spend the day before you begin mapping out your choices, going to the market, and setting aside the time you need to spend in your kitchen. You might designate Sunday as your prep day during which you take an hour or two to get ready for the upcoming week. I recommend making a dozen hard-boiled eggs on Sunday that you can use in your meals and as snacks throughout the week.

Note that you can just as easily craft simpler meals based on the guidelines presented here (e.g., roast or steam a bounty of fresh vegetables, add a few ounces of high-quality protein, and include a mixed greens salad with lots of olive oil). For those of you who need more calories or who feel like you need more carbs, try adding additional coconut oil or olive oil first. If you still feel you need more carbs, go with non-gluten grains such as quinoa or wild rice and keep the portion small (8 tablespoons). Or try my Sunchoke Fritters (page 234), which are an excellent substitute for the carbs (e.g., potatoes, bread, pasta) you will not be eating.

When preparing a salad of mixed greens, be sure to add lots of cooked or raw vegetables (see below). You might not want to eat raw asparagus and broccoli, for instance, but you can cook those veggies and add them to your leafy green salad with cucumbers, jicama, radishes, and such. I don't suggest which type of dressing to use in all instances. A fallback staple is olive oil and balsamic vinegar. Avoid processed, commercially made dressings. These can be loaded with sugar, bad fats, fillers, and artificial ingredients. Read your labels.

You don't need to toss your cookware, cutting boards, utensils, and so on that have been used with gluten-containing products in the past. Use what you've already got. Think about investing in some fun kitchen equipment in the future to make the art of cooking all the more enjoyable.

Get to know your grocers and local farmer's markets; the people there can tell you what just came in and where your foods are coming from. Go organic, grass-fed, and wild whenever possible. Aim to choose produce that's in season in your hemisphere, and be willing to try new foods you've never had before. Take one to three breaths with your eyes closed before you eat and express gratitude for the food that will nourish you from the inside out.

The most essential lesson to learn as you commence this new way of eating (and living!) is to begin to listen to your body. It knows what it needs. When we clear the slate of processed, inflammatory foods, we begin to guide ourselves toward our best selves.

14 DAYS OF DELICIOUSNESS

Recipes in boldface are included in Chapter 11. Recipes marked with an asterisk (*) can be found on my website, www.DrPerlmutter.com.

Day 1:

> Breakfast: 2 poached eggs topped with salsa or pico de gallo + half an avocado drizzled with olive oil and a pinch of sea salt
>
> Lunch: **Layered Vegetable Salad** (page 226) with 75g diced grilled chicken mixed in
>
> Dinner: **Mixed Greens with Toasted Walnuts** (page 228) + 75g baked or grilled fish
>
> Dessert: 2 squares of dark chocolate dipped in 1 tablespoon almond butter

Day 2:

> Breakfast: skip!
>
> Lunch: **Onion Soup** (page 220) + 2 roasted chicken drumsticks + side of mixed greens
>
> Dinner: **Tuscan-Style Pork Roast** (page 255) + sautéed spring greens + 100g quinoa (optional)
>
> Dessert: **Coconut Pudding** (page 258)

Day 3:

> Breakfast: **Broccoli, Mushroom, and Leek Frittata** (page 210) + 250ml almond milk

Lunch: leftover pork roast tossed into mixed greens salad with at least 3 raw vegetables (e.g., broccoli, radishes, green beans) + half an avocado + drizzle of olive oil

Dinner: grilled steak + roasted vegetables + leftover onion soup

Dessert: 60g fresh berries topped with coconut milk

Day 4:

Breakfast: leftover frittata + 250ml almond milk (optional)

Lunch: mixed greens salad with at least 3 raw or cooked vegetables topped with grilled fish or chicken

Dinner: **Roast Leg of Grass-Fed Lamb** (page 253) + unlimited steamed vegetables + 100g wild rice (optional)

Dessert: **Ricotta with Berries and Toasted Almonds** (page 260)

Day 5:

Breakfast: **Strawberry Power Smoothie** (page 213)

Lunch: leftover lamb tossed into mixed greens salad with at least 3 raw vegetables (e.g., broccoli, radishes, green beans) + half an avocado + drizzle of olive oil

Dinner: **Steamed Wild Salmon with Sautéed Leeks and Chard** (page 248) + 100g rice or quinoa (optional)

Dessert: skip!

Day 6:

Breakfast: Greek-style yogurt topped with raw walnuts and fresh berries

Lunch: mixed greens salad with 2 hard-boiled eggs, at least 3 raw vegetables (e.g., celery, spring onions, water chestnuts), half an avocado, crushed walnuts, and shredded or diced cheddar cheese + 1 piece whole fruit

Dinner: grilled fish, chicken, or steak + grilled courgettes + **Braised Kale** (page 233)

Dessert: **Easy Chocolate Mousse** (page 259)

Day 7:

Breakfast: **Baked Eggs and Greens** (page 212)

Lunch: mixed greens and vegetables sautéed in butter and garlic + grilled chicken or fish

Dinner: **Lamb Meatball Soup** (page 223)

Dessert: 2 or 3 squares dark chocolate

Day 8:

Breakfast: 2 fried eggs topped with diced avocado, diced vine-ripened tomatoes, and drizzle of olive oil + unlimited sautéed greens and other vegetables

Lunch: Leftover lamb meatball soup

Dinner: **Broccoli, Mushroom, and Feta Toss** (page 242) + **Herb-Roasted Wild Salmon** (page 247)

Dessert: whole fruit

Day 9:

Breakfast: 3 scrambled eggs with at least 3 vegetables (e.g., spinach, mushrooms, onions) and goat cheese + 250ml almond milk (optional)

Lunch: **Jicama Salad** (page 230) + side of roasted turkey

Dinner: **Thai Vegetable Curry** (page 239) + 75–115g ounces
chicken or steak

Dessert: **Coconut Pudding** (page 258)

Day 10:

Breakfast: coconut milk or plain yogurt topped with nuts and
seeds + 2 hard- or soft-boiled eggs

Lunch: **Layered Vegetable Salad** (page 226) with 75g diced grilled
chicken mixed in

Dinner: **Roasted Chicken Thighs with Parsley Sauce** (page 256)
+ unlimited steamed vegetables + 100g quinoa (optional)

Dessert: skip!

Day 11:

Breakfast: Eggs Benedict with Courgette Pancakes* or **Breakfast
"Porridge"** (page 214)

Lunch: leftover roasted chicken thighs + mixed greens and
vegetable salad

Dinner: grilled fish of your choice + roasted asparagus and
brussels sprouts + **Sunchoke Fritters** (page 234)

Dessert: 25–50g cheese

Day 12:

Breakfast: skip!

Lunch: mixed greens salad with at least 3 raw or cooked

vegetables topped with grilled fish or chicken + **Sunchoke Gratin** (page 236)

Dinner: grilled chicken or fish + **Mixed Vegetable Kraut** (page 243)

Dessert: **Easy Chocolate Mousse** (page 259)

Day 13:

Breakfast: coconut milk yogurt topped with nuts and seeds + 2 hard- or soft-boiled eggs

Lunch: leftover vegetable kraut tossed into mixed greens salad or beside grilled fish or poultry

Dinner: **Grass-Fed Beef Burgers** (page 252) + mixed green salad or **Fish Fillets with Black Olives, Artichokes, and Shaved Brussels Sprout Slaw** (page 250)

Dessert: skip!

Day 14:

Breakfast: **Strawberry Power Smoothie** (page 213) or Oatless Oatmeal* + 2 eggs any style

Lunch: **Creamy Cauliflower Soup** (page 221) + mixed greens salad with shredded chicken mixed in

Dinner: **Pea and Goat Cheese Custards** (page 218) + mixed greens salad + 75g meat or fish

Dessert: whole fruit

Congratulations! You've made it through two weeks on the Grain Brain Whole Life Plan eating nutrient-dense foods that fill your heart and soul. Hopefully you've incorporated other elements on that check-list (see page 173) into your new lifestyle, too. I'm confident you can keep going. If you don't know what to eat after these two weeks, just repeat the same 14-day meal plan until you get used to cooking and eating this way and feel confident enough to start experimenting in the kitchen. Now let's get to the recipes.

CHAPTER 11

The Recipes

GET READY TO MAKE SOME delicious meals using the recipes in this chapter. When buying ingredients, remember to choose organic, grass-fed, GMO-free, gluten-free, and wild whenever possible. Reach for extra-virgin olive and coconut oils. Check labels on all packaged goods to be sure they don't contain anything suspicious (see page 88). Most of the ingredients you'll need are now widely available and found in supermarkets. Some of these recipes are more time-consuming to make than others, so plan ahead and feel free to swap one for another if you don't have the extra time. Ultimately, have fun with these recipes and enjoy being your own personal chef.

EGGS AND OTHER BREAKFAST DISHES

Broccoli, Mushroom, and Leek Frittata

Serves 4

A frittata can be made with almost any combination of vegetables and/or meat, even leftovers. Some tasty combinations might be pumpkin-mint, tomato-basil, asparagus-salmon, onion–chopped greens, summer squash–feta, chopped pork–Gruyère — the list can go on and on. Frittatas are perfect for breakfast, brunch, lunch, or dinner and can be eaten hot out of the oven or at room temperature.

1 tablespoon unsalted butter, preferably from grass-fed cows

1 tablespoon extra-virgin olive oil

225g diced leeks, white part only

6 large mushrooms, stems removed, cleaned, and thinly sliced

1 teaspoon minced garlic

120g finely chopped tenderstem broccoli or broccoli

Sea salt and freshly ground black pepper

5 large eggs

4 tablespoons grated Parmesan cheese

2 large egg whites

Preheat the oven to 180°C/gas 4.

Generously butter a 20cm deep-dish pie plate or ovenproof frying pan. Set aside.

Combine the butter and olive oil in a large sauté pan over medium heat. Add the leeks and cook, stirring frequently, for about 4 minutes or just until wilted. Add the mushrooms and garlic and continue to cook, stirring frequently, for about 12 minutes or until the mushrooms have exuded their liquid and begun to brown. Stir in the broccoli and continue to cook, stirring frequently, for another 3 to 4 minutes, until the broccoli is slightly soft. Lightly season with salt and pepper.

While the vegetables are cooking, place the whole eggs in a medium bowl, whisking to lighten. Add 2 tablespoons of the cheese and season with salt and pepper.

Place the egg whites in a medium bowl and, using a handheld electric mixer, beat until firm, but not dry. Fold the beaten egg whites into the egg mixture, folding only until small pieces of egg white are still visible.

Scrape the broccoli mixture into the eggs, stirring to blend. Pour into the prepared pan, gently smoothing out the top with a spatula. Sprinkle with the remaining 2 tablespoons of cheese and transfer to the oven.

Bake for about 20 minutes or until the center is set and the top is golden brown and almost crisp around the edges.

Remove from the oven and let stand for a couple of minutes before cutting into wedges and serving.

Nutritional Analysis per Serving: calories 278, fat 15 g, protein 18 g, carbohydrates 20 g, sugar 6 g, fiber 6 g, sodium 286 mg

Baked Eggs and Greens

Serves 6

This is a terrific Sunday brunch dish. The recipe is easily doubled; just use two baking dishes. Make sure that you remove the dish from the oven before the eggs are fully cooked, as you want the yolks to be runny when served so that they can be mixed in with the greens.

   1 tablespoon extra-virgin olive oil

   1 tablespoon unsalted butter, preferably from grass-fed cows

   115g chopped leeks, white part only

   1 tablespoon chopped garlic

   Sea salt and freshly ground black pepper

   2 bunches Swiss chard, tough stem ends removed and cut into large
     pieces

   4 tablespoons chopped sun-dried tomatoes

   1 tablespoon chopped fresh basil

   75ml double cream, preferably from grass-fed cows

   12 large eggs

   60g grated fontina cheese

Preheat the oven to 200°C/gas 6.

Generously coat a 23 by 32 by 5cm baking dish with butter. Set aside.

Heat the oil and butter in a large frying pan over medium heat. Add the leeks and garlic, season with salt and pepper, and cook, stirring occasionally, for about 8 minutes or until the leeks are quite soft.

Begin adding the chard, a couple of handfuls at a time, tossing to soften and wilt before adding another batch. When all of the chard has been added, add the tomatoes and basil. Season with salt and pepper and continue to cook, tossing and turning, for about 10 minutes or until very soft.

Stir in the cream and continue to cook for about 6 minutes or until the cream has almost evaporated. Taste and, if necessary, season with additional salt and pepper.

Spoon the chard mixture into the prepared baking dish, spreading it out into an even layer. Using the back of a soup spoon, make 12 small indentations in the chard. Crack one egg into each indentation. When all of the eggs are nestled in the chard, season each one with salt and pepper and sprinkle the cheese over the top, covering both eggs and chard.

Transfer to the oven and bake for about 15 minutes or until the whites are not quite firm and the yolks are still very runny.

Remove from the oven and let stand for 5 minutes to allow the whites to set before serving.

Nutritional Analysis per Serving: calories 297, fat 21 g, protein 17 g, carbohydrates 10 g, sugar 3 g, fiber 3 g, sodium 585 mg

Strawberry Power Smoothie

Serves 1

Most traditional smoothies and shakes are filled with sugar, but this one lives up to my standards and is an excellent recipe to have on hand for those mornings when you don't have time to create a regular breakfast meal. This smoothie can go with you to work, too, and keep you satisfied for hours.

4 tablespoons unsweetened coconut milk

4 tablespoons water (or more for desired consistency)

40g frozen strawberries

¼ ripe avocado, pitted and peeled

1 tablespoon raw unsalted sunflower seeds or almonds

1 tablespoon hemp seeds

1 tablespoon sunflower seed butter or almond butter

1 teaspoon chopped fresh ginger

½ teaspoon ground cinnamon

Combine all of the ingredients in a blender jar. Blend until completely smooth, scraping down the sides as needed. Serve immediately.

Nutritional Analysis per Serving: calories 380, fat 32 g, protein 10 g, carbohydrates 17 g, sugar 7 g, fiber 7 g, sodium 23 mg

Breakfast "Porridge"

Serves 1

Once you taste this bowl of deliciousness, you'll never want to go back to your old-fashioned oatmeal. To accompany this dish, have a cup of coffee or kombucha tea, or drink some kefir, almond milk, or coconut milk. This breakfast will keep you satisfied all morning long.

125ml hot water (or more for desired consistency)

1½ tablespoons chia seeds

1½ tablespoons hemp seeds

1–2 tablespoons sunflower lecithin (optional)

1 tablespoon coconut oil

1 tablespoon almond butter

1 teaspoon ground flax seeds (optional)

1 teaspoon ground cinnamon

5 drops stevia, or to taste

Sea salt

60g blueberries, raspberries, and/or blackberries

Combine all of the ingredients except for the berries in a bowl. Stir well. Top with the berries and serve.

Nutritional Analysis per Serving: calories 460, fat 37 g, protein 12 g, carbohydrates 26 g, sugar 9 g, fiber 11 g, sodium 330 mg

APPETIZERS

Wild Salmon Crudo with Shaved Artichokes

Serves 4

This light but beautiful artichoke salad is the perfect complement to the unctuous raw salmon. If you can't find tender baby artichokes, the salad can be made with raw asparagus or thinly sliced fennel. Eating both the salmon and the artichokes raw gives you many health benefits.

    225g wild salmon fillet, skin and pin bones removed
    75ml white vinegar
    3 baby artichokes
    4 tablespoons extra-virgin olive oil, plus more as necessary
    2 teaspoons fresh lemon juice
    2 tablespoons chopped fresh chives, tarragon, or flat-leaf parsley
    Sea salt and freshly ground black pepper
    Lemon wedges, for garnish (optional)

Using a very sharp knife, cut the salmon crosswise against the grain into 5mm-thick slices. Place an equal number of the slices in a single layer on each of four chilled plates.

Cover each plate with a sheet of plastic wrap. Working with one plate at a time and using the bottom of a small frying pan (or any flat object), gently press down to flatten the salmon so that it covers the entire plate. Do not press too hard, as you don't want to make the salmon mushy. Leaving the plastic wrap on, transfer the plates to the refrigerator.

Fill a large bowl with cold water. Add the white vinegar and set aside.

Working with one at a time, pull off the tough outer leaves of each artichoke. Then, using kitchen scissors, cut off the pointed, spiked tips of each artichoke and about 5mm off of the top. If the artichokes have stems, cut them off completely also.

Using a vegetable slicer or very sharp knife, slice each artichoke crosswise into paper-thin slices. Immediately drop the slices into the cold, acidulated water to keep the flesh from oxidizing.

When all of the artichokes have been sliced, remove them from the water and pat very dry. Place the well-drained slices in a medium bowl and add 2 tablespoons of the olive oil, along with the lemon juice. Add the herbs, season with salt and pepper, and toss to coat.

Remove the fish from the refrigerator and unwrap. Drizzle an equal portion of the remaining 2 tablespoons olive oil over each plate. Season lightly with salt and pepper. Scatter an equal portion of the shaved artichokes over each plate. If using, garnish with a lemon wedge, and serve immediately.

Nutritional Analysis per Serving: calories 260, fat 17 g, protein 17 g, carbohydrates 13 g, sugar 2 g, fiber 6 g, sodium 260 mg

Pea and Goat Cheese Custards

Serves 4

This very elegant dish can be served as a first course for a dinner party or as a lovely lunch when accompanied by a green salad. Although it's quite rich, the crisp peas and fresh herbs add an unexpected lightness.

Butter, for ramekins

150g frozen petits pois

75g mild creamy goat cheese

4 extra-large eggs, at room temperature

250ml double cream, preferably from grass-fed cows

2 tablespoons grated Parmesan cheese

Sea salt and freshly ground black pepper

2 tablespoons finely chopped spring onions white part only

2 tablespoons minced fresh dill

4 sprigs fresh dill, for garnish (optional)

Preheat the oven to 180°C/gas 4.

Generously butter the interior of four 175ml ramekins. Set aside.

Bring a small pot of water to a boil, and boil the peas for 1 minute. Drain well and pat dry. Set aside.

Place the goat cheese in the bowl of a food processor fitted with the metal blade. Add the eggs, cream, and Parmesan. Season with salt and pepper and process to a smooth puree.

Scrape the cheese mixture into a medium bowl. Add the spring onions and minced dill and stir to blend well.

Season the peas with salt and pepper and spoon an equal portion into the bottom of each of the buttered ramekins. Then spoon an equal portion of the cheese mixture over the peas.

Place the ramekins in a baking pan. Add enough hot water to come halfway up the sides of the ramekins and carefully transfer the baking pan to the oven.

Bake for 25 minutes or until the custards are set in the center and lightly browned around the edges.

Remove from the oven and place the ramekins on a wire rack to cool for 10 minutes.

Garnish each ramekin with a dill sprig, if desired, and serve while still very warm.

Nutritional Analysis per Serving: calories 390, fat 34 g, protein 14 g, carbohydrates 8 g, sugar 1 g, fiber 2 g, sodium 370 mg

SOUPS

Onion Soup

Serves 6

This is about as rich and delicious as the classic French onion soup, even though it lacks the traditional topping of toasted baguette. Although it can be made with all red or all sweet onions, the combination creates a rich color and a slightly sweet flavor.

115g unsalted butter, preferably from grass-fed cows

550g thinly sliced red onions

550g thinly sliced sweet onions

2 bay leaves

1 star anise

125ml brandy

2 liters beef stock or low-sodium beef broth

Sea salt and freshly ground black pepper

175g grated Gruyère cheese

Place the butter in a large saucepan over medium-low heat. Add the onions, bay leaves, and star anise and cook, stirring frequently, for about 20 minutes or until the onions have begun to caramelize and turn a rich golden brown.

Stir in the brandy, raise the heat, and bring to a boil. Boil for 3 to 4 minutes so that the alcohol can cook off. Add the stock and season with salt and pepper. Bring to a boil, then lower the heat and cook at a gentle simmer for 30 minutes or until the onions are meltingly soft and the soup is deeply flavored. Remove and discard the bay leaves and star anise.

Taste and, if necessary, adjust the seasoning. Ladle into deep soup bowls and immediately top each bowl with an equal portion of the cheese so that the heat can begin melting it.

Serve immediately.

Nutritional Analysis per Serving: calories 360, fat 24 g, protein 14 g, carbohydrates 15 g, sugar 9 g, fiber 2 g, sodium 370 mg

Creamy Cauliflower Soup

Serves 4

Although called "creamy," this soup does not have an ounce of cream in it. It is pure velvety vegetable flavor that is perfection in a bowl. The addition of the brown butter adds extraordinary richness to what is otherwise a very simple soup.

The soup may be made up to 2 days in advance and stored in the refrigerator in an airtight container. Reheat it and make the brown butter just before serving.

- 1 head cauliflower, trimmed and broken into small pieces, including the tender core
- 115g chopped leeks, white part only
- Sea salt
- 115g unsalted butter, preferably from grass-fed cows
- Freshly ground white pepper

Reserve 8 tablespoons of the cauliflower pieces and place the remaining cauliflower in a medium saucepan. Add the leeks, along with 1 liter cold water. Generously season with salt and place over medium-high heat. Bring to a boil, then cover and simmer for about 12 minutes or until the cauliflower is very soft.

While the cauliflower is cooking, heat the butter in a small frying pan over medium-low heat. Add the reserved cauliflower pieces and sauté, stirring frequently, for about 7 minutes or until the butter is golden brown with a nutty aroma and the cauliflower is lightly browned and just barely cooked. Remove from the heat and keep warm.

Remove the cauliflower and leek mixture from the heat and, using a slotted spoon, transfer the vegetables to a blender jar or the bowl of a food processor fitted with the metal blade. Add 250ml of the cooking water and reserve the remaining water.

With the motor running, begin pureeing the cauliflower, slowly adding additional cooking water until the mixture reaches a soup-like consistency. Season with salt and white pepper.

Ladle an equal portion of the soup into each of four large shallow soup bowls. Spoon a dollop of the sautéed cauliflower in the center of each bowl and drizzle an equal portion of the brown butter over the top.

Serve immediately.

Nutritional Analysis per Serving: calories 240, fat 23 g, protein 3 g, carbohydrates 8 g, sugar 3 g, fiber 3 g, sodium 314 mg

Lamb Meatball Soup

Serves 8

This dish comes courtesy of Seamus Mullen, chef-proprietor of Tertulia restaurant in New York City. It's a great recipe to use for dinner parties or to make on a Sunday night. Use the leftovers for lunches in the upcoming week.

For the meatballs:

2 large eggs

135g almonds, soaked in milk for 30 minutes, then drained and finely chopped

8 tablespoons chopped mixed fresh herbs, such as oregano, rosemary, and/or thyme

1 tablespoon red wine (optional)

2 cloves garlic, minced

2 tablespoons sea salt

1 teaspoon cayenne pepper

1 teaspoon ground coriander

1 teaspoon ground cumin

1 teaspoon ground fennel

½ teaspoon freshly ground black pepper

1.1kg minced lamb

For the soup:

2 tablespoons extra-virgin olive oil, plus more for garnish

1 bunch (4 to 6) small carrots, chopped

4 cipollini onions or shallots, peeled

100g diced king oyster mushrooms

1 fennel bulb, trimmed and cut into 2.5cm pieces

2 cloves garlic, sliced

250ml white wine

1.5 liters chicken stock

2 bay leaves

2 sprigs fresh thyme

1 sprig fresh rosemary

Sea salt and freshly ground black pepper

170g red quinoa, rinsed

1 jalapeño pepper, stemmed, seeded, and sliced as thinly as possible

200g sugar snap peas, cut diagonally in half

40g coarsely chopped radicchio

Freshly chopped dill, coriander, basil, fennel fronds, and/or mint, for garnish

For the meatballs: Whisk the eggs in a large bowl. Add all of the remaining meatball ingredients except for the lamb and mix thoroughly. Add the lamb, then, using your hands, blend everything together. Pinch off a piece of the lamb mixture and gently roll between your hands to form 4cm balls. Continue shaping until all the meat mixture is used.

For the soup: In a large saucepan, heat the olive oil over high heat and quickly brown the meatballs evenly. Transfer to a plate lined with paper towels. Add the carrots, onions, mushrooms, and fennel to the saucepan, and sauté for 3 minutes, then add the garlic and cook for

1 minute. Deglaze with the white wine and allow the alcohol to cook off, about 3 minutes. Add the chicken stock, bay leaves, thyme, and rosemary, and bring to a boil. Reduce the heat to a simmer, and season with salt and pepper.

Add the quinoa and simmer for 15 minutes, until it's just tender, then add the meatballs and gently simmer for 2 minutes. Check the meatballs for an internal temperature of about 48°C; if touched to your lower lip, they should be warm, but not superhot. Once they have reached 48°C at the center, add the jalapeño, sugar snap peas, and radicchio. Simmer for another 3 minutes or until the vegetables are just barely tender but still vibrant.

Serve immediately, finishing each bowl with a healthy drizzle of olive oil and a generous sprinkling of chopped herbs.

Nutritional Analysis per Serving: calories 650, fat 35 g, protein 40 g, carbohydrates 45 g, sugar 8 g, fiber 13 g, sodium 680 mg

SALADS

Layered Vegetable Salad

Serves 6

This is a terrific salad to make when company is expected, as it can be made ahead and tossed at the last minute. The red onions add some nice color, but if you don't have them on hand, white onions will work just fine. However, don't replace the softer savoy or chinese cabbage with ordinary green or red cabbage, as the latter is a bit too tough.

3 red onions, peeled and trimmed

675g thinly sliced savoy cabbage or chinese leaves

1 large jicama or celery heart, peeled, trimmed, and shredded

500g thinly sliced radish, preferably red, but any type will do

125ml organic, cultured, full-fat plain yogurt

125ml Grain Brain Mayonnaise (recipe follows)

2 tablespoons chopped sustainably sourced anchovies packed in olive oil (see next recipe for details)

2 teaspoons chopped mixed fresh herbs, such as mint, basil, parsley, and/or thyme

Sea salt and freshly ground black pepper (optional)

Using a vegetable slicer or a very sharp knife, cut the onions crosswise into paper-thin slices. Place the slices in a large bowl of ice water and let soak for 10 minutes. Pour off the water and pat the onions dry.

Place a thin layer of cabbage in the bottom of a large salad bowl. Top with a thin layer of onions, followed by the jicama, and finally the radishes. Continue making thin layers, ending with radishes, until all of the vegetables have been used.

Combine the yogurt, mayonnaise, anchovies, and herbs in a small bowl and whisk until well combined. Pour the dressing over the salad, spreading it evenly over the top. Cover with plastic wrap and refrigerate for at least 6 hours or up to 24 hours.

When ready to serve, toss the salad. Taste and, if desired, season with salt and pepper.

Nutritional Analysis per Serving: calories 232, fat 16 g, protein 5 g, carbohydrates 17 g, sugar 7 g, fiber 6 g, sodium 390 mg

Grain Brain Mayonnaise

Makes about 500ml

The secret to this mayonnaise is in its oil. Rather than traditional mayo, which typically uses rapeseed oil, this one calls for avocado oil, which creates a much more delicious, nutritious experience. Use this mayo like you would traditional mayo—as a spread, as a dip, and in dressings. Be sure to buy organic avocado oil. Sustainably sourced anchovies are available online.

3 large egg yolks, at room temperature

½ teaspoon sea salt

¼ teaspoon mustard powder

1 tablespoon champagne vinegar or fresh lemon juice

375 – 500ml avocado oil

1 tablespoon hot water

Fill a blender jar with boiling water and set it aside for a couple of minutes. You just need to heat the jar to help the eggs thicken. Pour out the water and quickly wipe the jar dry. Place the jar on the blender motor. Add the egg yolks and process on medium speed until very thick. Add the salt and mustard powder and quickly incorporate. Add the vinegar and process to blend.

With the motor running, begin adding the oil in an excruciatingly slow drip; the slower the drip, the more even the emulsification. When about half of the oil has been added, you should have a sauce that is like double cream, and you can then begin adding the oil just a bit quicker, as curdling will no longer be an issue. If the mixture seems to be too thick — you want a soft, creamy mix — add just a smidge more vinegar. Continue adding the oil until all of it has been absorbed into the eggs. Then, add just enough hot water (but no more than 1 tablespoon) to smooth the mix. Scrape the mayonnaise into a clean container with a lid. Cover and refrigerate for up to 5 days.

Nutritional Analysis per Serving (1 tablespoon): calories 105, fat 11 g, protein 0 g, carbohydrates 0 g, sugar 0 g, fiber 0 g, sodium 34 mg

Mixed Greens with Toasted Walnuts

Serves 4

Caramelized onion dressing, crunchy walnuts, and slightly bitter greens combine to make an aromatic and satisfying salad. It works well as a lunch main course or as a side dish for grilled fish or poultry.

1 large red onion, peeled and cut lengthwise into 8 wedges

125ml cup plus 1 tablespoon walnut oil

1 tablespoon balsamic vinegar

4 tablespoons chicken stock or canned low-sodium chicken broth

3 tablespoons white balsamic vinegar

Sea salt and freshly ground black pepper

500g finely chopped mixed bitter greens, such as endive, radicchio, dandelion, mustard, and/or kale

115g chopped toasted walnuts

1 small red shallot, peeled, cut in half lengthwise, and thinly sliced

Preheat the oven to 200°C/gas 6.

Place the onion wedges, cut side down, in a nonstick baking pan. Combine 1 tablespoon of the oil with the balsamic vinegar and drizzle the mixture over the onions. Transfer to the oven and roast, turning occasionally, for about 30 minutes or until golden brown and caramelized.

Remove from the oven and set aside to cool slightly. You want the onions to still be quite warm when you make the dressing.

While still warm, place the seasoned onions in a food processor fitted with the metal blade. Add the remaining 125ml oil along with the stock and the white balsamic vinegar. Process to a smooth, thick puree. Season with salt and pepper. (The dressing may be made in advance, but if so, you will need to warm it slightly before adding to the salad.)

Place the greens in a large salad bowl. Pour the dressing over the top, adding just enough to coat and wilt the greens. You may not need all of the dressing. Toss well.

Add the toasted walnuts and shallot and again toss to combine. Taste and, if necessary, season with additional salt and pepper.

Serve immediately.

Nutritional Analysis per Serving (if all the dressing is used):
calories 600, fat 53 g, protein 14 g, carbohydrates 30 g, sugar 5 g, fiber 17 g, sodium 140 mg

Jicama Salad

Serves 4

The zesty dressing is a perfect match for the slightly sweet, crisp jicama. When paired with the bitter radicchio, it makes for a salad of complex textures and savory flavors.

4 tablespoons finely chopped sun-dried tomatoes

1 tablespoon chopped fresh coriander

1 tablespoon chopped fresh chives

3 tablespoons champagne vinegar

2 teaspoons fresh lime juice

1 teaspoon fresh lemon juice

2 teaspoons extra-virgin olive oil

Freshly ground black pepper

350g julienned jicama

40g shredded radicchio

Parmesan or ricotta salata cheese, for shaving

Combine the tomatoes with the coriander and chives in a small non-reactive container. Stir in the vinegar, along with the lime and lemon juices and the olive oil. Season generously with pepper and stir to blend well. Cover and refrigerate for at least 1 hour or up to 4 hours.

Place the jicama in a large bowl of ice water and refrigerate for 1 hour.

When ready to serve, drain the jicama very well and pat dry. Place in a medium bowl and pour the tomato dressing over the top. Toss to blend well.

Place a layer of radicchio in the center of each of four salad plates. Mound an equal portion of the jicama salad in the center of each plate. Shave the cheese over each plate, and serve immediately.

Nutritional Analysis per Serving: calories 180, fat 9 g, protein 10 g, carbohydrates 12 g, sugar 3 g, fiber 5 g, sodium 350 mg

Tomato-Basil Tower with Kefir Dressing, Bacon, and Fresh Dill

Serves 1

This recipe is from my good friend Fabrizio Aielli, chef at Sea Salt restaurant in my hometown of Naples, Florida. Enjoy it as an appetizer, a refreshing snack on the weekend, or a side to a meal. When you find that perfectly ripe tomato, make this recipe.

    1 vine-ripened tomato, sliced into 3 slices, top and bottom discarded
    2 fresh basil leaves
    2 tablespoons Kefir Dressing (recipe follows)
    2 slices bacon, cooked until crispy and finely chopped
    1 tablespoon extra-virgin olive oil
    Sea salt

Stack the tomato slices on a plate, tucking a basil leaf between each layer. Drizzle with the dressing, sprinkle the bacon on top, and finish with the olive oil and salt.

Nutritional Analysis per Serving: calories 273, fat 24 g, protein 9 g, carbohydrates 9 g, sugar, 6 g, fiber 2 g, sodium 480 mg

Kefir Dressing

Makes about 500ml

Kefir has a tart and refreshing flavor. Its texture is similar to a drinking-style yogurt, so it makes a great dressing.

500ml kefir

2 tablespoons red wine vinegar

1 sprig fresh dill, chopped

2 tablespoons extra-virgin olive oil

Sea salt and freshly ground black pepper

In a medium bowl, whisk together the kefir, vinegar, and dill. Whisk in the olive oil, a little at a time, until it is fully incorporated. Season with salt and pepper. Store in an airtight container in the refrigerator for up to 1 week.

Nutritional Analysis per Serving (2 tablespoons): calories 34, fat 3 g, protein 1 g, carbohydrates, 1 g, sugar 1 g, fiber 0 g, sodium 50 mg

VEGETABLES

Braised Kale

Serves 4

After years of being ignored, except in Portuguese cuisine, kale is having its day in the sun. It is high in fiber, filled with antioxidants and vitamins, and a great detoxifier. It has been shown to help lower the risk of many cancers. I think that this is a particularly delicious recipe to add to your kale repertoire.

> 2 bunches lacinato (or other type) kale
> 3 tablespoons extra-virgin olive oil
> 1 large sweet onion, peeled, trimmed, and cut into slivers
> 1 tablespoon (about 5 large cloves) roasted garlic puree (see Note)
> Sea salt
> Red chilli flakes
> 2 tablespoons red wine vinegar

Trim off the tough lower stems of the kale. Stack the leaves and cut them crosswise into thick pieces. Wash very well in cold water, taking care that all dirt has been rinsed off. Drain well, but do not spin off all of the water, as you need it to make the braising liquid.

Heat the oil in a large deep sauté pan over medium heat. Add a layer of kale, along with the onion slivers, and let wilt; then continue adding kale and tossing to incorporate until all of the kale has been added to the pan. Toss in the garlic puree and season with salt and chilli flakes. Cover and braise for about 10 minutes or until very, very tender.

Remove from the heat and uncover. Drizzle in the vinegar and toss to blend. Serve immediately.

NOTE: To make roasted garlic puree: Preheat the oven to 180°C/ gas 4. If roasting whole heads, lay the head on its side and, using a sharp knife, cut about 3mm off the stem end. Lightly coat the entire head(s) or cloves of garlic with extra-virgin olive oil. Wrap tightly in parchment paper and place in a baking pan in the oven. Roast until soft and aromatic; whole heads should take about 25 minutes and individual cloves about 12 minutes. Remove from the oven, unwrap, and let cool slightly. Using your fingertips, squeeze the flesh from the skin. The cloves may or may not pop out whole, but either way, it doesn't matter, as roasted garlic usually gets mashed or pureed before use. Use immediately, or cover and refrigerate for up to 1 week.

Nutritional Analysis per Serving: calories 210, fat 12 g, protein 6 g, carbohydrates 24 g, sugar 9 g, fiber 6 g, sodium 140 mg

Sunchoke Fritters

Serves 4

Sunchokes, also known as Jerusalem artichokes, have nothing to do with artichokes or Jerusalem, although they do have a flavor profile quite similar to artichokes. Although often eaten raw in salads, when cooked they can be used in place of potatoes, as they are in this recipe, which is similar to the traditional Jewish dish latkes.

900g Jerusalem artichokes, scrubbed and dried

1 shallot, peeled and minced

4 tablespoons unsalted butter, preferably from grass-fed cows, melted, plus more as needed

Sea salt and freshly ground black pepper

Using a vegetable shredder, cut the artichokes into julienne. (Alternatively, you may use a food processor fitted with the shredding blade, but this will create wetter shreds than the small, drier strips you desire.) Place the strips in a medium bowl and toss them with the shallot.

Place the mixture into a clean kitchen towel. Pull up the sides of the towel and tightly twist it closed. Continue tightening as you press out any excess liquid from the vegetables.

Add 2 tablespoons of the butter to a 25cm nonstick frying pan placed over low heat. Add the drained artichoke mixture, patting it down with a spatula to make a dense cake. Season with salt and pepper. Cook over low heat for about 12 minutes or until the bottom is crisp and golden brown. Adjust the heat as necessary so that the cake does not get too dark before the artichoke begins to cook through. Add more butter as necessary to keep the cake from sticking.

If you feel like living dangerously, lift the cake up from the pan and turn it over using two spatulas. If not, slide the cake out onto a plate. Then use a second plate inverted over the cake and carefully turn the plate upside down so that the whole cake flips around, browned side up, and then slide it back into the pan.

Return the pan to low heat and again pat the mixture down into the pan. Drizzle the remaining 2 tablespoons butter around the edge of the pan and continue to cook for another 7 minutes or until golden brown and crisp on the bottom and the artichoke are cooked through.

Place a double layer of paper towels on a clean, flat surface. Gently tip the cake onto the paper towels and let rest for a minute or so to allow some of the excess butter to drain off.

Transfer to a serving plate, cut into quarters, and serve.

Nutritional Analysis per Serving: calories 200, fat 8 g, protein 3 g, carbohydrates 29 g, sugar 16 g, fiber 3 g, sodium 150 mg

Sunchoke Gratin

Serves 4

In this gratin, the mellow flavor of the artichokes is nicely enriched by the yogurt and cheese. If you can't find Jerusalem artichokes, you could use artichoke hearts instead. Either way, this is a terrific supper dish served with a big salad.

2 tablespoons unsalted butter, preferably from grass-fed cows

1 tablespoon extra-virgin olive oil

2 large shallots, peeled and cut crosswise into thin slices

1 teaspoon minced garlic

450g Jerusalem artichokes, peeled and cut into thin slices

1 teaspoon fresh thyme leaves

1 teaspoon chopped fresh tarragon leaves

Sea salt and freshly ground black pepper

75–125ml vegetable stock or low-sodium vegetable broth

4 tablespoons organic, cultured, full-fat plain yogurt

50g mature cheddar cheese, grated

Preheat the grill.

Combine the butter and oil in a large frying pan over medium heat. When hot, add the shallots and garlic and cook, stirring occasionally, for about 6 minutes or just until soft and beginning to color.

Stir in the artichokes, thyme, and tarragon. Season with salt and pepper and add 75ml vegetable stock. Cover, reduce the heat to low, and simmer, stirring occasionally, for about 15 minutes or until the artichokes are very tender but not mushy. If the liquid evaporates, add a bit more stock. Uncover and continue to cook, stirring frequently, for about 4 minutes or until the artichokes are nicely glazed.

Remove the artichokes from the heat. Add the yogurt and gently stir to distribute evenly. Taste and, if necessary, season with additional salt and pepper. Sprinkle the cheese over the top and transfer to the grill.

Grill for about 3 minutes or until the cheese is melted and golden brown. Remove from the grill and serve immediately.

Nutritional Analysis per Serving: calories 222, fat 14 g, protein 6 g, carbohydrates 19 g, sugar 10 g, fiber 2 g, sodium 266 mg

Indian-Spiced Cabbage

Serves 6

A little spice added to sautéed cabbage lifts it from the ordinary to the sublime. If you don't like heat, feel free to eliminate the chilli. You may need to add a bit of water along with the cabbage to keep it from browning too quickly. But don't add too much, as a bit of color adds caramelization and savoriness to the mix.

3 tablespoons ghee or clarified butter, preferably from grass-fed
cows

1 teaspoon mustard seeds

1 tablespoon minced garlic

1 teaspoon ground turmeric

¼ teaspoon ground cumin

675g red or green cabbage, trimmed, cored, and shredded

1 small green chilli, stemmed, seeded, and minced

Sea salt

Heat the ghee in a large frying pan over medium heat. Add the mustard seeds, cover, and cook for a couple of minutes, just until the seeds begin to pop.

Remove from the heat, uncover, and stir in the garlic, turmeric, and cumin. Return the pan to medium heat and cook, stirring constantly, for about 2 minutes to soften the garlic somewhat. Add the cabbage, chilli, and salt. Cook, tossing and turning, for a minute or so or until all of the cabbage is lightly coated with the seasoned ghee. Cover and cook for about 5 minutes or until the cabbage is still slightly crisp; if you prefer well-done cabbage, cook for an additional 20 minutes or until it is very soft and almost mushy.

Remove from the heat and serve.

Nutritional Analysis per Serving: calories 102, fat 7 g, protein 2 g, carbohydrates 9 g, sugar 4 g, fiber 3 g, sodium 31 mg

Thai Vegetable Curry

Serves 4

Although you can purchase both red and green curry pastes that give that identifiable Thai flavor to curries, I prefer to make my own. It keeps very well and is great to have on hand for last-minute curries. If you want to keep the curry completely vegetarian, you can eliminate the shrimp paste and fish sauce from the recipe. Or, if you prefer, replace the fish sauce and shrimp paste with about 100g shredded wakame or other seaweed to give a hint of the sea without the flavor of seafood.

1 tablespoon coconut oil

75g chopped onion

1 teaspoon minced garlic

1 teaspoon chopped fresh ginger

3 tablespoons Red Curry Paste (recipe follows)

500ml vegetable stock or low-sodium vegetable broth

1 (400ml) can unsweetened coconut milk

1 small aubergine, trimmed and cut into small cubes

1 small red bell pepper, stemmed, seeded, and cut into cubes

500g small broccoli florets

200g baby spinach, tough stems removed

Heat the oil in a large frying pan over medium heat. Add the onion, garlic, and ginger and cook, stirring frequently, for about 4 minutes or until soft. Add the curry paste, along with the stock and coconut milk, and bring to a simmer. Stir in the aubergine, bell pepper, and broccoli florets and cook, stirring frequently, for about 10 minutes or until the vegetables are just tender. Add the spinach and lower the heat. Cover and cook for 5 minutes or until the vegetables are very tender.

Serve immediately.

Nutritional Analysis per Serving: calories 290, fat 19 g, protein 7 g, carbohydrates 24 g, sugar 8 g, fiber 8 g, sodium 332 mg

Red Curry Paste

Makes about 250ml

Once you see how easy it is to make homemade red curry paste with this recipe, you'll never buy packaged curry pastes again. This Thai-inspired red curry paste is tastier, richer, and healthier than any you can buy in a store. It can be used in a variety of dishes, including those that feature seafood, poultry, and beef. You can also add a dollop of this paste to soups to add a punch of mouthwatering flavor.

    10 dried red chillies, stemmed and seeded
    250ml boiling water
    10 black peppercorns
    1 teaspoon caraway seeds, toasted
    1 teaspoon coriander seeds, toasted
    ½ teaspoon ground turmeric
    ¼ teaspoon ground cinnamon
    1 large shallot, finely chopped
    2 tablespoons minced lemongrass or 1 tablespoon grated lemon zest
    2 tablespoons fresh coriander leaves
    1 tablespoon minced garlic
    1 tablespoon shrimp paste
    1 tablespoon additive-free fish sauce
    1 teaspoon grated lime zest

Place the chillies in a heatproof container. Add the boiling water and set aside to rehydrate for 15 minutes. Drain well and pat dry.

Combine the drained chillies with the peppercorns, caraway seeds, coriander seeds, turmeric, and cinnamon in a spice grinder or the small jar of a blender. Process until finely ground.

Scrape the chilli mixture into the bowl of a food processor fitted with the metal blade. Add the shallot, lemongrass, coriander, garlic, shrimp paste, fish sauce, and lime zest, and process to a thick paste. If necessary, add cool water, a tablespoon or so at a time, to smooth out the mix.

Scrape the mixture from the processor bowl and place in a nonreactive container. Use immediately, or cover and refrigerate for up to 1 month.

Nutritional Analysis per Serving (1 tablespoon): calories 27, fat 0 g, protein 2 g, carbohydrates 4 g, sugar 0 g, fiber 0 g, sodium 210 mg

Broccoli, Mushroom, and Feta Toss

Serves 4

This one-pot meal is quick to put together and cook; nothing is easier to put on the table after a long day at work. The broccoli can be replaced with a head of cauliflower and the feta with almost any semi-soft or hard cheese you like.

1 head broccoli

2 tablespoons extra-virgin olive oil

1 tablespoon unsalted butter, preferably from grass-fed cows

350g mushrooms, cleaned, stems removed, and sliced

1 teaspoon minced garlic

Sea salt and freshly ground black pepper

225g feta cheese, crumbled

2 tablespoons chopped fresh basil

Cut the broccoli into florets. Trim the outer tough skin from the stalks and then cut the stalks, crosswise, into thin coins. Set aside.

Preheat the grill.

Heat the oil and butter in a large frying pan over medium heat. Add the mushrooms and garlic and cook, stirring occasionally, for about 10 minutes or until the mushrooms begin to exude their liquid and brown around the edges.

Add the broccoli florets and stems and continue to cook, stirring frequently, for another 5 minutes or until the broccoli is crisp-tender. Season with salt and pepper.

Add the feta and basil, stirring to blend. Cover and cook for about 2 minutes or just until the cheese has begun to melt.

Remove from the heat and place under the grill for a couple of minutes to brown slightly. Remove from the grill and serve immediately.

Nutritional Analysis per Serving: calories 300, fat 20 g, protein 15 g, carbohydrates 25 g, sugar 5 g, fiber 6 g, sodium 830 mg

Mixed Vegetable Kraut

Makes 2 liters

Time required to prepare: 1 week

The addition of kale and chilli to the traditional cabbage makes this mixture particularly high in vitamin C, with the liquid as nutritious as the vegetables. Even just a tablespoon will boost your daily intake of the vitamin. For a hint of sourness and even more nutritional value, you can add the juice and zest of 1 Meyer lemon, and for added sweetness, the juice and zest of 1 medium orange. Use the kraut as a side dish for grilled meats, fish, or poultry; toss it into mixed greens as a salad; or eat it as a snack.

450g shredded cabbage

450g jicama or white radish, peeled and shredded

100g shredded kale

75g shredded Granny Smith apple

115g shredded leek, white part only

1 teaspoon minced garlic

1 teaspoon minced hot red chilli

1½ teaspoons fine sea salt, preferably fine Himalayan pink salt

4 tablespoons whey, or 1 package vegetable starter culture

Distilled water, as needed

Combine the cabbage, jicama, kale, apple, leek, garlic, and chilli in a large bowl, tossing to blend. Add the salt and, using your hands, begin massaging the salt into the vegetable mixture, working until the vegetables exude some liquid.

Pack an equal amount of the vegetable mixture and the liquid it has exuded into each of two sterilized 1-liter glass canning jars with clean, unused lids or two 1-liter crockpots with tight-fitting lids. Using your fingertips, a smaller jar or glass that will fit down into the larger jar, or a potato masher, press the mixture down as firmly as you can to allow the liquid to rise up and cover the vegetables. Add 2 tablespoons of the whey to each jar, leaving 2.5–5cm of space between the vegetables and the top of the jar to give them room to expand as they ferment. If the liquid and the whey do not cover the vegetables entirely, add enough cool distilled water to completely cover.

Place a bit of cool water into a small resealable plastic bag. You need just enough water to create a weight to keep the vegetables under the liquid. Seal the bag, eliminating all the air inside, place it on top of the vegetables, and push it down to ensure that the water bag is serving as a weight. Place the lid on the container and seal tightly.

Set aside in a cool, dark spot for 1 week. Check the fermentation process daily to make sure that the vegetables have remained covered with liquid. If the liquid level is low, remove the water bag and set it aside. Remove and discard any scum or mold that has formed, noting that it is not harmful, just unappetizing. Add distilled water to cover. Push the vegetables back down into the liquid, place the water bag on top to press them down, seal tightly, and set aside as before.

After 1 week, the kraut will be ready to eat, but it may also be transferred to the refrigerator and stored for up to 9 months.

Nutritional Analysis per Serving (125ml): calories 30, fat 0 g, protein 2 g, carbohydrates 7 g, sugar 2 g, fiber 1 g, sodium 230 mg

Asian-Scented Greens

Makes 1 liter

Time required to prepare: 3 days

Pickled greens, most frequently mustard, are served throughout Asia— alone or as components of soups, stews, or rice dishes. This recipe carries quite a bit of flavor with the combination of peppery greens, hot chillies, and aromatic ginger and garlic. All the ingredients offer health benefits, and the fermentation makes the whole batch even better for you.

225g dandelion or mustard greens, or kale

1 tablespoon slivered fresh ginger

1 teaspoon slivered garlic

2 hot red or green chillies, cut in half lengthwise

500ml distilled water, plus more as needed

4 tablespoons natural apple cider vinegar

2 tablespoons coconut sugar (see Note)

1 tablespoon fine sea salt

3 star anise

Trim the leaves from the stems of the greens. Cut the stems crosswise into 5cm-long pieces and chop the leaves. Pack the cut stems into a 1 liter glass measuring jug and then add enough chopped leaves to fill the measuring jug when packed down gently. Transfer the greens mixture to a bowl. Add the ginger and garlic, tossing to blend well. Then pack the greens mixture into a clean, sterilized container, such as a 1-liter glass canning jar with a clean, unused lid or a 1-liter crock with a tight-fitting lid, randomly placing the chillies among the greens as you go.

Combine the distilled water, vinegar, sugar, and salt in a small saucepan over medium heat. Bring to a boil, then immediately remove from the heat.

Add the star anise and let the brine cool for 3 minutes. Pour the hot brine over the greens, taking care that the greens are completely covered. Leave 2.5–5cm of space between the greens and the top of the jar to give them room to expand as they ferment. If there is not enough liquid to cover it, add enough cool distilled water to completely cover.

Place a bit of cool water into a small resealable plastic bag. You need just enough water to create a weight to keep the greens under the liquid. Seal the bag, eliminating all the air inside, place it on top of the greens, and push it down to ensure that the water bag is serving as a weight. Place the lid on the container and seal tightly. Transfer to the refrigerator and allow to ferment for 3 days before serving. The greens may be stored, refrigerated, for up to 6 months.

NOTE: Coconut sugar is available at health food stores, at specialty markets, at some supermarkets, and online.

Nutritional Analysis per Serving (125ml): calories 25, fat 0 g, protein 0 g, carbohydrates 6 g, sugar 2 g, fiber 1 g, sodium 600 mg

FISH

Herb-Roasted Wild Salmon

Serves 4

About as simple as you can get, but also as elegant. The salmon is a wonderful main course for a dinner party, as it cooks quickly and looks so inviting that the cook will be the star of the evening. Always purchase your salmon from a reputable fishmonger, as farmed salmon are often labeled wild. Note that a recent investigation by the conservation group Oceana found that about 43 percent of the salmon labeled in stores as wild was, in fact, farmed, so buyer beware.

1 tablespoon coconut oil

1 tablespoon fresh lemon juice

4 tablespoons chopped fresh herbs, such as parsley, tarragon, chervil, and/or dill, plus more for garnish

1 large shallot, finely chopped

1 (675g) 2.5cm-thick salmon fillet, skin and all pin bones removed

Sea salt and freshly ground black pepper

Lemon wedges, for garnish

Preheat the oven to 230°C/gas 8.

Place the oil and lemon juice in a baking pan large enough to hold the salmon. Transfer the pan to the oven and heat for about 4 minutes or until the oil is very hot.

Working quickly, remove the hot pan from the oven and stir in the herbs and shallot. Season the salmon with salt and pepper and add it to the pan. Carefully turn the salmon a couple of times to coat it with the herbs and liquid, ending with the skinned side down. Roast, basting two or three times, for about 10 minutes or just until the fish is slightly underdone in the center.

Remove from the oven and carefully transfer to a serving platter, spooning the pan juices over the fish. Garnish with the extra herbs and lemon wedges.

Serve immediately.

Nutritional Analysis per Serving: calories 240, fat 10 g, protein 34 g, carbohydrates 2 g, sugar 1 g, fiber 0 g, sodium 230 mg

Steamed Wild Salmon with Sautéed Leeks and Chard

Serves 4

The sautéed chard makes a colorful base for the pink salmon, but you can use almost any green that is in season. In the spring, dandelion greens will give a slightly bitter contrast to the rich, succulent fish.

2 tablespoons unsalted butter, preferably from grass-fed cows, melted

4 (175g) skinless, boneless wild salmon fillets

Sea salt and freshly ground black pepper

8 thin slices lemon

2 tablespoons extra-virgin olive oil, plus more for drizzling

450g thinly sliced leeks, white part only

675g chopped rainbow chard, tough ends removed

Preheat the oven to 230°C/gas 8.

Place a wire rack large enough to hold the salmon in a rimmed baking sheet. Set aside.

Cut four 25cm square pieces of parchment paper. Using a pastry brush, lightly coat the paper with the melted butter. Set aside.

Lightly season the salmon with salt and pepper. Place a slice of lemon on each piece of paper, top with a piece of seasoned salmon, and top the salmon with another slice of lemon. Tightly wrap each piece of paper around the salmon by folding in the seam and twisting the ends together. Place the wrapped salmon pieces on the rack in the prepared baking sheet.

Place in the oven and allow to steam in the parchment paper for about 8 minutes or just until the fish is slightly underdone in the center.

While the salmon is steaming, heat the olive oil in a large sauté pan over medium-high heat. Add the leeks and sauté for about 4 minutes or until soft but not colored. Add the chard and, using tongs, cook, tossing and turning, for about 4 more minutes or until the leeks and chard are tender. Season with salt and pepper and remove from the heat. Tent lightly with parchment paper to keep warm.

Remove the salmon from the oven and carefully open the paper packets. Be cautious, as the steam will be very hot.

Spoon an equal portion of the chard mixture in the center of each of four plates. Place a piece of steamed salmon on top of each chard mound. Drizzle with olive oil and serve immediately.

Nutritional Analysis per Serving: calories 324, fat 19 g, protein 35 g, carbohydrates 3 g, sugar 0 g, fiber 0 g, sodium 330 mg

Fish Fillets with Black Olives, Artichokes, and Shaved Brussels Sprout Slaw

Serves 2

Chef Fabrizio Aielli, of Sea Salt restaurant, brings us this elegant and tasty dish that uses the local catch of the day. You could use sea bream in lieu of the snapper. Find what's fresh in your area. Feel free to double this recipe for a party of four.

    2 (175g) snapper fillets
    Sea salt and freshly ground black pepper
    4 tablespoons extra-virgin olive oil
    2 cloves garlic, smashed
    2 sprigs fresh rosemary, chopped
    Juice from half a lemon
    2 artichokes preserved in oil, quartered
    12 pitted kalamata olives
    8 tablespoons Shaved Brussels Sprout Slaw (recipe follows)

Season the fish with salt and pepper. Heat a large frying pan over medium-high heat. Add the olive oil and bring to about its smoking point. Add the fish fillets to the pan, skin side down. Turn the heat down to medium and cook for 2 minutes. Using a fish spatula, flip the fillets and add the garlic, rosemary, and lemon juice. Cook for 2 more minutes or until the desired doneness is reached and the fish flakes easily with a fork. Remove the fish from the pan and place on two plates.

To the same pan, add the artichokes and olives and cook for 1 minute. Scatter around the fish, and top each with the slaw. Serve immediately.

Nutritional Analysis per Serving: calories 625, fat 44 g, protein 40 g, carbohydrates 23 g, sugar 3 g, fiber 12 g, sodium 670 mg

Shaved Brussels Sprout Slaw

Serves 2

This delicious slaw goes well with fish dishes. Double or triple the recipe if you're serving more people. You can also store the ingredients separately in airtight containers in the refrigerator and dress the slaw just prior to serving.

    225g brussels sprouts
    2 tablespoons liquid olive dressing (see Note)

Thinly shave the brussels sprouts on a mandoline. Toss with the liquid olive dressing. Serve.

Note: To make the liquid olive oil dressing, simply whisk together 1 large egg yolk and 125ml extra-virgin olive oil, adding the oil a little at a time until fully incorporated. Add a squeeze of fresh lemon juice and sea salt to taste. Double or triple the recipe to have the dressing on hand for several days. Store in an airtight container in the refrigerator for up to 1 week.

Nutritional Analysis per Serving: calories 290, fat 29 g, protein 4 g, carbohydrates 8 g, sugar 2 g, fiber 3 g, sodium 170 mg

MEAT AND POULTRY

Grass-Fed Beef Burgers

Serves 4

Rather than using just plain beef, I like to spice up my minced beef with some heat. Make sure that your beef is not too lean, as you need a good amount of fat to create a juicy, flavorful burger. For an extra treat, sauté some onions in butter until they are just beginning to soften; then, pile them on the grilled burger.

675g minced grass-fed beef

1 serrano or other hot green chilli, stemmed, seeded, and minced, or to taste

2 tablespoons minced shallot

1 teaspoon minced garlic

Sea salt and freshly ground black pepper

Extra-virgin olive oil, for brushing

Preheat and oil the grill or preheat a stovetop griddle pan over medium-high heat.

Combine the beef with the chilli, shallot, and garlic in a medium bowl. Using your hands, squish together to blend well. Season with salt and pepper.

Divide the mixture into quarters, then shape each portion into a patty of equal size so they will cook evenly. Using a pastry brush, generously coat the outside of the patties with the olive oil.

Place the burgers on the grill and grill for 4 minutes. Turn and grill for another 4 minutes for medium-rare.

Remove from the grill and serve immediately.

Nutritional Analysis per Serving: calories 350, fat 24 g, protein 33 g, carbohydrates 1 g, sugar 0 g, fiber 0 g, sodium 400 mg

Roast Leg of Grass-Fed Lamb

Serves 6

I think everyone has a favorite way of roasting a leg of lamb—mine is quite simple. I make any number of slits in the meat and then fill each one with a clove of garlic. Not only does it scent the meat as it roasts, but the garlic also adds flavor to the pan juices, further enriching the sauce.

    4 tablespoons extra-virgin olive oil
    Juice and zest of 1 lemon
    1 tablespoon chopped fresh rosemary
    2 teaspoons fresh thyme leaves
    1 (2.7kg) leg of grass-fed lamb
    About 20 cloves garlic, peeled and, if large, cut in half
    Sea salt and freshly ground black pepper
    3 leeks, finely chopped, white part only
    125g chicken stock or low-sodium chicken broth
    4 tablespoons dry white wine
    50g unsalted butter, preferably from grass-fed cows, at room
        temperature

Preheat the oven to 230°C/gas 8. Place a rack in a roasting pan large enough to hold the lamb and set aside.

Combine the oil with the lemon juice and zest, rosemary, and thyme in a small bowl.

Using a small sharp knife, make 20 small slits in random spots all over the lamb. Fill each slit with a piece of garlic. Using your hands, generously coat the outside of the lamb with the oil mixture, patting it into the meat. Generously season with salt and pepper.

Place the seasoned meat on the rack in the roasting pan. Transfer to the oven and roast for 40 minutes. Reduce the oven temperature to 190°C/gas 5 and continue to roast for another hour or until an instant-read thermometer inserted into the thickest part reads 57°C for medium-rare (or 65°C for medium).

Transfer the lamb to a cutting board, tent with parchment paper, and allow to rest for 10 minutes before carving. Note that the lamb will continue to cook while it rests, increasing the internal temperature by about 10 degrees.

Transfer the roasting pan to the stove top over medium heat. Add the leeks and cook, stirring up the browned bits from the bottom of the pan, for about 3 minutes. Stir in the stock and wine and bring to a boil. Boil, stirring frequently, for about 3 minutes or until the liquid has reduced somewhat. Add the butter and cook, stirring, for about 3 minutes or until a rich sauce has formed. Taste and, if necessary, season with salt and pepper.

Using a carving knife, cut the lamb into thin slices and place on a serving platter. Drizzle some of the sauce over the top and serve with the remaining sauce on the side.

Nutritional Analysis per Serving: calories 540, fat 29 g, protein 58 g, carbohydrates 5 g, sugar 0 g, fiber 0 g, sodium 550 mg

Tuscan-Style Pork Roast

Serves 6

Like many Italian recipes, traditional or inspired, this is a very simple dish to prepare, but it requires superb ingredients. Pasture-raised pork is now usually a heritage breed that has been allowed to roam freely in pastures and woods. It is richer in flavor than farmed pork, but it can also be almost as lean. With the heritage breeds, I prefer the Berkshire for its high fat content and juiciness when cooked.

1 (1.1kg) boneless pasture-raised pork loin, preferably with a layer of fat

4 tablespoons extra-virgin olive oil

10 juniper berries, crushed

8 cloves garlic, minced

1 tablespoon dried rosemary

1 tablespoon cracked black pepper

Sea salt

250ml chicken stock or low-sodium chicken broth

225g thinly sliced onions

135g thinly sliced fennel

Zest of 1 orange

1 teaspoon chopped fresh rosemary

Preheat the oven to 200°C/gas 6.

Place a rack in a roasting pan large enough to hold the pork and set aside.

Place the pork on a cutting board. Combine the oil with the juniper berries, garlic, dried rosemary, and cracked pepper in a small bowl. When well combined, rub the mixture over the pork, pressing it down to adhere to the meat and fat. Season with salt and transfer to the rack in the roasting pan, fat side up.

Place in the oven and roast for 45 minutes. Add the stock, onions, fennel, and orange zest and continue to roast for an additional 40 minutes or until an instant-read thermometer inserted into the thickest part reads 65°C for medium-well done.

Transfer the pork to a cutting board, tent with parchment paper, and allow to rest for 10 minutes before carving.

Using a sharp knife, cut the roast crosswise into slices. Spoon the onion gravy onto a serving platter and lay the slices, slightly overlapping, over the onions. Sprinkle with the fresh rosemary and serve immediately.

Nutritional Analysis per Serving: calories 270, fat 10 g, protein 37 g, carbohydrates 6 g, sugar 1 g, fiber 1 g, sodium 390 mg

Roasted Chicken Thighs with Parsley Sauce

Serves 4

If you keep hard-boiled eggs on hand, as I do, this is a quick and easy supper for a busy work night. Chicken thighs are quick to cook, juicy, and flavorful. The sauce is a classic, but combined with the roasted chicken, it creates a totally new and exciting dish.

8 bone-in, skin-on chicken thighs (about 900g)

125ml plus 2 tablespoons extra-virgin olive oil

Sea salt and freshly ground black pepper

3 hard-boiled egg yolks

1½ tablespoons white wine vinegar

3 tablespoons chopped fresh flat-leaf parsley

2 teaspoons minced shallot

Preheat the oven to 200°C/gas 6.

Place the chicken thighs in a baking pan or on a rimmed baking sheet. Drizzle with 2 tablespoons of the olive oil and season with salt and pepper. Transfer to the oven and roast, turning occasionally, for about 25 minutes or until golden brown and just cooked through.

While the chicken is roasting, make the sauce.

Combine the egg yolks and vinegar in the bowl of a food processor fitted with the metal blade and process until smooth. With the motor running, slowly add the remaining 125ml olive oil, processing until well emulsified.

Scrape the egg mixture into a small bowl. Stir in the parsley and shallot, season with salt and pepper, and stir to combine.

Remove the chicken thighs from the oven and place on a serving platter. Spoon some of the sauce over the top and serve any remaining sauce on the side.

Nutritional Analysis per Serving: calories 600, fat 52 g, protein 35 g, carbohydrates 1 g, sugar 0 g, fiber 0 g, sodium 450 mg

DESSERTS

Coconut Pudding

Serves 4

Chia seeds not only add nutrients and fiber to this dessert, but they also thicken it without the addition of starches. Unfortunately, they also need time to hydrate, so the pudding needs to be made a few hours in advance of serving.

250ml almond milk

2 teaspoons stevia

250ml unsweetened coconut milk

4 tablespoons white chia seeds

¼ teaspoon ground nutmeg

2 tablespoons unsweetened coconut flakes, toasted

Combine the almond milk and stevia in a medium bowl, whisking vigorously to incorporate. Add the coconut milk, chia seeds, and nutmeg, whisking to just combine.

Cover with plastic wrap and transfer to the refrigerator. Chill for at least 4 hours, whisking every hour for the first 4 hours to ensure that the seeds are fully hydrated. The pudding may be chilled for up to 24 hours before serving.

When ready to serve, sprinkle the top with the toasted coconut flakes.

Nutritional Analysis per Serving: calories 170, fat 15 g, protein 3 g, carbohydrates 7 g, sugar 1 g, fiber 4 g, sodium 66 mg

Easy Chocolate Mousse

Serves 6

This is so quick to make and is the equal to more elaborate mousse recipes in terms of its airiness and flavor. Although it can be refrigerated for a couple of days, it gets firmer and firmer as it sits. It will still be delicious, but it will have quite a different texture.

> 200g extra-dark (72% cacao) chocolate, finely chopped
> 500ml chilled double cream, preferably from grass-fed cows
> 4 tablespoons organic, cultured, full-fat plain yogurt (optional)
> Chocolate shavings, for garnish (optional)

Place the chocolate in a heatproof bowl.

Select a saucepan that will hold the bowl snugly inside, like a double boiler. Fill the saucepan about half full with water, taking care that the water will not touch the bottom of the bowl. Place over medium-high heat and fit the bowl into it. Bring the water to a simmer, frequently stirring the chocolate. By the time the water comes to almost a boil, the chocolate should be melted. Ideally, the chocolate should register no more than 48°C on a candy thermometer. (If the chocolate is too hot, it will instantly melt the whipped cream. At 48°C you should be able to do a heat test with your finger without any discomfort. It will be more than lukewarm, but not hot.) Remove the bowl from the saucepan and, using a wooden spoon, vigorously beat for about 30 seconds to aerate and even out the temperature.

While the chocolate is melting, whip the cream. Place the cold cream into a chilled bowl and, using a handheld electric mixer, beat for about 4 minutes or until soft peaks form.

Whisking constantly, slowly pour the cold whipped cream into the warm melted chocolate, beating until well blended. The mixture will be soft and almost airy.

You can either scrape the mousse into one large serving bowl or spoon an equal portion into each of six individual dessert cups or bowls. Refrigerate for at least 30 minutes before serving.

Serve as is, or garnish with the yogurt and some chocolate shavings.

Nutritional Analysis per Serving: calories 500, fat 46 g, protein 5 g, carbohydrates 20 g, sugar 11 g, fiber 4 g, sodium 35 mg

Ricotta with Berries and Toasted Almonds

Serves 4

Another easy dessert that is very satisfying. I usually make my own ricotta so that I am assured of its quality and flavor, but you can also find high-quality ricotta in the markets today. The cheese is rich, while the berries add a touch of sweetness and the almonds a nice finishing crunch.

- 240g full-fat ricotta cheese, preferably from a grass-fed animal (cow, goat, or sheep)
- 120g raspberries, strawberries, or blueberries
- 4 teaspoons flaked almonds or unsweetened coconut flakes, toasted

Spoon a quarter of the ricotta into each of four small dessert bowls. Sprinkle a quarter of the berries over the ricotta in each bowl. Spoon an equal portion of the almonds over the top. Serve immediately.

Nutritional Analysis per Serving: calories 135, fat 9 g, protein 8 g, carbohydrates 7 g, sugar 0 g, fiber 2 g, sodium 52 mg

Acknowledgments

I am truly blessed and in deep gratitude to be working with what has proven to be the absolute dream team in publishing. It is through the creative and artistic dedication to the craft of writing that Kristin Loberg so skillfully weaves the raw material I deliver into empowering text that changes the health destiny of so many. Bonnie Solow, my literary agent, maintains the vision for the entire team. Her highly skilled and compassionate guidance has allowed all of our goals to manifest. And Tracy Behar, our Editor at Little, Brown, with her gentle demeanor coupled with unparalleled literary acumen and experience, has made the process of creating this work a joyful event for all involved. And to her entire crew: Michael Pietsch, Reagan Arthur, Nicole Dewey, Craig Young, Genevieve Nierman, Lisa Erickson, Kaitlyn Boudah, Zea Moscone, Ben Allen, Julianna Lee, Valerie Cimino, Giraud Lorber, Olivia Aylmer, Katy Isaacs, and Dianne Schneider.

James Murphy — for your incredible ability to embrace the big picture and then bring about the manifestation of our shared goals.

Andrew Luer — for your day-to-day commitment to our short- and long-term goals, your ability to adapt to the ever-changing demands placed upon us, and your thoughtful council, which I highly respect.

Digital Natives — for so effectively navigating the constantly shifting landscape of social media and keeping our message in the forefront.

Judith Choate — for making magic happen in the kitchen and

creating such delicious recipes that live up to the Grain Brain Whole Life Plan principles.

Gigi Stewart—for contributing some of your own tasty kitchen concoctions that abide by my rules and make cooking fun.

Fabrizio Aielli and Seamus Mullen—for providing me the recipes to some of my favorite dishes from your respective restaurants, Sea Salt in Naples, Florida, and Tertulia in New York City.

Jonathan Heindemause—for performing the nutritional analyses on the recipes and making yourself available to handle all the last-minute changes to the menu.

Nicole Dunn—for hitting the ground running as the newest member to our team, and doing an amazing job in public relations.

And finally, to all of those who have inspired, helped, and supported me on my own journey. You know who you are. Thank you.

Selected Bibliography

The following is a selected list of papers and writings that have been useful in crafting this book, organized by chapter. This list is by no means exhaustive, since each of these entries could be complemented with dozens if not hundreds of others, but it will help you learn more and live up to the lessons and principles of *The Grain Brain Whole Life Plan*. This bibliography can also open other doors for further research and inquiry. For additional references and resources, please visit www.DrPelrmutter.com.

Introduction: You've Come to This Book for a Reason

Roach, Michael, and Christie McNally. *How Yoga Works*. New Jersey: Diamond Cutter Press, 2005.

Part I: Welcome to the Grain Brain Whole Life Plan

Chapter 1: What Is the Grain Brain Whole Life Plan?

Alzheimer's Association, "2016 Alzheimer's Disease Facts and Figures." www.alz.org/facts/ (accessed July 6, 2016).

Bournemouth University. "Brain Diseases Affecting More People and Starting Earlier Than Ever Before." ScienceDaily. www.sciencedaily.com/releases/2013/05/130510075502.htm (accessed June 14, 2016).

Centers for Disease Control and Prevention, Chronic Disease Prevention and Health Promotion. "Statistics and Tracking." www.cdc.gov/chronicdisease/stats/ (accessed June 14, 2016).

Centers for Disease Control and Prevention, National Center for Health Statistics. "Leading Causes of Death." www.cdc.gov/nchs/fastats/leading-causes-of-death.htm (accessed June 14, 2016).

Keith, Lierre. *The Vegetarian Myth: Food, Justice, and Sustainability.* Oakland, CA: PM Press, 2009.

Laidman, Jenni. "Obesity's Toll: 1 in 5 Deaths Linked to Excess Weight." Medscape.com. www.medscape.com/viewarticle/809516 (accessed June 10, 2016).

Perlmutter, David. "Bugs Are Your Brain's Best Friends." *Extraordinary Health.* Vol 24, 2015: 9–13.

Pritchard, C., A. Mayers, and D. Baldwin. "Changing Patterns of Neurological Mortality in the 10 Major Developed Countries 1979–2010." *Publ. Health* 127, no. 4 (2013): 357–368.

Chapter 2: The Chief Goals

Blumberg, R., and F. Powrie. "Microbiota, Disease, and Back to Health: A Metastable Journey." *Sci. Transl. Med.* 4, no. 137 (June 2012): 137rv7.

Braniste, V. et al. "The Gut Microbiota Influences Blood-Brain Barrier Permeability in Mice." *Sci. Transl. Med.* 6, no. 263 (November 2014): 263ra158.

Brogan, Kelly. *A Mind of Your Own: The Truth About Depression and How Women Can Heal Their Bodies to Reclaim Their Lives.* New York, NY: HarperWave, 2016.

Cahill Jr., G. F. and R. L. Veech. "Ketoacids? Good Medicine?" *Trans. Am. Clin. Climatol. Assoc.* 114 (2003): 149–61; discussion 162–3.

Carding, S. et al. "Dysbiosis of the Gut Microbiota in Disease." *Microb. Ecol. Health. Dis.* 26 (February 2015): 26191.

Cheema, A. K. et al. "Chemopreventive Metabolites Are Correlated with a Change in Intestinal Microbiota Measured in A-T Mice and Decreased Carcinogenesis." *PLoS One* 11, no. 4 (April 2016): e0151190.

Crane, P. K. et al. "Glucose Levels and Risk of Dementia." *N. Engl. J. Med.* 369, no. 6 (August 2013): 540–8.

Daulatzai, M. A. "Obesity and Gut's Dysbiosis Promote Neuroinflammation, Cognitive Impairment, and Vulnerability to Alzheimer's Disease: New Directions and Therapeutic Implications." *J. Mol. Gen. Med.* S1 (2014).

David, L. A. et al. "Diet Rapidly and Reproducibly Alters the Human Gut Microbiome." *Nature* 505, no. 7484 (January 2014): 559–63.

Earle, K. A. et al. "Quantitative Imaging of Gut Microbiota Spatial Organization." *Cell Host Microbe* 18, no. 4 (October 2015): 478–88.

Fan, Shelly. "The Fat-Fueled Brain: Unnatural or Advantageous?" ScientificAmerican.com (Mind Guest Blog). blogs.scientificamerican.com/mind-guest-blog/the-fat-fueled-brain-unnatural-or-advantageous/ (accessed June 10, 2016).

Gao, B. et al. "The Clinical Potential of Influencing Nrf2 Signaling in Degenerative and Immunological Disorders." *Clin. Pharmacol.* 6 (February 2014): 19–34.

Gedgaudas, Nora T. *Primal Body, Primal Mind: Beyond the Paleo Diet for Total Health and a Longer Life.* Rochester, Vermont: Health Arts Press, 2009.

Graf, D. et al. "Contribution of Diet to the Composition of the Human Gut Microbiota." *Microb. Ecol. Health. Dis.* 26 (February 2015): 26164.

Holmes, E. et al. "Therapeutic Modulation of Microbiota-Host Metabolic Interactions." *Sci. Transl. Med.* 4, no. 137 (June 2012): 137rv6.

Jones, R. M. et al. "Lactobacilli Modulate Epithelial Cytoprotection through the Nrf2 Pathway." *Cell Rep.* 12, no. 8 (August 2015): 1217–25.

Kelly, J. R. et al. "Breaking Down the Barriers: The Gut Microbiome, Intestinal Permeability and Stress-Related Psychiatric Disorders." *Front. Cell. Neurosci.* 9 (October 2015): 392.

Kresser, Chris. "9 Steps to Perfect Health—#5: Heal Your Gut." ChrisKresser.com. February 24, 2011. chriskresser.com/9-steps-to-perfect-health-5-heal-your-gut/ (accessed June 14, 2016).

Kumar, Himanshu et al. "Gut Microbiota as an Epigenetic Regulator: Pilot Study Based on Whole-Genome Methylation Analysis." *mBio* 5, no. 6 (December 2014): pii: e02113-14.

Li, H. et al. "The Outer Mucus Layer Hosts a Distinct Intestinal Microbial Niche." *Nat. Commun.* 6 (September 2015): 8292.

Mandal, Ananya. "History of the Ketogenic Diet." News-Medical.net. www.news-medical.net/health/History-of-the-Ketogenic-Diet.aspx (accessed June 14, 2016).

Mu, C. et al. "Gut Microbiota: The Brain Peacekeeper." *Front. Microbiol.* 7 (March 2016): 345.

Perlmutter, David. *Brain Maker: The Power of Gut Microbes to Heal and Protect Your Brain—For Life.* New York: Little, Brown and Co., 2015.

Perlmutter, David. "Why Eating for Your Microbiome is the Key to a Healthy Weight." MindBodyGreen.com guest blog. March 24, 2016. www.mindbodygreen.com/0-24285/why-eating-for-your-microbiome-is-the-key-to-a-healthy-weight.html (accessed June 14, 2016).

Reger, M. A. et al. "Effects of Beta-Hydroxybutyrate on Cognition in Memory-Impaired Adults." *Neurobiol. Aging* 25, no. 3 (March 2004): 311-4.

Rosenblat, J. D. et al. "Inflamed Moods: A Review of the Interactions Between Inflammation and Mood Disorders." *Prog. Neuropsychopharmacol. Biol. Psychiatry* 53 (August 2014): 23-34.

Schilling, M. A. "Unraveling Alzheimer's: Making Sense of the Relationship Between Diabetes and Alzheimer's Disease." *J. Alzheimers Dis.* 51, no. 4 (February 2016): 961-77.

Shenderov, B. A. "Gut Indigenous Microbiota and Epigenetics." *Microb. Ecol. Health Dis.* 23 (March 2012).

Slavin, Joanne. "Fiber and Prebiotics: Mechanisms and Health Benefits." *Nutrients* 5, no. 4 (April 2013): 1417–1435.

Sonnenburg, J. L., and M. A. Fischbach. "Community Health Care: Therapeutic Opportunities in the Human Microbiome." *Sci. Transl. Med.* 3, no. 78 (April 2011): 78ps12.

Stulberg, E. et al. "An Assessment of US Microbiome Research." *Nature Microbiology* 1, no. 15015 (January 2016).

Sunagawa, S. et al. "Ocean Plankton. Structure and Function of the Global Ocean Microbiome." *Science* 348, no. 6237 (May 2015): 1261359.

University of California—Los Angeles Health Sciences. "Gut Bacteria Could Help Prevent Cancer." ScienceDaily. www.sciencedaily.com/releases/2016/04/160413151108.htm (accessed June 14, 2016).

Vojdani, A. et al. "The Prevalence of Antibodies Against Wheat and Milk Proteins in Blood Donors and Their Contribution to Neuroimmune Reactivities." *Nutrients* 6, no. 1 (December 2013): 15–36.

Zhan, Y. et al. "Telomere Length Shortening and Alzheimer's Disease—A Mendelian Randomization Study." *JAMA Neurol.* 72, no. 10 (October 2015): 1202–3.

Zonis, S. et al. "Chronic Intestinal Inflammation Alters Hippocampal Neurogenesis." *J. Neuroinflamm.* 12 (April 2015): 65.

Chapter 3: The Food Rules

"GMO Foods: What You Need to Know." *Consumer Reports.* March 2015.

Bawa, A. S. and K. R. Anilakumar. "Genetically Modified Foods: Safety, Risks and Public Concerns—A Review." *J. Food Sci. Technol.* 50, no. 6 (December 2013): 1035–46.

Bazzano, L. A. et al. "Effects of Low-Carbohydrate and Low-Fat Diets: A Randomized Trial." *Ann. Intern. Med.* 161, no. 5 (September 2014): 309–18.

Catassi, C. et al. "A Prospective, Double-Blind, Placebo-Controlled Trial to Establish a Safe Gluten Threshold for Patients with Celiac Disease." *Am. J. Clin. Nutr.* 85, no. 1 (January 2007): 160–6.

Catassi, C. et al. "Non-Celiac Gluten Sensitivity: The New Frontier of Gluten-Related Disorders." *Nutrients* 5, no. 10 (September 2013): 3839–53.

Di Sabatino, A. et al. "Small Amounts of Gluten in Subjects with Suspected Nonceliac Gluten Sensitivity: A Randomized, Double-Blind, Placebo-Controlled, Cross-Over Trial." *Clin. Gastroenterol. Hepatol.* 13, no. 9 (September 2015): 1604–12.e3.

Fasano, A. "Zonulin and Its Regulation of Intestinal Barrier Function: The Biological Door to Inflammation, Autoimmunity, and Cancer." *Physiol. Rev.* 91, no. 1 (January 2011): 151–75.

Guyton, K. Z. et al. "Carcinogenicity of Tetrachlorvinphos, Parathion, Malathion, Diazinon, and Glyphosate." *Lancet Oncol.* 16, no. 5 (May 2015): 490–1.

Hollon, J. et al. "Effect of Gliadin on Permeability of Intestinal Biopsy Explants from Celiac Disease Patients and Patients with Non-Celiac Gluten Sensitivity." *Nutrients* 7, no. 3 (February 2015): 1565–76.

Lawrence, G. D. "Dietary Fats and Health: Dietary Recommendations in the Context of Scientific Evidence." *Adv. Nutr.* 4, no. 3 (May 2013): 294–302.

Levine, M. E. et al. "Low Protein Intake Is Associated with a Major Reduction in IGF-1, Cancer, and Overall Mortality in the 65 and Younger but Not Older Population." *Cell. Metab.* 19, no. 3 (March 2014): 407–17.

Mason, Rosemary. "Glyphosate Is Destructor of Human Health and Biodiversity." Available at www.gmoevidence.com/dr-mason-glyphosate-is-destructor-of-human-health-and-biodiversity/ (accessed June 14, 2106).

Nierenberg, Cari. "How Much Protein Do You Need?" WebMD.com feature, Guide to a Healthy Kitchen. www.webmd.com/diet/healthy-kitchen-11/how-much-protein?page=2 (accessed June 14, 2016).

Pan, A. et al. "Red Meat Consumption and Mortality: Results from 2 Prospective Cohort Studies." *Arch. Intern. Med.* 172, no. 7 (April 2012): 555–63.

Perlmutter, David. *Grain Brain: The Surprising Truth about Wheat, Carbs, and Sugar—Your Brain's Silent Killers.* New York: Little, Brown and Co., 2013.

Shai, I. et al. "Weight Loss with a Low-Carbohydrate, Mediterranean, or Low-Fat Diet." *NEJM.* 359, no. 3 (July 2008): 229–241.

Suez, J. et al. "Artificial Sweeteners Induce Glucose Intolerance by Altering the Gut Microbiota." *Nature* 514, no. 7521 (October 2014): 181–6.

Thongprakaisang, S. et al. "Glyphosate Induces Human Breast Cancer Cells Growth via Estrogen Receptors." *Food Chem. Toxicol.* 59 (September 2013): 129–36.

Toledo, E. et al. "Mediterranean Diet and Invasive Breast Cancer Risk among Women at High Cardiovascular Risk in the PREDIMED Trial: A Randomized Clinical Trial." *JAMA Intern. Med.* 175, no. 11 (November 2015): 1752–60.

Valls-Pedret, C. "Mediterranean Diet and Age-Related Cognitive Decline: A Randomized Clinical Trial." *JAMA Intern. Med.* 175, no. 7 (July 2015): 1094–103.

Want, Liqun et al. "Lipopolysaccharide-Induced Inflammation Is Associated with Receptor for Advanced Glycation End Products in Human Endothelial Cells." *FASEB J.* 28, no. 1 (April 2104).

Part II: The Grain Brain Whole Life Plan Essentials

Chapter 4: Getting Started: Assess Your Risk Factors, Know Your Numbers, and Prepare Your Mind

Brandhorst, S. et al. "A Periodic Diet That Mimics Fasting, Promotes Multi-System Regeneration, Enhanced Cognitive Performance, and Healthspan." *Cell Metab.* 22, no. 1 (July 2015): 86–99.

Leslie, Mitch. "Short-Term Fasting May Improve Health." ScienceMagazine.org. June 18, 2015. www.sciencemag.org/news/2015/06/short-term-fasting-may-improve-health (accessed June 14, 2016).

Perlmutter, Austin. "5 Ways to Thrive While You Wean Off Carbohydrates." DrPerlmutter.com. www.drperlmutter.com/five-ways-thrive-wean-carbohydrates/ (accessed June 15, 2016).

Seshadri, S. et al. "Plasma Homocysteine As a Risk Factor for Dementia and Alzheimer's Disease." *N. Engl. J. Med.* 346, no. 7 (February 2002): 476–83.

Torgan, Carol. "Health Effects of a Diet That Mimics Fasting." National Institutes of Health, NIH Research Matters page on nih.gov. July 13, 2015. www.nih.gov/news-events/nih-research-matters/health-effects-diet-mimics-fasting (accessed June 15, 2016).

Youm, Y. H. et al. "The Ketone Metabolite β-hydroxybutyrate Blocks Nlrp3 Inflammasome-Mediated Inflammatory Disease." *Nat. Med.* 21, no. 3 (March 2015): 263–9.

Chapter 5: Step 1—Edit Your Diet and Pill-Popping

Azad, M. B. et al. "Infant Antibiotic Exposure and the Development of Childhood Overweight and Central Adiposity." *Int. J. Obes.* (Lond.) 38, no. 10 (October 2014): 1290–8.

Babiker, R. et al. "Effects of Gum Arabic Ingestion on Body Mass Index and Body Fat Percentage in Healthy Adult Females:

Two-Arm Randomized, Placebo Controlled, Double-Blind Trial." *Nutr. J.* 11 (December 2012): 111.

Björkhem, I., and S. Meaney. "Brain Cholesterol: Long Secret Life Behind a Barrier." *Arterioscler. Thromb. Vasc. Biol.* 24, no. 5 (May, 2004): 806–15.

Calame, W. et al. "Gum Arabic Establishes Prebiotic Functionality in Healthy Human Volunteers in a Dose-Dependent Manner." *Br. J. Nutr.* 100, no. 6 (December 2008): 1269–75.

Chowdhury, R. et al. "Vitamin D and Risk of Cause Specific Death: Systematic Review and Meta-Analysis of Observational Cohort and Randomised Intervention Studies." *BMJ.* 348 (April 2014): g1903.

Culver, A. L. et al. "Statin Use and Risk of Diabetes Mellitus in Post-menopausal Women in the Women's Health Initiative." *Arch. Intern. Med.* 172, no. 2 (January 23, 2012): 144–52.

Durso, G. R. et al. "Over-the-Counter Relief from Pains and Pleasures Alike: Acetaminophen Blunts Evaluation Sensitivity to Both Negative and Positive Stimuli." *Psychol. Sci.* 26, no. 6 (June 2015): 750–8.

Frenk, S. M. et al. "Prescription Opioid Analgesic Use Among Adults: United States, 1999–2012." NCHS Data Brief no. 189 (February 2015): 1–8.

Graham, D. Y. et al. "Visible Small-Intestinal Mucosal Injury in Chronic NDSAID Users." *Clin. Gastroenterol. Hepatol.* 3, no. 1 (January, 2005): 55–9.

Hegazy, G. A. et al. "The Role of Acacia Arabica Extract As an Antidiabetic, Antihyperlipidemic, and Antioxidant in Streptozotocin-Induced Diabetic Rats." *Saudi Med. J.* 34, no. 7 (July 2013): 727–33.

Holscher, H.D. et al. "Fiber Supplementation Influences Phylogenetic Structure and Functional Capacity of the Human Intestinal Microbiome: Follow-Up of a Randomized Controlled Trial." *Am. J. Clin. Nutr.* 101, no. 1 (January 2015): 55–64.

Kantor, E. D. et al. "Trends in Prescription Drug Use among Adults in the United States from 1999–2012." JAMA. 314, no. 17 (November 2015): 1818–31.

Kennedy, Pagan. "The Fat Drug." *New York Times*, Sunday Review. March 9, 2014, page SR1.

Lam, J. R. et al. "Proton Pump Inhibitor and Histamine 2 Receptor Antagonist Use and Vitamin B12 Deficiency." JAMA. 310, no. 22 (December 11, 2013): 2435–42.

Liew, A. et al. "Acetaminophen Use during Pregnancy, Behavioral Problems, and Hyperkinetic Disorders. JAMA *Pediatr.* 168, no. 4 (April, 2014): 313–20.

Littlejohns, T. J. et al. "Vitamin D and the Risk of Dementia and Alzheimer's Disease." *Neurology* 83, no. 10 (September 2014): 920–8.

Matthews, L. R. et al. "Worsening Severity of Vitamin D Deficiency Is Associated with Increased Length of Stay, Surgical Intensive Care Unit Cost, and Mortality Rate in Surgical Intensive Care Unit Patients." *Am. J. Surg.* 204, no. 1 (July 2012): 37–43.

Mazer-Amirshahi, M. et al. "Rising Rates of Proton Pump Inhibitor Prescribing in US Emergency Departments." *Am. J. Emerg. Med.* 32, no. 6 (June 2014): 618–22.

Mikkelsen, K. H. et al. "Use of Antibiotics and Risk of Type 2 Diabetes: A Population-Based Case-Control Study." *J. Clin. Endocrinol. Metab.* 100, no. 10 (October 2015): 3633–40.

Million, M. et al. "Correlation between Body Mass Index and Gut Concentrations of *Lactobacillus reuteri, Bifidobacterium animalis, Methanobrevibacter smithii* and *Escherichia coli.*" *Int. J. Obes.* (Lond.) 37, no. 11 (November 2013): 1460–6.

Mor, A. et al. "Prenatal Exposure to Systemic Antibacterials and Overweight and Obesity in Danish Schoolchildren: A Prevalence Study." *Int. J. Obes.* (Lond.) 39, no. 10 (October 2015): 1450–5.

Newport, Mary. "What if There Was a Cure for Alzheimer's Disease and No One Knew?" CoconutKetones.com. July 22, 2008. www.coconutketones.com/whatifcure.pdf (accessed June 14, 2016).

Park, Alice. "Too Many Antibiotics May Make Children Heavier." Time.com. October 21, 2015. time.com/4082242/antibiotics-obesity/ (accessed June 14, 2016).

Pärtty, A. et al. "A Possible Link between Early Probiotic Intervention and the Risk of Neuropsychiatric Disorders Later in Childhood: A Randomized Trial." *Pediatr. Res.* 77, no. 6 (June 2015): 823–8.

Perlmutter, David. *Grain Brain: The Surprising Truth about Wheat, Carbs, and Sugar—Your Brain's Silent Killers.* New York: Little, Brown and Co., 2013.

Reyes-Izquierdo, T. et al. "Modulatory Effect of Coffee Fruit Extract on Plasma Levels of Brain-Derived Neurotrophic Factor in Healthy Subjects." *Br. J. Nutr.* 110, no. 3 (August 2013): 420–5.

Reyes-Izquierdo, T. et al. "Stimulatory Effect of Whole Coffee Fruit Concentrate Powder on Plasma Levels of Total and Exosomal Brain-Derived Neurotrophic Factor in Healthy Subjects: An Acute Within-Subject Clinical Study." *Food Nut. Sci.* 4, no. 9 (2013): 984–990.

Sass, Cynthia. "The 5 Most Confusing Health Labels." Huffington-Post.com. www.huffingtonpost.com/2014/08/02/health-food-labels-confusing_n_5634184.html (accessed May 1, 2016).

Schwartz, B. S. et al. "Antibiotic Use and Childhood Body Mass Index Trajectory." *Int. J. Obes.* (Lond.) 40, no. 4 (April 2016): 615–21.

Shah, N. H. et al. "Proton Pump Inhibitor Usage and the Risk of Myocardial Infarction in the General Population." *PLoS One* 10, no. 6 (June 2015): e0124653.

Sigthorsson, G. et al. "Intestinal Permeability and Inflammation in Patients on NSAIDs." *Gut.* 43, no. 4 (October, 1998): 506–11.

Simakachorn, N. et al. "Tolerance, Safety, and Effect on the Faecal Microbiota of an Enteral Formula Supplemented with Pre- and Probiotics in Critically Ill Children." *J. Pediatr. Gastroenterol. Nutr.* 53, no. 2 (August 2011): 174–81.

Slavin, Joanne. "Fiber and Prebiotics: Mechanisms and Health Benefits." *Nutrients* 5, no. 4 (April 2013): 1417–1435.

Swaminathan, A., and G. A. Jicha. "Nutrition and Prevention of Alzheimer's Dementia." *Front. Aging. Neurosci.* 6 (October 2014): 282.

University of Exeter. "Link between Vitamin D, Dementia Risk Confirmed." ScienceDaily. www.sciencedaily.com/releases/2014/08/14 0806161659.htm (accessed June 15, 2016).

Velicer, C. M. et al. "Antibiotic Use in Relation to the Risk of Breast Cancer." JAMA. 291, no. 7 (February 2004): 827–35.

Vesper, B. J. et al. "The Effect of Proton Pump Inhibitors on the Human Microbiota." *Curr. Drug. Metab.* 10, no. 1 (January 2009): 84–9.

Weinstein, G. et al. "Serum Brain-Derived Neurotrophic Factor and the Risk for Dementia: The Framingham Heart Study." JAMA *Neurol.* 71, no. 1 (January 2014): 55–61.

World Health Organization. "WHO's First Global Report on Antibiotic Resistance Reveals Serious, Worldwide Threat to Public Health." WHO.int news release, April 30, 2014. www.who.int/mediacentre/news/releases/2014/amr-report/en/ (accessed June 14, 2016).

Wu, A. et al. "Curcumin Boosts DHA in the Brain: Implications for the Prevention of Anxiety Disorders." *Biochim. Biophys. Acta.* 1852, no. 5 (May 2015): 951–61.

Zaura, E. et al. "Same Exposure but Two Radically Different Responses to Antibiotics: Resilience of the Salivary Microbiome versus Long-Term Microbial Shifts in Feces." *mBio.* 6, no. 6 (November 2015): e01693–15.

Zhang, H. et al. "Discontinuation of Statins in Routine Care Settings: A Cohort Study." *Ann. Intern. Med.* 158, no. 7 (April 2, 2013): 526–34.

Chapter 6: Step 2 — Add Your Support Strategies

American Academy of Neurology (AAN). "Heavy Snoring, Sleep Apnea May Signal Earlier Memory and Thinking Decline." ScienceDaily. www.sciencedaily.com/releases/2015/04/150415203338.htm (accessed June 15, 2016).

Andrews, S. et al. "Beyond Self-Report: Tools to Compare Estimated and Real-World Smartphone Use." *PLoS One* 10, no. 10 (October 2015): e0139004.

Balogun, J. A. et al. "Comparison of the EMG Activities in the Vastus Medialis Oblique and Vastus Lateralis Muscles During Hip Adduction and Terminal Knee Extension Exercise Protocols." *Afr. J. Physiother. and Rehab. Sci.* 2, no. 1 (2010).

Barclay, Eliza. "Eating to Break 100: Longevity Diet Tips from the Blue Zones." NPR.com. The Salt page. April 11, 2015. www.npr.org/sections/thesalt/2015/04/11/398325030/eating-to-break-100-longevity-diet-tips-from-the-blue-zones (accessed June 14, 2016).

Berman, M. G. et al. "Interacting with Nature Improves Cognition and Affect for Individuals with Depression." *J. Affect. Disord.* 140, no. 3 (November 2012): 300–5.

Buettner, Dan. "The Island Where People Forget to Die." *New York Times*, Sunday Magazine. October 28, 2012, page MM36.

Clarke, S. F. et al. "Exercise and Associated Dietary Extremes Impact on Gut Microbial Diversity." *Gut* 63, no. 12 (December 2014): 1913–20.

Dennis, Brady. "Nearly 60 Percent of Americans — The Highest Ever — Are Taking Prescription Drugs." *Washington Post*, To Your Health section. November 3, 2015. www.washingtonpost.com/news/to-your-health/wp/2015/11/03/more-americans-than-ever-are-taking-prescription-drugs/ (accessed June 14, 2016).

Dimeo, F. et al. "Benefits from Aerobic Exercise in Patients with Major

Depression: A Pilot Study." *Br. J. Sports Med.* 35, no. 2 (April 2001): 114–7.

Environmental Working Group. www.ewg.org. Research section and Consumer Guides.

Erickson, K. I. et al. "Exercise Training Increases Size of Hippocampus and Improves Memory." *Proc. Natl. Acad. Sci.* 108, no. 7 (February 2011): 3017–22.

Eriksson, P. S. et al. "Neurogenesis in the Adult Human Hippocampus." *Nat. Med.* 4, no. 11 (November 1998): 1313–7.

Halden, Rolf. "Epistemology of Contaminants of Emerging Concern and Literature Meta-Analysis." *J. Haz. Mat.* 282, no. 23 (January 2015): 2–9.

Jarrett, Christian. "How Expressing Gratitude Might Change Your Brain." NYMag.com. Science of Us section. January 7, 2016. nymag. com/scienceofus/2016/01/how-expressing-gratitude-change -your-brain.html (accessed June 14, 2016).

Kini, P. et al. "The Effects of Gratitude Expression on Neural Activity." *Neuroimage.* 128 (March 2016): 1–10.

Lautenschlager, N. T. et al. "Effect of Physical Activity on Cognitive Function in Older Adults at Risk for Alzheimer's Disease: A Randomized Trial." *JAMA.* 300, no. 9 (September 2008): 1027–37.

Lee, B. H., and Y. K. Kim. "The Roles of BDNF in the Pathophysiology of Major Depression and in Antidepressant Treatment." *Psychiatry Investig.* 7, no. 4 (December 2010): 231–5.

McCann, I. L., and D. S. Holmes. "Influence of Aerobic Exercise on Depression." *J. Pers. Soc. Psychol.* 46, no. 5 (May 1984): 1142–7.

National Sleep Foundation. www.sleepfoundation.org. Sleep Disorders and Sleep Topics.

Osorio, R. S. et al. "Sleep-Disordered Breathing Advances Cognitive Decline in the Elderly." *Neurology* 84, no. 19 (May 2015): 1964–71.

Perlmutter, David, and Alberto Villoldo. *Power Up Your Brain: The Neuroscience of Enlightenment*. New York: Hay House, 2011.

Preidt, Robert. "Bonding with Others May Be Crucial for Long-Term Health." U.S. News & World Report Health, January 8, 2016. health.usnews.com/health-news/articles/2016-01-08/ bonding-with-others-may-be-crucial-for-long-term-health (accessed June 14, 2016).

Raji, C. A. et al. "Longitudinal Relationships between Caloric Expenditure and Gray Matter in the Cardiovascular Health Study." *J. Alzheimers Dis.* 52, no. 2 (March 2016): 719–29.

Richtel, Matt. "Digital Devices Deprive Brain of Needed Downtime." NYTimes.com. August 24, 2010. www.nytimes.com/2010/08/25/ technology/25brain.html (accessed June 14, 2016).

Sandler, David. "Dumbbell Wide Row for Serious Back Muscle." Muscle & Fitness. www.muscleandfitness.com/workouts/backexercizes/ dumbell-wide-row-serious-back-muscle (accessed July 19, 2016).

Srikanthan, P., and A. S. Karlamangla. "Muscle Mass Index as a Predictor of Longevity in Older Adults." *Am. J. Med.* 127, no. 6 (June 2014): 547–53.

University of California—Los Angeles Health Sciences. "Older Adults: Build Muscle and You'll Live Longer." ScienceDaily. www.sciencedaily.com/releases/2014/03/140314095102.htm (accessed June 15, 2016).

Weinstein, G. et al. "Serum Brain-Derived Neurotrophic Factor and the Risk for Dementia: The Framingham Heart Study." *JAMA Neurol.* 71, no. 1 (January 2014): 55–61.

Yang, Y. C. et al. "Social Relationships and Physiological Determinants of Longevity across the Human Life Span." *Proc. Natl. Acad. Sci.* 113, no. 3 (January 2016): 578–83.

Chapter 7: Step 3—Plan Accordingly

Garaulet, M. et al. "Timing of Food Intake Predicts Weight Loss Effectiveness." *Int. J. Obes.* (Lond.) 37, no. 4 (April 2013): 604–11.

Chapter 8: Troubleshooting

Azad, M. B. et al. "Gut Microbiota of Healthy Canadian Infants: Profiles by Mode of Delivery and Infant Diet at 4 Months." CMAJ. 185, no. 5 (March 2013): 385–94.

Blustein, J., and Jianmeng Liu. "Time to Consider the Risks of Caesarean Delivery for Long-Term Child Health." *BMJ.* 350 (June 2015): h2410.

Couzin-Frankel, Jennifer. "How to Give a C-Section Baby the Potential Benefits of Vaginal Birth." ScienceMag.org. February 1, 2016. www.sciencemag.org/news/2016/02/how-give-c-section-baby-potential-benefits-vaginal-birth (accessed June 14, 2016).

Mueller, N. T. et al. "The Infant Microbiome Development: Mom Matters." *Trends Mol. Med.* 2014. dx.doi.org/10.1016/j.molmed.2014.12.002.

Part III: Let's Eat!

Chapter 9: Final Reminders and Snack Ideas

Otto, M. C. et al. "Everything in Moderation—Dietary Diversity and Quality, Central Obesity and Risk of Diabetes." *PLoS One* 10, no. 10 (October 2015): e0141341.

University of Texas Health Science Center at Houston. " 'Everything in Moderation' Diet Advice May Lead to Poor Metabolic Health in US Adults." ScienceDaily. www.sciencedaily.com/releases/2015/10/151030161347.htm (accessed June 15, 2016).

Index

acacia gum, 104, 108–9

acetaminophen (Tylenol), 114–15

acid-reflux drugs, 30, 114

Adams, John Quincy, 157

ADHD (attention deficit hyperactivity disorder), 12, 14

Advil (ibuprofen), 115

aerobic exercise, 123–25, 128, 169

Agriculture, U.S. Department of (USDA), 4–5, 93, 97–98, 161

Aielli, Fabrizio, 231, 250

air quality, indoor, 162

Aleve (naproxen), 115

almonds, ricotta with berries and, 204, 260

alpha-lipoic acid (ALA), 105, 112

ALS (ammonium lauryl sulfate), 162

aluminum chlorohydrate, 161

Alzheimer's disease, 5, 7, 12, 13
    brain-derived neurotrophic factor and, 106
    diabetes and, 36–37
    exercise and, 120–21
    glycated hemoglobin and, 73
    homocysteine and, 74
    sleep disturbances and, 137, 140
    telomeres in, 41

American Academy of Physical Medicine and Rehabilitation, 136

American Board of Sleep Medicine, 138

American Diabetes Association, 36

amino acids, 79

ammonium lauryl sulfate (ALS), 162

amyloid-beta protein, 37, 137

anchovies, 227

antibiotics, 30, 116–18, 184–85

antidepressants, 13, 138, 186

antioxidants, 40, 105, 115

anxiety, 13, 186

appetite, 37–38, 166

appetizers, 216–19

AquaBounty, 56

artichokes
    fish fillets with, 207, 250–51
    salmon with, 216–17
    See also sunchokes

ASD (autism spectrum disorder), 14, 33

aspirin, 181

atherosclerosis, 74

attention deficit hyperactivity disorder (ADHD), 12, 14

autism, 12, 14, 33

autoimmune disorders, 13–14, 46–47

back pain, 69, 132–34

bacon, tomato-basil tower with, 199, 231–32

bacteria, vaginal, 184
  See also gut bacteria; probiotics
Barclay, William, 157
BDNF (brain-derived neurotrophic factor),
    106, 111, 122
beauty products, 161–62
beef, 93
beef burgers, 207, 252–53
berries, 97
  frozen, 98
  ricotta with almonds and, 204, 260
beta-amyloid protein, 37, 137
beta-hydroxybutyrate, 79
beverages, 99–100
bicep curl, 129
bicycle crunch, 131
Bifidobacterium, 111, 112
bisphenol-A (BPA), 160, 178
blood-brain barrier, 32
blood glucose, 25–26, 35–36, 72–73
  See also glucose; sugar
blood pressure, 52–53, 151, 169
blood tests, 68, 72–76
Blue Zones, 119–20
body fat, 23, 24, 79
body mass index, 151
BPA (bisphenol-A), 160, 178
brain
  acetaminophen and, 114–15
  cholesterol and, 50
  exercise and, 120–21
  fuel sources for, 24–25, 78–79
  gluten and, 44, 47
  gut bacteria and, 26, 27, 32
  neuroplasticity of, 142–43
  probiotics and, 111–12
  sleep and, 136, 140–41, 170

statins and, 113
  vitamin D and, 106–7
brain-derived neurotrophic factor (BDNF),
    106, 111, 122
brain disorders, 12–13
  ketogenic diet and, 25
  risk factors for, 27, 36, 49, 69–71
Brain Maker (Perlmutter), 3–5, 9, 27, 33
breakfast
  plan for, 203–7
  recipes for, 210–15
  routine for, 194
  skipping, 80
breast cancer, 51–52
breast-feeding, 104, 183–84
broccoli, mushroom, and feta toss, 205,
    242–43
broccolini, mushroom, and leek frittata,
    203, 210–11
Brussels sprout slaw, fish fillets with, 207,
    250–51
Buddhism, 78, 156, 158
burgers, beef, 207, 252–53
butyric acid, 31

cabbage
  Indian-spiced, 237–38
  vegetable salad with, 226–27
caffeine, 99, 138, 193
calf exercises, 131
calories
  carbohydrate, 36
  fat, 119
  protein, 62
  restriction of, 40
  timing of, 166
Campbell, Joseph, 156

cancer
    diet and, 51–52, 60, 61–62, 81–82
    gut bacteria and, 27–28
caprese salad, 198
carbohydrates, 26, 43, 48–52
    body fat and, 23
    cravings for, 181–82
    cutting off, 81–85
    gut bacteria and, 30–31
    need for, 24
    processed, 91
    recommendations for, 36
    substitutions for, 201–2
    See also glucose; sugar
cardiovascular disease, 48–50, 60, 74
cardio workout, 123–25, 128, 169
cauliflower soup, creamy, 207, 221–22
celiac disease, 44
cell phones, 153–54
ceteareth, 161
chemicals, toxic, 159–62
    See also glyphosate
chest exercises, 130
chia seeds, 258
chicken thighs with parsley sauce,
    206, 256–57
children
    antibiotics for, 118, 185
    dietary protocol for, 186–87
    diet-related disease in, 11
chocolate mousse, 205, 207, 259–60
cholesterol, 23
    cardiovascular disease and, 24, 49–50
    drugs lowering, 113, 138
    eggs and, 63
    low-carb diet and, 48
choline, 110

chromosomes, telomeres on, 41, 74, 75,
    107
circadian rhythm, 139, 166, 169
cleaning products, 162, 163–64
coconut oil, 95, 105, 112, 183, 193, 209
coconut pudding, 203, 206, 258
coconut sugar, 246
coffee, 50, 99
coffee fruit extract, 105–6, 112
cognitive function
    Mediterranean diet and, 52
    mild impairment of, 121, 140
    See also Alzheimer's disease
Cole, Nat King, 146
compassion, 146, 150
condiments, 96, 110–11
Confucius, 158
cookware, 160, 202
core exercises, 127, 131
corn, 55
corticosteroids, 138
CPAP (continuous positive airway
    pressure), 141
cravings, handling, 82, 83–84, 181–82
C-reactive protein, 49, 74, 151
C-sections, 184
curcumin, 105, 143
curry, Thai vegetable, 206, 239–41
custards, pea and goat cheese, 207,
    218–19
cytokines, 44, 47

daily checklist and schedule, 173–74
dairy products, 96, 97–98, 109–10
Dalai Lama, 156
David, Lawrence, 32–33
DBP (dibutyl phthalate), 162

death
protein intake and, 59–62
top causes of, 11, 12–13
deep-breathing exercises, 139, 155
dementia, antibiotics and, 117
See also Alzheimer's disease
depression, 12
drugs for, 13, 138, 186
exercise and, 122
inflammation and, 22
probiotics for, 112
desserts, 203–7, 258–60
DHA. *See* docosahexaenoic acid
diabetes mellitus, 12
Alzheimer's disease and, 36–37
antibiotics and, 116–17
inflammation and, 47
protein intake and, 61
tests for, 72–73
zonulin and, 47
dibutyl phthalate (DBP), 162
diet, 42
carbohydrates in, 26, 81–85
cheating or straying from, 178–80, 194–95
children and, 186–87
diversity of, 193–94
editing, 68
eggs in, 63–64
fasting and, 77–80
gluten in, 44–48
GMO foods in, 55–59
goals for, 19
government guidelines for, 4–5
gut bacteria and, 30–33
hormone balance and, 35–38
hunter-gatherer, 23, 31, 33, 52, 77
journal for, 43, 167, 200

ketogenic, 24–25, 26
low-carb, higher fat and fiber, 43, 48–52
low-fat, 48–49, 51
Mediterranean, 51–52
Nrf2 pathway and, 40
protein in, 44, 59–62
rules for, 43–44, 64
side effects of, 180–82
sleep and, 141–42
stress and, 143
sugar in, 52–54
testimonials for, 9, 65, 81–82, 141–42, 175–77, 179, 186–87, 189, 191–92
vegan or vegetarian, 61, 182–83
weight loss and, 65
Western, 3, 11, 31, 33
See also foods; meals; supplements
diethyl phthalate, 161
dill, tomato-basil tower with, 199, 231–32
dinner
hunger after, 182
plan for, 203–7
routine for, 194
disease
biomarkers of, 151
chronic, 11, 12–15, 17–18
gut bacteria and, 27–28, 29, 32
hormone imbalances and, 34
inflammation and, 21–22, 50
knowledge about, 15–16
risk factors for, 5, 68, 69–71
disinfectants, 162, 164
DNA (deoxyribonucleic acid), 16–17
evolution of, 77
expression of, 38–39
GMO foods and, 55
microbial influence on, 28

docosahexaenoic acid (DHA), 104, 112
  brain health and, 143
  Nrf2 pathway and, 40
  vegan diet and, 182, 183
Dominguez-Bello, Maria Gloria, 184
downtime, personal, 153–58
dressings, 202
  kefir, 199, 231, 232
  mayonnaise, 198, 226, 227–28
  olive oil, 202, 251
  zesty tomato, 230, 231
drinks, 99–100
drugs. *See* medications

eating. *See* diet; foods; meals
EDCs (endocrine-disrupting chemicals),
    161
Edison, Thomas A., 156
eggs, 210–13
  embracing, 44, 62, 63–64
  fermented, 111
  frittata of, 203, 210–11
  greens and, 205, 212–13
eicosapentaenoic acid (EPA), 104
Einstein, Albert, 157
electronic devices, 152, 153–54
Elliot, Walter, 156
Empowering Neurologist, The (video), 37
endocrine-disrupting chemicals (EDCs), 161
endocrine system, 34
environment
  detoxifying, 69, 120, 159–64, 173
  microbiomes in, 29
  natural, 159
  sleeping, 138
Environmental Working Group (EWG),
    161, 162

EPA (eicosapentaenoic acid), 104
epigenetics, 16–17, 39
epilepsy, 25, 189
Erikson, Peter, 142–43
Excedrin, 138
exercise, 19, 69, 120–32
  aerobic, 123–25, 128, 169
  benefits of, 120–22, 126
  checklist and schedule for, 173–74
  for cravings, 181
  deep-breathing, 139, 155
  goals of, 132
  leptin, insulin, and, 38
  outdoor, 159
  pain related to, 134–35
  plan for, 69, 124, 165, 168–70, 172
  sleep and, 139
  strength-training, 126–31, 169
  stress and, 143
exercise journal, 169, 172

fabrics, natural, 163
Fasano, Alessio, 32, 46
fasting, 40, 77–80, 86, 166
fat, body, 23, 24, 79
fat, dietary, 43, 48–52
  healthy, 92, 95
  metabolism of, 21, 23–26
  omega-3, 40, 74, 92, 104, 143, 182
  saturated, 24, 49–51, 63
  sources of, 87–88, 196
  trans, 50, 92
  vegan diet and, 183
  See also cholesterol; oils
FDA. *See* Food and Drug Administration
    (US)
fecal microbial transplant (FMT), 33

fermented foods, 94, 96
  probiotic, 110–11
  recipes for, 199, 201, 243–46
feta cheese, broccoli and mushroom toss
    with, 205, 242–43
fiber, 43, 51, 52
  gut bacteria and, 30–31
  juicing and, 53, 193
  prebiotic, 31, 104, 107–9, 112, 184
fish, 96, 207, 247–51
  fermented, 111
  pregnant women and, 183
  See also salmon
FMT (fecal microbial transplant), 33
folic acid, 75
Food and Drug Administration (FDA), 194
  acacia gum and, 109
  gluten and, 90
  GMO foods and, 56
  "natural" foods and, 93
  supplements and, 103
food journal, 43, 167, 172, 200
food labels
  fat on, 92
  gluten on, 90–91
  for GMOs, 55, 57
  "organic" on, 97–98
  reading, 195, 209
  sugar on, 52, 54
foods
  buying, 98–99, 168, 196–97, 202,
    209
  canned, 160, 178
  epigenetics and, 16–17
  fat in, 50, 92, 95, 196
  fermented, 94, 96, 110–11
  gluten-containing, 46, 88–91, 92

GMO, 43, 55–59, 93, 99
  microwaving, 160
  "natural," 93, 98
  "no," 88–93
  organic, 91, 93, 97–98, 161
  prebiotic, 108
  probiotic, 109–11
  processed, 11
  snack, 83–84, 178, 181, 197–99
  sugar in, 52, 53
  "yes," 93–99
  See also diet; meals; recipes
formaldehyde, 161
formalin, 161
Frank, Anne, 158
free radicals, 36, 39–40
free weights, 127, 129–31
frittata, broccolini, mushroom, and leek,
    203, 210–11
fritters, sunchoke, 201–2, 206, 234–36
fructosamine, 73
fructose, 52–53
fruits, 98–99
  low-sugar, 94, 199
  pickled, 110
  sweet, 97

gardening, 163
garlic puree, roasted, 233, 234
Gedgaudas, Nora, 23, 37, 38
genes, 16–17, 77
  control of, 21, 38–41
  microbial influence on, 27, 28
genetically modified organisms (GMOs),
    43, 55–59, 93, 99
ghrelin, 37, 38, 166
glass cleaner, 163–64

gliadins, 30, 46

gluconeogenesis, 79

glucose, 24

blood, 25–26, 35–36, 72–73

metabolism of, 26, 35, 78–79

See also carbohydrates; sugar

glutathione, 115

gluten, 43, 44–48

blood-brain barrier and, 32

cravings for, 181

deli meats and, 198

gut bacteria and, 30, 51

sensitivity to, 44–45, 46

sources of, 88–91, 92

glutenins, 46

glycation, 36, 53, 73

glycogen, 35, 78

glyphosate, 57–59, 160

foods without, 93

meat with, 61

urine test for, 59, 73–74

GMOs (genetically modified organisms), 43, 55–59, 93, 99

goals, 3, 19–21, 86

exercise, 132

setting new, 155–56

goat cheese, custards with, 207, 218–19

golfing, 124

Gould, Robert, 56–57

Grain Brain (Perlmutter), 3, 4–5, 6–7, 9, 36, 44, 176, 181

Grain Brain Whole Life Plan, 16, 17–18, 21

grains, 14, 97, 201

Grant, Ulysses S., 157

gratitude, 19, 144–46, 150

gray matter, 121

Great Plains Laboratory, 59, 73–74

greens

Asian-scented, 201, 245–46

baked eggs and, 205, 212–13

salad of mixed, 202, 203, 228–30

green tea, 99

grocery shopping, 98–99, 168, 196–97, 202, 209

growth hormone, 136

gut, 26–27

inflammation of, 47

leaky, 29–30, 32, 33, 44, 45, 46–47

NSAID damage to, 115–16

gut bacteria, 4, 21, 26–34

acid-reflux drugs and, 114

antibiotics and, 116

artificial sweeteners and, 54

autism and, 33

causes of unhealthy, 30

fiber and, 30–31, 51

gene expression and, 28, 40–41

glyphosate and, 58

supplements supporting, 107–12

vitamin D and, 107

gut dysbiosis, 27, 33

habits

creating new, 8

non-negotiable, 153

reverting to old, 178–80

turning off, 68, 76–77

hamstring muscles, 135

Hanson, Jaydee, 56

headaches, 13, 180–82

heart disease, 48–50, 60, 74

heart rate, maximum and target, 123–24, 125

hemoglobin A1C, 73

HEPA air filters, 162

herbicides. *See* glyphosate

herbs
    list of, 100–101
    salmon with, 205, 247–48
Hillel, Rabbi, 156
hippocampus, 25, 36
homeostasis, 42
homocysteine, 74
hormones, 21, 34–38
    glyphosate as, 58
    sleep and, 136, 139
    steroid, 35, 50, 168
houseplants, 163
How Yoga Works (Roach and McNally),
    7
Huffington, Arianna, 141
hummus, 96
hunger, pre-bedtime, 182
hyperinsulinemia, 37
hypertension, 52–53, 151

ibuprofen (Advil), 115
immune system
    gut bacteria and, 27–28, 29–30
    inflammatory response by, 21, 22
    sleep and, 137
infants
    breast-feeding, 104, 183–84
    C-section delivery of, 184
inflammation, 21–22
    brain disorders and, 36
    coconut oil and, 95
    C-reactive protein and, 49, 74, 151
    gluten and, 44, 46, 47–48
    gut bacteria and, 27, 29
    low-carb diet and, 49, 50
    social network and, 151
insulin

carbohydrates and, 23
    fasting, 72
    fructose and, 53
    leptin, ghrelin, and, 37–38
    reducing surges in, 21, 35–37
insulin resistance, 35–36, 38, 47, 73
intestines. *See* gut; gut bacteria
I Read Labels For You (website), 161

Jerusalem artichokes. *See* sunchokes
Jesus Christ, 158
jicama salad, 205, 230–31
John XXIII, Pope, 156
journals, 156, 171–73
    exercise, 169
    food, 43, 167, 200
juicing, 53, 193

kale, braised, 205, 233–34
kefir, 110
kefir dressing, 199, 231–32
Keith, Lierre, 14
Keller, Helen, 156, 158
Kennedy, John F., 157
ketones, 24–26, 79
ketosis, 25
Keys, Ancel, 49
kitchen clean-out, 87–102
knee pain, 69, 134–35
knee replacement surgery, 134
kombucha tea, 99–100
kraut, mixed vegetable, 199, 201, 207,
    243–45
Krishnamurti, Jiddu, 158

laboratory tests, 68, 72–76
Lactobacillus, 40–41, 111, 112, 185

lamb
    meatball soup of, 205, 223–25
    roast leg of, 204, 253–54
Lao Tzu, 156
lat row (exercise), 130
leeks
    frittata with, 203, 210–11
    salmon with, 204, 248–49
leftovers, using, 201
legumes, 96
leptin, 21, 37–38
    fructose and, 53
    resistance to, 38, 47
    sleep and, 166
life, balance in, 21, 41
life expectancy, 11
lifestyle, 16, 17
    brain health and, 143
    changes in, 19–20, 64, 67–69, 86
    healthy, 3, 119–20
    low-carb, 81–82
    microbiome and, 27
    unhealthy, 60
Lincoln, Abraham, 158
Lindbergh, Anne Morrow, 157
lipopolysaccharide (LPS), 47, 111
lipoprotein lipase, 23
liver disease, nonalcoholic fatty, 52
love, power of, 146–50
lunch
    away from home, 178
    plan for, 203–7
    routine for, 194
    timing of, 166–67
lunges, 130–31

mayonnaise, Grain Brain, 198, 226, 227–28
McDonnell, Mike, 146–48, 149, 150
McDonnell, Nina, 147
MCI (mild cognitive impairment), 121, 140
meal plan, 14-day, 8, 194, 200–208
meals
    away from home, 84, 177–78, 195
    checklist and schedule for, 173–74
    frequency of, 77
    planning, 69, 165, 172
    plate model for, 87, 196
    timing of, 166–68
    See also diet; foods; recipes
meat, 59–61
    deli, 198
    fermented, 111
    healthy, 93, 95–96
    organic, 97–98
    recipes with, 223–25, 252–56
meatball soup, lamb, 205, 223–25
medications, 69, 113–18
    discontinuing, 185–86
    gut bacteria and, 30
    homocysteine and, 74–75
    pain, 114–16, 118, 181
    sleep-disrupting, 138
    supplements and, 103
meditation, 173
Mediterranean diet, 51–52
melatonin, 139
menopause, 35
mental illness, 13
    See also depression
Merzenich, Michael, 143
metabolism
    diet diversity and, 193–94
    fat burning in, 21, 23–26

metabolism *(cont.)*
glucose production in, 78–79
hormones related to, 35–38
microbiome, 4, 27–28
dietary change and, 32–33
global, 29
gluten and, 48
probiotic bacteria in, 111–12
See also gut bacteria
microwave, 160
migraine headaches, 13
mild cognitive impairment (MCI), 121, 140
minerals, 58, 183
mitochondria, 25
Monsanto, 160
mood disorders, 13, 22
See also depression
motivation, leveraging, 83
mousse, chocolate, 205, 207, 259–60
Mozaffarian, Dariush, 194
Mullen, Seamus, 223
multiple sclerosis (MS), 12, 13, 36
muscles
breakdown of, 79
grouping of, 127
stretching, 123, 169
See also strength training
mushrooms
broccoli and feta toss with, 205, 242–43
frittata with, 203, 210–11

naproxen (Aleve), 115
National Institute of Health (US), 28
National Sleep Foundation (US), 138
nature, getting out in, 159
"Nature Boy" (Cole), 146
neurodegenerative disease, 27, 95

See also Alzheimer's disease; brain
disorders
neurogenesis, 142–43
neuroplasticity, 143
nicotine, 138
90-10 rule, 180
non-celiac gluten sensitivity (NCGS), 45
nonsteroidal anti-inflammatory drugs
(NSAIDs), 30, 115–16, 181
Nrf2 pathway, 39–40, 79

oats, 97
obesity
antibiotics and, 116–17
brain disorders and, 12–13, 36
circadian rhythm and, 166
fat consumption and, 23
inflammation and, 47–48, 49
leptin or insulin resistance and, 38
prebiotic fiber and, 31
sleep apnea and, 141
social network and, 151
See also weight loss
Oceana, 247
oestrogen, 35, 58
oils
avocado, 227
coconut, 95, 105, 112, 183, 193, 209
healthy, 95, 209
olive, 51, 183, 193, 209
unhealthy, 92
olive oil, 51, 183, 193, 209
olive oil dressing, 202, 251
Oliver, Jamie, 11
olives, fish fillets with, 207, 250–51
omega-3 fats, 92
DHA, 104, 143, 182

homocysteine and, 74
Nrf2 pathway and, 40
omega-6 fats, 92
onion soup, 203, 220–21
opioids, prescription, 118
orange juice, 53
organic foods, 91, 93, 97–98, 161
oxidative stress, 39–40, 41

pain, 120
back and knee, 69, 132–36
headache, 13, 180–82
pain relievers, 114–16, 118, 181
pantry, restocking, 102
papaya, GMO, 55
parabens, 161
Parkinson's disease, 12, 27, 36
parsley sauce, chicken thighs with, 206, 256–57
partnership, 195
patellofemoral syndrome, 134–35
Patton, George S., 158
PC (polycarbonate), 161
peas, custards with, 207, 218–19
Pediasure Enteral formula, 58–59
PEG (polyethylene glycol), 161
perfluorooctanoic acid (PFOA), 160
Perlmutter, David, 5, 6–8, 12, 146–50
Brain Maker, 3–5, 9, 27, 33
Grain Brain, 3, 4–5, 6–7, 9, 36, 44, 176, 181
online resources of, 7, 37, 63, 72, 74, 111, 123, 128, 173, 199, 203
Power Up Your Brain, 142
Perlmutter, Leize, 147, 148
Perlmutter, Reisha, 147, 148
physiatrist, 135–36

physical activity. *See* exercise
physical therapist, 135
pickles, 110
pills. *See* medications
piriformis syndrome, 133–34
pituitary gland, 136
plastics, chemicals in, 160–61
Plato, 77
polycarbonate (PC), 161
polyethylene glycol (PEG), 161
polysomnogram, 138
pork, 255
pork roast, Tuscan-style, 203, 255–56
"porridge," breakfast, 206, 214–15
portion size, 87–88, 196, 200
poultry, 93, 95, 256–57
Power Up Your Brain (Perlmutter), 142
PPIs (proton pump inhibitors), 30, 114
prebiotics, 107–9, 112
acacia gum, 104, 108–9
in breast milk, 184
gut bacteria and, 31
PREDIMED studies, 51–52
pregnant and lactating women, 115, 183–84
Primal Body, Primal Mind (Gedgaudas), 23
probiotics, 103–4, 109–12
antibiotics and, 185
breast-feeding and, 184
hormone balance and, 35
prostaglandins, 115
protein, 44, 59–62
gluten, 46
healthy sources of, 95–96
portion size for, 87, 196, 200
requirement for, 61, 62
vegan diet and, 183

proton pump inhibitors (PPIs), 30, 114
pseudoephedrine (Sudafed), 138
pudding, coconut, 203, 206, 258
push-ups, 130

quadriceps muscles, 130–31, 135
quotations, inspirational, 153, 155,
    156–58

Reagan, Ronald, 157
recipes, 209
    appetizer, 216–19
    breakfast, 210–15
    dessert, 258–60
    fish, 247–51
    meal plan for, 203–7
    meat and poultry, 252–57
    nutritional data for, 200
    salad, 226–32
    soup, 220–25
    vegetable, 233–46
red curry paste, 239, 240–41
religions
    fasting in, 78
    quotations from, 156–58
restaurants, 84, 177–78, 195
ricotta with berries and toasted almonds,
    204, 260
ringspot virus, 55
Roundup, 57, 73, 160
    See also glyphosate
routine, daily, 152–53, 165, 194
    See also habits
Rumi, Jalaluddin, 158

salads, 226–32
    artichoke, 216–17

Brussels sprout slaw, 207, 250–51
    caprese, 198
    jicama, 205, 230–31
    layered vegetable, 203, 206, 226–27
    mixed green, 202, 203, 228–30
    tomato-basil tower, 199, 231–32
    See also dressings
salmon, 247
    artichokes with, 216–17
    genetically modified, 56
    herb-roasted, 205, 247–48
    leeks and chard with, 204, 248–49
Santayana, George, 158
sauerkraut, 110
SCFAs (short-chain fatty acids), 31
Schilling, Melissa, 36–37
Schwartz, Brian S., 116
sciatic nerve, 133
seasonings, 96, 100–101
seeds, 57, 95
seizures, 25, 189
Serenity Prayer, 157
Seven Countries Study, 49–50
Seventh-day Adventists, 120
shellfish, 95
short-chain fatty acids (SCFAs), 31
shoulder lifts, 129
sit-ups, 131
sleep, 120, 136–42
    diet and, 141–42
    eating before, 166, 182
    leptin and, 38
    plan for, 69, 165, 170–71
    requirements for, 171
    schedule for, 19, 137–38, 173–74
    strategies for, 137–40
    stress and, 143

sleep apnea, 139–41, 166
Sleep Revolution, The (Huffington), 141
sleep study, 138, 139
smartphones, 153–54
smoothie, strawberry power, 204, 207, 213–14
snacks
  away from home, 178
  healthy, 83–84, 181, 197–99
  plan for, 168
social media, 152
social networks, 146–53
sodium lauryl sulfate (SLS), 162
Sonnenberg, Justin, 30
soups, 220–25
  creamy cauliflower, 207, 221–22
  lamb meatball, 205, 223–25
  onion, 203, 220–21
sour cream, 96, 111
soy products, 55, 92–93
spices, 100–101
starches, 91–92
statins, 113, 138
stem cells, 142–43
strawberry power smoothie, 204, 207, 213–14
strength training, 123, 126–31
  equipment for, 126–27
  exercises for, 123, 129–31
  muscle groups in, 127
  plan for, 169
stress, oxidative, 39–40, 41
stress reduction, 19, 69, 120, 142–59
  checklist for, 173
  gratitude and, 144–46
  nature and, 158
  personal downtime for, 153–58

social networks for, 146–53
  techniques for, 143–44
stretching, 123, 169
stroke, 74
Sudafed (pseudoephedrine), 138
sugar, 43, 52–54
  coconut, 246
  cravings for, 83, 181–82
  names for, 52, 54
  processed, 91
  See also carbohydrates; glucose
sunchokes
  fritters of, 201–2, 206, 234–36
  gratin of, 207, 236–37
supplements, 69, 102–12
  cheat sheet for, 112
  checklist for, 173
  general, 104–7
  for gut health, 107–12
  melatonin, 139
  for pregnancy and lactation, 183, 184
  See also docosahexaenoic acid; prebiotics; probiotics; vitamins
Sutton, "Slick Willie," 26
Sweeney, Paul, 157
sweeteners
  artificial, 53–54
  natural, 97
Swiss chard, salmon with, 204, 248–49

Tagore, Rabindranath, 157
tamari soy sauce, 93
tea, 99–100
TEA (triethanolamine), 162
telomerase, 74
telomeres, 41, 74, 75, 107
temptation, avoiding, 84, 194–95

Teresa, Mother, 158
testosterone, 35, 168
thigh exercises, 130–31
thyroid hormones, 35
toiletries, 161–62
toluene, 162
tomato-basil tower, 199, 231–32
trans fats, 50, 92
triceps extension, 129
triclosan and triclocarban, 162
triethanolamine (TEA), 162
triglycerides, 48, 95
tryptophan, 58
turmeric, 104, 105, 112
Twain, Mark, 77–78
Tylenol (acetaminophen), 114–15
tyrosine, 58

Unified Microbiome Initiative (US), 28
urine test, glyphosate, 59, 73–74
USDA (U.S. Department of Agriculture),
    4–5, 93, 97–98, 161

vegan or vegetarian diet, 61, 182–83
vegetable curry, Thai, 206, 239–40
vegetable kraut, mixed, 199, 201, 207,
    243–45
vegetable oils, 92
vegetables, 93–94, 233–46
    buying, 98–99
    pickled, 110
    portion size for, 87, 196, 200

snacks with, 198–99
    starchy, 92
vegetable salad, layered, 203, 206, 226–27
Vegetarian Myth, The (Keith), 14
Vieira da Silva, Marta, 157
Villoldo, Alberto, 142
vitamins, 102–3
    B, 74–75, 182
    C, 53
    D, 58, 74, 75, 106–7, 112, 182
vitiligo, 81

walnuts, mixed greens with, 203, 228–30
water, 19, 99, 192–93
water bottles, plastic, 161
weight-bearing exercise. *See* strength
    training
weight loss, 5
    acacia gum for, 109
    diet and, 48, 65
    meal timing and, 167
    probiotics for, 112
    See also obesity
white matter, 141
wide row (exercise), 130
wine, 99, 100, 193
women, pregnant and lactating, 115,
    183–84

yogurt, 109–10

zonulin, 46–47

About the Author

Dr David Perlmutter has dedicated his professional career to advancing the science underlying brain disorders, with an emphasis on disease prevention. He is a board-certified neurologist and Fellow of the American College of Nutrition, and has contributed extensively to the world medical literature with publications appearing in *The Journal of Neurosurgery*, *The Southern Medical Journal*, *Journal of Applied Nutrition*, and *Archives of Neurology*. Dr Perlmutter lectures worldwide and is a frequent speaker at symposia sponsored by such institutions as Harvard University, Columbia University, and New York University. He is a popular guest on national media programs and has appeared on *20/20*, *Larry King Live*, *CNN*, *Fox News*, *Fox and Friends*, *The Today Show*, *Oprah*, *Dr. Oz*, and *The CBS Early Show* and serves as a medical advisor to the *Dr. Oz* show. In 2002 Dr Perlmutter was the recipient of the Linus Pauling Award for his innovative approaches to neurological disorders and in addition was presented with the Denham Harmon Award for his pioneering work in the application of free radical science to clinical medicine. In 2006 he was named Clinician of the Year by the National Nutritional Foods Association, which was followed by the Humanitarian of the Year award from the American College of Nutrition in 2010 as well as the 2015 Media Award from the same institution. He is the author of seven books including the #1 *New York Times* bestseller *Grain Brain*, now published in twenty-seven languages.

The 44 Most Closely Guarded Property Secrets

3rd Edition

Mark Homer & Rob Moore

www.progressiveproperty.co.uk
www.robmoore.com

Order this book online at www.progressiveproperty.co.uk or on Amazon and in Waterstones or email rob.moore@progressiveproperty.co.uk. "The 44 Most Closely Guarded Property Secrets" 3rd Edition is also available as an Audiobook.

Other books by Rob Moore and Mark Homer can be ordered at www.progressiveproperty.co.uk including "Make Cash in a Property Market Crash".

Cover design by Jason Duckmanton
Photography by Roland Eva

Published by Progressive Property Ltd
Printed in Peterborough, Cambridgeshire, UK

ISBN: 978-0-9559712-7-3
A catalogue record for this book is available from the British Library

www.progressiveproperty.co.uk

Progressive House
9 Office Village, Forder Way, Cygnet Park
Peterborough
PE7 8GX

01733 898550
ask@progressiveproperty.co.uk
Skype: rob.progressive

For everyone who wants to be something, for those who want to make a difference and for those who have the courage to stand up for what they believe in.

If it wasn't for you

If you're anything like me, you probably just want to dive into the nuts and bolts, and you don't want to read long Oscar speech-style thank you's.

So let's keep it simple – thanks to Mark, co-author of this book. He didn't actually have anything to do with this 3rd edition, because he's too busy buying property. But the foundation of the secrets, tools and techniques in this book are from the 10 years and 20,000 odd hours he personally dedicated to the property investing community.

And thank you. Yes, you. You're committed, focused, passionate, you've taken a risk buying this book, you could have bought the cheaper, more flimsy ones out there, and you may not know us well yet. You're putting a lot of faith in us.

I'm very grateful to you for that; humbled and honoured to share this journey with you, and I'll give it everything to add value, inspiration and support to your life as a successful property cashflow investor and Entrepreneur.

Let's get straight in.

Rob Moore & Mark Homer

rob.moore@progressiveproperty.co.uk

Contents

Section 1: Introduction   11

Section 2: The Fundamentals of Property   25
1. Why invest?   28
2. The Law of compounding   38
3. Why property & not the lottery   41
4. Leverage   50
5. Potential pitfalls   61
6. The property buying process   68
7. [Have a] Strategy   74
8. Interest only vs. repayment   78
9. Due diligence   83
10. Don't read the papers   86
11. Why 95% of people get it wrong   88
12. Take action: Start Now   90

Section 3: The Psychology of Successful Investors   94
13. Know your purpose   96
14. Focus   98
15. Belief   102
16. Anyone can do it   109
17. Faith, passion & desire   113
18. Be realistic [& unrealistic]   115
19. Think mid to long term   118
20. Trust your instincts   120
21. Expect the unexpected   122
22. Delay gratification   126
23. Never give up. Ever   128

Section 4: Strategies to Profit in Property   133
24. The Language of property   135
25. Multiple streams of property income   136
26. Be a relationship expert   139
27. R.E.A.S.O.N   143
28. C.A.S.T.L.E.D   153
29. Your Goldmine area   168

30.	Finance fundamentals	170
31.	Creative finance & JV's	177
32.	Yield & returns on investment	179
33.	Never sell [Buy to Let]	184
34.	Never let [Buy to Sell]	187
35.	Cashflow strategies	190
36.	Letting, tenancy & management	202
37.	Protect the downside	210
38.	Sales [without selling]	215
39.	Dealmaking & negotiation	222
40.	Finding the deals [marketing]	229
41.	Joint Ventures & your network	248
42.	Become an expert	253
43.	Exit strategies & tax [how to pay less of none]	256

Section 5: What Are You Going to Do Now?   267

44.	Time: your most precious commodity	268
44a.	To know & not to do…	272
44b.	Decide on your strategy	273

Bonus Section 1: Your next steps	277
Bonus Section 2: Are you sitting on an asset?	
About Mark & Rob	281
Your figures & projections	295

What others have said about "The 44 Secrets..."

"As a direct result of one of the many secrets in the book, I purchased a property in Brighton & have made £27,000 in 3 months, all whilst having a baby daughter! Rob & Mark actually do what they teach rather than the so called Guru's who talk the talk but still work in Sainsbury's at the weekend. If you have any interest whatsoever in setting yourself financially free you have to read this book now."

Neil Asher, MD New Insights: www.life-coach-training.co.uk
E-mail: neil@life-coach-training.co.uk

"Mark & Rob made me £21,000 in my first deal, saved me £1,350 in stamp duty, found and completed on the property with an instant tenant after just 76 days and I did not have to do anything except sign papers."

Richard Bellars, Inner Action Coaching: www.inneraction.co.uk
E-mail: richard@inneraction.co.uk

"What a well-written and inspiring book. I was quickly able to apply some of the techniques I learned from it to acquire an investment property which will generate profits for many years to come. I now look forward to mirroring the success of Rob and Mark, and having a substantial portfolio of income-generating properties in the not too distant future."

Richard Clifford
richard.clifford@gmail.com

"One of, if not the best investment I've ever made! This information is not only timely and informative, but it actually works. I've learnt more from your book than all of the courses I've attended. I wish I'd have read this before spending £7,000 on property courses! I'd be a few steps closer to my dream of becoming financially free! I'm Looking forward to reading the next one, and making a killing off the 'Property Crash'! Keep up the good work"

Dan Atkins
www.atkinsinvestment.co.uk

"I just couldn't put it down. I read the whole book cover to cover in less than 5 hours. I now realise you can make money in a boom or a crash and not to listen to anything the

papers say! This book makes me want to go out and get cash and invest NOW. For very little money you can build a portfolio worth millions of pounds."

Adam Sargeson:
adam_sargeson@jpress.co.uk

"Gents, I have just finished the above book and I must congratulate you. My synopsis would be "An holistic approach to Property investment for long term financial security. I personally followed your model and bought 3 local properties which have proved to be excellent buys."

Gary Moore

"A very well written, insightful look in to the world of property investing.

They cover all the topics an investor starting out will be interested in, but also have some great little strategies for more experienced investors too. I regularly go back and re read the progressive books for little bits of wisdom/motivation as and when I need it!

Since reading this book I have gone on to build a portfolio of 24 properties with a net value in excess of £2.5m, and definitely contribute a large portion of my success to Rob Moore and Mark Homer."

Jonathan Woolley

"A must read for all those wanting to invest in property. A practical easy read that covers all aspects of property investment. It includes the Psychological aspects of mindset, the fundamentals of area and property choice and financial knowledge plus more

Highly recommended and well worth the investment both time to read & cost to buy."

Julie H

"I've been investing in and managing property for 15 years, and it's only after reading this book that I began to make some serious headway. Rob and Mark have divulged massive amounts of hugely important material in this book and I honestly urge you to buy this book, regardless of your current position. This book is so reasonably priced, that you could not fail to use it profitably!"

Ed H-J

"I had invested in property for many years before reading this book. Due to being burnt a couple of times in the past, the recession, lack of funds and trust and due to sheer panic I had really slowed down my investing and nearly stopped. Since reading this book I have learnt more than I ever thought possible and the knowledge gained was so valuable which gave me the confidence to push on.

This book is truly amazing and inspiring. The information given totally shows you the "how to" do it for yourself and explains it really well. I totally recommend reading this book as it will open your eyes to many opportunities!"

James Mason

Section 1: Introduction

The original version of this book was written in 2007 by the two people you see named on the front cover. That's us: hi! Rob is the tall one with the crazy shirt and slightly red beard. Mark has hair on his head and not on his face; it's a pleasure to meet you.

Now, this 3rd, fully updated, semi future proofed edition has been updated by Rob. It's unofficially outsold any other property book by 5 to 1. You've got a combined 12 years of on the ground, front line in the trenches experience of the reality here, presented to you in a unique and interactive way. Well that's the feedback we've had, anyway.

And so throughout the course of talking to you, we flick between I and we. This must surely break all literary rules, but we feel this is the best way to get across the voices of both of us, and to give you alternative perspectives. All will become clear why as you read; and some rules are just there to be broken.

But more about us a little bit later. If you do want to read more about us, the authors, because you may not know us well yet, you can go straight to the back. It's all there, and Mark has taken the bits out about Rob's ego, because this book is about you.

A huge and special thanks to everyone at Progressive, Suneep Nayee for his content contribution and being a fantastic agent and our Mums for being here from the start. We love you :-)

And on the next page we have something special for you, as another thank you...

Special upfront offer

Joint Ventures [JV's] are the big thing right now, to invest in deals with other people's money and none of your own .

When you get a minute, go on over to the page linked below, and there we have the Progressive *Be Your Own Bank* Joint Venture Blueprint – the 7 steps to successfully nailing the JV's and getting other people's money in your bank for business and investing, without banks.

Plus you'll find a 40-odd page document specifically detailing how to find the partners, where to find them, how to 'sell' to them gently but effectively, the different types of partners, and a whole lot more, for free.

It's our way of thanking you, and a way we can stay in touch with each other:

www.beyourownbank.co.uk

What you can expect from this book

This book, with the sister book, "Make Cash in a Property Market Crash" has been designed to be the most comprehensive guide ever written for making profit from investment property, and to be accessible to most people.

A big claim perhaps?

We are by no means professing to be the biggest pair of 'Gurus' the world has ever seen. We're both still relatively young [which is why you can do it too], having started in our mid 20's, with over 55 years left in the property business – a very exciting prospect. Our aim is to help you leverage this experience to shortcut your route to your goals, and possibly dreams.

We have, however, read most of the property books out there. Twenty three in fact, on the subject of property alone. Rob reads/listens to over 60 books/programmes a year, and has dedicated his life to continual learning. But there seemed to be a gap for the entire step by step process of property investing, mixed with the real life experiences, and some mindset and support that was lacking in other publications.

Since 2004 we've invested over £600,000 on training and education, all over the world, in multiple fields, a lot of that specifically in property. We now have a £120,000 a year budget for training and education. 30% of it pays a 919% ROI [Mark worked that one out!]. 70% of it sits on the 'shelf.' You can probably relate to that.

What we aim to achieve for you is a leveraged mix of all the reading, the investment in training and education, the 'shelf development,' the missed opportunities, the mistakes and the big [sometimes accidental] wins, all focused on how you can actually apply this experience and money making strategies in your own life. All wrapped in a book or two. Condensed and detailed. Simplified. And more than just the concepts; the specifics, the non-sugar coated, to the point reality:

The on the ground experience that gives you that last 5% that is the difference between a fluffy concept that 'sounds about right' and a strategy you can cut, paste and apply to get exactly the same results, in quicker time, with less risk.

After all, that's how we've done it. We got to the people actually doing it, hounded them, sought out the very best when books and courses, like you're able to access now, didn't then exist, paid them huge amounts of money, and copied them: property, business, sales and marketing experts. And we gave them £10,000's. And as painful as it was, and as hot as those credit cards got, it worked. And it was the only way.

So we wanted to write a book for you, to save you the mistakes or the £10,000's in errors that you wouldn't have been able to predict, because you don't know what you don't know. And if you think what you read is valuable enough, we may have the chance to work together personally. After all, if a pair of cheeky 20 [now 30] something year olds can do it, then so can you, right?

You really can, and we believe in you.

If, after reading this book, you feel that we have not lived up to this, or that there has been no realisable value in what we have written, we will give you your money back, no questions asked.

Actually we probably will ask why, because your opinion matters to us, but we'll still stand by our guarantee.
Why would we offer a money back guarantee on a book?

It's a commitment we are willing to make to prove to you, before you start, that we feel there is so much truth out there that you are not being told and that if you don't educate yourself the right way, it could cost you a lot of time and money in your life. We don't want that for you.

If you do decide to return it, please send it back to Progressive Property where we will refund your investment. All of our details are at the front and back of the book.

The fact is that you have put your hand in your pocket, even if it is only a small investment [in yourself], and that says a lot. Thank You. We think you'll want to use this book long into the future for reference to build your portfolio. And you should. You might even enjoy it too.

Check out what Heather Self did:

...my property investments which are quite small by your standards! :-)

However I was inspired by the ideas in your first book because although I had often thought about investing in property, I never actually got as far as DOING anything about it until you and Mark made it sound so simple (though not always easy), in the "44 Secrets".

Basically I have adhered quite closely to your rules and I now have a definite strategy for my investments with specific criteria, (eg. No more than 3 miles from my home, 2 or 3 beds, have a certain ROI etc), which have to be met before I will consider a purchase. I have just completed my 8th purchase and I bought my first property in May 2008.

Here are the basic details about each purchase;

Property	Purchase Price	Comparable Property in same area (at time of purchase)
1	72k	85k
2	70k	85k
3	£64,950	£79k
4	£70k	£90k
5	£57k	£85k
6	£70k	£95k
7	£90k	£125k
8	£41,950	£67

Of course some of the values of the earlier ones may have gone down but it doesn't matter because they are all cash flowing positively and I will not be selling them. 3 are on variable rates so are giving particularly good yields at the moment though I do realise that eventually the rates will go up again, and I am budgeting for this.

I buy in the areas where the properties are at the lower end of the market and where there are always going to be plenty of people who will want to rent.

I have made some errors and haven't always got my deposits out particularly with regard to the more recent purchases. One of the mortgages was expensive and I shouldn't have agreed the deal because of that but I have learned (hopefully) from my mistakes and at least I've made a start.

I still work as a teacher for 3 days each week. I now purchase jointly with my eldest son who is 21 and as soon as my youngest son is 18 he wants to be included in any future purchases as well. Of course I NEVER intend to sell!

That's about it except to say a big thank you to both you and Mark because I don't think I would ever have made that first purchase if I hadn't read your first book. Both of your books are so user friendly, easy to read and explain the property purchasing process clearly and simply. I know that if I can do it anyone can. I wanted to invest in property to secure the future for my family - so I was already motivated but it was the ideas in your book which gave me the confidence to take the necessary ACTION.

Thanks again,

Heather

Use it as a manual, use it as a guide, use it as a checklist of do's and don'ts, use it to motivate and inspire you to take action. Use it as a warning as to what, and who, to watch out for, use it as a beer mat or use it to reach the Jaffa cakes on the top shelf of the cupboard.

Just make sure you use it.

"To know and not to do, is not to know – just go" – Rob Moore

And if at the end of the book you still think to yourself:

'I don't have the time'

'I'm not interested in doing it myself'

Then get in touch and we will help you. You can 'leverage' us.

Or if you feel you need more personal help, support, a community to help you through the challenges and the negative people, then get in touch, we can help you.

Fair enough?

But you must read all the way to the end of the book to qualify for this, and you will be very glad that you did!

What's new?

We believe that there should be more practical, how-to training and education in the areas of investment, property and Entrepreneurial strategies to help you take personal responsibility in a changing world, and secure your financial future [not get rich quick]; hence writing this book.

We hope that this book fills this educational void for you that we felt there is [was!] in property education. We intend that you will be able to take what you've read here and go out straight away and get the same results. Believe us; you really can if you choose to. Commit to it now. Decide.

This book will reveal all: the good, the bad and the downright ugly about property investing. You simply must read this before you even think about investing. Do not part with your cash until you have finished whatever you do. Chain yourself to the sofa and don't get up until you're done! With lots of gaps, big writing and some pictures it shouldn't be that difficult :-)

If we had learned the 'secrets' [there are no real secrets, just things most people don't know] within this book before investing [and looking back, we'd have paid thousands for it], we would have saved ourselves many mistakes. Mark wouldn't have lost over 50,000 Euros in a deal in Bulgaria in the early 2000's. We wouldn't have bought those overseas, off-plan, new build properties on the other side of the planet. We would have saved hundreds of thousands of pounds too in deals left on the table and missed opportunities. However, all mistakes are part of our journey. We paid our 'entrance fee.' We needed to, as painful as it was. We all do. But you can leverage us. You can benefit now from the dues we've paid, our humble, fun, crazy journey and learn from our mistakes, in the hope that you can get it right from the start and make property investment work for you [even quicker than we did]. And save a wad of cash in the meantime.

Jon Woolley did exactly that. A Progressive VIP community member with 24 properties and £4,900 NET cashflow per month from his portfolio, at the age of 21!

At 19 years old, before he started, he was working at a BP Garage, and then worked at Burger King. He told us that he felt he was really letting himself and his family down, as his dad had him reading Entrepreneurial books at age 12, invested in him and supported him in working for himself.

But he lost his way. Within one year of becoming part of the Progressive community, investing in his education and taking action, he had bought a portfolio of over 20 houses and garages for a 70% discount, had them rented out, flipped 2 properties for cash, bought a brand new Audi TT — and did all of this with a JV partners' money!

Much quicker than us, not that we're jealous ;-) We're just honoured to be part of his journey.

You can watch his full story here, click on his name at the top: **www.progressiveproperty.co.uk/inspiration**

What you won't get from this book

You won't get unrealistic get rich quick — sit-on-a-Beach-drinking-Pina-Colada-in-Marbella-and-come-back-a-millionaire BS.

It doesn't exist. Seriously. Sure, there is the shortest route to success, and we give you that straight line approach in this book. But that straight line is in fact full of hurdles that you must go through, or over.

"You have to work hard enough not to have to work hard" – Richard Templar

We won't delude you about this. If you're not prepared to work, you're in the wrong business.

what people think
it looks like

what it really
looks like

That's the bad [real] news. The good [real] news is that if you treat property as a business, leverage wherever you can so that others are doing the work for you and helping you to your results using their time, build a great [leveraged] power team, leverage the Progressive community, pick the right strategies for you, and make the fewest mistakes possible learning from others who've been there...

Then you'll actually succeed way beyond your goals, and possibly dreams; certainly quicker than you'd have ever thought possible. Just like Jon, and many others we'll talk about in this book.

You won't get unrealistic dreamy fluff, but you won't get grumpy sceptical moaning either – a healthy small dose of both at the right times is perfect. You won't get reams of boring stats of a book full of stories about us and our ego's – a healthy small dose of both in between facts and strategies is what you'll get.

Our disclaimer:

We have taken care to make the figures and specifics in this book as accurate and relevant as possible at the time of writing; and of course we hope you understand that these can change dependent on market and economic forces.

The content, projections, figures and indications contained in this book are based on opinion and cannot be relied upon when making investment decisions. As with any investment, property values can fall as well as rise.

The Authors offer this information as a guide only and it cannot be considered as financial advice in any way. Please refer to your independent financial advisor who is qualified to give you complete advice based on your circumstances.

The authors Rob Moore and Mark Homer are not qualified to give mortgage, legal or financial advice. Please seek legal and financial advice from a qualified advisor before making commitments. Neither its authors nor 'Progressive Property Ltd,' or any other Progressive companies, accept liability for decisions made based on the content of this book.

Of course that was necessary to get out of the way and it is something that you know already. This book is a guide and you have ultimate *choice*.

About Rob & Mark

At the end of this book, there are a few pages that tell you about us. Because this book is for you, we thought that the back is the best place for them. What we do think is relevant to you now, is how we got to where we are and how you can do the same. A small introduction:

Mark bought his first Property in 2004:

I started buying small houses because I realised that the smaller properties [under £125,000] in our area were growing in value quicker when compared to anything over £150,000. I saw it as a reduced risk to chop my money into smaller properties rather than buying expensive ones, and knew that most people want to rent cheaper houses rather than 5 Bed Mansions with swimming pools and cinema rooms [which I couldn't afford anyway].

Having spent ages researching [I have a bit of a habit of over-analysing according to Rob] I found one street in one area that I felt was massively undervalued compared to other streets in the same area of the same type.

I must have bought most of this street and was only spending about £3,000 on a full refurb. I was buying the properties at around £75,000, and was able to add a lot of value to them.

"The more 'minging' they were, the more money I made"

I was getting them cheap anyway because I was negotiating good discounts, and I was convinced that they were worth up to £100,000.

I wanted to get all of my money back out of the properties so that I could keep buying more on the same street without any extra cash. I put them all on the market at the same time for what I thought they were really worth. I then got a surveyor round to value them and gave him the comparables of my other houses that I had recently put on the market. I had a couple that were not valued as high as I wanted, so once I got a surveyor who valued one of my properties at the price I wanted, I got him to value all of the others. He valued them all at the price I believed they were worth.

As a result I was able to remortgage these properties almost instantly after revaluation and get all of my money back [deposit, all fees and refurb costs] and extra cash on top, because of the discount I had got and the value I had added by doing some small refurbishment work.

I kept going until I had pushed the value of the whole street so high that I could not get the properties as cheap anymore. But that was fine because I owned a load of them and they were all free!

And sure enough, as I had predicted, the market grew and the properties continued to go up. In 2 years the properties I bought had gone up over 50% pre crash in 2007/8. Even after the crash these properties still have equity. But better than that, and my main consideration, is the cashflow.

The equity is great, and I know that in time the mortgages will erode and the values will continue to rise, but I also see equity as a protection against a downturn. Rob'll tell you, I'm a bit paranoid, and always look at numbers pessimistically. We'll detail all this later.

I knew I now had a *system* that I could now replicate and scale up, both in our local area, and then in other areas in the future. All I had to do was locate the areas that were undervalued with good rents using the model, software and system I had built and tested, and buy as many as I could using the same strategy.

I've been using this model since 2004. We call it the BRR model [detailed later]. I bought over 30 properties in 2 years using this model before the crash, and refined it in 2008 to buy another 250 plus in 4 years, and counting, including large Multi-Lets, commercial and office blocks.

"I like to test, test, test, protect, replicate then aggressively scale up" – Mark Homer

We have leveraged this model too to sweat it more – since 2007 we've been helping JV partners and clients own portfolios by enlisting us to use this model for them. Rob will share with you how to build your own business from property investing later.

Since the downturn, and after an initial panic on my part [Rob says it's all about mindset, I say it's all about reality], the properties we were buying became much cheaper – £70,000 for the same house we'd pay £90,000 for, and the yields and cashflow shot up. The lending costs reduced, and as banks slowed with lending, we accessed more and more private funding sources.

I now spend a lot of my time buying commercial property [perhaps the subject of our next book], office blocks and bank buildings, and helping our lettings MD grow Progressive Lets. It's our 6th business now, and 4th that is an offshoot of buying our 1st buy to let in 2003/4.

The properties and business now bring in many millions of pounds a year, and to be honest I never would have believed it in 2007 when Rob and I partnered, starting from a little 2 bed house when Rob was over £30,000 in credit card debt.

He had these huge [what I thought were dreamy] plans of many property businesses and many millions [millions — a term I think quite frankly is overused and generic]. I didn't really believe him, but played along, as I was just looking for a few properties, some future security, and not to have a boss. I guess by default I felt property was my best chance. Oh how things can grow if you just stick at it, because we didn't really do anything ground breaking except start, keep going, constantly test, keep investing in ourselves, and just give things a go.

Rob started Property investment in 2005 having thought about it for 4 years without taking any action. Every year in those 4 years my Dad kept prodding me to buy a house in a new development down the road from his pub.

'I can't afford it Dad. And even if I could, I wouldn't have a clue what to do and how to buy a house.'

'Just give it a try, the prices keep going up, you'll make money. I'll put half the money up.'

'But I don't have any money.'

So this continued for years, and those new houses on Swan gardens went from £50,000 for the smallest ones when the plans were unveiled, up to over £150,000 in less than 10 years.

£100,000 left on the table because I said 'I can't.' Expensive word that.

Within 3 months of learning the strategy from Mark that he shared with you, I had already remortgaged my house that I [finally] bought with Dad [4 years too late, but not too late]. My house had gone up from £125,000 to £170,000 in 2 years pre 2007. The funny thing is that I had made £45,000 in 3 years doing nothing at all, from that one property. Yet as you'll read in the back of the book, I never made that amount of money in 3 years as a full time artist, working 14 hours or more a day.

I was an 'accidental investor' as are so many people who own their own house. I didn't even know that I was literally sitting on a Goldmine, and that one house would help me build an asset base worth now many millions.

Now anyone who doesn't know our world might say that it was all because of the boom years. Actually Mark and I bought our first 20 properties pre crash and they are the worst 20, and not because we didn't buy well. The crash that hurt so many people was the biggest guardian angel we could have hoped for.

But we were ready. Are you?

I didn't even buy that first property at a discount; I was really good at negotiating the full asking price ;-) And that is what I paid because I loved it and really wanted it! Maybe you can relate to that, and maybe you're smart enough to know why that was dumb! My Dad helped me raise the deposit. My diligence and market research went as far as: it's next door to Mum and Dad's pub, I want it!

When I remortgaged this house my repayments went down from £750 per month to £550 per month, and I released £26,000 cash. This was because I had not got the best rate at that time, and because I went from capital repayment to interest only. A good decision? Well there's a whole chapter coming up on it.

With that single remortgage I paid off much of my credit cards and loans [which saved me around £1500 per month] and with what was left I bought another 7 properties, with Mark, in the space of 4 months [and the amount wasn't even enough for 1 deposit].

We built a portfolio that was worth well over £1million [which keeps going up] before that year was even over. We bought another 20 in 2006, and now have bought and sold over 350 properties, with over 250 left in a portfolio with Mark and other JV partners. We have never stopped buying property together and I can't see why that would ever change.

I literally went from being over £30,000 in credit card debt to having a portfolio that could fund the rest of my life [before the crash kicked in, when things changed], all in less 9 months. I am certainly nothing 'special', I was no expert at the time, and Mark had most of the knowledge back then. The one thing I am proud of is that I was decisive. I found the strategy that worked and I took immediate action. All the mistakes were necessary, and even action through mistakes is better than inaction.

I have never looked back.

And to be honest, partnering with Mark was the best thing I could have done, and I'm really grateful to him and all he knows and does.

I had no experience or knowledge, no money, and failed attempts at setting up my own business behind me. I was able to leverage his knowledge, shortening the time it took me to catch up with him. I was able to watch, listen, and learn every day. All the money we made I put back into the business or into Mark and our Entrepreneurial education, because I wanted more and more and more of it.

Since the crash, and the building of our portfolio, I've taken a backward step on physical buying, because Mark does that, and quite frankly I found viewing properties boring. My focus now is on growing the businesses around property – which I share with you in detail in this and in the sister book "Make Cash in a Property Market Crash."

I really had no idea that you could package deals, write books, run courses and trainings, build communities and develop so many [fun] ways of adding value to the world, and bringing in many millions of pounds with more free time, and then give a load of it away.

This all just spun off buying properties well and having people spread our message and a desire to help you do the same. I now spend my time building the team at Progressive and driving the vision and values, where we run about 150 days of events per year. The Progressive brand has also grown into the personal development and business world, Lettings and public speaking with the same vision and values, and it's the most fun thing to run businesses that require no work.

Don't worry I'll share the strategies on how you can do the same in these 2 books.

Enough sizzle, where's my steak?

So that is more than enough about the two of us. Hopefully that has helped you feel excited over what you are about to learn now.. What you are about to read, if applied and continued, will absolutely guarantee your future financial success, security and happiness.

Bring it on? You want it? Well here we go…

One more thing: a huge thank you for buying our book, it really means a lot to us.

Section 2: The Fundamentals of Property

In this section, we cover the fundamental basics you need to get you going buying property. Some of this might seem quite obvious if you have some experience, which is just fine, because it is very important. It won't be a bad thing to go over it again and embed it in your subconscious now.

"To know and not to do is not to know. Just go" – Rob Moore

However there are many things that are regarded as basic or fundamental, that many investors either ignore or do not understand. Fundamentals are fundamental.

You wouldn't believe how many supposedly experienced investors have come unstuck ignoring the basics or overcomplicating things. Perhaps we'll share some of those real stories later.

More of the tricks, secrets and specific strategies to come in Section 4. You will need the knowledge in this section before moving on through. You wouldn't build a house without a foundation, would you? Remember this is your money at stake.

If all of this is new, then be excited because you are about to embark on a life-changing journey. Be excited that you're about to save yourself years of mistakes that we would have loved to avoid, and warp speed the knowledge that took us over 25,000 hours and over £600,000 to compile.

The world is a different place right now. Gone are the days when it was easy for anyone who watched the property ladder to be a property investor. The novices have been scared off. The first time buyers [FTB's] can't get finance. Vendors are in pain and motivated to sell. Public confidence is low. Spending is low. Debt is high. Inflation is high. Panic and fear are rife.

And perhaps, before you picked up this book, you got sucked into all this? You believed what you read in the Daily Mail, and despite your positive thinking you just couldn't convince yourself that 'observing the masses and doing the opposite,' was the right thing to do.

Or perhaps you believed there IS a BIG opportunity, but you're scared. What if it gets worse? What if prices go down further? How do I protect the downside risk *and* take this opportunity.

Because you do know that this could be the biggest contrarian opportunity to make cash in property, don't you? More millionaires are made in times of recession than any other time [Google it].

"Be greedy when others are fearful and fearful when others are greedy" – Warren Buffett.

That time is now. But let's not kid each other, you need courage and conviction. You need to have confidence that what you are doing will make you money, when others around you think you're just a little crazy.

But it's gotta be difficult, right? Property investing is for the professionals. It's risky, and you could make big mistakes. That's why you're reading this book, because a part of you, no matter how small, believes that you **could** get the results of the wealthy. You have something about you. You want to know more and you were destined for more. You just don't know *how* yet?

When Arnie decided he was going to be a movie star, he didn't know *how*. In fact, he was a terrible actor. His first attempt, at a live sitcom was not going to be nominated for any awards.

He didn't need to know how, because he just knew he could. If one person can, anyone can, right? He was so sure, without any evidence or talent whatsoever, that he went around telling everyone he already was an actor, when he wasn't yet.

Deluded? Perhaps. Crazy? Certainly a little bit. The rest of the story is history.

Enjoy and know that just by reading this it is all starting to happen…

Why invest?

Why not just spend your money on cars, conservatories, holidays, handbags, sex, drugs, feed eBay and online gambling addictions and be done with it? After all, you only live once and you can't take it with you, right?

And waste the rest.

Fair enough. Go and join the lottery winners who won it all, spent it all, and ended up in more debt 3 years down the line [there was one chap who lived just a few miles from us who did exactly that]. Oh, and don't forget your one in 3 squillion chance of success [or 14,000,000:1 actual figure – thanks Chris!].

What we are talking about here is financial security, independence and ultimately freedom. When you get to the stage where your expenses are covered and the risk of losing your job or not having enough income to cover expenses is gone. Then you have security plus disposable income to do some of the things you enjoy – that's independence. Then the ultimate freedom is to do what you want, when you want, with who you want.

Without investing in assets, you'll always be exchanging time for money. Without investing, your income will be directly related to your hourly worth. You'll always be tied to working, and never get a residual return on those hours you work. You'll only earn more by working more: there are only a limited number of hours in the day, and you'll be 'set' at an income level that will take years to grow out of, if ever.

And how sad is it that most people spend their whole life working to 'earn' the time and money to do the things they want to do, yet because they are so busy working they can't ever do the things they love to do.

And then they die.

And that is how our society sets us up. Work hard. Earn a living. Do it for 55 years. And then have no support, not enough money to retire, and none of your life left. Then die.

To free your time to do the things you love, you need residual income from assets, and not earned income from a job. Investing is about building an asset base steadily and properly; investing your time and money at the start so that you can reap the rewards in the future through a continual income stream.

Build assets that you can set up once and earn on forever, rather than continually exchanging your time for money that only comes if you continue to 'sell' yourself and your time. Time you can NEVER get back.

Earn residually and continually on your time, not just once. Earn recurring income that becomes [virtually] passive once set up.

People work to free up time, but working takes up time. They work more and more to try and keep up with bills and debt, and have less and less time they are trying to create by working. It's in inescapable loop that is self fulfilling. The ONLY way to break the loop is to change the habit. The ONLY way to free your time is to have income without 'spending' your time.

Financial independence: it has been said that you cannot work or save your way to financial independence, which is defined as the 'length of time that you can comfortably live without the need to work or exchange time for money.'

Statistically, more than 99% of the working population have at one point in time thought about taking the first steps to financial freedom and achieving a vehicle to self sustainability, yet so few ever achieve it. These statistics are not good.

At Progressive it is our lifelong vision to help you to financial independence, by *"investing for freedom, choice and profit."*

This is inherent in our mission and one of the big reasons for writing this book. We believe anyone can achieve financial independence; trouble is not everyone does.

Don't get us wrong, we do have personal motives for helping. We want testimonials. We want success stories. We want to grow the Progressive community further. We want to help your friends and family too. Perhaps we might JV with you in the future like we have with many of the Progressive VIP community members.

Go out there and make a success of yourself; we'd love to have a small part in that. Perhaps you might allow us to promote your story to inspire others. You can be part of our success and help us grow.

Like Nick Hague.

Nick has raised over £600,000 of JV finance, using other people's money, and has 2 property JV partners in the Progressive community. He has a portfolio of well over 20 properties and net income enough to replace his corporate job, which he did.

Now it's not just people who start with low amounts of money that have a real desire and need to become successful in property investing. Nick had a good job working for a developer, and an expensive lifestyle to maintain.

Then when the crash kicked in, he got made redundant which came as a big shock. His redundancy package was not what he had hoped and the funds were dwindling fast, so he needed to do something about it, and fast.

Nick learned the same system that we've used since 2003/4, and has total financial independence now. He is also training others, he's now a mentor in the same VIP community that helped him achieve his goals, running a deal packaging business with his partners that did over £24,000 in one month, and has his own brand, which we've no doubt he'll leverage for more passive income.

You can watch an interview with him here, just click his name at the top: **www.progressiveproperty.co.uk/inspiration**

We believe everyone has what it takes to gain financial independence. You probably know that there's enough money in the world for everyone to be a millionaire, so it begs the question which is:

'Who's got your bloody money?'

In reality, there's a simple *system* you can follow, a system we've developed over 25,000 hours in the business, and which we've learned from other experts, that can give you financial security, independence and ultimately freedom.

Investing, like everything, is a learned skill, not an inherited fantasy. Investing is the **only** route to financial and time freedom. Working never gets you there, because although you could have money you simply won't have the time to enjoy it, and your living expense will always creep up to consume all the extra money. We know plenty of poor people with expensive toys, and it doesn't make them happy.

Investing in property, in your power team and community, in your education and training, in your knowledge and experience, pays the best rate of interest and return.

A savings account is no longer enough due to low interest and high inflation. As soon as you start to live from savings they diminish, and money from earnings will only come for as long as you can work. By investing your money you are not spending it, like most of the population think, but putting it into a vehicle that will increase the monthly amount of money which will flow into your bank account.

And over time it compounds as values rise, debt reduces, cashflow increases and compounding increases the capital that churns out the income.

People become wealthy not because of their earned income, but because of their investments. Take a look in the Times Rich List, sure, not all of them have their primary income from property, but all of them have property and *every single one of them* uses property to grow their wealth.

Think of a wealthy person you know. Do they have a big house? Do they own an office? We don't know any successful person who doesn't.

Lord Sugar, our guest and partner at the 2011 Property SuperConference said this:

"While I was stupidly messing around with the FA, these young property guys were making a fortune, it was a waste of my time and talent"

Lord Sugar sees technology as the risky part of his business, and property, in which he has a JV with his son in his company Amsprop, as the secure part. He has over £300M of property as a part time property investor. Tells you something, right?

Property is a vehicle that is going to increase your income every month through cashflow and capital growth, whether you are Lord Sugar or Lord of the Manor, whether you start with £millions or you start with minus £30,000 of debt and no knowledge.

You can do it too.

Knowing that you do have a *choice*, what choice is it for you now?

And what if you were to lose your job? As soon as you lose your ability to work [through burn out, illness, injury, loss of motivation, family commitments, lack of desire, laziness] you no longer have income. You are only as wealthy as your last month's pay cheque.

According to the moneysavingexpert site, the average person in the UK has £15,960 savings and according to UK debt statistics an average debt of £29,634. Figures do vary slightly from source to source, but a consistent theme is that the average person has almost twice as much *bad* debt as savings.

It is also consistent that most people have just a few months of no work before they are penniless. In fact the average person under the age of 34 only has around 2 months of savings before they totally run out of money.

These are seriously worrying statistics, and if you fit into these, you must do something now.

Another thing that really hit us was the relationship between money and stress. We looked at all the people we knew: our parents, friends, mentors, business associates and so on. We realised that those who were stressed were the ones who were working longer hours, and much 'harder' for their money.

In fact the richest people we know [some billionaires] work less than people we know who don't ever get to six figures. We're talking a few calls, emails and the odd board meeting per month. And lots of holidays.

And the more these poorer persons work for their money, the more stressed they become. The more they worry about money, the more this leaks into other areas of their life, including relationships with their loved ones.

What if you could earn money without working so hard? What if you could earn money without doing something you hate over and over and over, and without most of the stress? You can imagine what people who read the tabloids thought about that. Of course, stubborn as we are, we ignored them. We shall deal with 'pub talk' later.

Our lives have changed dramatically since investing in property, business, and our personal education. We owe it a lot, and succeeded in spite of our flaws, because property is so leveraged and forgiving. We have grown to have a burning passion for property investment, not just because it is a great business, but because it enables you to do all the other things you love to do, were born to do, and will leave a legacy from.

Your first aim should be to have an income stream equivalent to your minimum monthly outgoings. This is because if you lose your job you will know for certain that all your debts/liabilities will be paid for. This is financial security.

Enough income to live a comfortable lifestyle and do the things you would like to do without the stress of earning is known as financial independence.

Enough income flowing to do anything and everything you want is known as financial opulence.

You can have either of these, and they can take less income than you think, depending on your needs.

So write down **now** on a piece of paper what your total outgoings are. Include everything and don't kid yourself. One of Mark's top tips is that it is better to kid yourself by overestimating expenses and underestimating profits, than the other way around.

Do it now.

Once you have this figure, your goal should be to become financially secure by matching this level with income from assets, without increasing your costs of living.

Once you achieve this, your next goal should be financial independence, which usually means having an income stream that will be equivalent to [roughly] twice your total outgoings.

You will be able to stop work, do something you love and know all your monthly bills will be paid for. You will have enough income to do the things you want to do, and re-invest some to compound the effects. You'll be surprised how quickly it compounds into financial opulence.

Take for example; your monthly outgoings are £1500 per month. Your target would be to first to replace this figure by creating a rental income in excess of this after ALL costs, then keep going until you double it.

To replace this figure and to be secure, you would need 7-8 rental properties churning out £200 net each or 2-4 Multi-Lets. To become financially independent you would need 15-20 single lets, or 6-8 Multi-Lets. This is very real and possible, even if you start off with just a few hours a week of time input, and you don't start with any capital.

Just like Alan & Alison Graham.

When they started back in 2008, they could only spare around 5 hours per week each. Alison, a GP and Alan a head teacher PhD. Both busy. Three children to look after. Both had good reasons not to get into another vocation. Both already successful.

Mark ran a mentorship for them back in 2008 when he used to do them, and they got themselves educated, as well as getting out there and taking action. They viewed many properties and forged great relationships with Estate Agents locally.

In their first year, starting on a combined 10 hours per week, they built a portfolio worth over £1 million. At the end of that first year they both went down to part time, and set up the Buy to Let Doctors, to help other doctors build property portfolios. They hired Estate Agents to work for them and never looked back.

It was great to see their development starting so fast with just a few [focused] hours per week. You can see their story on the Progressive Property YouTube channel. **www.Youtube.com/progressiveproperty**

Of all the investment vehicles we have looked at [and we have looked at many] property is the best, in our opinion, from the following viewpoints:

The leverage that you can attain through property is like no other investment vehicle available. We explain leverage in more detail later on. You can leverage your money a minimum of 3-4 times over with just a standard 70% mortgage, and that is without factoring in any growth on your portfolio. That leverage can become infinite when you build your knowledge and experience and learn how to invest with other people's money.

Stocks and shares do not enable the average investor to leverage their money; nor do savings accounts. You earn only on your money invested, not the bank's money [all explained later].

With inflation currently somewhere near 3.7% [the RPI is over 5% at the time of writing, and real inflation without Governmental PR is believed to be much higher] the value of your money is going down at more than 3% per year.

The cost of food, petrol, many commodities, and general living, are on the rise at a far greater rate than 3%!

A half-loaf of sliced white bread from Tesco has gone up from **60p** to **93p** in a very short period of time. Prices of electricity, gas and other fuels have risen at an annual rate of **20.9pc**, the fastest pace since February 2009.

Households only saved just **6.4%** of their disposable income in the first three months of the year, down **0.5%** from the previous quarter. The continued rising cost of goods and services means that the UK's 26 million households would collectively need to spend an extra *£33 billion* just to enjoy the same standard of living as 12 months ago!

Immediately cash is worth much less every year, so at least 3% of your 0.5% interest has just been eaten. Damn it! You end up being poorer every year.

Currently the cost of living is going up at a greater rate than salary rises, so more money is lost to the expense of general living. Many people's salaries have actually taken a hit in the years since the crash, to compound the relative loss. Annoying.

Then there is tax. Oh tax. Bloody tax. The Government charge you tax on interest gained at your tax rate of up to 50%, so that eats another 1-2%, leaving you with less money than you had last year.

So if anyone tries to tell you that leaving your money in the bank will make you a nice tasty sum each year, then I'm afraid that they are wrong [or on narcotics]. They certainly don't have any. Leave your cash under your mattress and you are losing around 5% per year at the moment [and going insane with paranoia].

That's inflation. Interestingly, as inflation goes up, and the value of money goes down, the values of property continue to rise. Surely then it makes sense to leave the majority of your money there in your portfolio?

But won't the Government look after me? Won't my pension see me right into my old age?

Yeah right. Let's get real. Things are not as they used to be. Get a good job. Work hard for 55 years, pay into your pension. Retire and your company will pay you for your service until you die.

No fluff alert: *no-one is going to look after your future but you.*

We don't need to talk too much about pensions in this book as we all seem to agree that pension stability and security are relics of the past, getting dusty in Museums. Gone is the industrial age. You can't get your money out of pensions like you can property. You can't re-invest it. You can't control it. You can't gear it and you can't leverage it.

So forget it.

A pension stops when you die. The income stops. Whereas you can leave property to your next of kin who will benefit from the tenants paying rent, and the increasing capital growth, for decades and generations to come.

Two very close family members put faith into their IFA to invest their money securely, as they approached retirement age. They didn't want high risk, in fact their specific requirement was low to low-medium risk, and this is what happened:

Their investment via their IFA was placed into what was meant to be, as requested, a low risk product. The details of the product didn't say who it was backed by, and the IFA didn't tell them. The investment, £105,000, was over 50% of their total investment pot, and was recommended as a low/medium risk investment. This was important to them coming into retirement.

The first they even knew who Lehman Bros were was when they received a letter to say they'd lost the £105,000 that 'they had invested.' They've been fighting now for 4 years with the ombudsman that they were mis-sold the product by their IFA, and as of yet have not had a penny back.

You earn an income right away from a property. With a pension you will have to buy an annuity and the first payment will be made some time in the next 40 years [if you are alive to benefit from this].

Property is a tangible asset and history proves property values double every 10 years. This takes into account all previous crashes, recessions and downturns. You don't need to put your financial future in the hands of a biased fund manager or IFA who get commissions.

You can leverage using O.ther P.eople's M.oney [OPM] to invest in property. You cannot borrow in the same way to buy a pension fund. The yields are generally lower from a pension pot and you are in total control of the properties that you buy.

Do we really need to go on..?

The government increase taxes year on year to repay their national debt. Many of our greatest assets have been sold off [British Gas, BA, BT, Jaguar, Aston Martin] and the last point of financial return for our government is the tax-paying public.

That's you my friend. And your family.

When you actually work it out, some people [mostly employees] pay upwards of 70% of their money in taxes, it's staggering. Tax on what you earn, on what you buy, on what you sell, on services you provide and receive. On what you eat and drink. You pay tax on places you go and methods in which you travel.

Think of a car: we pay tax on our income to raise the money for it. We pay tax to the bank for saving it. We pay tax to buy it. We pay tax to insure it. We pay tax to tax it. We pay tax to put fuel in it. We pay tax to fix it. The bigger the car we get the more tax we pay. We pay tax to drive it to some cities. We pay tax when we drive it too fast. We pay tax to park it. We pay tax to park it 5 minutes longer than we said we would park it.

You get the picture. End of rant.

Summary

The only way to achieve financial independence is to invest. The government won't look after you. Savings aren't enough. Stashing cash under the mattress will make you paranoid. Pensions are dying. You control your future; no one else will. Assets produce recurring income to free your time to do the things you love.

The Law of compounding

Money attracts Money.

It is said that like attracts like, and money is no different. Einstein called the Law of compounding the 8th wonder of the world. He believed it was a Law, and that is what we would like to discuss here, if that's OK with you.

A great analogy is one of a bet on a golf course: betting £1 per hole and doubling your bet on each hole seems like a fairly innocuous challenge. However that £1 bet compounded over each hole turns into £256 in 9 holes.

Quite a compounded effect isn't it? Well that's nothing. After hole 15 that amount has compounded to £16,384. Look at how much more money is being attracted now, in a shorter time, because of the compounded effect. Once you get to hole 18 the compounded total is £131,072.

Property assets work the same way. Cashflow and income work the same way too. Your time input into this business rewards you the same way.

It is just this straightforward: the more time or money you invest, the greater the return you will get. And the beauty of it is that it all started from £1, but it was not spent; the returns were re-invested [and compounded].

A water lily also obeys this rule, it seems. Each day it covers double the water surface it covered the day before. The first few days it covers very little, and the results are not obvious. But after 30 days it has covered an entire pond, regardless of size.

The law of compounding states that the maximum benefit comes the longer you are doing it, so remember this:

"You have to work hard enough not to have to work hard" – Richard Templar.

There's a great book on this called the 'Tipping point' by Malcolm Gladwell. Read it. And you know what the sad thing is? Most people stop just short of the time when compounding kicks in and starts to pay them back.

Even more relevant for you when thinking about property and the money you invest is, 'The Rule of 72.' This law, or formula, demonstrates the Law of compounding very well. We use it here for purposes of illustration and to show the impact of the Law of compounding, and of course you could use this in many of your future investments.

To estimate the amount of time required to double an original investment, divide the most convenient "rule-quantity" [72] by the expected growth rate, expressed as a percentage.

For instance, if you were to invest £1000 with compounding interest at a rate of 9% per annum, the rule of 72 gives 72/9 = 8 years required for the investment to be worth £2000; an exact calculation gives 8.0432 years.

We like playing with this. If we add some relevant property figures to this equation it starts to get very interesting:

You buy a £100,000 Property for £75,000. This is something that you can easily do in today's market compared to the pre-crash era, using the principles in this book.

We know that property grows at an average of around 10% per year [source: Nationwide house price statistics]. You can put in some figures based on your expectation of growth or your attitude to risk.

It would probably cost you about £3,000 to £5,000 in cash; explained later. We can use the rule of 72 and put our figures in like this:

5% growth: 72/5 = 14.4 years to turn £5,000 into £10,000
8% growth: 72/8 = 9 years to turn £5,000 into £10,000
11.74% growth = 72/11.74 = 6 years 48 days to turn £5,000 into £10,000

Once you start adding leverage to this, borrowing against a bank or a private investor, or Joint Venturing with OPM, you'll very quickly indeed see just how powerful this can become. More about that later.

It doesn't matter where you are in your current position. If you have very little money [or quite a lot of debt] you can still apply this Law. Everyone starts somewhere, whether £1 or 1 Lily. You just obey the Laws and keep going, and it happens.

As we shall discuss frequently as we go, always be looking at how you can leverage what you have and compound it to make very large sums of money. If you have equity in your home, or know someone who does, then you should be particularly excited to get investing as you read on now.

Don't we always hear people pointing out how the rich get richer and the poor get poorer? Well this is generally the case as they are attracting more of what they already have; be that wealth and abundance or bills and more bills a 'lack' mentality. And they understand the principles that we have just shown you in this section.

In fact, the rich have a problem with too much money: they can't reinvest it fast enough, and because they reinvest it, more money comes in. Yes, the rich do get richer.

We want to help you to think mid to long term. This will be mentioned many times in the book. When you plant a seed you can't come back the next day and say "where's my frickin' tree?!"

You have to water it, give it sunlight and rich nutrients in the soil. You have to look after it and be patient with it. When you are, it will bear fruit for you, year after year after year.

The 'Law' of compounding works just this way. And remember, it works just as powerfully and dangerously in reverse with debt. Treat it with total respect and you can grow your property portfolio to look after you and your family for generations to come, without you having to work again and again and again. And die.

Summary

Money attracts money. Invest and re-invest and watch your money multiply like Gremlins [just add water]. By holding on to your properties for the long term, you can reap the effects of compounded capital growth and rental income, and even inflation erosion. Understand and apply the Law of compounding and build a solid foundation that you can live from for the rest of your life.

Why property & not the lottery?

Now we are starting to talk about property and the benefits over saving and other investment vehicles. Very nice indeed; we love talking about property.

You know, so many people tell us that they have been thinking about investing in property for years and years, but have never done anything about it [for whatever reason]. Here are just a few we've heard first hand:

'I haven't got any money. If [when] I had more money I could invest.'

'Other people don't want me to. My Mum/Dad/mates think I'm insane to even think about it.'

'I don't have the time. I'm just too busy.'

Time poverty is an excuse. Time is the one thing we all have that is equal, so why are some people billionaires working 3 hours a day [Warren Buffett] and others working 15 hours a day for £5 per hour? We all have the same 24 hours in a day, right?

'Money will change me and people won't like me.'

'I'm not educated enough. I don't know how to do it?'

'What if I lose money?'
'The market is going to crash. I have been saying it for the last 10 years, d'ya know wha' I mean?'

Well only one is actually right ;-)

So what makes property so good that we keep on shouting about it? And what do we know about other vehicles of investment to compare it to? Here are all the reasons nicely broken down for you:

The basics: first and foremost property [shelter] is a basic human requirement. It is just below the need for air and food, and on a par with the need to interact with other human beings. It is way above the need for money, cars, designer clothes, handbags and matching shoes, the latest golf clubs, cosmetic skincare products, botox and body part augmentation.

As long as we're alive we'll need housing. We will always need shelter from the cold and the rain and the snow and the wind.

So what? What does that mean in investment terms for you? It means consistent and perpetual demand. Demand drives the economy. Add to that the fact that we are an island here in the UK, and the population is growing year on year; what do you think is going to happen to that demand? You guessed it. We'll talk about demand later.

Touch it, feel it: property is tangible. It is real. You can see it, touch it, visit it, walk through it, and as a result control it much more than many other investments.

With shares in companies you do not have that added security. Look at the dotcom crash and the fall of the Nasdaq. Look at Marconi and Lehman Bros. Many of those so called multi-billion dollar companies were so intangible that their true values were highly volatile, questionable and easily hidden. Many of them were ultimately proven to be speculative and worth very little.

The control freak in you and me: anything you can see and you're close to, you have a certain amount of control over. If your dog is on a lead you can guide her, pull her away from the kids that walk by, and scoop up the mess she leaves behind. No analogies intended. Other dogs can even follow her trail and sniff exactly the path she has been down.

OK, let's leave the analogies alone.

Take a speculative company based in someone's bedroom in Taiwan; how can you control that? How can you feel comfortable about your money being in companies you will never ever see?

The answer is that you can't. As will become very apparent, anything that can't be reasonably controlled will not provide you with the kind of investment you want [if you are looking for mid to long term financial independence and security that is]. Even if you buy them well.

Property vs. shares: pound for pound, stocks and property perform quite closely, unleveraged, though the last ten years has seen no growth in the stock market. Some will tell you that property will outperform shares every time and others will tell you vice versa.

In our experience it is far easier to utilise *leverage* in property. We've met many people who have told us that you can make 6% per month on shares by renting them out; all you have to do is turn your computer on once a month!

Funnily enough they sell these educational packs that take 2 people to carry them at big seminars and charge thousands of pounds for them. They would tell you that now, wouldn't they?

Out of all the people that we've met who have bought these, or been exposed to them, we have never actually met anybody who has made them work or given us evidence. Even many of these 'Gurus' don't seem to be doing it themselves

You cannot go to a bank and ask for a loan for £100,000 to go and put on the stock market, on trap 6, or all on black. Interesting, isn't it, that banks for decades have queued up to loan the average Joe or Jo money against a house, but no one will touch anyone who is not Warren Buffet [with a bargepole] to lend money to invest in shares.

How about some figures? With property, a non expert has the ability to borrow, gear and use other people's money [OPM]. Low barriers to entry like this mean anyone can get started without 7 year degrees. Take the example of £25,000 [savings, equity, pension release etc]. You can either buy £25k worth of shares or use that lump sum to buy a property worth £100k, through a 75% BTL mortgage [depending on loan to values at the time], with your £25K making up the deposit [let's not get into loan to values of buying costs yet, we'll do that later].

Let's forget the fact that the stock market hasn't grown for a decade, and assume it doubles in 5 years. Your shares would give a rough compound rate of 12% per year − £25K to £50K in 5 years with a big back wind and lots of luck going your way.

Put that same £25k put into property in the same time frame at the same 12% per year, and the value of the £100k property will have doubled to £200k. Plus all the net cashflow for 60 months!

Of course neither asset class gets that growth every year, which for property brings huge advantages we'll discuss later in the book.

To the average, even novice, investor property offers the best solutions. I know that there are people who really are experts in the stock market who are making cash and using other people's money to make that cash. But these guys have been doing it for 30 years. They are real and proven experts and not ordinary people starting out.

History: history tells us that property is one of the most sound and powerful investment vehicles available.

Since records began on house prices through Nationwide in the 1950's, property has performed remarkably well, doubling in value every 7-10 years as an average. This is with the current correction included.

In fact, you can track land prices all the way back to 1086. William the Conqueror commissioned a survey to work out which land was being used in England [and by whom], for taxation purposes. This survey provides a great point to compare modern day property values and the land and property price growth that has taken place. It is estimated that since the survey property values have increased at over 10% per annum. This represents around 1,000 years of data, and if history is seen as a good long term predictor of the future, then this has to provide some clue as to what should happen moving forward.

Using history and fact as an effective gauge, it tells us that property is, has been, and therefore is likely to continue to be, a superb investment.

You wouldn't believe how excited Mark gets over 1,000 years of data! His spreadsheets would set on fire. Mark even once had a spreadsheet for all the attributes his ideal woman should have. Mr. Paranoid and his spreadsheets are best of friends.

Anyway, history is not a guarantee of what is to come, but it is possibly the best indicator of what is likely to happen over a long period of time. This is what we, as investors, need to know.

According to The Halifax plc: UK Property prices have risen in 36 out of the past 44 years, seeing an average annual increase of 10.3%. **Demand for property is currently high:** 'demand for housing is increasing over time, driven primarily by demographic trends and rising incomes,' according to the Barker report. With the typical family unit breaking up much more frequently; larger families, higher divorce rates, a huge influx of migrants – demand is outweighing supply at around 120,000 homes per year.

In fact in 2012, 250,000 houses was the target to keep up with current homes and around 100,000 new houses were built.

This lack of supply pushes prices up as competition gets greater, in prices and rents.

Market movements: in the UK we have a far greater chance of property investing success than the vast majority of the rest of the world. We experience strong property ownership rights and in general our property market is very strong. In Europe and in many other parts of the world this is not the case, where properties don't really go up and people rent for life.

In Australia properties are negatively geared for apparent tax benefits. In the US where the crash has hit really hard there is so much land, that demand is lower. In the UK long term demand is based on an acute shortage of properties [homes].

Opportunity is massive but most people will miss it all and wonder what on earth happened. The secret to buying property at 25-50% below market value is still unknown by the majority. The details of cashing in during a crash are in the sister edition of this book. You can find it on Amazon or the Progressive website.

Affordability in the market: "aren't properties just too expensive for first time buyers at the moment?"

Well yes, house prices went up significantly until 2007 and many FTB'ers were priced out. This is great news for those of us who are buying, because there is less competition.

Then if things weren't bad enough for FTB'ers, post crash has gotten even worse for them, because the banks have stopped lending them money, and they can't get on the ladder.

Post crash rents have rocketed too, increasing yields and cashflow for investors – the FTB'ers have no choice but to rent, which creates an increase in demand and decrease in rental supply. They have to pay more because of a scarcity of houses for rent.

In fact in one of our prime investing areas there are over 15,000 people on the waiting list for a council house.

This is great news for [Contrarian] investors.

As a side note: between 2004 and the back end of 2007 we personally experienced very strong growth in our own portfolio. Obviously good, right? However, what miffed us was that our rents across the board had not gone up a penny in that time.

There's always a lag between the increase in property values and the rise in rents. Between November 2007 and March 2008 our average rents shot up by 20%! They've steadied since then up around 25%. Add to that the reduction in interest rates and lower cost of finance and buying prices, and the significant increase in cashflow.

The market has to adapt to this. As much as people [and the press] might scaremonger, it is highly unlikely that, all of a sudden, all first time buyers will be out on the streets. There is evidence to suggest that people are living in smaller [and smaller] properties in this country, as the availability of property decreases and prices rise. This has forced the market to adapt to provide ways in which first time buyers can afford to get on the ladder, such as shared ownership, Lease Options, 2 + 2, Instalment contracts and renting by the room [which creates great opportunities for investors to get even more cashflow] to reduce living costs.

The average size of homes in London and Tokyo are extremely small compared to the rest of the world, but this wasn't always the case. They have had to adapt over time for the same reasons.

For an example of market adaptation, look at the change in residential developments: we have smaller plots, where gardens and plan footprints are compensated by additional storeys. Many houses are now 'town houses' with 3 floors as opposed to 2.

As demand for land and property [price per square foot] has increased, there has been a shift to living in smaller properties. This has allowed prices to continue rising whilst not pricing people out of the market. People who have already bought have benefited from these increased property values.

What if you had built a portfolio of your own 10 years ago, or bought double the amount that you have now?

And remember, we live on a very small island. Land will always be at a premium, especially when compared to countries like the US. This should keep driving the price of property upwards, taking into account corrections every 15 years or so [that you'll want to be ready and waiting for], enabling investors like us to continue to gain long term returns.

Demand outweighing supply: the shortage of homes which we now face here in the UK [great news for rental demand] has been brought about by a number of factors:

Migration into the UK has affected demand, along with an increase in people living alone. This creates a smaller average household size, as do divorce and larger family units that split.

The rate of house building in the UK is not keeping pace with demand. In 2005 193,000 new homes were built. Although this was the highest for 15 years, it is still only 3/4 of the number that the Government's independent report estimated would be required each year to bring house price inflation down to 1%.

The current shortfall is around 120,000 new homes per year according to the 2003 Barker Report. By 2021 The Halifax predicts that the shortfall will have reached 400,000 per year.

The Government made house building one of their centrepieces, promising three million new homes by 2020 [240,000 a year until 2016]. Building has fallen short of this; in 2009 only 123,000 were built making it the lowest for 87 years and in 2011 less than 100,000 out of a necessary 250,000 were built.

To reiterate: the demand for Property is *far* outweighing supply, keeping prices high in growing markets, and reducing severe drops in corrections. In fact many areas of London are still rising through the recessions! All very positive, real evidence for future investment in property *for the long term.*

Growth in Buy to Let in the UK: the UK rental market has grown significantly since the introduction of Assured Shorthold Tenancies [AST] and Buy to Let mortgages in 1996. Between 1995 and 2003 the number of people needing to rent doubled from 46,000 to over 93,000, according to the Barker report.

This means more tenants for investors like you. This trend has continued, with demand for **the right types of rental properties** in the **correct areas** remaining strong. We give you the model for this later.

Another effect of continuing Buy to Let growth has been the increased difficulties first time buyers face when buying property. This has fuelled rental demand even more as more of the population need to rent for longer periods before being able to buy.

Increased levels of personal spending, borrowing on credit at payday loan rates and instant gratification has led to people saving less, and so they don't have the deposit monies available to gain a mortgage.

Mortgages are now being offered over longer periods as a natural response to reduced affordability. The old maxim of a 25 year mortgage is now being stretched with more than a quarter of lenders offering terms for up to 40 years. Split mortgages can also be obtained where up to 5 people can share the ownership of a single property.

Despite this, mortgages are not as easy to come by any more, so the market adapts again. Now you have private investors, professional money lenders, bridgers, Angels and V.C's replacing the gap in the market that the banks used to own.

Many of these offer competitive rates, faster access to funds, easier applications, more personal touches and more flexibility on terms. Just like it was in the good old days.

Back in 2008, when everything changed in the world as I [Mark] was looking for guidance, I had a frank, somewhat penis-envy style conversation with one of my [GBP100M+] mentors – happens to be a JV partner too:

'Mark, back in my day, if you wanted folding [his term for funds] you asked your bank manager.

If you have a good relationship with him, he gives you fowwwlding, and you go and play. If not, you go hungry.'

Because it was 2008, I [naively] asked the same question everyone does now:

'But the banks aren't lending now'

Imagine you're seated with us, and you know I've just told my girlfriend that the dress she's just bought looks a little tight on her – this was his reaction [deep breath]:

'Mark, haven't you listened to anything I've been showing you? The world of 'computer says noooooooooooooooooo' applications processed by Katherine Tait & David Walliams is dead. It's owwver.

Finance is going back to the good ol' days, like it was in the 60's, or as far back as the Wild West. You want fowlding? You build relationships with real people, not faceless banks. That world is now the past.'

At the time, because the crash was so raw, I didn't fully get what he meant. Four years later and the picture is so clear.

When things become great for the FTB'er, they'll be harder for you, the investor. From 2001 to 2007, when Property Ladder was popular, you had every amateur, owner occupier [OO] and FTB'er 'Buying to Let,' or 'Tarting and Turning.'

When the man in the pub is telling you to get into property, you know it's not the best time. Sit on your hands! You'll get outbid by naive competition and over-emotional house buyers. There'll be too many of them flocking to properties that no one is looking at now.

Enjoy this time while it lasts, because it won't last forever. You best fill your boots while you can my friend.

Rental increases: on average, rents in the UK have doubled every 9 to 12 years through history, and we have one of the most competitive Buy to Let mortgage markets in the world, regardless of what part of the market cycle we are in.

Interest rates are relatively low anyway, and with the crash they've fallen off a cliff. According to many predictions, swap rates, Libor rates and so on, interest will stay low for many years to come.

All great evidence and positive news for property investment, don't you think? Provided you can 'observe the masses, and do the opposite.'

More importantly, we think, is that property gives you freedom and choice. Just as we explained the benefits of investing over spending and saving, property is the vehicle that will allow you to live the life that you choose. Because your properties will be growing year on year over time without you having to work on them, as will the income and the rents, and as inflation erodes your debt, you are free to do as you please, with all the money you need and more.

Summary

Property is tangible and real. You can see and control it. It is secure and much less volatile compared to other investments. Rents are rising, interest rates are low, private investors are financing the market, supply is low, demand is high, prices are low, yields and cashflow are high. History and demand all point to a great future for property investment.

Leverage

Leverage is an art form in a scientific guise.

Put simply, it is achieving more, with less. More money with less money. More time with less [of your personal] time. More results with less [of your personal] effort.

To many this concept is just not believable. They've been brainwashed to believe that 'working harder' means you'll earn more money. But everyone experiences leverage in acceleration or reverse.

You see you're either utilising leverage in your favour, earning on OPM [bank, JV partner], getting results on *time invested* and OPT [other people's time], and these leverage points are helping you to your vision.

Or this is happening to you, in reverse, and you working for someone else's vision, being leveraged by them, getting paid an hourly wage for time you've given up and will never get back.

If you work for someone else and you're not happy, or you work for money and that money stops when the work stops, and no one works for you, then you are being controlled by others' leverage. They are earning from you, you're bottom of the food chain, and earning the least while probably working the hardest.

You probably have the least control too, and possibly you're the unhappiest.

Now this is not to say that working for someone else is wrong. We all need eachother, and we are all interdependent. The banks need us and we need them. The cleaner needs the boss and the boss needs the cleaner. And if you're happy at the hand to mouth end of leverage, then you are happy, and who are we to judge?

You're probably just reading this book for fun and you'll go back to living a happy working life.

But perhaps that is not you, and perhaps you want more, but you don't want to kill yourself doing it, or make huge sacrifices over the things you love and the people you love.

If you can master the Art of leverage then you will be wealthy beyond all of your expectations, plans, goals [and quite possibly dreams]. You will earn on your portfolio almost infinitely more than you would using your own money.

This is what millionaires and billionaires know and do. And you can learn the same strategies and systems they know, and have learned.

Leverage is becoming more and more important in our society. First there was the wheel, the donkey, the camel, the horse and the Elephant. We're not great on history, so we can't tell you which one came first. Did prehistoric man use the mammoth to get from his Ice house to the local Ice Bar? You get the picture; we used animals to make a journey quicker and easier.

Then there was the wheel 3000 odd years B.C. Then the bicycle, then the train, then the car, then the plane, then the shuttle. Who knows what will come next, but whatever it is will make journeys even faster and easier.

In the modern day we have the internet; a huge vehicle for leveraging time. You can outsource any task for pounds and pence on sites like elance. You can employ a VA [virtual assistant] who you can pay by the hour or even by the minute, to do tasks for you to free your time to focus more on Income generating activities [IGA's]. 5 hours a week leveraging non IGA's that might cost you £40 can be spent viewing and offering on properties that might bring you in £30,000.

Leverage really is easier and more accessible to the everyday person. The main things holding people back are lack of knowledge, lack of belief, overwhelm and information overload and fear.

It can be a hard shift; many people take real ownership of things that they have built, they have identity and importance from being the boss and getting stuck in, they can get precious about handing tasks over to other people because no one can do their job as well as they, they think they can't afford to pay people to do things, or that they can 'save money' by doing it themselves.

Of course we're not saying that's you ;-) But perhaps you can relate to this?

When I [Rob] first got into property, I thought viewing properties, buying them and dealing with mortgage brokers, and refurb-ing and renting out and managing tenants was going to be my daily grind.

Property can be a job like any other, with crappy stuff to deal with and people who don't value you, if you let it. I decided early that I didn't want to have my property business like this, and looked at ways I could get other people to view, offer, buy, rent, refurbish, manage and maintain my properties, whilst still making most of the income. More later on *how*.

Leverage is the non-get-rich-quick, get-rich-quicker strategy for property investors. Property investors' success is down to how much or how little they leverage, and this section will help you start with your outcome clear in your mind, and give you the shortest possible route to financial independence, or even financial opulence.

You see, when we first started in property, we did everything ourselves. We probably didn't do too badly, because we kept costs really tight, we protected the downside and we reduced risks. But looking back, we could have achieved more, faster and smarter, without increasing risk too much, if we got out of our own way and farmed out most of the boring and difficult jobs to others far better than us, at a much lower rate of pay than for us doing it ourselves.

This is shown in how fast the Progressive community members and VIP's get results – the proactive ones do so well so quickly if they pick up on leverage early, and fast. Many of them are now full time property investors and many are even now training others and respected experts in the industry.

If you'd have been with us in December 2006, you'd have seen us sourcing our properties, arranging and doing the viewings, finding the tenants [to save the money on fees – poor leverage], checking the properties, even doing the maintenance and ongoing management.

We were also doing all our websites ourselves, our own admin, management accounts, post, going to networking events, you name it, we did it, ourselves, the hard way. Sweat beats regret – we said.

After a year or so the time we were spending doing everything was actually holding our business back, costing it money, and repelling huge amounts of money we didn't know we were losing, because we couldn't see it. We were in so deep, there was no view outside.

The business couldn't grow because we only had so many hours in a day. As we got so busy our time was taken away from IGA's, and we started making mistakes through fatigue and lack of focus. We kept getting in our own way.

And besides, the whole point of working for ourselves was so we could free up some time to do the things we really loved, right? But we were too busy working to be able to do these things, and the dream of property financial independence was starting to slip.

We thought it was how every business was. Work hard or go home. We didn't realise that it was our behaviour.

We needed to create our business so it would work independently of ourselves, if it was to grow, and be congruent with our lifestyle. We needed to continually increase our IGA value by ensuring we were totally strict with what we did, and what we leveraged. Anything that brings in less that our IGA [you'll work out yours in a minute], must be outsourced, or you go backwards and become poorer.

Fast forward to now, and property for us, and for Progressive, is a leveraged business. Katherine, the Progressive GM, manages the business, and the team of 35 at Progressive House. Wayne, ProgressiveLets manager, manages 230 tenants who rent our properties. Personal assistants and team members in every department take on the roles in the business we tried [and failed] to juggle in the early days.

Refurbs are managed by Caroline, buying by Mark P using our Deal Scrutiniser™ software, accounts by Sue, Sue and Anita, events by Gemma, Hollie, Gary and Trina, some of Rob's email accounts by Sharon [his Mum], though you can still get me personally on: **rob.moore@progressiveproperty.co.uk**

The list goes on, but we certainly don't say this to blow our own Trumpets. When we started we did everything, and it cost us a lot of money. I'd say we'd be twice the size if we started again, read this section, and stuck to the rules and models we're about to share with you.

But before we do, this is just as important in your private life too. If you iron your clothes, that's time away from making money. If you cut the grass or clean the house, that's time away from IGA's. If you drive to an event rather than have a driver or get the train, that's dead time you can't leverage or earn from.

I [Rob], once read a book that said that millionaires cut their own lawn. I feel that this is a bit out of date now. If a millionaire can do a property deal in a few hours, time spent on non IGA's actually blocks out and repels the IGA's. You save £30 mowing the lawn but leave £30K on the table by not doing a deal.

That's the 'secret' most of the world doesn't understand.

And if you saw either of us iron a shirt, you'd see us lose 7 months off our life, 17 minutes wasted and burn marks in perfectly acceptable stripy Duchamp shirts. Yet pop down to Peter's cleaners and you get 3 shirts pressed for £5. That's cleaned and ironed! That's 51 minutes saved, 7 months of your life back and £5 *invested.* In 51 minutes we could probably make 4 or 5 figures doing some kind of property or business deal from that £5 invested if the time was used wisely.

Plus we add to the flow of the economy in our area and support local businesses too, giving many 100's people jobs and houses and contracts, which we believe will in turn come back to us.

But you might think it's OK for us, we're in the position to do that, but you don't have the resources for that. Yes, and that's exactly why we're spending a good amount of time telling you this, because the longer you leave leverage out of your life, the longer people leverage you. The longer you stay poor.

Yes Rob & Mark, but how do you actually do it?

Well here's how:

Calculating your IGA: the first stage is to calculate your Income Generating Value [IGV]. When you know exactly what an hour of your time is worth, you can calculate accurately what tasks you should do yourself, and what tasks you should leverage out, pay for, or inspire others to do for you.

Taking a step back though, the following exercise is important. This is a book of action, not just a book of hypothese, so are you prepared to take some action?

"When all is said and done, more is said than done"

Good, then let's begin:

For the next 2 weeks create a simple work log of how you are spending your work time [career of property]. Have a word doc open or a sheet of paper or notes folder on your smart phone. Every hour that you work in a day, note briefly what you did. Be honest with yourself, and at the end of the day put the letters IGA next to the parts that were income generating.

At the end of the 2 weeks, work out what percentage of your time is spent on IGA's. If you're anything like us, you'll probably be shocked at how just a few hours bring in most of the money and results, and a huge amount of time is virtually wasted, with little or no financial benefit.

Back to your worklog in a minute.

Now, to calculate your IGV, total the amount of hours you spend working every week. That includes your job/career, any part time work, and any time you're putting into property or asset building – the entire amount of time attributed to earning money. You might have something like 55 hours.

Now calculate, or roughly guess, how much money you earn in that timeframe. If you find it easier, calculate the same figures: hours worked and income generated, in a month, it doesn't matter as long as there is consistency. You may have £850 in a week. Make sure that all income that is not a loan is added, any asset or passive income should be included.

Now divide the amount of income by the amount of hours, and you have your IGV – your time value per hour. Every hour you work brings in, on average, £x.

Now you have to be strict with yourself, and have faith in this algorithm. OK, it's not that fancy, but still you should be disciplined: any task that comes your way that you feel will or could earn you more than your IGV, then do it yourself, because it will pay you to do it. If you keep doing that, your IGV will go up and up and up.

But even more importantly, every task that comes your way that will or could bring in less than your IGV, you **must** leverage or outsource it. Either blag a favour, do a reciprocal deal, or pay for the task to be done. If you don't, you'll get poorer and you'll actually repel more money that you pull in. We promise you this – stick to this and it will change your life forever.

"What you earn has nothing to do with what you're doing, and everything to do with what you're not doing" – Rob Moore

And to monitor your time, to check that you are using it well, do your worklog for a couple of weeks to make this time restructuring a habit. It's a habit of successful people, you can make it a habit too.

The greatest business people in the world understand this concept, because they have had to learn it through experience. If you ever want to grow, or upscale to the next level, whether in business or investing, you need the help of people; their money, time, resources, systems and contacts.

Many of the greatest investors never actually use any of their own money, but invest millions. Many of the biggest business owners don't work day to day, yet employ thousands of people.

In investing terms, relating this concept to property, leverage is "utilising other people's time, money and skills to gain greater advantage, result or wealth than you ever could on your own."

Think of buying a property now. Do you think you would be able to find it, survey it, do the conveyancing, find a solicitor, organise the mortgage, do the gas safety check, vet the tenant, do the inventories and so on, all on your own?

The more people you can 'utilise,' especially experts in the areas that perhaps you aren't as strong or as specialised, the better the results you will get. You'll find your property business will grow into an automated *system* and run much more on autopilot without you.

In property investment we can look at leverage from 4 angles:

1. Leveraging other people and their time
2. Leveraging money [OPM, bank, JV, private investors]
3. Leveraging systems and software
4. Leveraging other people's contacts and resources

All of which are detailed in these 2 books.

And it is very important to understand that leverage is not 'using' other people; that will end up more expensive in the long term, guaranteed. It's about having a vision, helping people through leadership and giving them hope and belief, adding value to their lives, providing them with incomes and security, and making them feel valued and important.

The first person we recruited at Progressive was Mark's Mum, Catherine. She helped us because she loved her son; it was a cost effective way for us to leverage. She still works at Progressive [though she gets paid now before you say it!].

The second person we recruited at Progressive was Rob's Mum. She still works with us too. We hired Estate Agents to buy for us and paid commission only, we offered properties for design work and IT services and a host of other 'contra' deals – we did what we had to do to get leverage even when we didn't have much spare cash to pay people.

But looking back we were far slower than we should have been, and you don't have to be.

We managed to get people working for Progressive's vision because they felt part of it. That was more important than the money, and still is today for many of the team.

Every person you meet has the ability to help you to your financial goals. You can help them to theirs. You can help each other. These rules apply not just in your handling of agents and vendors, but in all areas of life.

Here's another model for leverage. It's changing one or two small words in your thought process, but a huge difference in your results and outcomes. Most people, when they have a task to do, ask themselves:

'How can I do that?'

Fair question, right? Better than "I can't do that." But still, the problem with this is that they are asking themselves to do the task, and if they are asking themselves that, the likelihood is that they don't have the answer. It's likely to take some work.

If you ask a different question, you get a different result. Here's how to ask the same question, a question that you probably have 100 opportunities a day to ask:

'Who can I get to do that?'

Train yourself to do this. Give yourself diary reminders or stick it on post-it notes on your desk. If you make this a habit, you'll make success a habit too.

Gentle word of warning: not **everything** can be leveraged ;-)

Make your money and your wealth work for you. If most of it is stuffed under your mattress then it may be going down in value by 5% or more per year. The average inflation figure since 1948 has been 5.8%. More about inflation later but remember this: you could be investing that cash for an infinite return using other people's money. And you can sleep easily!

A simple Buy to Let mortgage in today's market will require a 25% deposit [subject to weekly change it seems]. Yes there are other mortgage products that allow 80%, and there are bridging loans and such that use leverage, and we'll talk about these in forthcoming chapters. The bank will lend the other 75% [in the current climate, this may go up or down in the near future] of the purchase price needed so that you can buy a given property. Banks are willing to lend such a great amount on property [as opposed to shares, bonds and other vehicles] because it's secure and stable. The banks know they have a good chance of getting their money back if things go wrong as their loan to you is secured on an historically stable asset.

You will use the money received from your tenant renting out your property to pay the bank [mortgage] back. Here you have twice effectively used leverage. Then you will have net cashflow remaining that the tenant is paying you too. More leverage.

You will earn your return on the full value of the property having only paid out 25% of the full price. That is leverage. And that is only the start.

Later in this book and "Make Cash in a Property market Crash" we'll show you how to leverage the 25%, so you are 100% infinitely leveraged!

Do you remember just a few moments ago we we're talking about the Law of compounding? This is where leverage really comes into its own.

We discussed the Rule of 72 working on the amount of capital that you invest, and we used the simple example of a £100,000 Property bought for £75,000.

We kept is simple, stating that a deal like this would probably cost you about £3,000 to £5,000 in cash.

And we gave you the figures below based on your ROCE [return on capital employed − spent]:

5% growth: 72/5 = 14.4 years to turn £5,000 into £10,000

8% growth: 72/8 = 9 years to turn £5,000 into £10,000
11.74% growth: 72.11.74 = 6 years 48 days to turn £5,000 into £10,000

Using the leverage you can obtain through property, we can dramatically improve these figures:

Taking the example of your £100,000 Property, in 10 years at the 3 given growth figures, the results are as follows:

5% growth: £100,000 becomes £162,889

8% growth: £100,000 becomes £215,892
11.74% growth: £100,000 becomes £303,450

So instead of taking between 6 to 14 years to double your cash and get a 200% return, you could be getting an ROCE [return on capital employed – return on the cash you spent] of over 4000%. If you want to see exactly how this is worked out, please turn to the back of the book on page 299.

We still know many investors who buy property for cash. They are not effectively utilising leverage and could buy 4 to 7 times as much property for the same money. Just imagine earning 4 to 7 times as much money with just a few simple tweaks in what you're doing. How would that feel?

Are you sitting on an asset right now that you can leverage? That asset could be cash, investment, or even your own time or experience. Or simply your desire and drive.

Think of your own property now. If you don't own one, perhaps you have friends or family who do. Over half of the people we regularly speak to at Progressive events and in the Progressive community, have enough equity in their home to buy more property [and earn much more using leverage]. And if not theirs, their friends' or families'.

Get a specific property in mind, and think back to how long you or they have owned it; perhaps 5 years, 10 years or more. Think back to what you bought it for; perhaps less than £100,000? Think now to what it is worth. If you don't know, look for what similar properties are selling for on www.nethouseprices.com or www.rightmove.co.uk.

You could also get an Estate Agent to value it for you [if you are even just thinking of selling your home, they will do it for free]. There is a great chance that the value of your home has gone up in value £50,000, £100,000 or more in a very short space of time.

In fact, some of our investors' and community members' homes doubled in the 5 years before the crash. Some are still going up in London.

You probably have enough equity, or other assets sitting idle, or those of potential JV partners, to buy more property, get the tenants to pay your mortgages and your monthly cashflow, and generate additional equity on perhaps 2-5 properties or more, rather than just your own home. Leverage baby!

Whatever equity you have made on your house now, multiply that by 2 or 10 and imagine what that means to you. Think of £500,000 to £1million now. Imagine 5-10% of that per year for the rest of your life. Would that help you for your retirement or the lifestyle you desire? Would that give you freedom, choice and independence?

At Progressive Portfolio builder, we effectively leverage the money loaned by the bank to purchase assets for investors up to 5 times the value you would be able to achieve with just their own money. They leverage us financially, but also leverage our time, knowledge and experience.

www.progressiveportfoliobuilder.co.uk

In "Make Cash in a Property Market Crash," 2 models for advanced leverage – Leverage 1st, manage 2nd, Do Last, and Time invested vs. Time spent, are detailed to take it to the highest level. You'll barely be doing a task ever again!

Summary

Always think of how you can use leverage. The difference between a successful person and a poor working person is how they use their time. Leverage time, money, resources, systems and contacts. Think "Who can I get to do it?" How can you earn maximum return on minimum time and and use other people's money for infinite ROI?

Potential pitfalls

Danger danger [don't panic].

There are, as with any kind of investment, potential banana skins that you should be aware of, if you want to make your investments work for you [for life].

There's always a risk to investing, and we're not here to kid you about that. But there's a risk to everything, and perhaps the risk of *not* investing is even greater to you and your future.

"If you don't risk anything, you risk everything" – Rob Moore

If you are totally averse to any risk, perhaps investing and business is not for you. Find a safe comfortable job [and let them make you redundant]. Get a safe secure pension [and let them spend it for you].

You see many people will not tell you this. You could accuse us of being negative here, but we believe in the 'warts and all' approach, because it's all about setting your expectations at the right point and being realistic from the start. Positively realistic!

If you know ballpark figures for your investments [purchase costs, maintenance, rentals etc] and what you can realistically expect, then there shouldn't be many flies turning up in your soup. No major surprises; no financial disasters.

"Be greedy when others are fearful, and fearful when others are greedy" – Warren Buffett

"Sanity in investing is overestimating costs and underestimating profit" – Mark Homer

The potential pitfalls of investing in property are as follows [and you should know them before moving forward]:

War/acts of terrorism/the Taliban/Kamikaze: yes it seems ridiculous, and yes it probably is, but there is a very slim chance that there could be a major war or other disaster that is not covered by your household insurance!

If there is a war or act of terror, then we're all likely to be hiding in bunkers living on tins of beans and condensed milk, rather than worrying about collecting rent.

Ok, so we *are* messing about a little here, but there are paranoid people out there [you know who you are - stop hiding with Mark!] and we said that we wanted to cover *everything*.

The 'market will crash even further': if you want to read some specific details about what happens when 'the market is crashing,' when London is burning and when all the rats are running out of town, you can read the sister book, "Make Cash in a Property Market Crash"

It is especially relevant if you want to make money right now, but you'll need to be quick, it may not last and you'll want to get stuck in. Not for the faint hearted though.

First of all we have to stand up, put our hands in the air and tell you that we didn't go through the 'crash' of the 1980's. We were about 2 years old when that kicked off and we didn't experience it first hand.

So before we go on a rant, let us give you some specific figures about the 'worst time for property in history.' And this is not because we believe one way or the other that the market will or will not continue to drop, but to look at the market as a whole, and the benefits and potential banana skins of each part of the cycle:

According to **www.communities.gov.uk**, the market as a whole did not drop through the 80's, as an average. In fact the lowest growth year was 1982 at 2.5% and the highest was 1988 at 25.6%! Even post current crash most areas are at worst 20% down on peak, still at least 60% up over the last decade.

And London has continued to rise, with many cities seeing an upward bounce this year.

In the 90's property did go down 4 years in a row between 1990 and 1993. The market never went down by more than 3.8% in any one of those 4 years and averaged over 2% per year over the 4 year period [10% less than the market had gone up in 1989 alone].

The point is markets do crash and correct, and with that comes huge, Contrarian opportunity.

But they always recover; they have since 1088. Corrections are almost always 'over-corrections,' so when they do start to go up, they often go up big. Double digit yearly growth is not unheard of.

The sensationalist 'crash' was not half as catastrophic as people believe, or as the newspapers reported. It also shows that with a mid to long term holding strategy, one year's growth can wipe out 5 years or more of downward movement, as it easily did.

Remember newspapers are there to sell stories, and that is it. That is how they make their money. They appeal to the masses, so you're never going to see the headline:

"Huge Contrarian opportunity for savvy investors in the crash" – Mark Homer

And you should be pleased that they don't print those headlines above, or everyone would be doing it, and there'd be way too much competition.

You make your money by finding and sharing the truth about property, knowing the facts and helping people. They make their money by adding spin and hype to everything with a little pinch of gross sensationalism. That is what sells newspapers.

Have you not noticed in the media that things are either absolutely amazing or verging on disaster? Nothing is ever just normal; nothing is like it is in real life. Celebrities are either 'flavour of the month' or 'dirty love rats' and nothing in between. The media spin around the property market is no different.

The media, and population as a whole, is absolutely obsessed with property here in the UK; it's major news, it's all we talk about. Everyone thinks they're an expert, be it the Sun editor or your friend down the pub.

This is obviously a good thing. We all want to own property here; it's the new handbag dog [except it's not new at all]. In other countries, and let's use Germany as an example, property ownership is far less prevalent; lending criteria is far more stringent and far larger deposits are often needed; many more people therefore rent and the papers don't write [scaremonger] about it all the time.

So we must put this into perspective; opportunity is there but what sells papers is not necessarily real. Be positive, with a healthy but small dose of scepticism. Question everything, and then trust once you decide or get the proof you need from the right sources. Look at the facts and the ulterior motives of others to make your judgements, and trust yourself and your instincts.

A fundamental rule here: only listen to those who know what they are talking about and can give evidence to backup their knowledge. You wouldn't give your baby to a butcher, or hire a personal trainer who gets knackered opening a door, so don't leave your investment decisions in the hands of journalists, or people who don't know what they're doing.

So history tells us that markets go up on average rather nicely and can drop a little [though only 7 years out of the last 61], but it is something to be aware of. It should not scare you. It should not put you off buying property.

There are so many people who we speak to who are still waiting to say 'I told you so' when the market crashes. They have been waiting 10 years and missed out on complete financial independence in that time. In fact, they're missing out on it right now, aren't they?

Surely we should want each other to succeed rather than fail?

"Don't wait to own property, own property and wait" – Mark Homer

In times of market downturn, skilled investors will make money. Skilled investors will make money regardless of the marketplace.

Whilst a market is 'bull' and riding high investors who have a good portfolio will experience healthy capital growth and benefit from this increase in the value of their property. When the market goes south, the average punter panics and wants to sell immediately, taking a hit on any losses and making them real. This is blindness and it is at this time that the savvy investor can pick up properties at discounted prices, thus making his or her profit from day one in equity; immediately at purchase, and reducing the downside risk and further drops.

Either way the educated investor wins. The sheep get skinned and lose their wool and are left out in the cold; going baa. We shall discuss this more later.

It is this simple; don't sell your property in a downturn, and buy as many as you can. Hold. Rent out and let them regain value and rise again; because they always do. **Think long term.**

Rents, vacancies and voids: A drop in rents and vacant properties could damage your profit in your portfolio. In the last 2 recessions, rents actually increased. From 2003 to 2008 rents didn't increase at all in one of our main buying areas. From 2008 to 2010 they went up 20% when the crash really set in. With demand so high for properties now, vacancies [in the right areas and with the right types of properties] are rare. Our portfolio rents on average in 8 days from completion for 2.7 years per tenant.

Negative equity: Negative equity occurs when the value of your home/property is lower than your outstanding mortgage; or the mortgage is higher than the value.

In 2009 the Bank of England reported that between 700,000 and 1.1 million households were in negative equity [and a few of ours were too]. Bad for those in that situation, Contrarian opportunity for investors like you.

The media create such a big hoo-rah and it is portrayed as a disaster. This coaxes novice investors or OO's to sell, and they cement the loss. Same thing happens in the stock market – fear influences bad decision making.

Negative equity is not an ideal situation, but it's only going to be a problem if you are trading [buying and selling] properties. As long as you don't sell, and you buy for income and cashflow, then variations of value don't matter to you.

If you trade properties, flip them, or buy to sell, you will be using the drop in the market to buy at a discounted price, so you won't be in negative equity: the bigger the discount, the greater the risk protection.

The properties in our portfolio that dropped into negative equity are now the best cashflowing ones we have. They are a better 'asset' to us than some of the properties with more equity in them. We'll hold out for the long term, and if we do ever want to sell or remortgage, we can make that decision when the time comes. And as long as the assets are cashflowing, you have the choice. As with every downside, there's an upside benefit.

Don't sell in a downturn otherwise you will realise the [paper] loss. The income a property provides is not relative to the value: some of our properties are worth less than they were in 2007 by as much as 30%, but they are producing significantly more income. Keep pulling in the cashflow and wait.: house prices will go up in the long run, by which time you'll probably keep it because rents would have risen and your cashflow will be too good to give away to someone else.

The tenant does not pay the rent: Across over 250 currently rented properties, less than 15 are in any kind of arrears with rents. We're not going to kid you, it does happen, it's an operational cost and commercial reality of being a property investor, but it can be radically minimised with increased knowledge and experience.

"The best way to reduce risk is to increase knowledge" – Rob Moore

If your cashflow is good, as we'll teach you later, then this reduces the risk of vacancies and arrears. Factor it in your figures in advance: Expect 2-3 weeks void a year, factor in 4-6 weeks in your figures and keep that cash as a contingency.

If you have the contingency, you probably won't need it, but you know what happens financially when you don't have any reserves, don't you? Details of how to manage this process come later.

Interest rate rises: now this one we do have to watch, as many people will tell you who were around when the interest rates almost tripled overnight [or so my Dad recalls! - Rob].

This is one of the biggest fears [common of course; it's hardly popular] of the investors we help and talk to, even taking into account how low rates are now, and how long they are projected to stay that way.

Just because we, and many other economic experts, don't think rates will go up for around 3 years, doesn't mean they won't, and doesn't mean you shouldn't protect yourself and your investments. If you want to get an idea of what interest rates may do over the longer term, you can look at www.swap-rates.com.

This looks at the future predictions of interest rates based on LIBOR rates, base rates, Euribor rates, Gilt rates, Historic rates and trends. Don't worry if most of those don't mean a thing to you, it's just a useful tool to look ahead and to see where the experts think the interest rates could be going.

That aside, it's really quite straightforward and sensible to think about fixing your mortgage rates on [some] of your properties. Your protection strategy will depend on your age and attitude to risk. Investors under 50 might think about getting lower rate variable mortgages, but banking the difference that you would have been paying on a fix as your own personal insurance policy. You offset the lower [short term] cost.

You can get competitive 10 year fixed rate mortgages at the moment that can actually work out to be cheaper than some variable rate mortgages.

If you want a good property investment broker who can help you with this, drop us a line at **rob.moore@progressiveproperty.co.uk**

It is smart practice to 'offset.' Use different lenders for different properties where possible, as different lenders have different rates and adjust to rate rises differently. By doing so, you are spreading your risk over a larger lender market.

Doing the same thing between fixed and variable rate mortgages, buying with big discounts, and on occasions taking lower loans to value [LTV], all reduce risk.

We will go into this in much more detail later. This is the most effective way of allaying fears when it comes to potential interest rate rises, and has you protected no matter what happens, as much as you can be.

Of course with every change comes opportunity, and remember as stated earlier, you can profit very nicely by helping people out of debt when the interest rates rise, and you can get increased cashflow when interest rates fall.

Summary

Know and beware of potential pitfalls before you invest. Be realistic, do your diligence and set your expectations at the right level. Know the risks upfront by increasing your knowledge, and determine your attitude to risk depending on your age, income and outcomes. You are the one in control, and most people don't have enough knowledge to be taken too seriously. Once you have made your choices and you're happy: take immediate action. Procrastination is a disease.

The Property buying process

Later on in this book we'll go over many of the processes of buying a property in much more detail. You may learn some useful secrets in transforming the performance of your existing portfolio [or saving time and money when starting to build it].

For now, see below the processes you will need to understand and go through as a serious property investor when buying a property. Not all of them will always apply, but knowing this in advance will save you a hell of a lot of time, pain and money:

Decide how much you want to invest: do you have equity in your property? Do you have savings or other investments? Have you sold a business or taken redundancy? The amount of capital you have to invest will determine your strategy. If you don't have much, or any, it doesn't stop you; it just impacts your strategy and rules, and you'll need partners.

The single biggest mistake that speculators and gamblers make, which holds them back from true investor status, is they buy without having a set of rules. In effect, they don't know what they are buying and how their 'investment' will turn out.

By the end of this book you will have a clear idea of how your rules will look to you, and what they will mean for you [as long as you follow and apply all that you read now].

And they'll change as you go on. They should; and that's good. You will be improving all the time.

Decide on what strategy to follow: Single let? HMO? Multi Let Without the Sweat? Buy to Sell? Deal Packaging? Lease Options? Installment contracts? Auctions? These strategies are revealed through the two books and on our educational web portal: **www.progressiveproperty.co.uk**

Decide on your area: we shall discuss the process of diligence to identify your area later in the book using the C.A.S.T.L.E.D model. For now just know that you should be sticking to a specific, local area.

Decide on your property type: most people find property by accident, or are lured by new build and off plan 'developers' discounts' and such like, and their emotions. There is diligence that should be carried out to find the best type of investment for you, and it is usually 'an area within an area.' All shall be revealed later.

Find your property? Are you going to use Estate Agents and build relationships? Drop leaflets in the right areas and to the right high yielding properties? Will you set up a website and advertise using Google Adwords [or other CPC/PPC engines]? Ageing technique, Blogs, Facebook [Multiple Ads], Debt forums, Biz Directories, Aggregators, WOM/Referrals, PR, affiliates, internet marketing or Guerrilla marketing?

Always run the numbers: this should be done before the offer and before the purchase stage. Determine the saleable value, the price you need to pay to get all the deposit and costs out on remortgage, the rental values and coverage percentage for lending purposes, the ceiling values on the streets and the cost of refurb.

Have you thought about all, all, the costs? All will be revealed and prepare to be surprised [especially if you have bought from some new builds in the past].

Find a good Mortgage Broker: this is vital for investors as specific mortgage products are often required. They may also refer you to a good solicitor. We have some contacts for you later.

Get a Decision in Principle [D.I.P] and be ready: most investors leave this too late. You must have this in place before your offer and to give the agent or vendor happy. Doing everything that is asked of you by the agent [details of your solicitor, mortgage proof, ID and proof of funds, sitting in front of their broker/mortgage advisor] can immediately make you the *Banker* investor.

If you are organised, efficient and on top of the buying process, even without previous buying history, you get the *first* call when a deal becomes available. Estate Agents get messed about by so many wannabe investors, that simply doing what you say you'll do, and completing on your purchase, accelerates you up the ladder fast.

View the property: always view the property. Does it need refurbishment work? Does it have damp? Check the windows [old windows can be expensive to replace] and check the boiler. Is the property mortgegable? Check the surrounding area. Check.

Never buy a property yourself without viewing it, no matter what anyone trying to sell you one 430 miles away will tell you, and no matter how many of the same type you have bought. If it's cheap, there's often a reason.

Make offer[s]: how are you going to negotiate your desired price and how are you going to know that the price is of genuine value? This might sound obvious, but a lot of people wait for the 'perfect' deal [that is never perfect enough or doesn't exist], and there's not much that winds up a vendor or agent more than a Procrastinator.

Make offers. Don't be scared, that's why you are doing the viewings! If you don't ask: you don't get [thanks Dad!].

It's a numbers game and you'll get some deals that you really didn't expect , and some that will surprise you [at how good they are]. Offer on everything structurally sound, of good yield and in your right area.

And if you don't really want the property, offer really low :-)

Get a survey on the property: this must be done to ascertain the value for mortgage lending purposes. Whether you do this before you offer or after, is up to you. It can be expensive to get surveys done too early if vendors then pull out. And a survey means an official RICS certified survey, not a 'desktop' valuation or opinion.

Find a tenant/Letting Agent: most people leave this very late and it costs them heavily. Start looking as early as you can and you'll save money. You want tenants lined up and ready even before completion.

Managing tenants yourself can be grief and we just don't bother with it. It's not good leverage either and will cost you because of IGA's it blocks out. Get a good agent to do it for you; it's their job and they'll be better at it than you.

You don't want to be paying mortgage payments because your property is empty, do you? Use a Letting Agent and pay their fees, it will end up saving you time and money.

But remember, you must find a good one, and you might have to kiss a few frogs — all part of the business, and it means it's also not easy for anyone else.

Agree a price: make an offer and agree a price. Once you do this and you're happy never pull out, especially if you are building relationships with Estate Agents and buying through them. You're only as good as your last deal.

You do not want to be the investor who got *Binned.* If you do, it is likely you will never get a deal from that agency again. You'll be biting the hand that feeds you, and even worse they'll tell all the other agents in the town.

Of course, if you have followed the steps here you will never need to pull out of a purchase, will you?

Find a good Solicitor for conveyancing and legals: there are specific legal requirements to purchasing a property; you'll need to find a good solicitor. We know some good ones and some not so good ones, and we're happy to pass you the details of the good ones. Most solicitors will seem quite efficient at first, but the service can very often tail off.

Full mortgage application: your broker will arrange this with you. A good one will make the process quick and easy. A bad one will take 6 months and you'll end up losing your deal. Details at the back for you.

Get 3 refurb quotes: it is important to get different quotes, as the difference in prices can be huge. Mark got quoted £800 and £7,500 by two Architects for a small piece of planning work, for the same job! Be strategic and tough with this, demand the highest possible standard at the lowest possible cost.

Instruct the Letting Agent: important to do it now. Get them working to fill your property before you own it. Every day a vacancy costs you money.

Chase the deal through again: keep in touch with the agent and broker to ensure everything is progressing as it should and there are no problems. Don't wait for them to contact you.

Pay your deposit over: required to receive the mortgage; your solicitor will sort this with you.

Exchange on the property: once application and legal work are completed and relevant fees are paid, then contracts are exchanged, at which time it is too late to pull out.

Complete any refurbishment work: [we are assuming that you have good tradesmen at your disposal. Don't get your hands dirty here, this is not property ladder and you are a leveraged investor].

Start this as soon as you can after exchange to save time on your mortgage payments [which have not started yet]. Start too early and your work could be in vain if the vendor pulls out. Start too late and you could make extra mortgage payments while the property is empty.

Check your costs: you should be keeping a good eye on costs ensuring that they don't spiral out of control. The quicker you are, the more efficient you are, and the better team you have around you, the less any deal will cost you. If you are unsure of costs, add on 25% and keep a cash contingency.

Chase the deal through [again]: chase and stay in the loop. The agent and vendor will appreciate regular contact.

Complete on the property: drawdown of funds. Your mortgage payments start now. You can house your tenant and complete any refurb work to make the property rentable.

Pay your insurances and gas safety checks [and perhaps even council tax for long refurb work]: We all have to do it.

Start your refurbishment works: project manage it through as quickly as you can.

Chase the Letting Agent until property is let: hard and fast ;-)

House your tenant: make sure you have an AST [Assured Shorthold Tenancy Agreement] signed between you and your tenant. The Letting Agent should have vetted your tenant properly, taken their deposit and their first month's rent upfront.

Set up a separate portfolio account: money flies all over the place in property investment so we recommend opening a separate bank account. Automate all payments in and out through D.D if you can.

Check rents are coming in: from your Letting agent. You'd think this is automatic right ;-) It can be random at times, especially with LHA tenants through the Council. Costs can also be sneakily added.

Get your property revalued: if you are finding discounts and using the tools we're teaching you in this book, then you'll be getting your [or JV partners'] deposits back out of the deal. You will probably need a different surveyor to value your property this time as you will require a higher valuation.

The original surveyor is not likely to accept an uplift of 30%, even when it really is worth it, because they surveyed it at the lower price just a few months ago [even if you have added value through refurb]. So find another surveyor.

At the moment most banks will require you to have owned the property 6 months before you can apply for a remortgage [this may change with time], unless it is cash purchase in and out, or sold to a FTB with a residential mortgage.

Organise your remortgage: just like you did your first one, ensuring you instruct a different surveyor, and getting as many comparables as proof, as possible.

Receive your deposit back and find your next property with the same deposit funds.

And that is just the start…

Summary

> The best way to sum up this chapter is to read it again :-)

[Have a] strategy

Define what wealth means to you: wealth means completely different things to each and every one of us. Mother Teresa's definition of wealth is probably a little different from that of Bill Gates, and again probably a little different from yours. It's a personal thing, and for many it's not all about the money. For some it's up there with oxygen.

Wealthy investors know exactly what they want, and how they are going to get it. Some call this law of attraction, some power of focus, some manifestation. Call it what you will, it works.

And it really doesn't matter what it is, and how much it is, as long as you're happy with it and it will give you the life of your choice. Your strategy is personal to you, and will come down to what you want for your life and the lives of those closest to you.

Think now, before you read on, about what you want for your life. How active or passive do you want to be? Is this a passion or simply a strategy to give you the money you want to do something else? What do you want your portfolio for? What is it that you want to do with the money?

Do you want wealth to change the world? To create a higher standard of living for you and the ones you love? Do you want to set up a shelter or a charity? Do you want to leave a legacy? Do those matching shoes and handbags have your name written all over them?

This is your vision and this needs to be thought about *before* you get down and dirty with your tactics and actions. Most people forget why they even started business, and end up being a slave to the very thing they used to be so passionate about. Not sure if you can relate to this?

Do you want 5 properties? 10 properties? 200 properties? 200 takes a lot more management than 5, and will require more people, more time and more leverage. Do you want passive income of £50,000 per year, tax free? Do you want more? Do you want a portfolio that you can retire on? Are you 28 or 58? [Or any other age for that matter.]

Start with your outcome in mind and work back, because no plan or anything accidental is also a strategy; just an ineffective one!

Do you want to leave your children with a large portfolio that can fund their retirement or a big nasty inheritance tax bill?! Do you want to be a full time investor or do you want someone to do it for you? Do you want to travel? You get the picture.

We have provided some space at the back of this book for you to write down your thoughts and motives, should you wish. It might be a good idea to write them down now, in this book, so that you have everything in once place.

Turn to page 296 and fill in the questions provided.

This is your confidential information. Use it as a reference, a guide, a rulebook, a checklist, a diary, a goal and as a useful tool to look back on to see just how much progress you have made.

If you want to be successful in property you need to have the skill of seeing your journey before you. This involves the following processes:

Where are you now? of course this sounds ridiculously obvious, but there are many people out there who could be described as 'delusional' when it comes to knowing where they are – lacking belief in their abilities or overestimating them.

Now it's time for you to get real. Honestly evaluate where you are [wherever it is, is just right for you], the skills, resources and talent you have, and need help with. Wherever you're at, know that's exactly where you're meant to be and be excited about the path you are about to forge.

Again, we have a section at the back of the book for you to write this down. Simply turn to page 297

Know your exact financial position to the penny: your monthly expenses, budgets and cash flow. Know the assets and liabilities [debt] you have and know your net worth. Your total net worth will be your marker for your wealth and your progress; it is *not* just about cash-flow.

Know where You want to go – Your goal: you must have a clear idea of where you want to be, as discussed earlier. It will grow and evolve; it is just at the very start now. Your goals *will* change, and that is fine. We know that life is a journey and not a destination, and each major goal will act as a significant milestone in your life.

You wouldn't get in a car and just drive, you'd set a destination in the Tom Tom, just like a pilot would do on a flight. Interestingly the auto-pilot function on an aircraft is off destination for virtually the whole journey – constantly tweaking and re-evaluating before it gets to its destination. You just need to know where you're going and keep the focus on it.

"Where focus goes energy flows and results show"

When you refer back to this section and define your strategy you must quantify your end goal: be specific with time scales, numbers and figures. The more real, tangible and specific you can make your goals, the more likely you are to attract them.

The reason that the majority of investors are in financial slavery is not because they don't have the ability to make or attract money; there are many people who make millions per year and are still broke. It is the lack of a specific plan and strategy. They don't have rules in place, or at least they don't stick to them.

Many buy property all over the place. We personally know an investor who bought 87 properties, all with good and genuine existing discounts, who went bankrupt because they were all over the country and he just couldn't manage them.

Many do not focus, get a little greedy or grow too quickly once they see progress, rather than sticking to the plan.

It is **never** too late to start planning, investing in property and becoming wealthy, but it's always too late to wait. Start now, get perfect later.

Of course analysis is important, but analysis paralysis is worse than just having blind faith.

We bought a couple of 'kippers' when we first started, and of course they look silly now, but the lessons we got buying them by just going for it were so fundamental in getting us where we are now. We wouldn't have bought ANY if we were waiting to get perfect.

Colonel Sanders is a great example. KFC Inc was formed in the late 1950's when 'Colonel Sanders' was nearly 70. We once helped an investor who was 76 get a Buy to Let investment property. Age is **not** an excuse.

Excuses are simply the stories that people who fail tell to make themselves feel better. The best and most fruitful, rich, loving and exciting years of your life could be the ones you still have left, and you could live until you are 105!

And you are **never too young** to invest and educate yourself to become very wealthy either. There are many great Entrepreneurs who are in their teens. The million dollar homepage that generated $1 million was created by Alex Tew at 21 and Facebook CEO Mark Zuckerberg was only 20 when he created the infamous social networking site.

And Jo Moore, a Progressive community member, started educating herself in property with Progressive at 17 years old. She wasn't even old enough at this stage to get a mortgage! But it didn't stop her.

She focused on packaging deals and selling them to other investors to make shorter term cashflow, until she became old enough to get a mortgage. She pulls in £3,000 a deal that she sells, she runs her own events, and she is an inspiration to young [and not so young] people in the Progressive community.

She has now got her partner/boyfriend involved in property too; helping him on his way to more financial independence. With the help of Progressive, they clearly defined their roles in their business so that they don't end up killing each other :-)

NOW is always the best time.

For our first 4 years in property, we used only one strategy. **One strategy only.** As will become clear, there really are 100's of opportunities out there when you look for them, and dozens of strategies. It's all about knowing which one to use; then sticking with it, focusing on it, and only expanding it when it is fully operational and leveraged.

Summary

Know what wealth means to you and what you want from your portfolio. Know where you are, where you want to be and see your journey before you. Set a clear strategy, goals and be specific. Use obstacles and setbacks as inspiration. Have a bigger picture vision; even bigger than you. Start now, get perfect later and keep tweaking your strategy as you go.

Interest only vs. repayment mortgages

This one sparks a great debate and thus warrants its very own section.

You will probably know that nearly all investment mortgages are interest only, rather than capital repayment. You only pay off the interest on the loan rather than the loan itself.

Firstly, if you try to get repayment mortgages on Buy to let, you probably won't. It's not that you can't, but the rent must be comfortably more than the mortgage, around 125%, for you to get a mortgage from the bank. So you'll need the deal of the century, or a much bigger deposit, because the repayments will be around one third more.

Secondly, the average repayment loan [mortgage] will take you 25 years to pay off. When you do eventually pay it off you will have paid off around 2.5 times the value of your property. Yes you will own your property outright, but for a £100,000 property you will have paid roughly £250,000 for it after the 25 years [at the time of writing, depending on interest rates].

That £150,000 is a lot of tied up capital that could have been invested, leveraged and making you much more money.

This is known as 'cost of capital.' A good example is the use of cash or finance to purchase a car. Many people will tell you it's foolish to get a car on finance. If it creates debt, then of course it is. But let's look at how you could have 'cost of capital' by buying it cash:

Let's make the assumption that you can easily afford a car costing £25,000; cash or finance [If you can't, it's a liability].

Option 1: You buy it on finance. You tie up a £5,000 deposit and raise the rest through finance, costing you approx £425 per month on a repayment loan for 60 months depending on interest rates.

You have left £20,000 to invest.

Option 2: You buy it cash. You have zero repayments and zero cash left to invest.

Option 1: You invest the £20,000 and with it, using your increasing knowledge, you can plausibly buy one property per year with the same capital. For ease of figures; these properties are worth £100,000 based on today's figures.

Compounded equity at end of year 5 [based on 5% growth]: **£168,461**

Go to the back of the book to page 299 if you would like to see how we arrive at this figure in more detail.

Option 1: Money made: £168,461
Money spent on repayments: £425 x60 = £25,500
Total profit deducting car loan payments: **£142,961**

Option 2: You save the £425 per month repayments and it takes 47 months to accrue the same £20,000 to invest. This leaves around one year to invest. You invest the £20,000 and buy one equivalent property for £121,550 [£100,000 Property + 4 years growth].
Equity at end of year 5 [or year one for this strategy]: £24,309

Option 2: Money made: £24,309
Money spent on repayments: 0
Total: £24,309

That's a difference of £118,652. A big cost of capital.

Interesting, isn't it?!

So back to property: in 25 years you would own your property outright with a repayment mortgage. In 25 years all of that money you've paid towards your repayment mortgage will actually be worth much less relatively than you paid for it. The £250,000 could have gone down in relative value by almost three-quarters.

Quick aside: don't be fooled by 'official inflation figures.' The actual rate of inflation figures can be [are] much higher. In our current economic conditions the price of food, commodities, petrol and general living are on the way up, alarmingly so, far more than the Government may openly admit. Taxes are increasing too, and wages are not going up at all, so every year your money is worth a lot less, if it isn't invested.

The average figure of inflation over the last 59 years has been 5.8%. A good source for this kind of information is www.statistics.gov.uk

We can actually work the impact inflation will have almost exactly using the 'rule of 70.' It is like using the rule of 72 in reverse, and it's a quick way of working out the time in which it will take the value of money to halve, knowing the figure of inflation.

Picking up on the example on the previous page of £250,000; to determine the time for money's buying power to halve, simply divide the "rule-quantity" [70] by the inflation rate. Let's look at some examples:

Inflation at 2%: 70/2 = 35 years for £250,000 to halve in value

Inflation at 4%: 70/4 = 17.5 years for £250,000 to halve in value

Inflation at 6%: 70/6 = 11.67 for £250,000 to halve in value

Here's a real example. Picture this: Imagine this.

My [Mark's] uncle bought his first property in 1967 for around £3,500 in Halesowen in the West Midlands. He decided to take out a 25 year capital repayment mortgage at 70% loan to value [or around £2500]. He put down the required £1000 [from money from my grandfather] and slaved away each day paying £17.87 a month in repayments. In those days one pound was worth a lot more, and his mortgage payment was about 40% of his pay. He had to go without holidays abroad, meals out, even clothes for the kids to make ends meet, such was life [hard] in those days.

In 1992 he made his final mortgage payment to the bank which was a great relief, the £2500 mortgage he had was now £0. Obviously by then the value of a £1 was much less as inflation had reduced its value hugely over the 25 years. I decided to ask him a question:

'If you had decided to take the mortgage out in 1967 on an interest only basis [the bank wouldn't have let him but let's say they did, because you can now] and the monthly payment had reduced by about £4 to £12.50 what would this extra money have meant to you?'

He replied, "A huge amount, for a start it would have been one more holiday a year for the family and probably a lot more."

Then I asked, "And in 1992 when you made your final mortgage payment how long would it have taken to clear the remaining £2500?"

"Well it would have been one pay cheque — I hadn't really thought of it like that."

The reality is that inflation had reduced the real value of his mortgage [as it will do again over the next 25 years] by so much that it had been almost meaningless when it was time to clear it off. In this story lies a good lesson about the power of inflation on mortgages for the future.

Thirty years ago properties could be bought for around £5,000. £5,000 doesn't even buy a garage now! Can you see how easy it would be to pay off that same £5,000 when your house is worth around £200,000?!

If you buy a house for £200,000 today and inflation stays relatively consistent to the last 25 years, then, like the situation with Mark's Uncle, that £200,000 could be worth, in relative terms, what one or two months' salary cheques are in 25 years time.

We'll discuss in just a second why most people will never actually get to the end of their repayment term; another reason for taking out interest only mortgages.

Capital repayment mortgages are not set so that you pay equal amounts of interest to repayment on a monthly basis [as you might expect]. Because mortgage companies are in the business of making money, because the market is so competitive and they know you'll be with another lender in 3 years, they make their loans 'top heavy.' This means that for the first few years of your repayment mortgage you are paying off nearly all interest and very little capital. It is not until you get right near the end of your 25 [+] year term that you are paying off a decent amount of capital.

The earlier you pay off the mortgage [as many people do by 'remortgaging'], the more you are penalised. This is the lenders' way of getting maximum money out of you in a minimum period of time.

They arrange the loans like this for profit. That goes without saying. Because the market is so competitive and transient, the lenders know that in 2-3 years you are likely to have remortgaged and changed mortgages in the search for a better rate or to release cash from your equity. People rarely stay with the same mortgage company for very long nowadays.

In short you are spending so much of your available and invest-able capital on a repayment mortgage which is going down in value over time. It makes far more sense to invest that money and compound the returns, and let it go up and up and up.

If you pay an interest only mortgage at 5% over 25 years, you'll pay £125,000 [and you'll still owe for the property, but only to the value of the deflated mortgage]. That's around half of the £250,000 on a capital repayment mortgage.

That £125,000 that you save by taking an interest only mortgage on a £100,000 house can be reinvested. Even if it only provided 5 properties in that time [semi-leveraged], you'd have another 5 properties, 6 in all, instead of one.

Assuming 5% growth over those 25 years, and having to pay back the existing mortgage values, you'd be up between £1.5 to £1.8million in equity, and a few hundred thousand in net cashflow. These figures are conservative.

So as you can see there is a huge cost of capital [cost of not investing] involved in paying back a mortgage. This is a fundamental concept for investing. If you have money tied up in your house it could be costing you millions in your lifetime by not investing it.

This is where leverage really comes into its own. The figures are quite breathtaking wouldn't you agree? And remember that you can take all of this growth incrementally [though not at the moment] if you remortgage [and not pay a penny of tax on it]. And you can offset your interest payments against your property related income to reduce your taxable profit!

Where else can you get almost 100% finance for an asset that pays you income every month and grows in value every year, and have the debt almost totally eroded over time while the income and value go up and up and up?

Seriously, you're in the right business my friend!

Summary:

Remembering leverage and the Law of compounding, keep your investment mortgages to interest only. Your cashflow will be higher, it will be easier to get mortgages, and if you re-invest saved capital you will build a multi £M portfolio from a single property.

Due diligence

Due diligence simply means 'The investigation and verification of the details of a particular investment.'

It doesn't mean analysis paralysis, or needless extensive research, but it does mean keeping well informed, and not taking anything at face value.

This is Mark's favourite subject. The right amount of diligence and action reduces risk and increases your bank balance. And Mark gets to create another spreadsheet to fantasise over.

Diligence is absolutely vital when going into any investment. Due preparation and research should be undertaken [or undertaken for you utilising someone else who knows how to do it] before you buy a property.

In property the following factors need to be considered, planned for, researched, and contingencies put in place for potential worst case scenarios:

- Market conditionsInterest rates and economic growth
- Demographics and your area to invest
- Location
- Property size
- Property type
- Property condition and potential refurbishment
- Property valuation
- Finance nuances
- Comparable prices
- Cost of repayments
- Running cost of property with contingencies
- Remortgage strategy
- Demographic and lifetime value of tenant
- Tenant management
- Growth strategy
- Exit strategy
- Tax strategy
- Competition
- Other things we may not have thought about from the start

Look at the prices: what are properties selling for in your area? What are they on the market for? If you want to find out what prices properties are selling for visit **www.rightmove.co.uk**. This is a great resource. You can also use **www.nethouseprices.co.uk**, though we find Rightmove is more complete.

You should know what properties are selling for. This is the only true indicator of real property values. Forget 'desk-top' valuations and guess work. Even official valuations can be wrong by up to 10%.

Rightmove: is also a great resource for the prices that properties are put on the market. If you find an area where properties are selling at considerably below the asking prices, then there might be something going on there that you want to be a part of. If they are all selling within a week for full asking, you know to move on.

Save these sites to your favourites. Are there properties that seem to have been for sale for months? Are there reductions in asking prices? Is there anything that gives you a sniff that the market might give you some deals?

A website called **www.propertybee.co.uk** enables you to track this history to spot deals that stick, and it plugs into Firefox.

Make some spreadsheets and put in the data. Or even better, use Mark's App version of his famous **Deal Scrutinser™** – you can get it free on the App store by searching 'property App' – our gift to you for buying this book.

If it costs anything, email me at **rob.moore@progressiveproperty.co.uk** and I'll make sure you get a free version.

Imagine being able to analyse any deal on the go, whilst viewing it or waiting outside, in around 40 seconds, using software on your phone that has the most complicated, detailed algorithm based on over 350 property purchases, yet is so simple to use in the palm of your hand.

Back to house prices: jump in your car and drive around your area. Are there many for sale boards? Are there many in any one particular area? Are there many that seem to have been there for months? Keep checking regularly.

A great resource for values of towns and cities is www.upmystreet.com. There you can find the average price of the average house in a given city. This helps you work out average yields in an area by comparing prices in cities versus the rent you might achieve. Areas vary considerably and this is important. You should be looking for gross yields of 8% upwards, finance depending.

But the best way of finding real sold prices is to ask the Estate Agents, as it is as 'real-time' as you will get. And they'll tell you for free because they want you to buy property.

Is the market moving? Much of what we have just explained will help you to get a feel for market movements. Make sure the Estate Agents you speak to are local as markets move in micro-economies. Ask them if there are many properties selling? Ask them if many are selling cheap, or any vendors with 'motives' to sell quickly. If there are, what areas are they in? You can get all of this information out of them simply by building some rapport and going on some viewings.

Remember they need you because they make money out of selling houses to you.

What are the general folk talking about? Is there a demand for tenants? It is all very well having all of the above, but if your property will not rent out in 3 months then forget it. Estate agents with their own Lettings departments might give you the information you need.

This becomes easier and replicable with every deal you buy, so if you don't really like research, don't panic! If you do, don't get carried away and use it as an excuse not to do anything.

Fundamental tip No.1:
Balance is vital. Diligence is important but analysis paralysis is a disease of progress. Do your diligence, take fast and decisive action and get perfect later. Start now.

Summary

Be diligent. Plan, prepare and research carefully. Know what you are buying, reduce the risk and question everything. But don't get caught up in analysis paralysis, you have to take action and get perfect later. Your diligence will improve and take less time the more properties you buy.

Don't read the papers

Absolutely one of the worst things that investors or success seeking people can do is to read the papers.

News is negative. It drains energy and it wastes time. The average person spends half an hour a day reading or watching the general news. That's 9,100 hours every 50 years.

Just think what you could do, and how many properties you could buy, with 9,100 hours! That's only half the time it takes to be a world expert in any subject.

Plus, the people who write articles for the newspapers do not have the same agenda that you have. They do what it takes to sell papers, and are not experts in the areas that you are interested in, so their 'reports' are irrelevant.

Let's get back to that in a minute. Of course you will know that it is absolutely vital that you read, study and learn from those who have done what you want, if you also want to become a successful property investor. So we're not saying don't read the following:

- The Land registry for sold Property prices
- The Economist for economic analysis
- The Financial Times for economic news
- The Communities and Local Government website for housing data
- The Halifax, Nationwide and Rightmove for house price data
- The Business Channel
- Biographies & Autobiographies of successful people
- Articles by industry experts

The commentators for these publications and websites are knowledgeable on the subjects on and around property, and base their news on facts rather than sensationalism, and subjects relevant to you.

Newspaper editors and journalists are trying to sell newspapers. They create stories. Have you noticed the 'lift them up chop them down' attitude our press seem to have? Life is not really the way it is depicted in many of these publications. Life is not all about the extremes; very often we simply tick along without too much happening of newsworthy note. You know, life as it really is. People don't die in your street every week like they do in Hollyoaks.

The papers would be out of business if they did not hype and spin everything. That is their business, but property is not.

We have, on numerous occasions, seen in the same day in the same newspaper that the market was both 'going to crash' and was 'booming.'

Stick to the reputable sources and avoid the rest. Re-invest that time into things that you can control, that you can leverage and get results from.

Especially take with a pinch of salt 'pub talk' where all the apparent experts on property hangout drinking their pints of bitter shandy.

Summary

Only listen to the property and finance experts and respectable industry publications and broadcasters. Don't take the newspapers seriously; their agenda is to sell newspapers. [Pub] talk is cheap. Do your diligence using reputable sources and make your own decisions.

Why 95% of people get it wrong

Don't be a Sheep. If you do what everyone else does, then you'll get the same result as everyone else. Sheople.

Unfortunately the statistics are not good. Most people **are not** wealthy, financially independent or in a position of choice in their life. Out of every 100 people by the age of 65:

- 25 will be dead
- 20 will have incomes of less than £5,000 [no kidding!]
- 51 will have incomes of less than £17,000
- 4 will have incomes over £17,000
- Only 1 will be a millionaire.

Most people who try property don't do anywhere near as well as they could; or perhaps should. Most people will make money in the very long term but they rely on property [and good old Father Time] looking after them, rather than getting it right and making serious money strategically. Most people's lives are out of control and they don't know what to do about it.

It is very important to be strong and to stick to your strategy and convictions. Only listen to those who have been there, done it and are doing it, and politely ignore everyone else.

Question the advice you're getting from someone, especially if it is the typical 'pub talk' scenario, or words taken straight from a daily tabloid. Do they have your best interests at heart, even if they mean well, and do they really know what they're talking about?

When there is a property crash the 'sheople' flock and they sell and they lose money. Now we know that this **could** sound patronising to those who aren't in our industry, but it is the truth. The truth hurts sometimes. But the truth and the pain give you opportunities to help people.

They need you, you need them. We appreciate all our vendors and tenants, they don't know what you know, but they all have the same opportunity to take personal responsibility, just like you are.

The ones who succeed are the ones who have a strategy and vision and are confident in that strategy [and themselves]. They have courage, conviction, confidence, nerve, strength and focus. They are the ones who buy and hold when everyone else is selling. And when there's chaos and crashes they keep their cool and focus on their goal.

Those who are successful are very often quirky, individual, different, sometimes excluded, sometimes ridiculed, very often creative, individual, perhaps stubborn and focused, definitely courageous, mature, educated, experienced, open minded and don't often do what people expect them to do. The rest stay with the herd because it is comfortable.

People can also be like crabs. Crab fishermen leave the lid off the boxes that they put crabs in because they know that when a crab tries to get out of the box, all the other crabs grab hold with their big claws and pull back into the box the crab that dares to venture.

Be successful, be courageous; don't be a sheep [or a crab].

Don't chase the glitz and the get rich quick – the route that looks too short is the longest. If it looks too good to be true then chances are it is. Trust your instincts; you know in your heart what is right and what is not.

So many 'investors' we have met are changing tack every 5 minutes; chasing MLM schemes, doing internet marketing, a bit of stock market trading, forex in the morning, some gold, silver, bronze, tin, carbon and soil investing, without working at the previous one long enough to make it work.

The biggest investors like Warren Buffet have built their wealth steadily over time through 'value' investing and sound principles. Many have portfolios generations old and continue to use strategies that have worked for them for decades. And you can too.

Summary

Be strong, be focused, and prepare to take some stick from those who don't know what you know. Continue to refine your strategy without getting lured by all that glitters and make your own decisions. Don't be a sheep.

Take action: Start Now

Decision.

"It's in your moments of decision that your destiny is shaped" -Tony Robbins

Fundamental tip No.2:
Start Now. Get perfect later. To know and not to do is not to know, just go.

Procrastination and indecision are diseases of progress and momentum. Both indecision and over analysis essentially lead to the same thing: a long and windy road to nowhere:

'I want to wait to see what the market is doing.'

'I don't have enough money yet.' *[So I might as well give up!]*

'I don't have enough time.' *[Less than everyone else?]*

'I do want to invest in property but don't know where to start.'

'What if I make the wrong decision?'

'My mate Jonny told me down the local pub the property market is going to crash, so I think I'll wait'

'It's too risky.'

We are all going to make mistakes. Mistakes are necessary. Mistakes are part of the journey to success that can't be avoided. Knowing that this is a fact of [successful] living, why not go out and make a few? Accept this as part of our journey; you can even start enjoying a few of them by seeing the funny side, or knowing that you've ticked another off the list and got one mistake closer to success, or you've got over one more hurdle that most people fall short of.

A great friend of ours *likes* to make as many mistakes as he can up front because he believes that the more mistakes he makes quickly, the closer to his goal he is getting, in less time. We really admire that attitude.

Fear, pride and ego are some of the biggest barriers to success. Enjoy listening, enjoy learning and growing, and know that we can all learn something from everyone. Do not fear the consequences of your decisions, and accept and enjoy mistakes. Be decisive.

You'll learn as you go with the right mix of studying and doing and reviewing.

We call this the 'entrance fee.' You have to make mistakes, and you have to 'pay' for your education, one way or another [education, mistakes, experience]. Wealthy people do not wait to make decisions; they make decisions and then refine their strategy and improve upon it.

Indecision leads to procrastination, which leads to frustration, which leads to more procrastination; and so the cycle continues. Ready, fire aim. Go. Just frickin' do it baby.

Fundamental tip No.3:
"Don't wait to own property, own property and wait" – Mark Homer

Perhaps you have thought about investing in property for many years now, but have not 'got around to it.' That wouldn't be the first time we have heard that. If we had just a pound for every time we heard that then we wouldn't need to buy any more property! That would be our main passive income stream ;-)

As Napoleon Hill puts it: "Do not wait; the time will never be 'just right.' Start where you stand, and work with whatever tools you may have at your command, and better tools will be found as you go along."

You will never be 100% ready to start in property, and you'll never be 100% perfect, no matter how much you learn or know, or however many you've bought.

If you're still 'getting all your Ducks in a row' you're probably just scared. We all start at the same point remember. We all have to earn the right in the same way, make the same sacrifices, look silly from time to time [Rob is good at that] and get back up.

It's just like having a baby. You can go to the doctors and see the scans, you can go to breathing classes, you can eat all the right foods, do incantations and play Dolphin music. You can get a pram and paint the spare room pink, but nothing will quite prepare you for the drop, and everyone says they were never really 'ready.'

But when it happens you get resourceful and any good parent will make it work. You'll learn and grow through doing and it will add so much more to your life. It's fun, it's exciting and it's real.

Decision is a mindset: Be a decision maker.

Take action now.

"The more action you take the more money you will make"

But we're all lazy gits from time to time. Sometimes we don't have the energy or desire.

Come on, let's be honest here. There are so many things we just can't really be bothered to do. I [Rob] can't be bothered to cook. I never ever cook. Not even for girls. I hardly go shopping and I'm quite well known for it. I can't be bothered to do any cleaning and my Mum has to come over to water the plants otherwise they die. I'm in my early 30's, in case I didn't tell you.

It is human nature to be lazy. The sad thing is that without actually doing anything about what you're reading here now, then there is no point in continuing.

But you can be as lazy as you want when you're rich and living off your income, right?

Most people can't be bothered to make money, be wealthy and attract success. They'd rather stay in their comfort zone of underachievement. It's much easier! Even if we try to pull some 'reverse psychology' on you and point out that **you will not** be one of those, 95% of you **will** be one of those! We just hope it's not YOU.

Don't just read this to humour us or because you have heard about us, or maybe even because you like us; or because you don't. Read it for you. Make a decision **right now** that you are going to take action on what you are reading in this book.

Consistent action is the **only** way we are going to achieve wealth and success. As Richard Branson states: *"Screw it, let's do it."*

No one ever had a bag of money fall on their head whilst asleep, watching TV, meditating or playing a games console.

It's all very well being great at visualisation and manifestation, but without doing anything about it, nothing will ever get done.

"The more you sweat in training, the less you bleed in battle." - proverb

It really doesn't matter how fast or slow you take action, what direction you go in, or which strategy you use at first, as long as you continue to take action and you are open to opportunities that will come your way, because you are taking action.

Summary

Be decisive, do a little more each day and always be moving forward. Think 'what action I am taking on a daily basis to get closer to my goal?' Use consistent action with never ending improvement and you will be as wealthy as you believe you can be. You have made that first important step towards being financially independent and taking action by buying this book. Procrastination is a disease — don't let this be you. Don't fear mistakes, enjoy them, knowing you're one step closer. Now is always the best [and only] time.

Section 3: The Secret Psychology of Successful Investors

Success, achievement, or however you want to classify the life that you want leaves tracks and clues, and is set up on fundamental concepts.

Success is something that you can mould or mimic. Wealth is exactly the same. Once you know the mould or the strategy it then becomes predictable. Just like failure is predictable.

Once you can find a pattern in something [a strategy] all you have to do is keep using that strategy over and over again to get your same, successful, predictable results. And then tweak and maintain it as it evolves and changes from time to time.

Tiger Woods does just that. How many times do you think he has practised [and visualised] the same shot? Not that type, I know what you're thinking! Andre Agassi said he won Wimbledon 10,000 times because he visualised himself winning it since he was 5 years old.

Those people who think that success is luck [luck is said by smart people to be a combination of knowledge, experience and preparation meeting opportunity] or co-incidence, are the people who are not where they want to be in their life.

Success, and the mindset of success, starts and finishes with you my friend.

If you want to change the world, it is generally your view of the world that needs to change.

"Be the change that you wish to see in the world." - Gandhi

If you want to be in a position to be able to give back to others, something we've been able to do thanks to property, then you need to be successful yourself first. Charity begins at home: get yourself successful, you have the ability, and then you can help as many people as you want.

It's funny how so many people we've met have had negative beliefs or guilt around making money. Not you, right? But if anyone thinks making money is a bad thing, you'll lose your friends or it'll make you a bad person, then no money comes your way.

Money can buy you happiness, and you can love money and be an amazing person too.

So in this section, and something totally unique to a property book, is a breakdown of your personal success strategies, specific to property investment profit. These probably have 80% of the importance of the tools, techniques and secrets within these pages. Don't skip over them, even if you have a successful mindset already.

Know your purpose

This is where everything is born. This is your reason for doing what you're doing and being who you are and why you're here. Do you know what it is? This may seem like a big step, and it can take time [and many say that it should], and that is just fine.

What are you investing for? Most people do not have a big enough purpose or a 'why' to invest in property. If they do not have a big enough reason guess what's going to happen: when things get too tough, they will quit.

We're fortunate to have the UK's biggest group of professional property investors in the Progressive VIP programme. These are people who've taken the big step up, and are succeeding beyond their expectations. These are not the 10,000's of people who have done our trainings, these are at a higher level: more committed, with bigger reasons.

Beckie & Martin Cooper had a burning desire to spend more time together, and as a family, and to put both their children through private [expensive] education. They realised that dream within 18 months of starting with Progressive, and now have almost £10,000 net cashflow from their portfolio and property businesses.

James Mason has a few months left before he retires [young] from the army. Had he not built his portfolio from within the Progressive community, his 'pension' from the Army for 2 decades of service [£800 per month], would be about one fifth of what he needed. His portfolio makes up the rest and more, all within one year. In fact his income from properties went from minus £1,000 a month net [pre Progressive], to plus £2,500 per month with Progressive. You can see both their stories in more detail here: **www.progressiveproperty.co.uk/inspiration**

So many people are living a life of quiet desperation, with no direction or meaning, dictated by someone else's vision, in a job they hate, with people that they hate, because they have no real purpose.

It really doesn't have to be like that. Life is a *choice*. You don't have to set this in stone now, but as you are formulating your strategy in your mind, also think about your purpose, the reason bigger than you, that outlasts you, that keeps you on your path when you'll have plenty of reasons to quit.

Is it to help your family? Is it to take care of the ones you love? Is it just to prove to yourself that you can do it? Is it to shut up all the negative people? Is it for a collection of super cars or matching shoes and handbags? Is it to spend on fast cars and fast women [and waste the rest]? Is it to leave a legacy or set up a foundation? Is it to grow a large business so that you can create many jobs? Is it to teach other people to do the same? Whatever it is, you need to know it.

Remember we have a section for you at the end of the book on page 295 where you can fill all of this in. I suggest you go to the back right now, and get scribbling.

The selfless life of Mother Teresa's purpose and drive was to help anyone who suffered anywhere in the world. She had a powerful enough reason why, which provided her with the necessary how.

Do you think that she could raise a few £mil in JV finance if she wanted to ;-) Of course she could. The purpose is the biggest magnet that people are attracted to

Money is just a consequence of the value we give to other people's lives. How can your purpose add to the lives of other people?

When you have a real purpose, when you are in your 'flow,' this will radiate and people will be attracted to your vision: to you [and many more properties will come your way too].

This is known as the 'why.' Once you have a compelling 'why' you will always find the 'how.' In fact, the 'how' becomes easy.

You'll build the best power team who'll fight your corner. You'll have people wanting to work for you, just to be associated with you. You'll attract the best people and the best deal, the best JV partners and the money, without having to go hunting for them.

If you have anything to add at the back of the book now, go to page 297 and write it down.

"Nothing is more powerful than a person who knows his destiny and has chosen now as the time to pursue it." - Jim Stovall.

Summary

Find your purpose in life so it gives you drive and fulfilment every day. Know why you are building your portfolio and your wealth, otherwise once all the obstacles show up you will give up. Reasons come first, answers come second. True purpose attracts success.

Focus

You get what you focus on.

But chase too many rabbits & you end up catching none.

Whatever it is that you think about most consistently is likely to become a reality in your life. You are what you think about consistently. Top professional sportsmen are just that because they have focused on their sport and being the best for the greatest amount of time, with the greatest level of commitment.

Anyone who is an expert in their field is not so by accident, but because they have read the most books, done the most study, had the most lessons, made the most mistakes, spent the most hours and gained the most experience. They have focused and thought for the most amount of time in their respective field.

Warren Buffet once said, *"I'm like a Tiger Woods, or a Michael Jordan....these people have an incredible ability to focus."*

Just think about flight. 500 years ago if you had told someone that anyone would be able to fly anywhere in the world in under a day you would probably have been voodoo'd, pinned to death and burned at the stake. Now it is common place because of people like the Wright brothers who believed that it could be done. They focused on making it happen, despite the fact that it had never been seen nor done before. And despite what everyone else said.

Thomas Edison said of the light bulb - *"I have not failed. I've just found 10,000 ways that won't work"*

If you want to be wealthy through property then you must think like the rich. The rich focus on wealth and money and business and success [without guilt]; learn how they think.

In order to think like the rich, find the rich and spend time with the rich. Find property investors with 20 or more properties; people to mentor and coach you, and work out exactly what it is that they focus on the most. Where do they go, where do they work, where do they eat and what people do they spend their time with the most? They are where they are because of their focus, and you can do and have exactly the same. There are 1,000's of these people in the Progressive Community, and they'd love you to be a part of it.

By the way this is not about comparing yourself to others. We're fortunate to work with some of the richest, most successful and most famous Entrepreneurs in the UK such as James Caan, Lord Sugar, Bob Geldof, Andreas Panayiotou, Karren Brady, Neville Wright, and other non-celebrity millionaires and billionaires.

If we compared the size of our penis, we mean office, to that of Andreas' whose conference table held almost as many people as our entire first office at Progressive, then we might feel a little insignificant ;-)

But he sold his entire portfolio for £1.2bn before the crash. Yet Mark is just as smart, he's just been doing it a lot longer.

It's about you, not anyone else. Don't compare, just learn.

There will always be someone bigger, faster, richer, slimmer, prettier and more intelligent than you [but don't forget that it is all just perception or opinion]. However you have unique qualities that can help add value to the rich and successful people who will be helping you.

Wherever you are, is just where you should be, and in 1, 2 or 5 years from now you could quite easily have a property portfolio that will look after you for the rest of your life, if you focus. It took Mark nearly 2 years, it took Rob 9 full time months; 15 hours a day. Use the unique qualities that you already have.

Certainly the mistake that many of us make, and I have been guilty of this in the past [Rob again], is not focusing on one thing long enough to become so good at it that wealth and success follow as a natural consequence.

I got 2 black belts at martial arts, I was one of the best artists in the country at GCSE and A-level, I played county cricket, played off single figures at Golf, and I don't say this to impress you. In fact it makes me look stupid, the fact that I converted none of them into anything useful, and kept making the same mistakes over and over, and don't do many of them anymore.

It's a waste of time and effort, because there's one thing I know for sure, if Mark had gotten to that level at any of those things, he would have gone on to become one of the best in the UK or world at them, because he has a great ability to stick to one path. I never became great at any of them, and gave up just as I had the chance to become great. I don't know if you can relate to this?

In fact, why not go to page 297 and list all your great qualities now. It really doesn't matter what they are, and no one is watching; you might be surprised how many things you didn't think you were good at.

Ask yourself now what unique skills you have. Take a minute right now. What can you do that most people can't? What are you better at than most people, so that you could become one of the best? You will be able to take many of these talents that you have focused on, and turn them into cash in your portfolio. As long as you focus on them with a Mark Homer style laser, and avoid distractions and shiny things.

Be opportunistic. It is in focusing on something [one thing] that you spot more opportunities. Have you ever noticed when you buy a new car that all of a sudden you see so many more of them on the road? Do you think that's because as soon as you buy your car everyone else copies you by buying the same car just to keep fashion with you, and then follows you around all day?

Or perhaps it is because that car has now come into your awareness? And what about the terrible realisation that three girls are wearing the same dress as you at a party [especially if you are a man]?!

Focus works just like that. Be open minded and ever aware of the 1000's of opportunities that are out there. Be thinking every minute of every day: 'How can I make the most of this situation?'

'How can I?' – What a great question to keep asking yourself.

Put a notebook by your bed, you might be surprised at how many ideas you wake up with. It's funny how things come to you with an even dose of focus and expectation.

Take a little time to define your strategy, and we can help you with that; then focus. Focus on a single property type [the one that works the best for you in your area], focus on a single area, focus on your one main strategy and the refining of it, focus on building relationships and offering value to people. Focus on your figures and you will be that financially independent property investor that you can and want to be.

You get to leverage all the testing, trial and error and strategy refining we've done over 25,000 hours. In all of our experience in property, and judging the performance of our own portfolio, focus is fundamental.

Discipline: focus really isn't that difficult, it just takes a few qualities we all have. I'm going to show you how easy it is by sharing the qualities I had to learn, but didn't have [at least not for long enough].

To be focused and become great, you need to be patient. It takes discipline to be patient, but you'll likely over-estimate what you can achieve in a short time and under-estimate what you can achieve in a lifetime.

I can hardly believe I am writing this as I'm one of the most impatient people you'll meet. But you gotta keep going, and you gotta have faith that it will bring results. It will, and the longer you keep going, the better it gets, the more people know your brand, the more good will you create and the more your outgoing efforts turn to incoming cashflow.

The next thing you must do is learn to do the mundane, boring and difficult things consistently well, and learn to enjoy them. Most people are ill-disciplined when it comes to the hard, the boring, the monotonous or the scary. It's these very things that get you the big, sexy, fun things that are waiting for you at the end.

And the third, and possibly most important thing, is you must create a forcefield to negativity. Negative people, news and energy will rot your enthusiasm, shake your belief, and distract you away from your goal. It is the thief of focus. Block it out.

I'm not saying be all faux-happy-clappy positive and only deal with positive things. But you can do hard things with enthusiasm, and you can ignore all that draining energy that eats you inside and steals your success.

Summary

Whatever it is that you want, focus on it intensely. Expect to achieve and you will. Stay on target in laser Mark Homer like fashion, don't chase too many rabbits and opportunities will come your way every day. Then grab them and shut out all other distractions [especially negative people] and keep going, you always get there in the end.

Belief

Wherever your 'ceiling of belief' is now, that is the limit to what you believe you can achieve.

You need to raise it. If you want more, then you need to believe you can achieve more. Believe first then receive, NOT the other way around.

"It is the mind that maketh good of ill that maketh wretch or happy, rich or poor" - Edmund Spenser.

If you currently earn a salary of £30,000, would you go and apply for a job that pays £130,000? Would you go and apply for a job that pays £3,000? Probably not, because your ceiling of belief in relation to earnings is unconsciously set somewhere similar to where you are now.

But if you want results you've never achieved before, you need to do things you haven't done, and have beliefs you've never had [before]. If you want to learn to be a billionaire, you need to unlearn all the things that made you a millionaire ;-)

If you want 5, 10 or 20+ properties then you need to believe you can have them *now*. That's right, before you own them. Some have found that tough, but if you're always waiting for evidence of something before you start, then you'd never get anywhere, right?

Did you know that if you catch fleas and put them in a jar they will jump to try and get out, only to hit the lid of the jar. If you leave them there for a while they will continue to do the same thing over and over: jumping and hitting the lid, expecting a different result [what was it Einstein said?].

Even more interesting is that when you take off the lid, the fleas will still only jump as high as where the jar lid was, even though they can jump higher and set themselves free. We are much more like fleas than we like to admit or realise, aren't we?

Itch. Scratch.

For 100's of years it was known that no human being could run a four minute mile; many people tried and failed, and the whole world set into a similar belief [which became a reality].

Then Roger Bannister came along, shattered this belief and ran a 3.59 mile. He visualised the images of breaking this belief until it became a reality. This new belief increased his willpower and built up his persistence and achieved physical results to match his mental picture. What is even more interesting is shortly after; over a 1000 people duplicated his feat. What changed? Did people suddenly become faster?

No, their beliefs changed.

Belief is the centre of everything, and it is our opinion [and we're not necessarily right] that we get what we believe we can achieve.

Our results are directly related to our level of belief. What do you think James Caan and Lord Sugar believe about money? That it's eeeeevil? That it is hard to get? That there's not much of it around at the moment? Are you kidding?

If you look at where you are now, the chances are you don't really believe that you could earn twice as much **now**. Be honest with yourself. If you did, you'd double your prices immediately, right? Or ask your boss for 100% pay rise. You'd have the money, right?

That has to change. Think about what having 20 properties would feel and look like to you. Think about 50. Think about the lifestyle that it will bring you now. That you deserve it. That it's easy when you follow a *system.* If anyone else can do it, you can do it too.

Geoff Whittaker did just that. He followed the Progressive 'flip' system and believed he could do it, despite not having done it before, and not having his own proof, only our word and some training from Progressive.

In the next 9 months he 'flipped' 3 deals in Manchester and made £58,000 cash. Geoff is over 60 years old and if you saw him, you'd never believe it.

While you are taking a moment to digest this, allow me to tell you another little story about that [Rob]. On the 3rd edition of this book, I considered taking this story out, as I look to keep the book on point and straight to the point to help you make more money through property. I've decided to keep it in, as I believe this can give you a bigger win than sweating your way to the top.

In 2004/5, when I realised that I had been living like a bit of an idiot for 25 years, a friend of mine just happened to give me two sets of personal development CD's. Something very exciting occurred for me.

I had been learning about visualisation, manifestation, attraction and incantations. Because I was kind of desperate, and felt that I was selling myself short, I figured I had nothing to lose, so I might as well give it a try. To be honest I was pretty sceptical of all the American rah-rah stuff, but hey, if you don't try, you'll never know, right?

I started to learn that if you tell yourself something enough times, you actually start to believe it [like being 'rich' before you are]. I also learned that you are far more likely to attract it through awareness and focus than having negative, 'can't do it,' thoughts, even if I didn't really believe it right away. After all I was trying to 'kid' myself that the last 25 years of belief [and reality] wasn't real, and this new way that I'd never experienced before, *is* real.

But I tried it. This is a true story of events that really happened. Do not read on if you think that the last page or two is hocus pocus.

Every morning I'd get up at 6:00am, and on the 115th day [that's how long it took] it became real. I'd get on my exercise bike in my front room and look out of my window onto my driveway.

'Every day in every way I'm getting bigger and better and stronger yes! I'm wealthy, successful and I have a Nissan 350Z with orange leather seats sitting on my drive.'

At the time of starting I had almost £35,000 worth of debt and no job or experience of any real money. But I just followed the script from the CD [with blind faith]:

'Every day in every way I'm getting bigger and better and stronger yes! I'm wealthy, successful and I have a Nissan 350Z with orange leather seats sitting on my drive.'

And there was no proof that any of this stuff actually worked because it was a whole new world to me:

'Every day in every way I'm getting bigger and better and stronger yes! I'm wealthy, successful and I have a Nissan 350Z with orange leather seats sitting on my drive.'

115 days later I had my gunmetal 350Z [by far my favourite car at the time, regardless of price, and the sexiest thing on 4 wheels] sitting on my drive with orange leather seats [I didn't even know that they made them with orange leather seats!]. It was mine, I owned it, and I loved it.

Since then I've become a little less 'fluffy,' but use a similar, slightly shortened technique, combined with consistent action, and it has manifested our Ferrari's and fleet of cars, property portfolio, £multi million businesses, being a pilot, great relationships and closeness of family, my son's golfing skills - he's two ;-) - and much more you don't need me to brag about.

But I used to **dream** about these things. Being a millionaire, driving Ferrari's like Magnum and flying helicopters like Airwolf. OK, so perhaps I am still a bit of a child ;-) But there was one key shift that turned dreams into reality. Because *dreams* are just dreams...

You see for 25 years I got what I focused on – not much, because I had warped beliefs around money and success. Perhaps you have beliefs that are creating your current results, and they can do with a change? Perhaps it was coincidence, perhaps it was taking action, but one of the main 'before and after' differences that has made a huge difference to my life is the belief change. At first I had to kid myself, now I've seen the proof. And I'll continue to 'kid myself' of the next thing, and the next thing, no matter how big. And it is something that I continue to practice every day before I go to bed, and you can too my friend.

Another story about this is of Major James Nesmet. He was a prisoner of war in Vietnam and was locked up for 7 years in a bamboo cage. To save himself from going mad, he visualised himself on a golf course playing a perfect 18-holes each and every day. He was your average golfer shooting an average round of no less than 90, but on the first round he played upon release he scored a personal best of just 74 strokes.

One major benefit of working with property investors [from total newbies to seasoned investors] in the Progressive community, is that you learn the common, consistent things that get in the way of people's success. In fact we'd have to be idiots not to recognise the signs, having educated over 150,000 eyeball to eyeball at live events or in the Progressive community. Here are some of them:

'I'm not smart enough to make money.'

'You have to do bad things to make money.'

'There's not much money around at the moment; things are really hard.'

'Friends, family and people won't like me if I make money.'

'I just wasn't born with the ability.'

'I'm not worth it and I don't deserve it.'

These are genuine common beliefs of ordinary people. It's what they know, what they've been taught or how they've been brought up. But the past does not have to dictate the future, right?

'I'm not smart enough to make money.'

Money doesn't care if you're smart, and it doesn't judge. Old or young, PhD or University of life, it doesn't judge. You're worth money just as much as anyone else.

'You have to do bad things to make money.'

Some of the wealthiest people in the world add the most value and do the best things for the most people. Could you accuse Virgin or Richard Branson of doing bad things for their money? Could you accuse people who run big companies of evil doings when they employ so many people who may not have jobs, pay more taxes than anyone else, and give more to charity than anyone else?

'There's not much money around at the moment; things are really hard.'

With the Governments of the world printing more money, do you think there's less money around at the moment, or more? Do you think it is harder to make money when it's moving faster from the big corporations to the Entrepreneurs, or easier? Would you rather it be easier for everyone else as well? Perhaps when it is more difficult for the masses, it's easier for those who help solve other people's problems?

'Friends, family and people won't like me if I make money.'

If you turn into an arrogant spanner then people won't like you whether you're rich or poor. If you're a great person who adds value, people will not like you any less if you have money, and lots of it. They'll probably respect how you got it, and want you to show them how to do it too.

And if they don't, they can put it in their pipe and smoke it.

The odd few will dislike you because you have money, but it's just a reflection of how they dislike themselves, it's nothing personal to you, it's all about them, and there's nothing you can do about it anyway. Let it motivate you. Perhaps you could challenge yourself to turn them around. Or just let them sail by.

'I just wasn't born with the ability.'

Here's the reality, no one is born with anything but potential. Tiger Woods didn't drop out of his Mum with a Golf club, Bill Gates didn't pop out with a PC and Sir Steve Redgrave didn't row his way out.

Anyone can be anything they want, if they take control. Get educated, move to the right environment, take consistent action and you can be successful at anything you want to be.

'I'm not worth it and I don't deserve it.'

Why not you? What's wrong with you? Surely you deserve it more than people who don't do things ethically? You're a good person, right? You've made mistakes, we all have, it doesn't make you bad, and it's just the action that was wrong. Not you my friend.

You get what you deserve, so perhaps you're selling yourself short on what you're really worth.

You might be surprised that in the one-to-one sessions on the Progressive VIP mentorship programme, we are dealing with challenges like this easily as much, if not more, than the strategies and tactics:

'The skillset without the mindset will leave you upset." - Craig Valentine.

The difference between the amount of money ordinary people make and what Bill Gates makes starts with belief. Gates' career was launched when he promised to deliver software he hadn't developed for a computer he had never seen. This sense of certainty led him to tap into all the resources he needed to successfully design the software and to build his billions.

By following all the strategies in this book and applying them with a heightened belief that you will achieve whatever you desire now your results will change accordingly.

When we started in property everyone was telling us it was too late. When we were buying with OPM everyone was telling us it couldn't be done. When Mark gave up a high paying job people thought he was nuts. When we set up Progressive to help other people do the same we were told we shouldn't:

'There aren't enough properties.'

'People won't pay you to help them.'

'You're too young; I've been doing it 30 years.'

"Be realistic."

People told us to be realistic! Can you believe that one? Most people who say 'try to be realistic' are living in fear. They let their past disappointments and other perceived failures of taking another shot hold them back, just in case they get their fingers burnt. Their [limiting] beliefs are developed to protect themselves, which lead to limited results. Do you think great leaders like Mandela and Gandhi were ever 'realistic'?

We refused to listen [crabs and sheep] and be held back. We used it to motivate ourselves, and still do, and it gave us a burning desire to succeed and to prove them wrong. No one will ever tell us we can't do anything, and they can't for you either.

You have to trust us on this one. Well actually you don't; it is your choice. If you do choose to trust us now, don't be like most people and wait to see results before you start to believe that you can have what you want. You could be waiting a very long time.

Summary

Believe now that you can achieve what you want to achieve and see the results change accordingly. Believe in yourself. The past does not equal the future. Don't listen to the crabs. Add commitment and hard work to that belief and you have the keys to great success in your portfolio and your life.

Anyone can do it

And yes that includes YOU :-)

You are your biggest chance of success and your biggest chance of failure. If you don't believe that you can have the wealth and property investment success that you want, then you won't. Sorry to be blunt.

Henry Ford best coined the phrase *"Whether you think you can or can't, you're right."*

Having just read about belief, let's assume that you believe [or are working on the belief] that you can achieve any goal you put your mind to.

It doesn't matter if you don't have all the answers right now: none of us have all the answers. Get perfect later. This book will give you a big leap forward, but the rest of your success will be down to your own belief and consistent action.

Remember that we used the analogy that buying a property is like having your first child. OK, to all the mothers out there, we are by no means saying that we could even begin to understand the pain you went through ;-) But at the end of the day when it happens for the first time we're all in the same boat; we all start from the same place and we all have it in us to be good parents; even though we might not know it yet!

And it's amazing how resourceful we become when we're actually doing it; when we're in at the deep end, getting the lessons the fastest, in real time.

You know that anyone can do it. Think about it. You know that most Entrepreneurs, multi-millionaire business people and property investors started from the start. Very often that somewhere is much further back than where you are right now. I [Rob] was almost £35,000 in credit debt when I started and James Caan built his business from a broom cupboard.

Just look at anything you have achieved in the past: anything at all. Everyone has unique talents and we know that you are good at **something;** many things in fact. Whatever it is that you are thinking now that you are good at, where you have achieved levels of success, you can replicate.

Napoleon Hill calls it 'transmutation.' Think of all that wayward sexual energy a lot of us have [speak for ourselves?!] and the huge amount of energy people expend [waste] on negative things that serve them no purpose. Imagine if you could rein that in and hone that energy in attaining wealth and success. We'd all be multi-squillionaires!

Our guess is you got really good at something through focus, belief, confidence, hard work, teamwork, commitment and concentration, overcoming obstacles, to name just a few. We shall be talking about these later.

There is enough money out there for us all to be millionaires many many times over. Go and get your share. There are enough properties out there for everyone who reads this book to have a nice profitable portfolio, go and buy some before your competition swallows up all the best ones.

Money does not choose where it goes and does not discriminate. There is no one single 'type' of person that becomes wealthy. Regardless of age, race, upbringing, creed, nurture and health, we can all become wealthy right now.

Take personal responsibility now: do you know anybody who is always blaming other people for things that go wrong? Perhaps even your boss or partner? Maybe you know people who always blame the weather or bad luck for their misfortunes. People who say 'it only ever happens to me:' or 'that's just my luck.' People who are never wrong and nothing is ever their fault.

I remember [Rob], being a competitive golfer in my youth. I consistently blamed my clubs, bad bounces, bad luck, and especially the wind for my poor scores. The irony is that the same wind blows on us all, doesn't it?

If only I knew then what I know now. If, but, when, maybe, shoulda, woulda, coulda: whatever!

The most wealthy and successful people, investors and business owners understand *responsibility*. The performance of their assets is not due to market movements, but their own diligence, faith, persistence and following of the 'rules' as discussed in this book.

And adapting and being resourceful.

Don't blame the market or the Estate Agent or the vendor or the surveyor. The more you take responsibility for everything that happens in your life, everything that you have control over, every decision you make, the more you will be in control of the things that happen in your life.

When Donald Trump was asked by reporters why he was in $900 million debt, he could have made excuses such as the real estate bubble burst, or blamed the economy, but instead he took complete responsibility for his results. He said:

"I took my eye off the ball. I stopped doing business the way I used to. So I got my eye back on the ball"

His personal responsibility propelled him to get back on the ball and to enjoy massive success. Similarly billionaire investor Warren Buffet [in his books] talks openly about the mistakes he has made, and how he has taken complete responsibility for his failures.

Are you fully in control? If not, do not worry [or blame someone else!] just read on with an open mind now.

Take responsibility for your life, your decisions and your finances now.

Money is not the answer, you are: If you think that money is the answer to all of your life's problems, then your problems are only just starting.

Money is not the answer.

Many of our business mentors state that with more money bigger problems come. Of course a problem is a perception, and the wealthiest see these so called 'problems' as challenges or opportunities. It is vital for us to realise that money doesn't solve anything.

Take a look at your money beliefs again:

"Money is one of the most important subjects of your entire life. Some of life's greatest enjoyments and most of life's greatest disappointments stem from your decisions about money. Whether you experience great peace of mind or constant anxiety will depend on getting your finances under control." - Robert Allen.

Money is easy to attract because you have the unique abilities to attract it. Money is not prejudiced and you can have whatever belief, religion or political standpoint you choose, and still be wealthy. You are the answer.

Money and happiness are completely unrelated. Some of the happiest people are the poorest and some of the most horrible, revolting, nasty people are wealthy beyond imagination. It probably won't last, but there we go. Don't look to money for the answers. You can choose to be whoever you want, regardless of how much wealth you have now and how much more you will make in the future. You are the answer.

Your portfolio is your vehicle to do the things you want in your life, but it does not depend on it. Wealth is merely a consequence of whatever it is that you do. The harder and faster and smarter you work, the more money you will attract, but it is still just a result of that.

The more value you give, the more money you'll attract.

Those who continually spend more than they earn [even when they earn a great deal] are chasing their tails in a self fulfilling vicious circle: always chasing more money to be happier only to spend more than they earn and feel empty.

You have everything now and you're ready right now to be as wealthy as you want to be. You can choose. You can have wealth and happiness and free time and a social life and a great family life and time with your kids and partner who you love dearly and who feels appreciated and holidays 3 times a year and regular sex and breakfast in bed [or both at once]…

You really can have it all, and it is only belief that will ever tell you otherwise.

Summary

Anyone can do it; especially you. Believe that you can and you will and know that you have the answers you need. Take personal responsibility for your life, your decisions and your finances and have what you want for your life.

Faith, passion and desire

Can you think of anyone who really loves what they do? Virgin founder Richard Branson once stated that if you can indulge your passion, your life will be more interesting than if you're working.

Every business Richard Branson enters, whether it is space travel, health clubs, music, airlines, it must be fun for him.

We don't see what we do as work. How can it be? It's far too much fun! Making money is fun. Buying property is fun. Training other people is fun. Watching them make money is fun. Spreadsheets are fun. Cough.

Passion: people who have passion and desire in what they do are radiant, attractive and successful in their own right and by their own definition. Think of Tony Robbins or Mother Teresa or Mohammad Ali or Will Smith; or anyone who really inspires you with passion. It's inspiring and infectious.

If it's fun when it's good, it will be fun when it's not so good. Or at least the passion will propel you through the tougher times, when negative people suck you dry and ordinary people just give up.

Have passion and desire in everything you do and faith that it will work for you, otherwise don't waste your time doing it. Remember everything is your **choice**. If you ain't got it yet, practice until you have, or do something else.

We love property. Property is King, God and religion. We live and breathe property because it makes us so much money, and it's fun, and we're in control, we're get to choose, we don't have to answer to too many people, and we get back what we put in, with limitless opportunity.

Sweet.

Faith: Faith in yourself [or a higher entity that you believe in] is another essential ingredient to personal and property investment success. If you do not implicitly trust yourself or believe in who you are, what you're doing and that you will get where you want to be, then who is going to?

You don't have all the answers yet, so you need a little, sometimes blind faith to get going, and to keep going, and that you'll get where you want to go.

True faith exists in people who believe even when there is neither reasons nor references to support it. We are all here for a purpose, there is a path for us all, and you simply have to take it.

It's often best not to know too much anyway, because if you knew the truth you may never get started ;-)

It sounds so easy in practice, and the truth is that it is, especially with a nice dose of passion and desire.

Colonel Sanders was over 65 before he even got the KFC brand off the ground. He spent 2 years travelling across America, sleeping in his car, taking his special recipe from restaurant to restaurant in the hope [faith/belief] that someone would like it. Do you think he had faith in himself and his recipe? You know the rest of the story.

Summary

Have faith in yourself and whatever you believe in; that you are and will become great at making profit through Property. Be passionate and have a burning desire for success and you will get it.

Be realistic [& unrealistic]

Set your vision and purpose big. Bigger than you. Then set goals and expectations realistically and take your time.

This was something that I found so hard in the beginning [Rob]. I was so focussed and excited and determined and energetic and impatient that I wanted everything yesterday and made these huge goals and felt amazing. It's not that the goals and dreams were unrealistic, but the timeframe and scale of them were.

Big vision; realistic goals.

Goals, dreams and vision are all essential parts of seeing your future before it happens and making plans to get there. Some of the greatest business people are those who can vividly picture their life in its future exactly how it looks, no matter how apparently far-fetched or in the future, or the lack of proof to back it up.

And with this ability, it is just as essential to understand what you consistently need to do on a daily basis, and how you're going to realistically achieve your goals. Being overly dreamy or unrealistic about the market, goals, projections or reality is dangerous, and will damage your long term wealth and security.

There are times when you need to keep your feet on the ground. Keep the big vision in mind and never lose the faith and belief, but don't get so far in the clouds you ignore the necessary day to day actions.

This is where our partnership has become more and more important over the years. Mark is very much a day to day, doing what is real, now, kind of person. Very operational and very realistic. Dislikes fluff. This is great for keeping your feet on the ground, staying focussed and getting the job done. But he's not a strategist, finds it difficult to imagine anything until he's seen the proof, and often over analyses and gets bogged down in [sometimes] unnecessary details.

Rob is hopeless with analysis — if the thing isn't top of Google, it doesn't exist, and he needs his assistant to search it for him. He gets bored quite quickly and doesn't always do enough research. But he makes quick big decisions well, can think years in advance, and sees the bigger picture to keep the direction of today on the vision of tomorrow.

Imagine the two of us in a confined space, and the conversations down the pub.

But these opposite traits have been one of the major things that have helped us get to where we are. Rob would have been off all over the place with 73 different businesses buying everything everywhere [and making some big mistakes], but Mark would still be an employed account manager stuck in the middle of a rigid corporate structure quietly rotting away but not doing anything about it, because of the risk.

And it was this realisation [not at the start of Progressive, by any means], that helped us get the best of both opposing skillsets. And you can do that too, by understanding your strengths and being honest about your weaknesses, and partnering accordingly with people in your powerteam. There's an entire section on exactly how to do that later :-)

You need to take consistent action to get to where you want to be; things are not always going to go your way, and you'll make mistakes. What are your expectations of these? How will you deal with situations when life throws you a curveball? It is always very wise to be realistic, and expect this.

But, be warned. You know overly 'realistic' people are usually cynical, cannot stand change, will often sneer at you in the beginning, stay stuck in a past mindset that existed 5 years ago, and are actually scared.

Perhaps, at this stage, you may be thinking 'these guys are contradicting themselves a little.' They talk about visualisation and big goals, yet they talk about being 'grounded' and 'realistic.'

Do you think it is realistic to earn £30,000 a month? Is it realistic to own 500 properties or to win a gold medal? Or to fly or step on the moon or sacrifice your life for someone you love? Imagine what the world would have been like if some of our greatest inventors would have been realistic [about their vision].

What you want from your life isn't realistic, because realistic is safe, boring and for everyone else. But wanting it all yesterday just isn't going to happen, and daily, realistic things need to happen consistently to get there.

Be realistic about your daily tasks and timeframe to success. Study what other successful people have achieved. Sam Walton of Wall Mart was an expert at watching his competition and taking on the things that worked well. If someone who has been in the industry takes 5 years to build 50 properties is it realistic to try to buy 100 in your first year?

Never stretch yourself too far. Do not invest money that you absolutely cannot live without and always have a contingency.

But have a huge vision, reason why and never sell it. Not to anyone. And make it HUGE. Because you can, and you've got a lot of time left in your life. So why not, eh?

"Most people over-estimate what they can achieve in a year but under-estimate what they can achieve in a lifetime"

Summary

Be realistic about what you can do in a day, but have a big vision that is bigger than you. You can change the world in your lifetime, just not every day. Set your expectations at the right level from the start, and take consistent action. Leverage others in your network to have complementary skillsets. Never stretch yourself too far and always have contingencies in place for worst case scenarios.

Think mid to long term

Anything that is for the long term is sustainable.

Rome wasn't built in a day. Nor were all of the wealthy property investors. If you want to get wealthy, be wealthy and stay wealthy, then you need to think long term sustainability rather than immediate gratification.

Property is not a get rich quick scheme; but investing time in assets and doing what is required will pay you forever. But the 'forget' needs to be 'set' first. Refer back to the previous chapter on the 'how-to.'

Building a portfolio takes time, regardless of what you might be told. Maybe a lot less time than 'realistic' people think, but time nonetheless.

Money attracts money and compounds [both ways]. If you keep spending all you earn then you'll never have long term wealth, because you're not saving/investing long enough to attract more of it. The more you put in, the more you get out.

If you're looking for the next big thing, quick fix, lazy way to save your life, you're reading the wrong book. Work smart. But you gotta work.

Property is exactly the same. If you keep selling for short term gains without holding some, delaying gratification and thinking for the future, then you'll never compound earnings long enough to be wealthy for the long term.

In formulating your property strategy think about this: will this or any decision aid my long term wealth? Is this sustainable? Will this create a good return on investment [ROI]? If not then leave and move on.

The principles set about in this book all gear towards long term wealth and sustainability, because that is the only way. Anyone can make a fast buck. Not everyone can make bucks for 6 decades.

Whatever you do, be careful of 'get rich quick zero to a million in no time' type offers, ads and 'opportunities.' We love the way most of them are sold: 'I have this great opportunity for you!' Oh yeah? What is it? Well I can't tell you now but what I can tell you…

Yes Ok. No thank you. If it seems far too good to be true, then the chances are that it is. By all means be open minded, but do your diligence. Every day we get approached with so many of these and when we do our diligence we've always found that the actual results are never the same.

Think 1, 5 and 10 years ahead and think about your future and your goals. Will your decisions to invest put you nearer or further away from these? Will that car, that conservatory or that 3 week holiday to Magaluf add to your long term wealth? In 5 years you can have as many material things and 'liabilities' as you want. If it's a Ferrari you truly desire, and you love the thought of driving in the summer evenings with the roof down and the music on full, then make sure you can afford it 10 times over so that you can actually enjoy it without worrying about the cost of the petrol and servicing.

If you want an 8 bed mansion with stables and a heart shaped bed with a Leopard skin throw, then make sure you work up to it; enjoy the journey without worrying about what the heating bills will be for the next quarter. Build your portfolio and wealth steadily, and over time, on solid financial and educational foundations.

If you can't be bothered with all of this then burn this book and try to sue a big company or marry a King or a Princess, but remember that everything comes at a price; and that might just be your happiness.

Summary

Think long term. Will any investment decision aid your sustainable success? If something seems too good to be true then it probably is, so walk on by and leave the gambling to the gamblers. Stick to your strategy and be forever wealthy for generations to come.

Trust your instincts

Your instincts and your intuition have been with you since the day you were born. They are part of you and who you are and have grown with you.

Everything that you have ever learned or experienced has been 'stored' in your subconscious. You have an innate ability to 'thin slice' any situation. Have you read 'Blink' by Malcolm Gladwell? This is a great book on this subject.

You can process millions of pieces of information in milli-seconds and make shrewd judgements that you may not have made so well had you stopped to think about it. This is your instinct and intuition at work. It is there to protect you and to help you. Trust it. Trust yourself and what your subconscious tells you.

If you get a bad feeling about something, absolutely don't go through with it. Do not work with or buy from someone you don't like, you don't trust, or who gives you an 'odd' feeling. There is a very good chance that your subconscious is telling you something. Trust it.

And if you like proof and evidence, and not fluff, then you'll be happy to learn that your 'instinct' is your subconscious, instant judgement totalling everything you've learned and experienced in your life before, micro-processing like a computer.

We can all get excited when an apparently amazing deal or offer is presented to us. Sometimes good [excited] feelings can lead us into problems because we are avoiding any due diligence. If you get a good feeling then by all means do the research to back up your feeling and pat yourself on the back if you are right. If you get a bad feeling then run like the bloody wind!

Stick to this strategy and you will not go wrong. The odd chance might pass you by, but all in all you will be right to listen to yourself. Trust yourself to trust yourself.

There are so many great, honest, skilled and trusted people out there. There is just no need to risk your wealth and future by working with people who are anything less than right for you.

Let's face it, you know when something is wrong, and you know you know, even if you try your hardest to tell yourself otherwise. We've all been in relationships we knew weren't right, haven't we? Life is far too short.

And if you are sitting here demanding evidence for all of this then create a strategy around your intuition and stick to it:

1. Listen to what you tell yourself.
2. Do your diligence. Find fact and respected opinion on your initial gut feeling.
3. Stay neutral and disassociate to the decision, just do what's right.
4. Make an informed decision as to whether you will act on your instinct or not, and get advice from those who have trodden the path.
5. Act fast or move on.

Summary

Don't get lured in by people or things that don't feel right; you just don't need to. Trust your instincts and intuition, they are reliable and are the sum of the evidence you've seen in your life. Live with your instinctive, informed decisions; they will end up being right most [enough] of the time.

Expect the unexpected

Planning and preparation are absolutely essential in property wealth and success.

"Fail to plan, plan to fail"

"Plan the work then work the plan"

There are very few people who had lasting wealth or a 20 + Property portfolio by total accident. Although it may appear that way on the surface, the fact is that wealthy people who are self made are great planners.

They may appear 'lucky'. In our experience, that is what envious or unsuccessful people say of those that have done well. If we take the time to look closely and to ask the right questions, we soon learn that there are principles that successful and wealthy people follow that anyone else can follow.

Wealthy and successful people do things 'subconsciously' that others are not even conscious of yet. They have done this through habit or repetition, experience or knowledge. Anyone can do this, anyone can get the experience or knowledge required to make these 'secrets' [what most people don't know that successful people do] become automatic and 'subconscious.'

Always do your diligence, but diligence can only get you so far. There are always unexpected factors that you'll never be able to account for, no matter how many times you re-analyse it.

Ensure you have a set contingency for each strategy you implement. Any deal should have a worst case scenario built in, so that no matter what happens nothing comes as too much of a surprise that it knocks you on your knees. Be prepared for many situations that could arise and not just the one that you expect [or desire].

If you don't prepare for the unexpected, you know it will happen, and it will catch you by surprise.

What's your financial contingency for the unexpected? What's your plan C? Know how much you want to invest and don't push it too far. Have a separate account for unexpected costs [that absolutely will come up; especially if you have not opened this account].

Know how much tax free cash you can save on an annual basis. Know how much you can afford to risk. Know the difference between investing and gambling and understand risk assessment.

Know what other people [vendors, agents, refurb men/women] want. Find out what they need. Know that people have their own agenda to any deal and make sure that you are aware of it so that a) you can strike the best deal, b) you can strike the best win-win relationship and c) you don't get ripped off.

Always check the small print on any contract or agreement. Check the interest rates, charges and fees of everything [especially when borrowing] and don't be afraid to negotiate and shop around as you can always find a better deal. Do not believe the first figure that you are told, and do not settle for a deal you are not happy with.

And, if like Rob, that sounds like torture to you, find your own 'Mark' in your powerteam, and leverage out these necessary steps.

Good people to listen to are the wealthy, the very successful, investors with a portfolio of 10 or more properties, the ones who have the skills and knowledge that you require, and the ones who are already doing what you want to do.

Don't listen to anyone else.

People you shouldn't listen to can very often be the closest to you, and this can be hard for some people. Friends and family may have [or think they have] the best intentions, but they can very often hold you back without even knowing that they are doing it. Are they experts in property? Are they rich and happy?

Grow and accept change.

If living things are not growing, they're dying. In this world, there is actually no such thing as standing still. It is forwards or backwards. Stagnation/lack of movement means you are actually falling behind.

"If you're green you grow and if you're ripe you rot" - Ray Kroc

Growth, evolution of the self and the acceptance that things don't stay the same are so important in your mindset and achievement of wealth and success.

Look at the internet. 20 years ago there was barely such a thing. Now you can do and find absolutely anything on the internet. Had you speculated about the evolution of the technological age 20 years ago, not even the most skilled forecasters could have predicted such phenomenal movement in technology.

And the sad and unfortunate thing for many is that those who do not stay up to date with the fast moving world get left behind. They stagnate. They die.

Many people have lived a life a certain way for such a long time and are so resistant to change, that they just fall behind helplessly. It is so counterproductive and such a waste of energy trying to fight the trends of change.

One thing that inspires us is youth. Youth, or the mindset of youth, is your position of strategic advantage in this game. Those who have a young and fresh mind very often lack fear and can adapt to change, regardless of physical age.

Being flexible is very important nowadays, more than ever, and it's only going to become more important. Those who are not flexible will get left behind.

If Avon had continued selling books door to door, if Colgate had continued to sell soap and candles, if Nintendo had continued selling playing cards and if Nokia continued as a paper mill, these companies would likely have failed. Because they adapted to change and could flex to what the world and their market wanted at the time, they were able not just to survive, but to thrive.

Your wealth and portfolio success depends on this flexibility, change and evolution for growth. This is not just accepting the things that are new, but growing and accepting change within yourself.

Buy to Let did not exist until the mid 90's, and then property investment changed. It changed again in 2006/7 when 100% mortgages stopped. It is changing all the time and now more and more houses are getting rented out room by room.

There are so many opportunities of earning income from different property related fields. Property is no longer just about buying and holding as it was just over a decade ago. There are new creative ways such as: AS, EDC, RMD, LO, S/LO, FF, PPB, QL, Uql, NMD, NMLI, MLWTS, JV's, brand, training, authoring books, property clubs, networking events and online communities...

All of which are covered in our 4th book, "Multiple Streams of Property Income," available on Amazon or the Progressive website.

Your needs *will* change over time too. A lot will depend on your age, education, family and social needs, health and your emotional mood. The people you know and deal with will change. Society will change. The rates from the bank and the value of money will change. The way you spend 'money' and what you want it for will change. The mortgage products will change and the economy will change. **Accept** and embrace it. Revise your strategy as you feel the need and know that you are on your path, and that growth and change are part of your journey.

"In property, the only certainty is change" – Mark Homer

Summary

Plan, prepare and be ready for the unexpected. Know that the market and your strategy will evolve and change over time. Don't resist it; accept it and embrace it. Be flexible, versatile and decisive.

Delay gratification

Discipline is the ability to control yourself and your desires/urges for instant gratification. It is the ability to stick to your strategy, and not be lured or tempted by anything that glistens or is coated in chocolate.

"Discipline is doing what you know you must do now, even when you don't feel like doing it" – Brian Tracy

"What you delay today, pays tomorrow"

Don't be lured by cash-backs and inflated prices and huge apparent new build discounts. Don't be lured by the easy or the quick fix or the get rich quick or the shortcut.

When you go out into the world to apply the things you are reading here, there will be offers and people and e-mails and all sorts thrown at you left right and centre about how you can be a millionaire in 10 minutes.

Be disciplined enough to push them all out of the way and focus on your own path.

Let your investments grow. Do not eat away at them too early. Set up solid foundations by understanding that wealth comes from delaying gratification. In the mid to long term you will be far wealthier than chasing short term fixes. You'll be richer with a bigger portfolio than those who over-borrowed, spent too much too soon, didn't do their diligence and were lured by the dark side of shiny objects and impatience.

A father and son who rejected a £50,000 offer for their wheelbarrow invention on Dragons' Den celebrated after netting over £1 million in orders during its first year on sale.

Father and son Mike and Joe Smith turned down offers by 'Dragons' Duncan Bannatyne and Hilary Devey who offered them £50,000 for 50 per cent of their Wheelbarrow Booster business.

The Dragons criticised the Smiths' attitude before they declared themselves out. But now the pair are struggling to keep up with demand, predicting sales of 100,000 units a year for their invention, a canvas product which increases the capacity of a wheelbarrow by 300 per cent.

DIY giant Homebase has placed an order of 5,000 units, Tesco Direct is also listing the product and there has been significant interest from companies as far away as Australia, New Zealand, America and Brazil. It is also now endorsed by professional gardener and broadcaster Alan Titchmarsh.

The 'Dragons' were left reeling when father Mike, 54, bluntly refused, telling them he would give away no more than 11.5 per cent of the company.

Son Joe, 32, said: 'I guess it could be seen as a mistake on our part but then again it may turn out to be the best thing we have done. Not many people turn down the Dragons, but we made the right call.

For the projections we gave them, we only needed to have sold 25,000 units for them to get their money back. They really undervalued it.'

"What you delay today, pays tomorrow."

Summary

> Be disciplined! What you delay today pays tomorrow.

Never give up

As Winston Churchill famously said [and repeated]: never ever ever give up!

Endearing persistence [not cat-like annoyance] is absolutely essential in your quest for personal success.

It took Thomas Edison ten thousand experiments to finally see the light in his invention of the light bulb. He did not give up, and knew that with every 'failure' he was one step closer to his goal. Failure is only an option when we give up, until then we are still moving forward.

"Nothing in the world can take the place of persistence. Talent will not; nothing is more common than unsuccessful men with talent. Genius will not; unrewarded genius is almost a proverb. Education will not; the world is full of educated derelicts. Persistence and determination are omnipotent. The slogan press on has solved and always will solve the problems of the human race" - Calvin Coolidge

There were many times when we could have given up; times when the deals we bought weren't the best; times when we had surveyors down-value perfectly good property, when people wanted us to fail, when cash was tight, when times were hard.

"The main thing is to keep the main thing the main thing" - Zig Ziglar

Our story of persistence is, to be honest, not as glorious as some, but it's ours and there have been plenty of times when we felt like throwing in the towel.

If you want to read a story of persistence, read up on Gerald Ratner and Christopher Reeve. Inspirational to say the least.

We would love to tell you that we had 3 near death experiences [I only had 2 – Rob!] and jumped through rings of fire, but most people's lives aren't really like that. Yes we got into debt at some points and it was hard. I [Rob] had to borrow money off just about everyone I knew to get by at times, and yes the market changed a few times and gave us a few eye opening surprises and seat of the pants moments.

But there really is no secret formula here other than attrition. Just keep on keeping on. You only fail when you stop; so just don't stop.

"Sweat beats regret"

What will motivate you when times get tough [as they will]? Is it the fear of going bust or the fear of failure? Having to go to work for somebody else, or beg for your old job back? How about what your friends and family will say and think about you when you succeed? To prove the doubters wrong? To give back to your family? To prove to yourself that you can?

The sad thing about persistence [or lack of] is that so many people actually get quite close to their desired goal. They get most of the hard lessons they need to toughen them up for the future, they are just around the corner from a big breakthrough towards success, and then give up.

Everything you do gets to a tipping point, where all the hard work you put in, [like getting the knowledge to go out and get great discounts or building a solid and reliable contact base to lend you JV cash for your next deal] will pay dividends. Once those foundations are set, then the money starts to roll your way; and it keeps on rolling, but not before you've earned the right.

Take this 3rd edition book, for example. It has taken around 4032 days and close to 26,000 hours to get from the ether to your hands. Now there are many people who are taking this information and turning it into cash. You have probably read many of our testimonials showing what can be done if you stick at it and break through that 'tipping point.'

Take Neil Asher, for example. Neil has one of the most successful global Life Coaching companies in the world, New Insights. I wouldn't be right to tell you in our words what he achieved, so this short passage is from an email he sent us as soon as he had read this book:

"As a direct result of one of the many secrets in the book, I purchased a property in Brighton & have made £27,000 in 3 months, all whilst having a baby daughter!

Rob & Mark actually do what they teach rather than the so called 'Gurus who talk the talk but still work in Sainsbury's at the weekend. If you have any interest whatsoever in setting yourself financially free you have to read this book now!"

Don't be one of those people who nearly got there, had great stories of how they nearly made it, or could have been, if, but, when, and maybe. Own yourself, not your story or excuses.

Summary

Never giving up and having faith in yourself will send you on your desired path and get you where you want to be. Stay elegantly persistent. The education you get along the way, and keeping on keeping on will get you to your destination as long as you don't stop. Don't ever ever give up. Ever.

What you have been given here are the tools to have the mindset of the wealthy and successful. Yes, this applies to property, but it is not exclusive to just bricks and mortar, it should carry through the whole of your life. Here's a reminder:

"The skillset without the mindset will leave you upset" – Craig Valentine

I [Rob] have to admit that it took me 25 years to get this. It took me that long to understand that I was responsible for my own life and my results, and that there are things that can be learned that will make you rich, happy and successful. I thought it was genetic; down to where someone lived and who had the most luck. I thought that it was everybody else who was lucky and that only drug dealers drive Ferrari's!

As I read now I can see its total nonsense. But I didn't know what I didn't know. The trouble is:

"Ignorance isn't bliss, it's ignorance" – Rob's Dad

We can all be anything we want to be. You can be all that you want to be. I know because I have done it for myself and I have coached 1000's of people and helped them do the same, all without silver spoons. When it comes down to it, we're all made of the same stuff. I don't take the credit; they do, because they did it. I just believe in them like I believe in you.

Think 'How can I do it?' rather than 'I can't do it,' believe that anything can be achieved, seek to learn new things daily and take consistent decisive action every day, and you're there.

And we're here every step of the way for you.

Section 4: Strategies to Profit in Property

This is where it all starts to get interesting. Most don't get this far. You know the basics and the principles and you can go out there and look after yourself on the street.

Mastery comes when you step it up a gear and things happen naturally: subconsciously. The following concepts, rules, laws, secrets, call them what you will, will be the difference that makes the difference to you. They will be the things that set you apart from those that do not do.

These following chapters are some of the things that we have spent many years refining. To be exact; over 25,000 hours, 350 properties bought and sold, at least a dozen duff deals, some great JV's and a failed one, 4 failed relationships, 6 companies, over 350,000 past and present community members and subscribers, and 55 years left of a lot more of the same: all endured and enjoyed because of a passion and belief in property and our commitment to investment.

And now our commitment to you.

Onward…

The language of property

If you wanted to get by in France [just a random example]: live, eat, shop, socialise, learn, have a loving relationship, do you think you would be able to if you could not speak a word of French [and did not have a translator for all you smart ones thinking leverage]? You would probably find it very difficult. You would need to spend time learning the language, wouldn't you?

So why is it that most people who want to be rich are not financially literate? Why is it that many property investors do not understand the language of property investing and the language of money? And they make no effort to learn it.

If you want to be wealthy, then you need to be able to speak the language of money. If you want your wealth in property, then you need to be able to speak the language of property.

Language is the gateway to our thoughts. It is the medium in which we communicate and we understand. Your continual study of the language of property will be directly proportional to the amount of money you earn.

Do you understand BTL, LTV, BMV, DIP, HMO, RICS, ROI, ROCE, NMD, NMLI, FF, RMD, QL, AS, BRR? Isn't it annoying when people use too many acronyms ;-)

But seriously, the nuances of language will put you across as someone who knows property, even if you don't. The difference between gross yield and net yield to an investor, neg or lister to an Estate Agent, who prefers DIP and who prefers AIP, ROCE or ROI?

What books and publications do you read and what websites do you use? What is your homepage? Who do you spend the most time with? This will all have a bearing on how quickly you pick up the language, how quickly you build and attract your powerteam, how quickly people take you seriously enough to deal with you, give you the best deals, give you the money and recommend you to others.

Summary

Improve your property and financial language. The language you use is a representation of your thoughts and your knowledge. Improve your knowledge on the specific language and acronyms of property and money and your results will be relative.

Multiple streams of property income

As you'll discover when you read the 'About us' section at the back of the book, when we started in property we thought there was one way to make money. You buy, you refurb, you rent out. The Progressive **BRR** strategy.

And it's served us well; we've bought and sold over 350 using this one strategy. But that was just the tip of the Iceberg.

You may have noticed that we've experienced turbulent times over the last few years. You might think there's plenty more to come. And you might be fooled into thinking that because of that, opportunities are more scarce.

Well, to be perfectly honest, for most people, this is true. Opportunities are scarce because confidence is low and the media is in a frenzy. But to the opportunists, the opportunities now are like you've never seen. Ever.

"Observe the masses, do the opposite" – Walt Disney

The recession hurts most people, yet they're printing more money, and more people become millionaires in a recession than at any other economic time in history. The High Street is hurting but second hand shops, pawn shops and charity shops are thriving better than they have for almost 2 decades. Record stores are hurting but iTunes rules the world.

So what does this mean to you?

Well first time buyers are hurting; they can't get on the ladder as they're still priced out and they can't get finance, but smart investors are using so many creative, Entrepreneurial strategies it's no wonder most ordinary people haven't got a chance.

But you don't know what you don't know, right?

Well, right now, in the property investment world, there's serious money to be made without even buying property, without needing a deposit, or even having to apply for a mortgage.

There's people cleaning up in a multitude of different property 'types,' and a variety of different add on businesses to the bread and butter single let residential **BRR**.

So what are they and how can you benefit from them?

Regarding the 'bricks and mortar' of property, you have single let buy to let, single let flipping, multi-let [Boutique, Blue Collar, Post Grad & LHA] financed through sub letting, JV partners, option purchases and long stop instalment completions.

There are many investors buying commercial property with commercial finance that have lesser barriers than buy to let finance – converting residential into commercial, commercial into residential, splitting title of bigger units into multiple flats, turning pubs into HMO's and offices into multi-purpose residential/commercial hybrids.

For every one of these, there are people [including Progressive] who are running courses on how to do them. We're partly to blame for this, because we teach the Progressive community members how to build their own businesses, and even train them how to be trainers. Why? Because it's a way to faster income through 'repackaging' your property knowledge – and it's just plain smart.

Then you have the different strategies of buying such as a variety of 'option' purchases which give 'control' rather than 'ownership' and remove many barriers, especially around needing deposits. Other variations on this such as delayed completions/instalment contracts are different ways to cut the 'no money in' cloth. Yes we run a training on that too, because it's sexy, and it helps people who wouldn't normally have a chance, to get started.

With finance being limited through conventional banks, people are getting creative and partnering with those who have money to form Joint Ventures [JV's]. Share 50% of your profit with a 'backer' or have 100% of nothing – your choice. Mark and I started this in 2006 before it was necessary and we didn't even really know it was a 'JV.'

Then there are the businesses that support buying, such as selling deals on for quicker cash, flipping deals through Estate Agents, building portfolios and creating bespoke end to end services for busy professionals, mentoring people to take the step from corporate to investor, and repurposing their knowledge and information into CD's, DVD's, online continuity programmes, mastermind and 'private equity' programmes and much more.

This is everything we do at Progressive. Stay with us long enough, and rather than just buying a few single lets [which will get you started and serve you well], you'll have a whole empire of businesses around property, and multiple streams of property income. You'll also reach more people, build a bigger brand around your name, and serve and contribute more than you ever dreamed you could.

Start with one strategy and get good. But also "start with the outcome in mind." Know that you're significantly underestimating what you can achieve in the long term in property.

And we're here to open your mind and let you get your large, multiple income piece of it.

But one final note [to the sceptics]:

Why would we share all our secrets? Why would we train people to train others in what we train them? And if we're so good at buying property and so rich, why don't we just do that and forget the rest?

In all honesty, we'd be a little more cagey about sharing everything if this was a cannibalisation business. If we were on the high street, selling the same thing next door to each other. We'd have to be a charity to do that, right?

The great thing about property is that to be properly successful at it, as you'll discover in the next couple of chapters, you have to work it locally. The Progressive R.E.A.S.O.N & C.A.S.T.L.E.D models will teach you that.

So we can teach you how to do everything we do, as long as you don't climb over our gated, barbed wire, electric, dog and rifle patrolled, fencing ;-)

Seriously though, for the most part the property world is an abundant industry, and all we want is for you to be as successful as you want to be, and we'd love to be a small part of that.

To cover all these strategies would be a book in itself. In fact some of the single strategies are a book in themselves. For more details on these more advanced methods, make sure you read "Make Cash in a Property Market Crash" and "Multiple Streams of Property Income" once you've finished this one. You can find them online by typing in the title on Google or Amazon.

Summary

There are multiple cashflow strategies in property – you just have to learn them. Focus on one strategy and build 'add-on' strategies as you go that take less time and area more leveraged. There are fewer opportunities for the masses but more opportunities than there have ever been for the creative, opportunistic, contrarian investors like yourself.

Be a relationship expert

You are your wealth. One of the biggest factors in your success will come down to the relationships you build, the leverage you get from your contact base working hard and in harmony with your vision, and ultimately the way you treat, motivate, insipre and make other people feel.

There are many people out there with what seems like big businesses treating people badly and using them. It never lasts, it comes back to get you, and it's not good long term business.

Every good relationship you build could be the key to setting up a deal that will make you money, no matter how insignificant or far removed it may actually seem. Someone always knows someone who knows someone who could be the link that you need for a JV partnership.

Everyone you meet knows a lot of people. Are they recommending you or are they moaning about you?

The person right in front of you may not necessarily have an immediate answer that you need now, or £200K liquid, but she may have in 6 months, or someone she knows may have, or someone he knows. Long term thinking is especially important in relationship building.

Always be fair and honest with people. What can you offer them and what value can you add to their lives? They will always want to help you in return.

Fundamental tip No.4:
"If you help enough people to get what they want, you'll get what you want"

We hope that you will agree that at Progressive we give away a lot of very valuable information for free. In fact, this book may have been the first time that you have actually paid [and we don't get much of that £15] to gain any property knowledge from us, having perhaps read our eBooks, eCourses, attended our web-classes and JV events.

This is the way we like to do business. We don't have to hide what we know; we should all be sharing it. Interestingly, our statistics actually prove that more of you will invest with us now or get educated with us because we have been open with our information and given you value, even though we had to invest more in you upfront.

This is despite the fact that we are actually teaching you to do what we do and that in the long run you don't even need us.

Mark's Mum helped us buy a property and save someone from repossession, because she always used to buy cakes from a lady at the cake counter at Sainsbury's. And it wasn't even she from whom we bought the house, it was a friend of hers who she recommended us to, all based on the strength of Mark's Mum's regular cake buying and kindness :-)

You're smart, so we don't want to patronise you, telling you how to do this; you know. You know when you've been great with people and got everything you wanted, and you know when you got emotional, lost your cool, shot from the hip or reacted, and you know how ineffective that was.

But we'll give you the top 3 that have worked the best in building a property portfolio and multiple property businesses. There are endless books on relationships and influence, if you feel the need to dig deeper.

Importance: people have an inherent and basic need to feel important and significant. We all have it, it's one of the 6 basic human needs hardwired into our neurology, according to many scientists.

Find out that the importance 'triggers' or 'drivers' are for your Estate Agents, Letting Agents, vendors, JV partners; everyone in your power team, and you'll get anything you want. And people will love you for it, because you make them feel great, and you hit their ego hot button square on.

In our experience some of the most common ways to make people feel important are compliments of success, power, how hard they work, that they're great with people, listening to them, highlighting what they're great at, talking about their kids, letting them rant and moan – whatever it takes for them, show genuine interest and agreement, and let them talk and talk and talk about it.

If I [Rob] want to make Mark feel important I know I can comment on his detailed, below market value buying skills, his driving skills [despite all his points and tickets, he thinks he's great] or how comprehensive and detailed his latest spreadsheet is looking ;-)

Listening: people talk too much. You have 2 ears and one mouth, so use them in that proportionate capacity. The great thing about listening is that it hits most people's importance trigger, so kills 2 birds with one stone. It makes people feel comfortable enough to trust you [despite the fact that you're not saying much so they don't know much about you], and they divulge all the valuable information you need to be able to get to your outcome and have them thanking you for it.

No-one really cares about [y]our boring mundane Groundhog Day life. People just want to tell you about theirs!

We've seen many nervous investors literally talk themselves out of a deal because they talked too much and didn't listen. People misunderstand deals and JV's fail when you don't listen.

Very often the seller may just talk themselves out of their own objections, especially if they like you. We regularly get objections about price, [if we didn't they would have sold the property already] but their desire to avoid agents' fees, the necessity of a fast sale and debt pressure soon convinces them that the price isn't so bad after all; and when they tell you that themselves, it's far more powerful that you trying to 'sell' them.

Great listeners build quick rapport, make people feel important and get the answers they need, fast, in a comfortable, trusting environment.

Asking questions: this has a lot in common with listening. A great way to get people to talk for two thirds of the conversation is to ask questions. It is amazing how simple this one is, yet most people are incessantabouttalkingaboutthemselveswithouttakingabreath.

The more questions you ask, the more answers you get. The better questions you ask, the better answers you get. Vendors open up when you ask [the right] questions. You get all the answers you need with the right questions, and you get people to think in a different way when you ask good questions. In fact:

"The quality of your life will be determined by the quality of the questions you ask."

The best leaders and relationship experts get the most out of the people around them. They motivate, inspire and create belief in others. They give others confidence in themselves, believe that they are worth something, and part of something big.

Then [and only then] can you go out and make a shed load of money in property, because to structure a property deal takes many people; far more than in many other areas of investment. You need brokers, solicitors, Letting and Estate Agents, refurb teams, vendors, electricians, plumbers and accountants, as an absolute minimum, just to buy a single house.

Summary

Treat everyone well and with respect. Think about how you can add value to their lives and become a relationship expert by finding importance drivers, listening and asking great questions. There are many people involved in a property purchase and everyone you meet could be the missing link you need for success and profit.

R.E.A.S.O.N

The Progressive R.E.A.S.O.N model is the formulaic 6 reasons not to buy property
– clever eh, us at Progressive ;-) If there's one big thing you could take from this:
knowing what to stay well away from will save you tens or hundreds of thousands
of pounds. Even more important, it will mean you won't have a bad first experience
that could put you off the best business we've ever seen.

Whatever you do, when you start out, without exception [unless you are a bona
fide expert in one of these areas], do NOT buy the following types of property:

R.undown - If the property is beyond economical repair or you don't have the
right contacts to do major building works, then you need to avoid them. We've
spoken to many new property investors who have fallen into this trap and it's cost
them tens of thousands of pounds. Even more painful, is they gave up, thinking the
investment class didn't work because of their first novice mistake.

*One of the really early properties we bought needed rewiring, underpinning and load
bearing walls supported. But it was c h e a p. So like the 2 naive investors we were
almost a decade ago, hunting the deals and discounts, and not knowing the can of
worms ahead of us, we bought it. The vendor must have found it hard to hide his smile,
and the costs, that we budgeted for, ended up being 3 times as much in reality. We were
forced into flipping it, and came out a few grand down with bruised egos, but valuable
'entrance fee' lessons learned. You can leverage our mistakes.*

I [Rob] have the belief that anyone can do anything they put their mind to, if they
want it badly enough. I [Mark] think you should stick to what you know, and keep
improving at it. Yes, anyone can do big and complex deals, but it is very risky to do
them first, without getting the necessary 'initiation' education.

Don't bite off more than you can chew. Don't do a deal that is beyond your current
skillset [OK, maybe just a tiny bit, after all if you've never bought a property, it's all
new].

In boxing, a coach will not put someone in their first fight against a world champion,
even if the fighter has huge talent. It is too early, and a big knockout can ruin a
great future career. A good coach will bring a new fighter through, giving them well
matched fights. Perhaps the first few would even be ones that the new fighter is
favourite for. Then as the fighter builds confidence he will step up in class, one step
at a time, until he has enough experience to fight with the best.

Property deals are exactly the same. Don't go too big too fast. Don't punch above your weight, because you risk hitting the canvas hard, and ruining your career. Start on smaller [safer and often better] cosmetic refurb projects, and build it up from there.

Mini Summary

Don't buy anything too rundown: the costs will spiral, you'll stumble across expensive repairs you couldn't spot before, and you'll lose all your profit. Stick to cosmetic work only.

E.xpensive – If a house has costs that are more than the rent it brings in, then it will cost you money every month, and is not an asset. Anything priced too highly [either actually or relatively] will take money out of your pocket. The basic rule for single lets is under the first level of stamp duty threshold, or £100,000. Anything that yields at less than 8% gross is likely to cost you some money every month, cost of finance and market dependent. You'll be shown how to exactly [and quickly] calculate costs and cashflow in the 'Yield' section.

The exception to this is with buy to sell strategies, Lease Options, and central London investing strategies. If you are more of a seasoned investor, and you want more advanced or varied strategies, these are detailed in "Make Cash in a Property Market Crash," the sister book to this.

Mini Summary

Don't buy anything too expensive: the rent won't cover the mortgage and you'll be subsidising it every month. General rule, stay under £100,000 or first stamp duty threshold.

A.broad - Risky strategy. Lack of local knowledge. Lack of control. The cost to visit the property - flights etc, legal fees and translation costs, managing the property remotely, the list goes on and on. All reasons [and unnecessary costs] for new and seasoned investors to avoid.

Oh we have some stories to tell here, but let's not bore you with the details. In the heady days pre 2008 big companies with bigger brochures were spending huge amounts of money, some millions per month, on getting you to emotionally desire overseas properties. A3 Glossy brochures of sunscapes, seascapes, beautiful beaches, big Dulux dogs and a couple in their 50's who look in their 30's running in slow motion in the sunset in their white linen clothes…

And yes, we fell for it in our naive youth. We put deposits down for 2 in Florida, please. We'll have a couple in the Caribbean too, thank you. A perfect holiday home AND an investment. Boom. Sweet. Kerching. All we have to do now is go and holiday in Marbella, and when we return we'll be millionaires Rodney.

As you can imagine most properties like this have 2 storeys – one before you buy and one after [boom boom]. Thankfully we got our deposits back and learned just in the nick of time. Many of these never rented out, larger deposits were to be put down, mortgages for overseas investors were pulled and dreams turned to nightmares.

The mistake that many first-time investors [including ourselves] make is that they confuse a holiday home or overseas dream with profitable property investment. If you want a second home abroad to live in at certain time of the year, then this is fine, but don't expect it to make any money at all for a long time. Expect it to cost you year on year and expect to get a few headaches; maybe even the odd heart attack! Many people get their emotions entangled with the concepts of investment and ultimately end up spending vast amounts of money for very little return.

Ignore the hype about the next hot spots: we'll talk about your Goldmine area in the next chapter. By definition a hot spot is an area where people speculate that the price will increase in value very quickly. The problem with hotspots is that they're often based on rumours, speculations and announcements by local Governments that an area will grow in value by a new regeneration project. This is mostly guesswork – it is a future prediction not a past result [like finding proven comparables in your local area].

If you have invested in an area as a result of the hype, miles away from where you live that you know nothing about, but the new railway link is not being built now, and the Government plans are being scrapped, or the predictions you were given by companies selling stuff didn't come true, then what do you do? You're left with unrentable properties that are too far away to be managed.

Leave the speculation to those who have more money than sense; they may make some money in a bull market if they get lucky once, but you will make money regardless of what the market is doing.

You can make overseas property investment work if you're an expert, if you live in the country you want to invest in and you know the area like your own town or city. You'll need to be able to speak the language, have a large contact base and know the intricacies of the legal system [and the differences from the UK market].

So keep it simple, save yourself all this time and wasted money. Are we saying you'll never make a mistake? Not if you want to get results, but you can minimise them significantly.

Mini Summary

Don't buy abroad: there are too many risks, variables and things out of your control. Management is virtually impossible, costs will escalate and you won't know the local area well enough to know the right types of properties and areas locally. Keep emotional, second home buying, and investing totally separate.

S. cattergun - Having properties dotted around the country when starting out is a recipe for disaster, for much the same reason as abroad. Start local, or have a local area managed for you, and build up from there. Diversify much later. The key to reducing risk is increasing knowledge, and it is harder to have specific knowledge of properties, areas, tenants, refurb teams and so on the further away from them you are.

We knew of one up and coming professional investor on the scene in 2008. A UK big shot who had sourced around 90 properties nationally through online advertising, dotted all over the country.

It all looked good and everyone was mystified by his fast rise. Within 18 months, when we picked up one of his properties in a repossession listing locally to us, and paid around 25% less for it than he had, we were able to dig enough to find out the reality.

Remote management of this portfolio had left half of his entire portfolio unrented, to the tune of around £25,000 per month! 90 properties in a 5 mile radius wouldn't have 5 of them in arrears if managed well. Needless to say he lost them all.

But you don't know what you don't know until it is too late.

This is one of the most misunderstood concepts in the property world. Seriously, there are so many people and companies out there investing all over the place: villas in Spain, ski flats in Bulgaria, second homes in Cyprus, and properties dotted all over the UK. And why do they do this?

"I want a diverse portfolio"

"It is good to spread your risk"

Well Warren Buffet would argue with that one. He says that focus and selection are what make wealthy investors. He is a billionaire [now the third richest man in the world, Forbes Billionaire Rich List] and he invests in companies like Gillette [men will always need to shave unless we go back to the dark ages]. We agree with him here.

We've been told that 'a deal is a deal' and it is 'good to buy all over to spread your portfolio far and wide.' Then we monitored and tested our portfolio. We compared the results, the costs and the pain-in-the-backside factor [official Progressive terminology].

No one really knows the reality of your own portfolio, or a new strategy you are using, until you can sit back and review 2 years of full management accounts. Anyone can say anything, but the accounts tell the reality.

People chase the deals across the country because they think they don't exist on their patch, or that the grass is greener on the other side and the deals are better elsewhere. They rarely, if ever, are. A big part of what makes a deal a great deal is its management, it being exactly what you thought it would be, and it being sustainable.

Something might look good on paper but the longer things take, the more they cost. The less you know, the more they cost. You end up with big headaches and bigger bills the further afield you go.

Mini Summary

> Don't buy all over the place: you'll have too many people to manage, you won't be able to become an expert on any of the areas, your costs will spiral and your time will get eaten. Stay local.

O.ffplan - Not as lucrative to do in the present climate, a few years ago the rising market added value to your properties before building commenced, but that's luck at best and gambling at worst. In this economic climate the value could go down and you'd be putting in good money after bad, plus getting finance on off plan/overseas properties is much harder. More money can be made from smarter investing in properties that are tangible, real and where values are proven.

Mark bought an off plan property in Bansko [influenced by the pretty artist impression of a luxury brochure] in 2003 which completed in 2007. It cost 70,000 Euros. The Net annual loss after the mortgage, service charges and maintenance worked out an equivalent of: 5000 Euros x 4 years = 20,000 Euros.

It was sold in March 2011 for 25,000 Euros. Net loss: 50,000+ Euros.

And here was the sting in the tail...

The property only rented for 3 weeks in total. What looked like a great rental market with a nice income stream and cash flow turned into an absolute nightmare as lots of other apartments were built which flooded the market.

Dishonest solicitors and rental agents and overpriced furniture packs didn't help either. Word is the developer has now evacuated from the building and rack and ruin is on the horizon as there is no management company!

An important lesson can be learned: don't invest in overseas off plan property unless you know the area, the legals, and a reputable bank which will lend on the property, otherwise just stay away, it's just not worth the hassle and risk.

And when you buy A.broad, O.verseas, N.ew build properties, all hell breaks loose!

Mini Summary

> Don't buy off plan: prices can go down in this market, further deposits may be required, and you could even find yourself not being able to get a mortgage, and losing your money completely. There are no comparables for off plan properties and there's no historical data, so you're speculating, not investing.

N.ewBuild — Expensive to buy, overpriced because of taxes, new premiums and developers margins [even with discounts]. Very difficult to prove valuations as there's nothing to compare them to, and easy to get emotional about new properties. When the shine comes off, that's money you've lost, and it takes decades oftentimes for values to start increasing.

The big problem with new build property is it's just like buying a new Mercedes straight from the forecourt. As soon as you drive it away you have lost 10-20% of its value.

There are sweet spots in the purchase of any object where the residual values are at their optimum, the point at which the relative value is at the greatest level. You can buy a brand New Range Rover for £70,000 plus, and you can buy a 4 or 5 year old one for £15,000. The model is exactly the same, no facelift, no improved models; still the same model in the same cycle.

If you had bought that brand new and fancy Range Rover you would have lost almost £55,000 in 4 to 5 years. For the next 4 to 5 years that car will lose much less value because the residuals are much better at this point.

Property is exactly the same. When you buy a new property you are paying a premium. You are paying over the odds so that the developers can take their profit [fair enough, but why pay that if you don't have to?]. You'll also be paying taxes and R&D budgets you won't be paying on an older property.

There is one big difference between buying a car and a property, and that is there are very few cars that go up in value over time, whereas there are very few properties that go down in value over time. However, the residual concept is no different in anything you buy.

Let's look at this relatively and go back a few years. Yes, right now, we don't think that new build property works on cash flow. It can often take much longer to grow and can cost you money on a monthly basis. We have regularly heard of shortfalls of £200 - £500 per month.

When BTL first started to become 'popular,' around the mid to late 90's, there were bargains to be had in the new build arena. You could perhaps buy a property right at the start of a development, and get it for the cheapest price, and by the time the whole development was finished, perhaps in 2nd or 3rd phase, the new prices would drag the value of your flat upwards.

This did happen.

And perhaps if you were to time your purchase just right, at the very end of the development, you could get a flat or two when developers needed desperately to report to shareholders with sales figures, when they might let the last couple go cheaper than 'market value.'

This is certainly what you will be told you can achieve through buying new property, and perhaps it has been done. However, we're in a very different world now.

The fundamental flaw with this strategy is that it is totally dependent on a rising market. The truth seems to be that rising markets can actually 'smooth over' poorly purchased investment properties; this has definitely been our personal experience. However this will only happen when the market is rising a good 15-20% per year, and in reality this is not sustainable over the long term, year on year.

When demand for new build has fallen significantly and the developer runs out of cash to pay the bank back, the big banks stop lending and often these developers go out of business very quickly. This has been a common story since 2007.

At this stage do you really think you can re-coup back your initial investment? It is very unlikely. If the development does go through, but investment has fallen in value, if you have already exchanged contracts you will be committed to complete.

Similarly, new builds had been built during the speculative years, when demand was at its peak. And guess what happened when the market changed? Nobody wanted to buy these over-supplied and over-priced 'swanky' new builds, because they could have easily bought older houses for far less money. Those landlords who were looking to rent out these new flats, either couldn't, or the rents came tumbling down because there were too many of them.

There will be other periods of time where the market rises heavily, and we should all look forward to that when we have built a good portfolio, but we must never rely on it to make money.

Fundamental tip No.5:
You must rely on your ability to buy well whatever the market is doing.

"You make your money when you buy"

Developers and 'new build re-sellers' now throw all sorts of 'incentives' your way to try to lure you in, and hide the reality that has become easier to spot in a market that isn't rising.

Free carpets, curtains, upgraded appliances, car parking spaces, cash-backs, guaranteed rentals, gifted deposits, stamp duty paid, are all hooks to reel you in. None of these have an impact on the value of the property. None of these all of a sudden [as if by magic] make an over-priced [for investment] new-build property a bargain.

Very often a '25% discount' in new build property actually equates to buying the property around 20-25% over its real value, and if you want to get a new build that is well priced, you need at least a 50% discount.

Developers are in it to make money: developers are not stupid. They are in the business of making money and are not just going to give their products and profit margins away. And why should they?

Developers charge premium rates for their new developments. We have personally seen specific examples where developers are offering 2 bed flats at the same price as older 4 bed houses opposite that have **twice** the square footage!

Older properties that have 'settled' offer better value because that developers' premium has gone. Some S-class Mercedes' were £100,000 when new and are now worth £30,000 3 years later. The same happens to new property, so why not buy it at £30,000 instead of £100,000 where the residual value is much better?!

Rate of growth: in addition to this [and in our very own personal experience] not only will you buy a property that you think is discounted, though in reality is not, but your new build property value will likely not go up for another 3-5 years, as it needs to recover a further 20-25% to get to parity with an older property.

Fundamental tip No.6:
Buy on logic, not emotion.

The deal is all about the numbers. Love the numbers if they work. Don't love the carpet and the wallpaper, the curtains or the gated video entrance; love the numbers.

So there you have it. Six seemingly simple staples of property buying — which, if adhered to, can save you years of mistakes and financial loss and pain. That's from experience, on the ground, down and dirty — we've been there. Not because we are biased, out to prove a point or are emotional about it. [Have you seen what some of our properties look like!] But the bank balance looks a lot better! It's all based on what gets real results.

Despite these obvious warnings, we still hear stories of people who got too cute, too emotional, forgot or plain ignored this advice. Look, it doesn't make any difference to us, we have no bias or reason to say anything other than what works and what doesn't in our experience. You can try for yourself, or you can leverage the 'entrance fee' we have paid over the years in mistakes that we've 'paid' to learn.

Sorry if all of this seems a little negative but we want you to know the truth. A little dose of reality with the best intentions for your success means we can crack on now together with being positive.

Knowing the truth will hugely increase your chances of building a steady and secure long term property portfolio that will look after you for the rest of your life, and for generations to come.

Property profit without the pain.

We've been there, and now you don't have to.

Mini Summary

Don't buy new build properties: the price will be premium and you'll be paying taxes and profits to someone else. There are few comparables for new builds, so you can't prove value. Let the premium come off and buy at the highest point in the value curve, a few years after the new shine has gone.

Summary

Observe the 6 R.E.A.S.O.N.S not to buy the wrong types of property. New build, off plan and overseas property will, more often than not, cost you more money and give you much more pain than existing property in your area. Stick to the C.A.S.T.L.E.D model in the next chapter and reap the rewards for the mid to long term.

C.A.S.T.L.E.D

So what does work then? What are the right types of properties, areas and strategies that will make money and save all the mistakes? Here's what to look for when buying, or having properties bought for you.

C.ashflow — Not treating your property acquisitions as a business is a recipe for disaster. Properties used to shortfall pre 2008, and people topped up each month because they knew [believed] they would get growth that paid it back and more.

The landscape is very different now, but yield and cashflow are better, and properties, if bought well, can produce a monthly income, even on a 70% mortgage.

"The number of properties you own is vanity, the cash flow you make is sanity and the cash you have in the bank is reality."

As a general rule, you should be looking at properties that are 8% yield minimum, depending on the cost of finance [your mortgage, opportunity cost of cash or deal with your JV partner]. This will ensure, with all your other costs, that the property positively cashflows from day one, and with better rates and future property and rental growth, that cashflow will keep going up.

This is detailed in a later chapter for you.

Mini Summary

> If a property takes money out of your pocket every month, it's not an asset and you shouldn't buy it in this market. Buy properties for income.

A.menities — The availability and accessibility to local amenities and facilities such as local transport links, employment opportunities, local businesses, retail parks, supermarkets, schools and colleges, new industry and technology, an influx of employment, bars, restaurants, clubs, culture, museums, art scene, sports facilities – all will ensure your investment has strong tenant demand & the highest capital growth potential.

Remember that all of these are worth thinking about, but analysis paralysis is a disease of momentum; don't get too hung up on the details, just be aware of them.

One of our first choice investment areas has a £1 billion regeneration programme going on – 7,500 new homes, 20,000 new jobs. Better to get in before and during than after, because that is where you get the 'forced' appreciation.

Although important, many novice investors place a disproportionate amount of importance on this, to the detriment of the other 6. Keep a balance. If you have a choice between good cashflow and good amenities, we know which you'd choose. Cash is king, baby.

Mini Summary

What amenities in your local area could add value or forced growth to your portfolio? Tick as many as you can in this section, but don't get too het up on this – cashflow is better.

S.upply - Ensure properties in your micro-area have the strongest [and fastest growing] level of demand that outstrips supply for the number of discounted properties it can supply, and number of available tenants.

Not enough properties means that you won't be able to buy enough for your end retirement goals, and too big an area will make it hard to 'own' your own 'patch.'

A high volume of properties, even at good discounts, could mean there are not enough tenants. You want to have 1,000's of tenants waiting for a house if possible. One of our chosen investment areas has 15,000 people waiting for a house.

The formula we use is as follows, adjust it to your area accordingly:

One of our local areas has a population of 185,000 people, give or take. That equates locally to around 65,000 houses, and from that volume around 10,000 houses fit our buying criteria. From those 10,000, we have bought around 190 in this particular area in the last 5 focussed years, and around 205 in total.

We currently buy minimum 5, maximum 15, in any given month, averaging 6-7. This monthly volume has grown as we have gotten bigger and better, and seems to be continually sustainable.

We're also not the only buyers in our local areas, so we're not buying all the deals, as much as we would like to mwahahahaha. This figure is what we can buy. If we spread our marketing, developed even more relationships with agents and redirected a few from the hands of our competition, we could probably double that number.

Calculate how many people live in the greater area of your locality, how many houses that breaks down to, and then how many of those fit your buying criteria. Use our ratio of say 6 per month from a volume of 10,000 homes, and you know your relevant, available buying volume.

If your local area has half the numbers, you're looking at 3 per month availability. At one sixth of the numbers, it's one per month. Do this first, and you'll have long term sustainability in your area.

Mini Summary

Ensure the supply levels of property in your local area are enough for your long term investing sustainability. Too many and you're not focussed enough, too few and you'll outgrow your area too quickly and have to move further afield.

T.enants - You can buy the best properties in the world with the biggest discounts, but have them empty long enough and you'll be giving the keys back, along with all your money.

Your tenants pay your mortgage, your cashflow and fund your lifestyle, so the right types of tenants managed the right way make the difference between income and shortfall.

Some simple things you can do to check high tenant demand in an area: talk to Letting Agents, find out where there is demand, gather on the ground data from people in the business. Ask them where they'd love to get houses to rent for the tenant demand they have.

And ask as many as you can. They all have specialised areas [high end, professional, student, LHA].

Put an advert in the local paper for a property which you propose to buy. List the type of property and the rent and put your mobile as the contact. Monitor the number of enquires. Clearly lots of calls means that it is likely to be a great area, none means that there may be low tenant demand.

There are more details of tenant specifics in the 'Letting, tenancy & management' section.

A tenant will usually be found more quickly if outsourced to a Letting Agent as they have greater marketing abilities and resources than if you are taking the property on privately. When you find a good Letting Agent, you'll realise their huge value, and it is well worth your IGA time to find a good one, even by kissing a few frogs.

We get asked a lot if you should manage your properties yourself. If you want to run around at the beck and call of everyone else's needs such as changing light bulbs in fridges, switching power back on when they can't find the switch, seed the lawn, come and close the loft hatch, put a padlock on the gate, let me in every time I lock myself out of the house [all real examples], for a few pounds a month, then go for it.

And check LHA waiting lists on your local government website. LHA specific Letting Agents may know that stats too.

Your risk is vastly reduced when you know rental demand BEFORE you buy.

Mini Summary

Before you buy any property, check demand for tenants in your local area. Ensure you have the right types of tenants for your property, and don't manage properties yourself, its poor leverage and IGA. Find a great Letting Agent, even if you have to kiss a few frogs.

Local - Buy as locally to you, or within a tight geographical area as possible. There are Goldmine areas all over the country, even in London, from top to bottom.

You'll have a better understanding of tenant demand, actual sale price, who the local surveyors are, best and worst Estate and Letting Agents, refurb teams, solicitors, competitors to keep close, actual achievable rentals, best streets with highest uplift potential, and so on.

It's taken us around 25,000 hours of being in the property business to get to where we are now. No need to show off here, it's just being in the business, and in addition to some of the good things we've been fortunate to do, we've got a list as long as an ancient scroll of what not to do, and the crazy things we've seen:

Letting Agents running off with deposits, dead people in properties, a Barn Owl in the cupboard of one our properties, many companies coming and going, Estate

Agents struggling, new strategies, regulation changes, rises and falls in rents, finance evolution, befriending [and sometimes not getting on so well] with competition, creating our own competition; the list is endless.

We'd just never have been able to learn one hundredth of these specifics, especially the 'how not to,' if we were investing all over the place.

Not only does buying in a tight area allow you control, as above, but it also ensures that you understand the prices of the local stock inside out, better than anyone else, including Estate Agents and surveyors!

This in turn means you can sniff out a deal better than anyone else. You can manage voids and any issues from the first day you hear about it, control costs, get multiple quotes and create local competition. Plus because you will be visible to everyone, you will always be at the top of their mind:

"Visibility is credibility"

There are property deals everywhere, including somewhere near you; possibly on your doorstep, probably being swallowed up by your competitors who are following these rules.

This is how not to do it: guess. Pin the tail on the donkey [map]. Choose an area that was reported to be a 'hotspot' 2 years ago. Choose somewhere that you can't get to easily. Choose somewhere too expensive or too trendy. In case you forgot ;-)

Regardless of the north/south divide, England vs. Scotland, the huge growth that you might have heard about in London and the huge yields in Ferry Hill, you need your own local patch. We call this your Goldmine area.

Look at Somewhere Within about a 15 mile Radius of You: don't be pulled too far away from where you live. If you are happy to travel further then fine, and we know successful investors who do travel a little further because they choose to have their Goldmine area more remote because it works for their strategy.

Gill Alton lives in Berkshire, and her Goldmine area is N*********m [she wouldn't want us giving away her trade secrets]! Although not 15 miles away from where she lives, they are all in a 15 mile radius of each other – thus obeying the rules. She can leverage and become an expert in that area, because they are all so close. Same strategy.

Since joining the Progressive community, Gill has built a significant property portfolio and business. She is doing so well that each time we publish her results, they go out of date!

Gill had a good corporate job for Xerox, and so for her it was difficult to quit because she would be leaving very good money on the table, and with 2 young children that was risky for her. Plus after the crash business become very hard for her husband's mortgage brokerage, with big clients going bust, they lost lots of proc fees.

But less than 20 months later she has bought a portfolio for her family worth in the millions, she has net cashflow well over £2,000 per month from her own portfolio, she packages deals for investors through the work we did together helping her build her property business model, and she mentors other people.

You now see her speaking at property events and she has a well known and trusted brand. She has JV's with many of the Progressive community members too; borrowing money, lending money and sourcing properties for her clients.

So if like Gill, you live in certain areas that may be too expensive or too run down and you have to travel further, it just needs to be put in your strategy. The main thing is to keep all of your investments close enough together so that they are manageable. The more you buy, the more you will be pleased that you followed this [common sense] strategy.

What is Your strategy: different strategies have different Goldmine areas. Single lets vs. student HMO's vs. High end HMO's vs. Multi-Let Without™ the Sweat all have different Goldmine criteria.

Your Area within Your Goldmine: London is not a Goldmine area, it is too big. A big town or city has streets that are priced far too high and the yields far too low, and conversely Bronx-type properties where maintenance and management are too time and money intensive.

You'll be focusing on inner suburbs, specific streets and postcodes, and these exist in almost every town and city in the UK. In fact, 93/100 people who do the 'Find your Goldmine area' one to one training on the Progressive Property Masterclass, find a local Goldmine area within an area, within 15 miles of where they live. Only 7/100 have to travel further afield.

There are some big advantages of finding Goldmine areas within areas: you are seen far more often by more people – you get recognised mindspace and so people pass you more deals and referrals. Your presence evokes action, you are perceived as an expert [even if you're not], you know the prices and intricate details well and you can become an expert on a specific area quicker and better than anyone else in the UK.

Mini Summary

Stay Local, ideally within a 15 mile radius of where you live. If your area doesn't work for your strategy, go further afield, but buy all your properties within a 15 mile radius of that area.

E.xisting - Focus on 1 or 2 Property types of not new [5 years to 150 years old] in a local area, say 1960's 2 or 3 bed terraced houses, or Victorian 4 beds that are HMO'able. You'll soon know the prices better than the surveyors, agents, vendors & investors. When something comes up that's 'priced to sell,' you'll be able to spot it right away, before anyone else, and have first mover advantage.

Price is what you pay, value is what You get: price and value can vary significantly. You *will* become an expert at buying on value rather than price.

If you buy a property that is 5 years old [or older] you are getting a habitable dwelling that is suitable for rent [provided you have done your diligence] that will cost considerably less than an equivalent new property. You are buying at the point of optimum value.

This would be a flawed strategy if you were buying computers or consumables, but the great thing about housing is that the value can last for 100's of years.

A new computer today at £1500 would probably be worth about £400 in 3 years time and worth next to nothing in 5-10 years. The optimum time to buy that computer would probably be after one year when the value had dropped because it was no longer new technology [and new technology had come out], but was still useful and not out of date.

With property you can buy 30, 60, even 100 year old properties and they still have high relative value. They are still useful and useable; unlike 30 year old computers.

Understand Yield: we have a whole section on this so we'll save the surprise. You should be looking for properties with 8% yield and above, finance dependent. That is gross [Gr] yield.

Properties in nice areas will be too expensive compared to the rent that you will be able to achieve, and so the gross yield will be low. Properties in slums might have an attractive gross yield but by the time you have replaced your windows 3 times, got rid of the graffiti and your Sat Nav [window smashed] has been pinched out of your car, you won't be left with much of that. More later.

Be specific with your property type: there are many types of properties that you can buy, which only goes to make things potentially confusing. In any one property expo or show, for example, you could buy land for planning, land for development, developments, overseas holiday homes, off plan, self build, auctions, rent to buy, rent to own, Buy to Let, buy to sell, new build flats, shared ownership, repossessions, HMO's, commercial. We could go on. You get the picture.

5 bed houses and 2 bed flats are very different investment propositions. What works best in terms of exact property type will vary from area to area. It might be 1 & 2 bed flats or 2 & 3 bed semi's or 4 bed 2 storey Victorian houses near the town centre.

We've still not found any areas where MTV crib houses provide a good yield. You will discover what works best in your area. Once you know it, stick to what works best and don't mess about with anything too expensive or too far out of what you now know to work.

Generally speaking, the properties at the cheaper end of the market will give you the best yields and are more likely to cover the mortgage payment with your rental income with a nice margin left. The higher you go the less likely this is.

With the lower end of the market you are buying properties wanted [or needed] by a bigger share of the market. How many people out there do you think want to rent 66 [or 6] bedroom houses? Of course there aren't many people who can afford 66 [or 6] bed houses, and those that can are more likely to buy than rent ;-)

The lower end offers far more demand. It also offers more long staying tenants. Newer and bigger properties attract transient families and single career minded people. Many of our tenants have never moved from our smaller existing properties as they will be in similar circumstances for most of their life. They are much less likely to buy as they may not be able to afford the deposits or have good enough credit to get reasonable mortgage products. They have a 'rental mindset' since that is the way they have been brought up. These are the kinds of tenants you want in your properties.

It is quite important to explain this 'rental mentality.' You or I may always have aspirations to buy one or many houses, as we understand the benefits, have the knowledge to get a mortgage and a belief that we can either afford it now, or some time in the not too distant future.

However, when dealing with people near the lower end of the market, things are very different. Knowledge, experience and education are lower in general, and the belief that one day they may be able actually to buy a house is very often never there, because their perception is that it will always be too expensive. It is also quite common for these people to see buying other 'things' [beer, Plasma TV's, the latest trainers] as more important.

They may have had a mortgage before and felt like it was onerous, or even been repossessed. These people still want a home and still want their home to feel like their home, whether they physically own it or not.

You'll only get your properties trashed if you go too near the Bronx [usually only a few streets per town] because we find that the tenants who we deal with have the belief that the house they rent is the house that they own; that it is **their** home.

Compare this to the higher professional rental mentality which is much more transient because they will look to buy as soon as possible or move frequently with their job, and you have an easy decision on preferred tenant.

Mini Summary

Buy existing properties at the highest point in the value curve, where history proves value and comparables.

D.iscounts-

Fundamental top No.7:
"You make your money when you buy Property"

Not only do discounts make you money on purchase, they reduce any risk of loss in a downturn. Buying BMV [Below Market Value] is one of the most important skills to being a professional property investor. It separates the novices from the professionals.

You can also utilise the **BRR** buy, refurb, remortgage strategy to leverage one deposit pot for multiple property purchases, which doesn't work without good discounts.

You can make every deal a no money left in [NMLI] or even a no money down [NMD] deal, with good discounts.

A real discount is one that is below the market value of a property that can be proven with comparables [evidenced]; that is the same type of property in the same area sold for the same price in the same resale market.

Not a price that a financially unsophisticated first time buyer has paid, which included the developer paying their 5% deposit: with carpet, curtains, free light fittings and a Plasma TV thrown in!

And not a speculative 'desk-top' [off-plan] valuation and forward priced properties.

Even if these valuations have been 'proven' by a 'RICS' surveyor, be wary. If there are no comparables for properties of the same type in the same resale market then it is guess work, not just for you but for a surveyor too [we learned that the expensive way].

Every pound that you can negotiate off the market value goes straight into your back pocket in future cash through equity, or cash through sale. If you pay full whack for something [even property], no matter how great the deal may seem, there's no 'instant profit.' Instant profit makes a deal real, reduces downside risk if the market changes or declines, and means you need to borrow less from a bank or JV partner to fund the deal, so your repayments are lower and your cashflow is higher.

Discounts are out there, and you choose what you pay. Be patient. Don't buy everything. Have a set of [achievable] rules and stick to them.

The skill of getting discounts separates would-be or novice investors [some with plenty of money] from specialist and expert investors. There are many investors we know who are buying properties for cash and buying them at full market value. Some of them are great at it.

Yes they will make money in the long run because most of us will in property, but they could be making up to 3-5 times [unleveraged] what they are making just using some skill, knowledge and education.

So how do you find these great BMV discount deals?

It's a numbers game: we discussed this earlier. Specific to achieving discounts, you need to be putting the offers in to get the deals you want. Putting in one or two offers that are rejected and then giving up is not going to make you rich.

We get one deal in approximately 6 offers through Estate Agents. It used to be one in 20 when we started. It could be one in 50, it doesn't matter, keep churning the numbers and the deals will come, predictably.

We get two deals per 45,000 leaflets that are posted out [from around 17 phone calls]. We used to get double the volume but half the discount pre crash, but things have changed. And they will continue to change. And we will keep testing and adapting.

Put in the offers, play the numbers game and you will get the deals. If you don't shoot, you don't score.

Be patient: don't go negotiation crazy. Know your price that you want to pay and don't break your rules. If your offer gets rejected then wait, be patient, and in 3 to 6 months when expectations have levelled, you may well get some offers back your way.

This actually happens quite frequently for us. In fact just recently I [Mark] helped an investor to buy a flat. We actually went to look at it nearly 4 months before and the vendor was adamant that he wanted [and was going to get] full asking price. Of course every vendors' house is worth full market value, right ;-)

We just waited and the market picked away at him, and now we have helped her [the investor] get the flat for around £30,000 less than the original asking price. The vendor is also happy because he needs to move fast and has had people pull out on previous offers.

We call this strategy [it *is* a strategy] 'pipelining.' This is specifically covered in our buying through Estate Agents training. The longer a deal drags out, the cheaper you will get it, and therefore it will actually cost you money to negotiate too fast and hard.

Know when to push [when it is time to agree the deal and get it exchanged], and when to let the natural energy of the deal, the economy and the pain of the vendor, evolve and cause the itch.

We know some bullish hot-headed 'dealmakers' who try to bully people on price and pressure on time. Perhaps when we were less experienced we were like that a bit too, but even with the best intentions it doesn't work. The people we speak to on the other end of those negotiations don't like it and it becomes counter-intuitive. People will sell to people they like at a lower price.

Always be improving: keep improving on your figures. Keep learning, reading, growing and testing your results so you know what you can improve on: this is most important. A small improvement in a chain of events can compound quickly to big profits.

Use multiple marketing methods: use Estate Agents, leaflets, social media, forums & biz directories, Google local, Rightmove aggregators, the ageing technique, lead gen websites, Google, Facebook PPC, word of mouth marketing, YouTube, print media, postcarding, take-away menus, 'birddog' referrals, billboards, JV's with window cleaners, and many more.

More than one strategy will bring many more deals and is less exposed to change in market conditions that one single strategy.

But don't go and do them all at once: ooooooooverwhelm. Have a primary and secondary strategy, splitting your marketing IGA time 70-20, and the other 10% on the third or researching new ones. These strategies are detailed in "Multiple Streams of Property Income" and on the Progressive Property Investing Masterclass.

Stick to what You know: now that you have decided on area and type of property, stick to it. You will become known for what you want by Agents, vendors and contacts and they will come to you with deals. If you chase everything and buy outside your strategy, then you won't get the results you want.

"If you do everything you'll be known for nothing" – Rob Moore

Know your numbers: this is one of the most important factors in buying a property. Before you even put an offer in you should know exactly what that property will cost you to buy, including all fees. You should know what the rental figures are and what it will cost you per month with a contingency put in.

What can you get the property revalued at? Do you know what the rental coverage is so you can get the maximum loan to value [LTV]? What about your completion costs: survey fees, local searches, legal fees, deposit financing, indemnity insurance, refurbishments costs? Ongoing management costs? Building insurance, gas safety, mortgage interest, and service charges/ground rent?

Thankfully, you have a partner [Mark] who loves figures and details. A little too much in fact with his sweaty typing figures. It's all been plugged into his Deal Scrutiniser™ and our gift to you [if you didn't get it last time], is the App version that you can use on the go, on viewings. We suggest you get it now by searching 'Property App' on the App store

Yield: There are always little pockets within towns and cities that offer the best net yield. Some areas will be too expensive and some will be too cheap [with high maintenance]. Read the section on yield, and focus on this when you are finding your Goldmine area.

Watch interest rates and costs: as interest rates creep up more people [especially in the lower end of the market] get into more financial difficulties as the repayments on their loans go up. More repossessions happen at this point and you can use all of your newly acquired skills as a relationship expert to lead them out of debt and pick up a bargain. More detail later on.

However, investors are not immune to increased costs and rises in rates, so ensure you have factored in current and future cost of finance to keep your net yield and cashflow high and sustainable.

Timing: in property buying timing is everything. If you can understand the best time to buy, from keeping your eye on the market, then you are one step ahead of 95% of the other property investors.

Our second book "Make Cash in a Property Market Crash" is all about making money when the market isn't moving upwards. It is far better to buy at these times that in a rising market. You can make larger profits quicker using 'contrarian' strategies.

Certain times of year dictate buying prices. For example, most people are not prepared to buy over Christmas as it is a huge upheaval. However you do, in some cases, get people who really need to sell quickly, and because there is not much going on, and a lack of competition, you can benefit. Summertime can be interesting too. If a lot of people are on holiday [including your competition] then this creates space for you to get to *Banker* status much quicker than normal. January is a great time to buy and help vendors because divorce, financial pain and repossessions are at the highest point of the year.

Know what makes vendors tick: understanding the psychology of your vendor [seller] will make a huge impact on the prices you get. You should always be thinking about getting as much information from the vendor [sometimes through an Agent] as possible. Why are they selling? Do they have to move quickly? Are they in debt? Is it a probate sale? Do they have bad neighbours [perhaps you should stay away]? Has their property been on the market for 3 months or more? Is there a chain in the sale? Could you help find them a new house? What is important to them?

The more you know the more leverage you have to negotiate, and the more solutions you can offer to help them specifically.

Follow all the previous rules: don't buy new, focus on area and property type so they have lowest possible void, buy well under market value, ensure your deal is net cash flow positive, have finance in place, be ready to buy fast with your broker ready and your DIP [decision in principle] in place. Never ever pull out of a deal, have the other person's interest in mind, offer value and offer solutions to their problems.

Now go out and find some great deals!

Keep on keeping on; make mistakes. So what. We all make them. If you don't shoot, you don't score [and that doesn't just go for football and members of the opposite sex!] It's all part of your journey, a journey that no one can cheat, but everyone can accelerate and leverage, as you are now. But there comes a time when you just have to do it. Even if you're not 100% ready.

Mistakes are essential in learning to be good at anything. It is said that those who make the most mistakes become the best. Remember Thomas Edison and his light bulb moment? It is the learning and the meaning we put on our mistakes that make us who we are, both as investors and people.

"Anyone who has never made a mistake has never tried anything new" - Albert Einstein.

Enjoy the process: hunting for deals should be fun. It is a game and we love it. You will too, especially when you see the cash coming in. You can get out there, help other people sell their house faster than anyone else and make some money yourself. And have them grateful and thank you for it.

You are not gazumping people or circling like a vulture; you are setting up win-win scenarios and enjoying helping others. At least we do and you should too.

Mini Summary

Be patient, let negotiations take their natural course, and buy at discounts. The better the deal, the more protected you are on downside risk, market changes and finance/interest rate adjustments. Plus you make more instant cash. Use multiple strategies to source your discounts, but build them up over time, focusing on 2 at any one time. The better the relationships you build, the more they'll sell to you at a lower price than offered to your competition.

Summary

Use the C.A.S.T.L.E.D model for buying properties. Buy for C.ashflow, considering local A.menities that add value or forced growth to your portfolio, with good S.upply of properties for long term sustainability. Find good T.enants, in your L.ocal Goldmine areas buying E.xisting, value-provable properties at the highest point in the value curve, with big D.iscounts.

Your Goldmine Area

Here are some great tips for finding those little gem properties with the highest yield:

Fundamental tip No.7:
Always look for the 'worst' house on the 'best' street.

When you buy a brand new car, let's say a Mercedes again as an example, the difference between a standard model and a fully spec'd up supercharged version can be very significant.

Specifically, a standard Mercedes s-class is around £60,000. However the S-500 is around £100,000 for the same platform with some extra toys and a bigger engine.

In 3 to 5 years nearly all that difference in price disappears, and the S-500 might only be a few thousand pounds more expensive.

Property works the same way. If you have two 3 bed houses on the same road, both the same size but one has video entry, a plasma TV and oak flooring and is £20,000 more, they'll still both rent for the same money give or take £25 because the value of rent achievable is dictated by the 'platform' [location, square footage, number of bedrooms].

The cheaper one offers much better value, and a greater yield.

Those who get emotional about property don't understand this hugely important concept.

Always look for value by buying the 'worst' properties in the areas that will pull the relative value and rentals up. This has a lot to do with land values. It is the land that very often holds the greatest amount of value, and it is the land that can influence the overall price of a property.

On any one street similar plots of similar sizes will hold similar values. This goes some way to explaining why apparently 'worse' properties can achieve similar rents in comparison with 'better' properties.

Buying property on good land will always be wise. It's not generally the primary reason we do it, but it will become ever more important. A lot of the stock we are buying nearer the city centre and redevelopment areas is on land that will continue to rise in value.

The one thing we can't get more of in the UK is land, and that keeps demand very high. There's a small chance that over the next 100-300 years your property could fall down [or at least degrade significantly], there's almost no chance you'll lose your land. A fallen down or derelict house is worth very little, the land will always be premium.

Net yield can be quite difficult to calculate, and your knowledge of property type and area and these concepts discussed in this chapter will be invaluable to you. The point about knowing net yield is that you can be lured by high [gross] yielding properties, but in reality most of that return will be spent on maintenance, management and voids.

As a general rule higher yielding properties over a certain point can end up having a lower net yield than other seemingly less attractive properties [when you do your numbers]. If you have to replace the windows every year or spend money because tenants do not look after your property, then you can end up with very little at the end of each year. Void periods can also have a big impact [drain] on your yearly return.

Remember that all costs come out of your *profit*. What you are essentially on the look out for [in your area] are those areas where the gross yield is good [properties that are not too expensive, not too big and rent out well] and the maintenance is low [not too grotty, no crime]. You will get to know which areas to avoid at all costs [if the helicopters fly over at night and the rats are running out of town then stay away] and stick to your strategy at the lower end of the market.

You can work out gross yield very quickly and it is a very handy selection tool. Net yield needs a little more research, some experience and a bit of a sixth sense of your area. As long as you keep moving forward with your strategy and follow the rules, you will find those little 'gem' areas. You will become better than 95% of the investors out there and you will make money.

You'll be the 1 in 100.

Summary

Find an area within an area, local to you, that has the right balance between gross yield, and net after costs. You will have to test and research to find the pocket areas. Don't get lured by emotions or fancy properties, it's all about the bottom line.

Finance Fundamentals

Your ability to obtain credit, deposits, cash, bridging finance or JV partner funds is paramount to the exponential growth of your portfolio.

Before we even start on this chapter always remember this: **guard your credit score with your life.** Nurture and protect it like a child. Cushion it. Wrap your arms around it and never let it go. Despite the fact that for many strategies you'll learn mortgages are soooo 2007, they're still an important part of your long term vision.

Never ever miss a credit card or especially a mortgage payment, and always keep well up to date with what you owe. One missed payment can black mark your credit and hinder future lending, or put off a JV partner, and the growth of your portfolio.

Only borrow to invest in income producing assets: there are many schools of thought [particularly that of the Industrial age] that you should never spend anything until you have it. This is a sound base on which to build a solid financial platform, and certainly far better than borrowing to buy petrol guzzling cars, go on fancy cruises and build conservatories.

Don't borrow money to invest in liabilities until you can afford to do so, or when they can be paid for by assets. And if you can afford them, then why are you borrowing money for them in the first place? The exception might be if borrowing is cheaper than buying or there is a cost of capital from using cash, but as lending and interest rates are relatively low and inflation is high, this is very unlikely.

Don't over borrow on assets: many home owners and investors pre-crash were 'geared' too highly. Over gearing [borrowing too much against the value of an asset] has caused much of the financial mess of the last few years, and the crash serves as a good reminder to smart investors that things can change quickly and you should have a buffer.

Everyone wants to put as little money down as possible into a property deal, but raising too much debt against it leaves you exposed to market movements and a lack of control of timing of sale. Pre-crash you could get a 90% mortgage, a 95% mortgage, a 95% mortgage with a 5% vendor gifted deposit [100% mortgage], and then the value of the property could get pushed up so that the borrowing was in fact more than the value.

Yet people forgot in a frenzy of buying with such little money down, that this was all **debt**. Debt that needs to be paid off. In this case the only way it will get paid off is through growth [unless they earn it in their wage!], and growth between 2007 and 2013 has been slow in most areas, and may not change for many years.

Things have changed, and most banks and lenders won't let you gear at 90% or more, even if you wanted to. Many won't let you gear higher than 65% or 70%. They want you to have skin in the game. We'll admit that in 2006 we probably did gear up a few properties a bit too much. We still own them, it didn't kill us, we didn't have to sell them, but because of the [relatively] high 'loan to value' [LTV], the mortgage is more than it could be, and therefore the cashflow is less than it should be. Some are saved by low interest rates, but others produce far less than we are getting now on more recent, better purchases. Other people were not so lucky and didn't have other good assets as protection.

Regardless of whose 'skin' is in the game [your money, a JV partners funding], a 70% loan [LTV] is high enough. You might want to push to 75% if the banks let you, but even when the market changes and banks forget the pain of the last few years, taking high LTV mortgages is not smart investing, even if it is NMD.

[Controlled] leverage: no one ever set up a big business or portfolio without leverage. The richer the investors are, the less of their own money they often use – life's so unfair, right ;-) If you were to try and build a property portfolio with your own money, buying cash, it would take you 3 lifetimes to match what many professional investors have done in 3 to 5 years.

Most people could never buy a house unless they leveraged and borrowed money. There can be great leverage in borrowing money to create something that could potentially generate a lifetime of income far beyond the repayments. Just don't stretch it too far.

Here are some important factors in finance and leverage:

Line up a credit line: whether you use it or not, having access to credit can mean a deal that needs to be bought quickly will not slip through your fingers and into the hands of the competition. Keeping your credit file clean [and knowing how to], having access to credit, loans, overdrafts and other vehicles to borrow means when that opportune moment arrives, you're ready.

"Don't get ready, be ready"

This credit can be with a bank or with a private investor or JV partner, or credit cards empty but ready.

This is not to say that you spend money you don't have – just have access to as much finance as you can. You never know when you might need funds for a short term refurb, or a quick cash buy that you can flip. When you use some of the other strategies in this section, before you know it you could have access to six or seven figures, waiting and ready for when the deals come your way.

Don't just use mortgages: mortgages aren't quite relics yet, but they are not the free flowing, done deal that they used to be. Banging your head against a mortgage brick wall, applying and re applying for loans you'll never get, does nothing other than marginally tarnish your credit score.

So you need other vehicles to raise OPM, or you'll forever be stuck where you're at right now. And it doesn't matter if you are a one man band or Mr. Trump, you'll always want and need more OPM for the next deal. There's a saying in the property world:

"It doesn't matter how rich you are, you always run out of money"
Keep putting in your cash to buy properties, you'll run out one day, even if you are a favoured relation of Steve Jobs [what a great man with a great vision, we can all learn from him].

Bridgers, private investors, JV partners, friends and family, peer to peer lending sites; there's a whole host, and we're going to show you the lot :-)

JV partners: anyone who can fund your deal, or partner with you by offering other value propositions such as contacts and complimentary skillsets, can act as a 'leverage partner' in your property business.

There are two main types of JV partner: Sophisticated and Non-Sophisticated. The Sophisticated Investor is a professional, investing and lending for a living, and the Non-Sophisticated is a non professional individual. Horses for courses and you'll discover in these 2 books.

The Sophisticated Investor:
1. Venture Capitalists [super heavy weight]
2. Angels [heavy weight]
3. Private investors [super middleweight]

These investors are the pros. They do it for a living. You don't need to teach or persuade them to lend their money, you'd be stuffing eggs in their mouths. The money flows. 7 figures, 8 figures, if the deal is good, the money is too.

You don't need to persuade them to lend or invest, you need to persuade them on you and the deal. But you'll pay for it. They'll demand more returns and more control than a Non-Sophisticated. But you'll learn from them. You'll get great contacts from them. They'll leave you to it [while it is going well]. They'll want to give you more and more [while it is going well].

But if and when it goes wrong, they'll apply more pressure than a Non-Sophisticated. You'll feel like you've borrowed from a bank. They'll have some nice tight security, and you won't mess them about.

The Non-Sophisticated Investor:
1. Family
2. Friends
3. Solo-Preneurs
4. Biz Opp Seekers

These investors are not professional lenders or partners. They may never have done it before. They need persuading on the fundamentals of investing first, you need to take a step back. Order another copy of this book and get them to read it. Sometimes they've been brought up to save, work hard, pay off their mortgage and retire – the exact opposite of leverage.

But, everybody with money has the same problem right now: they can't get a return in the bank, stocks are volatile, government backed investments aren't as secure as they used to be and people have lost faith. They're motivated. They need to do something with their money, they're losing on it right now and they just need to work with someone they trust. They need help.

They'll be a little more worried about where their money goes, they'll want more regular communication and they'll feel the ride of the rollercoaster. But you'll get more flexible terms, they'll be more forgiving to market changes, and if things go wrong [which they always do], you can talk to a real person and you can come up with solutions. They'll probably expect a little less return [bank beating 5% might be good enough] and you'll make a bigger difference to their life when you make a bit of money together.

If you want a detailed synopsis on JV finance, and the exact Blueprint how to, here's what you need to do: in the picture section of the book we've printed out the Progressive *Be Your Own Bank* Joint Venture Blueprint. This is a model built over 7 years and £26M of JV's [some failed ones that taught us the most]. Study it.

If you want to download this Blueprint, along with a detailed document on how to raise the finance and put the money in the bank, here's our gift to you: **www.beyourownbank.co.uk**

This is a subject on its own that could take up another 500 pages. When you've read the detailed section on JV's in "Make Cash in a Property Market Crash," drop me a line at **rob.moore@progressiveproperty.co.uk** and I'll point you in the right direction of what to do next, how and where to meet the people, and I'll put you in touch with the community members who might want to JV with you :-)

Someone like Halstead Ottley, for example, a member of the Progressive VIP community:

A sports centre manager, he has always been interested in property and over a period of two decades, bought 12 properties, the traditional non leveraged way. And of course, they've done OK for him, but not quick enough.

Halstead's real passion is sports and martial arts. In his spare time he teaches Karate, and gave an acquaintance of his some free 1 to 1 training sessions. Imagine a fairly small, light unassuming guy throwing people twice his weight all over the place [gently, of course] ;-)

And while this is happening, imagine discussions about property investing [in mid air perhaps]. Within a few months Halstead had released over £1 million from this person he trains, and none of it was while he had him in an arm bar!

Halstead has now built a £million plus cashflowing property portfolio, and he has achieved more in the last 18 months with his JV partner, who is 100% financing the deals, than in his previous 2 decades doing it the old fashioned way!

In over 20 years he bought 12 properties, and in just over a year with Progressive he bought another 8 to get him to over £3K net cashflow per month.

You can watch his video and get in touch with him to hear this personal story from the man himself, here: **www.progressiveproperty.co.uk/inspiration**

Bridging Loans: a bridging loan does exactly what it says – a 'short term' loan [one hour to one year] to fund deposits, cash purchases and give you the 'bridge' to owning a property portfolio.

A bridging loan will be worked out on an individual deal. The better the deal, the better the terms of the loan you will get. The more security you can offer, the better the terms. Like any finance raising strategy, you need to be careful not to over-borrow and put yourself at risk, and there are some thirsty bridgers out there! Many bridgers fall into the category of 'Private investors.'

Mortgage Hosts: even if you can get a mortgage, you might not be able to get many, as the banks chop and change how many they'll give you. One month it might be £10M of property, the next it might be 3 properties only! Depends what side of the bed they get out of!

Like it or not, you will need [someone] to get mortgages, even if it isn't you, to build your portfolio, so the 'Mortgage Host' strategy is very important now. What if you have 3 mortgages already with BM or TMW, and you can't get anymore? What other strategies do you have as a back up? A Mortgage Host is someone who will take a mortgage on your behalf. It might be because you have too many properties and the bank won't lend you anymore for anymore. It might be that you can't get a mortgage, and it might not be anything within your control. It might be that you don't want one in your name. It might be that you need to save them for a rainy day.

A Mortgage Host could be your JV partner, it could be your Mum. It is anyone who takes a mortgage on your or your partnerships' behalf, whether active or silent.

We sometimes take mortgages out in Rob's name, or Mark's name, or Sharon's name [Rob's Mum] or Catherine's name [Mark's Mum] or Ralph's name [Rob's Westie] – if only ;-) It gives you more flexibility and buying power, and turns deals that you couldn't finance into deals you can. Detailed in the *Be Your Own bank* Blueprint.

Get a good broker: forget high street banks, forget standard high street 'sausage machine' brokers; get a specialist who is fast, efficient, knows how to make things fit to get you a mortgage, and has property specific knowledge and experience.

A property specific broker will know how to 'position' you to the lender, they'll know the best products for your strategy, they will learn from other big investors for whom they broker, and they'll work with you as much as they will with the lender.

We have some great brokers in the Progressive community – independent but aligned with the members. Feel free to contact us to get in touch with someone who can help you raise capital to start investing or mortgage finance to build your portfolio.

Summary

Understand the fundamentals of finance and how you can use borrowed money to invest in assets. Use leverage but don't over gear, build a team of finance experts and a large credit line to call upon when the deals find you, and guard your credit score with your life. Use the 7 types of investor/JV partner to build a safer, quicker and more cashflowing portfolio.

Creative Finance & JV's

What's the big thing that stopped us all getting into property for so many years? What's the main thing that held us back in the recession? And what is the thing that most people complain about never having the most?

Not that ;-)

You guessed it; money. Or the lack of money.

Let's keep it simple, [all the mindset around money is for the JV Be Your Own Bank™ programme] there's more money around now than there ever has been. Fact. There are more people becoming millionaires and billionaires faster now, and younger now, than there ever has been. Fact. A 17 year old 'kid' just got $30M for selling an App to Yahoo. Most Entrepreneurs and investors are self made, starting with little or no money. Fact.

So the fact is that your lack of money is not a disadvantage. You'll run out anyway if you buy enough property, even Lord Sugar would. Fact. So what's this all about? Is it about the money you have or don't have in the bank, or is it about you and what you do?

I [Rob] started with minus £30K. Deena Honey in the Progressive community started with minus 6 figures and raised £500K within a few short months within the Progressive Community. And there are hundreds of other stories just like it in the Community.

They did it, you can too.

Creative financing is about creating value. It's about spotting an opportunity to make money, and providing value or service that benefits others to attract the money from them.

Creative finance is about detaching completely from how much money you have in a bank, and focusing on what will pull it in. And there's $55 Trillion flying about before you say there isn't any! If you're not finding it, you're either not in the right places or you're not creating the value.

A Joint Venture [JV] is a method of creating finance. You have the deal that has profit locked in, or value that can be added through refurb, your value is in finding it and managing it, and the JV partner will fund the deal.

An option purchase is a method of creative finance. You don't have the funds to buy and take out hefty mortgages, so you take an 'option' to purchase [which costs virtually nothing], giving you full control and benefit of the cashflow, equity and growth, and the responsibility, but without much of the downside risk. You can take income now and purchase later, should you choose.

Multi-Let Without the Sweat™ is a method of creative finance. You find large properties to rent from Landlords on a single let tenancy, and then let out the property by the room, thereby increasing the cashflow. You've added value by creating a service and profit centre that wasn't already there, and that has attracted the opportunity or the finance.

The range of specific JV strategies shared in "Make Cash in a Property Market Crash" create added value that pulls in cash. The '3 in a bed JV' where you put the deal together and the other 2 partners fund it. The 'Hague JV' where you take income and the partner/financier takes equity. Selling a deal on, to raise the cash for the deposit to buy, is a simple yet creative technique for funding deals when money isn't in the bank.

The *only* limit to creative finance is the limit of your own creative mind, or your mind to copy other creative people doing it.

Summary

You don't need money to buy property, you need a creative mind to add value where it didn't exist. Create value, offer a service, partner with people and detach from how much [or lack of] money you have in the bank

Yield & returns on investment

Yield is the investor's way of gauging a return on a property investment on a yearly basis, calculated as a percentage of its value.

A £6,000 yearly return on a £100,000 house is a 6% yield. It's the percentage cash you get out of your investment.

Yield actually has many variations. To a professional property investor, the two main and most universal calculations are **gross yield [Gr]** and **net yield.**

Gross yield is the gross return [before costs] on the value of your property through rent on a yearly basis, expressed as a percentage. As per the example above: £6,000 return in rent [£500 per month] on a £100,000 property is a 6% gross yield: the return before costs are taken out.

A nice easy way to calculate this is to multiply rent [500] by 12 and divide that by value [100,000] and you will arrive at a one hundredth decimal figure: In this case 0.06 [or 6%]. If you want to get Mark Homer anal, you then x 100.

The obvious difference between gross yield and net yield, is that the net figure has all the costs taken out, and so is the cash you are left with. If this is the case then why is gross yield even relevant? Surely the only relevant figure is net: the real cash that goes in your bank? Gross yield is the barometer: the gauge. You have to have a common, accepted way of benchmarking; a way of comparing asset for asset, like for like. You cannot compare net yield on properties on a like for like basis, because the costs are variable between any individual investor.

Variable costs that contribute to net yield are cost of finance, letting and management, voids, bad debt, insurances and regulations and maintenance, and these vary totally from investor to investor.

But a house is purchased for a fixed cost, and the rent is a fixed cost, and so properties can be measured against each other and compared.

In the instance of the £100,000 property with a £6,000 yearly income, to increase the yield, you either buy lower, or get a higher income [rent]. Buying at £60,000 would give a 10% yield, or getting £600 per month [£7,200 per year], would give a 7.2% yield [gross].

If you have a refurb on a property, we see that as a cost associated with the purchase price, and so you should add that on. If the refurb was £5,000, then you use £105,000 as your calculation for gross yield.

Why? Because it is a factor of the buy price: you got it cheap **because** it needed a refurb, and you needed to do the refurb to add the value. The refurb is part of the value.

So the updated calculation is rent x12 divided by purchase price plus yield x 100.

Net yield is the return on the value of your property through rent on a yearly basis as a percentage, **minus** any additional ongoing costs relating to the income [not the capital]. Those income costs are cost of finance [mortgage, bridging loan, JV funds, cash], letting and management, voids, bad debt, insurances and regulations and maintenance.

The calculation for this is rent x 12 − costs divided by purchase price minus refurb x 100.

This is all very well, but how does it help you?

The gross yield calculation enables you to quickly work out, on a beermat or on a viewing, if a property is a buy or walk away deal. And you need to be able to work that out quickly. Then you lose fewer deals and impress Estate Agents with your speed of decision, and how smart and professional you are.

But how do you know what a buy, or walk away, gross and net yield figure is? We're glad you asked :-)

In order to know what is a good gross and net yield [which varies area to area and strategy to strategy], the important figure is 'Cashflow Benchmark neutral.' This is the figure where the net yield is zero [neither positive nor negative]. Anything in the negative is a walk away deal, and anything in the positive [or a minimum positive] is a deal to buy [based on yield and not other factors].

There are 2.5 ways to calculate a 'Cashflow Benchmark Neutral.'

1. Work out all your own costs on the individual deal
2. Work out an average cost across your previous deal
2.5. 'Benchmark' our average cost across 350 purchases

Actual costs of running a portfolio will vary investor to investor, and actual properties in your portfolio will vary property to property. If you want to be specific, detailed and exact [as much as you can], calculate all the projected costs of running your property, project them forward through the year and deduct them from your gross yield.

How would you know **exactly** what those costs would be? You never will to the pounds and pence, no matter how long you've been doing it. The best gauge is experience of like for like properties, so following step 2, using your data from previous properties, will help you to project forward. Get all the costs for each area [listed in this section] and average them out over the years and properties.

What if you don't have much experience or historical data? Then use step 2.5, and benchmark us. I [Mark] have been tracking our properties bought, sold, still owned and in our JV portfolio, and have averaged out all costs based on this history. Although you might accuse me of being a bit anal here [at least Rob will], this is now very accurate – but only as an average.

Our figures show that 'Cashflow Benchmark Neutral' on smaller single lets is around 8%. This does change as costs of finance change. Here's how it breaks down:

1. Cost of finance:
This is the biggest cost, and can be anywhere from 0.5% a year [older rates linked to Bank of England base rate], up to 6% for a longer term fixed rate mortgage. Call it 5% now.

2. Management:
Based on 10% of rent, this works out to be around £700 a year, or 0.7%. There'll be other charges, so we call it 1% to be on the safe side. If you self manage you might think you'll save this cost – it will actually cost you a lot more in non IGA's.

3. Maintenance:
This usually adds up to around £200 per property per year for a flat, and £300 per property per year for a house. We have got this down considerably over the years and have good economies of scale. It could be more [or less] when you start out]. Call this 0.4% to be clear.

4. Insurances & regulations:
You'll need buildings insurance, gas and boiler safety tests and so on. 0.4% a year should cover it.

5.Voids and bad debt:

It takes us 8 days per property to rent it out, and we lose around the same in bad debt per property. Again we have dramatically reduced this over the years, so your figures may be different. Good tenants first time, and it will be less. Get your bad one right up front, and it will be more. 0.5% should be enough.

6. Contingency:

These figures will vary per property. Save 0.5% [£500 a year on a £100,000 house] just in case. If you don't have it, you'll need it. Known as Sod's law ;-)

The total of all of these is 8%. The best case will be around 7.1%, and others could cost you 8.5% plus. So any gross yield under 8% means your costs will exceed your rental income. Anything over 8.% and your rental income will exceed costs and you'll make money.

A 10.4% gross yield on a £100,000 house, will leave a 'Benchmark' net yield of 2.4% a year. That is £2,400 a year, or £200 clear per month. This is definitely achievable for you depending on your Goldmine area. We see yields of 6% or less in central London up to 13% plus in extreme northern areas.

Costs on a higher yield are often higher, so be careful not just to get lured by gross yields.

Return on Cash Invested/Employed: yield tells you the return against the value of your investment. It's also likely that you'll want to know the return on your invested cash [or the invested cash], so you can compare against other assets and convince JV partners and money lenders to lend to you for greater returns.

Return on Cash Employed [ROCE]: is calculated on your income return on your investment as a percentage of the cash you put in the investment. This has a gross and net calculation too.

Using the same example of a £100,000 property, let's say you invested £30,000 into that property. It gave you £600 per month gross rent, which translates to £7,200 per year, or 7.2% of £100,000. Because the investment only cost you £30,000 of your or your JV partners' money, your gross ROCE is £7,200 per year from £30,000, which is 24%.

This figure, presented to a private investor or JV partner, blows the return from a bank or other investment vehicle out of the water. Even split 50-50 with your JV partner, it's an excellent, market out-performing return. This doesn't even include any growth.

But it's not the 'in the pocket' story.

Net ROCE is calculated as the net income [after costs], as a percentage of the value of the cash invested [£30,000]. A net return of 2% of £100,000 [£2,000 after all costs], equates to an almost 7% return. Still better than the banks and many investment vehicles, and very secure.

How to create infinite ROCE/ROI: you're probably one step ahead of us, and have already worked out how to create an infinite ROI/ROCE on your investment. Using the Progressive *BRR* strategy, if you **B**uy at a discount, add value through a **R**efurb, then **R**emortgage to get your [or JV partners'] cash back out, and your ROI & ROCE is infinite.

Use these formulas to asses any deal [quickly], and to convince JV partners and private investors to give their money to you, as opposed to other, less secure and lower return investments. The numbers make you money, and guesswork and emotions lose you money

Summary

Gross Yield is your quick benchmark to asses a deal compared to other deals. Net yield is your actual cash return on the value of your investment. When you leverage, you can get double digit Return On Cash Employed, and when you use the Buy Refurb Remortgage strategy means you can get up to an infinite ROCE for your [or your JV partners'] cash

Never sell [Buy to Let]

If you buy well, at a good discount, with a good yield and a positive net cashflow, why would you ever sell a deal? For quicker, bigger lumps of cash, perhaps? Let's discuss.

Pre-crash, and in the first 2 versions of this book, the title of this section was simply 'Never Sell,' and the next section, 'Buy to Sell,' didn't exist.

Times have changed, new strategies develop, but fundamentals remain the same.

If you buy well, and make your money when you buy, then this 'Law' applies 100% for **asset building** purposes: for building a portfolio that will passively fund your future pension plan, lifestyle and freedom.

It should be obvious that if you buy and sell, you never actually grow a portfolio. Sure, you may make some [quick] cash, you may also not, but you are exchanging your time for money, like a job, and you only earn once on the asset.

You'll never achieve true wealth turning properties around on this scale. It is generally too time intensive, there are too many variables that can go against you: high disposal costs, low ROI's, risks and exposure to market changes and one off 'salary' or consultant type income payments as opposed to being passively and residually paid for life.

But, if you want or need to create income quickly, in the first year, and you need tens of thousands of pounds to replace your income or meet your needs as you transition from a job to an investor, flipping [the right way], can achieve these goals. Single let properties net cashflowing at 1.5% to 3% will not meet these short term needs.

This book focuses on a **mid to long term** strategy. One that will last your whole life. And if you sell a solid property investment, the person you sell it to gets that lifetime benefit, not you.

It's relatively easy, once you know how, to create a replicable system around buying single let properties at a 25% average discount [25% to 70% is our range over the last 250 properties since the beginning of 2007], and a net yield of 2%, or around £150-£200 net cashflow per month.

You might only need 20 of those to replace your earned income. You might only need 30-40 of them to be totally financially independent. And when you've owned that portfolio for a decade, you can at the very least double those figures with capital and rental growth. So every one you sell just takes you a step back in that pension plan.

Sure, you could make £5K to £20K for one or two of the 'flips', but they'll probably take you the best part of a year; you'll have to take more risk [which you might not want to do] and there's certainly no guarantee of the profit [expect one in 3 to make no money at all].

Building assets that you can get at discount to leverage your money will generate for you mid-long term wealth. It is this mindset, rather than instant gratification, that will guide you to financial success in your portfolio.

Here's a recap of the benefits of holding properties for ever:

1. You earn on it for life
2. The income is [virtually] passive
3. You can access larger lumps of cash through remortgage and never pay capital gains tax
4. You can retire on the income from a targeted amount
5. The process is systemisable, repeatable and predictable
6. The model is robust through market changes
7. You compound your income and growth as you build a portfolio. The longer you own it, the more powerful it becomes.

Of course there are exceptions, as there are to every 'rule.' If you've bought a 'kipper' [structurally defective, damp issues, lease problems, huge shortfalls, above a kebab shop, in a war zone] then by all means get rid of it. Learn your lesson [like we did] and move on — fast.

You wouldn't believe how many people we talk to wish they had not sold their house 10 years ago: people who tell us that their old house is now worth **double** what it was in that time, even after the crash.

Would you like some figures?

You own one house that is worth £200,000 [example: insert your own figures here]. That will go up £10,000 per year tax free [compounding — going up year on year] at 5% growth [realistic].

You build an asset base following the rules: 10 houses worth £200,000 each = £2million. Your portfolio will go up **£100,000** per year tax free [on average and compounding year on year] at 5% growth. If each one of those properties produces just a 1% net yield, that is a £20,000 [and growing] yearly income. You should even be able to double that. Better than exchanging time for money, right?

Then flip the odd low yielder, or out of area, property here and there and you have a semi passive, high income, robust property investing strategy.

If you have an asset [your house] with equity in it, then make sure you keep it. If you need cash to re-invest and buy more 'appreciating assets' then instead of selling it and paying all the disposal costs, consider remortgaging your property to access equity [tax free] to leverage more investments.

Summary

Never sell a good yielding, income producing property. Create long term wealth by buying and holding for ever, letting the rental income and capital grow, which you can access by remortgaging, tax free.

Never Let [Buy to Sell]

This is a new section to this book. There are some instances when you should never let, and only sell.

Out of area deals: if you find an out of area deal that would be a great deal if it was in your area, flipping is the best option, provided the numbers are right. It will cost you money owning out of area properties. Package and sell the property as a packaged deal, one such 'package' being a 'Flip' – Buy to Sell. Details in a moment.

Low Yield, high equity: you will come across deals that you can get good discounts on, but are low yielding. If you held them, they'd be negative cashflowing, but a 30% discount is hard to turn away, right? You don't want to leave all that money on the table.

Larger refurb projects: if you want to buy a property and turn it around quickly to sell, it's likely that you need to spend some money on it. You often get the biggest discounts when properties are dirty-ugly: as they put others off. The margin is in the 'added value,' through your refurb. The bigger the refurb job, the worse it is to other buyers, the cheaper you'll get it, and the more you can add value.

We don't like being doom-mongers, but it's our duty to serve you the best we can and give you the most relevant, honest guidance. So here it is: don't start too big too soon with too many risks, variables and cans of worms you've not seen yet, because you've not been doing it long enough to spot them.

And when you find your first decent looking refurb-flip, double the costs you anticipate and double the length of time you think it'll take.

So let's go through the necessary things to be aware of, and then you can just crack on and do it :-)

Ensure your 'refurb' is not a renovation: structural work, listed buildings, legislative matters, planning and legal issues should be avoided, unless you have good experience where it becomes an advantage. Even when you've been in the business decades, things will still pop up and surprise you when work gets this deep.

Over estimate the time and costs of flipping: we've had a flip take 18 months before. We've had another one take 12 months; then we ended up renting it out [it never even sold]. We had properties cost twice as much as we budgeted. We've had Estate Agents lead us down a garden path about how much we could sell some of our flips for: fake viewings, BS excuses about the market, knee drop strategies, gazundering, the list goes on...

Pause.

As I [Rob] write this section, do you feel that I am making it sound like it's not worth doing? I'd be put off by all this ;-) But, when you know this, the reality, you actually make **more** money than you predicted, and **more** than your competition who don't know this.

I [Mark] factor my figures in my 'Flip Analysis' tool, on 3 price variables: 'Worst case,' 'likely case,' and 'best case.' If I can make it work by £7,500 or more on worst case, I'll do it. I must be at least £20,000 on best case to hit the green light, and I always turn an Estate Agent's 'worst case' valuation into my 'Best case' price variable, because they're biased.

This is the sane, realistic way to make money from flips. It is not as important to be this careful with buy to let valuations, because the equity stays in the property. For flips, the values have to be real and achievable. Most Estate Agents will say what you want to hear, to have you list properties with them. It's their job. We've employed a few over years and learned to take at least 10% off their valuations!

You can get the 'Flip Analysis' App version on the Progressive Property App – search 'Property App' on the App store.

One in 3 makes no money: if you were to flip 3 single lets at the £125,000 - £150,000 mark, one would make £25,000, one £15,000 and one would barely break even, if at all. Sure, you'd probably want to hear that every flip will make £25,000, but it just doesn't work out that way. If it did, everyone would be doing it, right?

It's actually not a disaster to do a flip and break even. You learn a lot. You learn more than on the ones you make money from, and you end up making more money on the next one. You don't make the same misjudgements; you know that the deals have to be a little better and you pick more wisely. So work your profits out on flips in batches of 3. If you do 3 a year, you should make a minimum of £40,000 net after all costs, more in London.

Like Geoff Whittaker who we mentioned earlier who made £58,000, net after all costs, on his first 3 flips, with little previous experience.

Know your costs: there are way more costs associated with a flip than there are with a buy to let. In addition to the standard costs of purchase, you have added refurb costs for a higher quality refurb-to-sell, all the associated agents and selling costs as you'll be the vendor, mortgage or cost of finance to cover the durations from purchase to sale [factor one year], legals and valuation fees, council tax while it's empty and possible stamp duty.

You should factor 10% of the price of the property for all these costs, a figure most amateurs never realise. And if it ends up being 'best case' variable, then you win, but you'll cover yourself on the downside risk.

3+1 Combination strategy: a smart strategy for the modern professional is a 3+1 strategy. Buy 4 properties, hold 3 buy to lets/Multi-Lets, and sell/flip one. You combine long term asset building with short term, bigger chunks of cash. You know how to do it the right way now, too.

And for final downside risk protection, make sure you're always able to hold and rent the one flip if the market changes and you can't make a profit from it, and the worse that happens is a good lesson to help you make more money next time.

Summary

Use the 3+1 strategy: buy and hold 3 properties and flip one. Overestimate the costs and time it takes to refurb a property, and use the 3 variables to cover the downside risk in the worst case scenario. Expect one out of 3 deals to break even only at best, and target minimum £40,000 for every 3 flips, more in London. Use as a strategy to make chunks of cash while you build your portfolio for the long term.

Cashflow Strategies

Now, more than ever, cash is king.

And now, more than ever, it is easier to get going faster, and generate income quicker, with property as your main vehicle.

The first 2 editions of this book focused solely on property as a wealth building asset base, but times have changed, and more opportunities have arisen for you.

You'd probably ask why everyone isn't doing it then. The reason is that most don't know how, don't have the confidence, and they believe what they read in the papers and watch on TV.

Dose of reality: you can actually earn very good money, have clean credit with a score of 999, and still be refused a mortgage if your face doesn't fit. You can now have too many properties, as well as not enough evidence of finance, and even with a rental property you need to prove income.

If you are self employed then your task of getting a mortgage is harder still [though by no means impossible]. In 2007 and the 5 years preceding, banks were throwing out NINJA mortgage ten-a-penny [No Income, No Job] – no problem. Not anymore.

So having the knowledge to create the cashflow without relying on banks and mortgages is essential information in the current climate.

BUT the flipside of these difficulties are that this has provided great opportunity for 'Contrarian Investors.'

The main cashflow strategies you'll want to consider adding to your arsenal are:

BRR [Buy, Refurb, Remortgage]: this is a low to medium risk, time tested strategy which is the staple diet of a professional property investor. You should understand this before you start other more intricate cashflow strategies in this section.

BRR allows you to force the appreciation of the property through refurbishment, and 'cycle' one deposit 'pot,' getting all of your own money [or JV partner's money] out upon remortgage, making it a NMLI deal [No Money Left In].

Then you simply start again, rolling and recycling deposits from property to property without needing any extra cash

Professional, sophisticated investors have been doing this for years, and have built £multi-million portfolios on one single deposit [that they probably borrowed from a JV partner or took out of their own house as equity], therefore building a no money down [NMD] cashflowing portfolio.

Here's how it works.

1. You must get a discount that equates the Loan to Value [LTV], to be able to recycle your deposit back out upon a remortgage. You will be buying the property with your initial mortgage at an LTV [say 75%] of the purchase price. There is an example in a moment.

So your first mortgage is 75% of the purchase price, say £70,000. Your remortgage will then be for 75% of the real value, say £105,000. You will therefore be left with a mortgage of 75% of £105,000, the old mortgage of 75% of £70,000 will be paid off, and you will be left with an amount that 'pays you back' your initial deposit.

2. If you want ALL your money back [refurb costs, fees], you need an extra discount to match these costs.

In the above example, if your refurb and fees were £6,000, that would mean an approximate additional discount of 5% is needed to cover them on the [second] remortgage], otherwise you'll get the deposit 'back out' but not the £6,000 costs.

3. Your 2nd [remortgage] must have no ERC's [early redemption charges].

Most lenders [though not all, and the market is always evolving] will not allow you to mortgage with them, until you have owned the property for 6 months. And many of these lenders will charge you an ERC to pay off that mortgage [to remortgage to another lender]. This can be as much as 6% of the value of the loan.

You need to select a mortgage that has no ERC's. Very important or you'll be paying £5,000 - £10,000 extra on your 'remortgage.' 4. Getting the higher valuation. If the same surveyor is sent to value your property for the remortgage, 6 months or so after she values it previously for 30% less, do you think she's going to give you the extra 30% on the valuation?

No.

It is vital that you instruct a different surveyor [through a different mortgage company] to value your property on the remortgage. You're not being shifty here, you're simply getting another independent valuation, from a surveyor who is valuing the property on its merits and value, and not being influenced by knowing what you bought it for.

Surveyors are being pressured now to value quite low, and are also instructed to value on the basis of value or purchase price, whichever is lower, for their indemnity and protection. If they know the purchase price, they will value it at that level, even if you have genuinely bought it at a discount [which you have], and genuinely added value through refurb [which you have].

Using the BRR strategy you can buy one property every 9 months or so [6 months plus remortgage and valuation time] with one deposit. If you want to buy more, and build your cashflowing portfolio faster, simply raise more deposits.

In 10 years with just 2 deposits you could have a portfolio of 26 properties worth a conservative £5million valuation and likely minimum equity in the millions.

BRR example:
Purchase Price: £70,000
[1st] purchase mortgage @ 75%: £52,500
Deposit: £17,500 [equity in home, JV partner, stocks, savings]
Cost of refurb & fees £5,000 [approx]
Total money in: £22,500

Revaluation [value] after 6 months of mortgage: £105,000
New re-mortgage @ 75% of £105,000: £78,750

[No deposit needed, as this is a re-mortgage]

Money left after old mortgage is paid off by new mortgage [£78,750 - £52,500] = £26,250

Money back out to 'start again' on the next property: £26,250 [£3750 more than cash put in]

You have effectively bought the property, refurbished it and remortgaged it pulling out the original deposit leaving no money in [NMLI], even getting a little cash back. You then repeat the process over and over. Remember, you also have locked in equity of £25,000.

This is infinitive return on your investment [ROI]!

This property will now give you passive income from the cash flow from day one [approx £150 per property per month NET], and all there is to determine is how many of these 'money boxes' do you need to replace your current income through equity or cashflow?

Even if you could only get a valuation of £95,000, you'd have a cashflowing property with £25,000 equity, with only £6,250!

Further Advance [FA]: a further advance is very similar to BRR, except you don't need to remortgage to another lender. In the case of an FA, you simply apply to the same lender [as long as they offer this service] to 'advance' you the uplift in value. This is like a remortgage, based on the fact that the property is worth more, but with the same lender.

The benefit of this is that you don't incur double fees [as you are only using 1 mortgage company, and it is quicker]. You do have to ensure that you have shown an increase in value, for the same surveyor to be happy to lend you more money to get your deposit back out.

HMO's/Multi-Let's: the demand for rooms is growing fast. People can't afford to buy like they used to, access to lending for ordinary people is hard, and rents and prices are very high compared to salaries.

The population is exploding through larger families and immigration, and towns and cities are becoming more and more densely populated, without the available land to build on.

It has gotten harder and harder for developers to make margins, so they build smaller and smaller houses and flats to reduce costs.

People are more transient in their careers now and do not hold down jobs or relationships for as long as they used to, so they need more flexible living accommodation to match the changing lifestyles.

The reaction to this is obvious and necessary. You'll notice many more houses are being converted into room lets, especially in and around the town centres. You'll notice more and more people renting out a room in their house. You'll notice more and more investors talking about HMO's/Multi-Lets, and the changing regulations concerning it.

There are 5 main Progressive HMO/Multi-Let strategies, and 5 main finance strategies to acquire them, 4 that don't need a deposit. Progressive are currently the only people training you on all of them.

Which strategy or strategies work for you will depend on your available cash, your local Goldmine area, and your local planning regulations. It is important that you research to find these before you scale up your chosen HMO strategy or strategies, and something that many investors are getting wrong now.

It's not smart to get drawn in by a sexy NMD HMO strategy, educate yourself on it and spend time working it out, only for it to work in every other area other than your locality.

*The Progressive 5 step HMO *strategy* model:*

High end 'Boutique:' the most profitable room by room model is the 'Boutique.'. It is also the model that requires the largest initial outlay of cash [especially sexy to JV partners]. This model provides Boutique, mini hotel room accommodation for high end professionals near the town centre or more affluent parts of a town or city. This model commands the highest room rent, attracts the best tenants, and needs to be furnished accordingly.

Post grad/professional: one step down in 'quality' to the 'Boutique' model, but with a slightly larger market, with less input costs to you or your JV partner.

Blue collar: a larger market than professional/post grad, and not as necessary in the town centre, where prices are often higher, as these can be located close to the main industry of the town/city, for example near the hospital or a large manufacturing plant.

Less input cost, less fussy about the quality of the accommodation and perhaps an extra room can be squeezed in per house. The lower down the 5 step model you go, the more management the tenants need.

Student: especially effective in University cities, and usually within one mile of campus. Voids are higher because of holidays, and maintenance and management are also higher, but tenant expectations lower and a greater tolerance of higher numbers.

LHA/DSS: the 'lowest' end of the market, needing the lowest amount of capital outlay, but commanding the lowest rent per room, and requiring the highest management in time and costs. Space can be maximised to great effect, and the market is wider than 'Boutique,' and 'Post grad/professional,' but tenant turnover can be high and management intensive.

The Progressive 5 step HMO *Finance* model:

BRR: as explained in this chapter, you buy with a deposit, refurbish, then rent out. You own the bricks and mortar. And in some cases, you can recycle ALL your cash back out, for NMLI.

Multi-Let Without the Sweat/Rent to Rent/Corporate Letting: excuse all the terminology, but you need to know the language. Corporate letting is a smart strategy which involves you renting an 'HMO-able' property from a Landlord on a single let basis, and then 'HMO-ing' it yourself. You create all the cashflow of an HMO, yet you don't buy it. No deposit needed. No big upfront costs.

Big upside is it's virtually NMD. Trade off is you don't own it, so don't want to spend much refurbing it. You can mix and match this finance strategy with one of the 5 Progressive HMO strategies above.

Lease Options: rather than buying the HMO and needing the big deposit, you take an option to purchase it. You take control of it through an option that excludes all other potential buyers, but you don't 'pay' for it until you 'complete,' which could be many years down the line. Virtually NMD HMO control except for legal costs, and a great way to generate significant cashflow with limited finds.

Trade off is that you'll need to learn and master this strategy, get the legals right and 'educate' vendors, Landlords and agents. But that's the same for most things anyway.

Lease Options and other option variations such as purchase and sandwich are detailed in "Make Cash in a Property Market Crash."

Delayed Completions [EDC's]/Instalment Contracts: a variation on an option where you exchange on a property, thereby negating the risk of lost refurb costs. Once you exchange, you basically own it, but you can then 'delay' completion, or own in 'instalments' over a period of time, often many years.

LO's & IC's are as relevant to single lets as they are to HMO's, and are a creative and evolutionary finance strategy that negates the need for mortgages or large chunks of cash.

JV's: Any property buying strategy becomes NMD when a JV partner fronts all the costs. A big advantage of working with a JV partner is that you can still own properties by using more traditional purchasing methods with your partner's money, and you have a partner where other benefits such as knowledge, experience that you wouldn't have working alone.

Cashflow: with a single let property, you're doing well if you can clear £200pcm net income. In some low yielding areas around London, it's virtually impossible to achieve cashflow on single lets without a 50% deposit. Not a great use of leverage or cash.

With HMO's, you should be looking at minimum £400pcm net, and with the higher end models, you can be looking at £800 plus per property per month, even with a repayment mortgage.

The more rooms you have [5 or more] the more your cashflow increases, and many old commercial units, old hospital and council buildings, clubs, nursing homes, retail and pubs are prime for HMO conversion.

You may need single let 20 properties to get to your income target, whereas 4 larger HMO's can achieve the same goal. We recommend that total beginners cut your teeth on a few single lets before stepping up, but if you're reading and you have a few already, perhaps it's time to step up and accelerate your cashflow, my friend?

Deal Packaging: when buying any type of property, it's likely that you view between 5 and 50 before you get a deal accepted, depending on your experience, criteria and area.

So this begs the question: what are you doing with the 4 to 49 properties that you're NOT buying? Are you making any money from them, or is someone else buying them?

What if you could make just £3,000 on each one? Or even just £1,000? In your professional property career you're going to view 100's or 1,000's of properties: you do the maths!

Strange though it may sound, there's a great advantage to having no money, or not being able to buy yourself [a problem you may have had before reading this book].

The fact that Jo Moore, Progressive VIP member, was 17 when she joined the Progressive VIP community should have zoned her out, if you talked to ordinary people or banks.

At 17 you can't buy property. Game over, right? Well no, not for Jo. Without cash or the ability to get a mortgage, you have to be creative. Jo started sourcing and packaging for others first, until she turned 18, so that she could learn property as a business, and make cash while doing it.

She did this by 'packaging' deals and selling them to other investors for immediate, upfront cash profit. More than £3,000 per month. Not bad for a 17 year old, right?

Many more of the Progressive community members double or triple their property income from selling deals they don't want, or would have previously rejected.

Kris & Jayne Carpenter, a brother/sister partnership in the Progressive Community, now have over 25 properties and a Letting Agency with over 120 lets, and still did their best month ever recently of £25,000 in deal packaging fees in one month!

Deal packaging gives you faster access to liquid cash that could free you from your job in 30-90 days; certainly much quicker than buying 20-30 single lets. And if you are really grasping the idea that property is a business, you can see how powerful, leverage-able and cash generating this strategy is.

This is one of the strategies that's allowed Progressive to grow from a personal portfolio of ours to a multi-million business empire. This has also allowed 1,000's of Progressive community members the same luxury.

You might think it's too early for you, or you don't have enough experience, or any other excuse you could make, but where else can one deal sold replace your monthly gross wage? We have been packaging 5-15 deals per month every month since the start of 2007, and you can too. We started with limited experience, helping out friends and family, and it grew from there.

And the power of compounding really kicks in when you combine deal packaging with HMO's/single lets with a well financed JV partner.

The fees you can get from deal packaging vary from £50 a lead, to £20,000 plus per property, depending on the strategy, time input, and customer type. uQL, QL, RMD's, FF, PPD, AS, LO/SO & PB are detailed in "Make Cash in a Property Market Crash"

Lending your money to other property investors: If you have cash to invest, and want a better return than the bank, and want to be more passive in your investing, you can consider lending your money to other property investors.

Most bridging/private lenders get between 1% and 3% a month on their money, depending on the term of the loan. With loans of six months or more 1% to 1.5% is easily achievable and with relatively low risk.

You can secure your loan on the property in question, and your investment is likely to be almost as safe as if it was in the bank, except you'd be making 5 to 10 times the return.

Many investors who become successful in property and make big lumps of cash, often use lending money to other property investors as another stream of their property multiple income strategy.

It's also a great way to 'buy in' great contacts and learn how to invest from people who are already doing it very well. You can use some cash to partner with an experienced investor, shadow them, and learn exactly how they do it, whilst they make money on your money.

You should very realistically and with low risk be able to make 12% a year using this strategy.

You can call upon any contacts in the Progressive community if you require help with the strategy, the legals, the contracts, the agreements, keeping the risk low and setting clear expectations from the start.

Gill Alton has been both money lender and recipient of funds in the Progressive community. She loaned out a deposit to another Progressive community member at 8% per year, and borrowed from her parents at 5% per year. As have Francis and Jane Dolley, who's £9,500 net cashflow per month has been leveraged by the funds they have borrowed and loaned within the community.

We often 'bridge' money to friends and business associates, and sometimes even act as money lenders to ourselves.

Sharing your knowledge and selling the information: Information is one of the most important and valuable commodities in the new age and economy that we're in.

Information is accessible faster than ever on demand, and people are craving to know the 'how to.' Property investing, making money and Entrepreneurship are some of the most popular topics people desire right now, especially with the money problems many people have, and recent property crashes and credit crunches.

In years gone by the facilitation of this information was only for the very top experts in their respective fields. But today where 'people buy people' and look for trust more than ever, people with less experience are positioning themselves as experts and being rewarded handsomely [financially] for it.

One of the unique things about the Progressive community is that we teach and actively encourage you to become an expert as quick as you can, and help and train others. We believe the world needs more trainers and leaders right now, and why shouldn't it be you?

Sure, you're not going to go out and teach someone how to build a multi-million pound property portfolio if you've never bought anything before, and still rent off your Mum at the age of 56, but with each step up the ladder you go, there will always be someone a level below you who needs the information that you have. Information they'll pay for.

The packaging of information has no limits. At whatever level you're at, you can 'repurpose' this information and sell it to others and help them make money. Even after your first property purchase, you can teach people how to let their first property. When you've bought 5 properties you can teach people the fundamentals of building a solid portfolio. When you've bought 50 properties you can teach advanced investors the intricacies of building a multi-million pound portfolio.

When you have a multi-million pound business you can teach other people how to build businesses around property.

Even more exciting than this are multiple ways in which you can package this information for people with different learning styles, therefore 'selling' the information many times over.

This is the exact journey we and Progressive have embarked upon, and the thing that helped us make far more money than we ever dreamed we could when we were keen but green. Buying houses alone would still have been great, but it may have taken us a few years to become financially opulent. With the help of training courses, mentorships, CD programs, DVD programs, online memberships, retreats, accountability programs and many other ways of repackaging the information we've been able to create many more, multiple streams of income.

Genuinely as good as the money is, the enjoyment and satisfaction and meaning you get from helping other people achieve the same results as you. Your sense of pride, humility and importance in life grows not so much with more money but with more contribution.

Mark has always said that training other people in property is what I [Rob] was born to do, because making money talking about myself all day is one of my favourite things :-) It's certainly more enjoyable and rewarding than dealing with tenants' minor issues, reading all legal contracts and other necessary details in property investing that really should be leveraged to other people.

Many of our competitors have said that we're crazy to share this information, reveal our 'ulterior motives' and train others to do what we do, thus creating more competition in the market place. However we believe in abundance and the more people we help helping more people, we believe can only be positive for the Progressive brand. The community grows faster this way and more people that want to learn from Progressive will be attracted to us. Not everyone wants to learn from Progressive, and you have unique skills and personality that people would prefer to learn from you.

Some people place us on high pedestals and feel that we will always be way ahead of where they could possibly ever be. This is not the case and we believe we're ordinary guys who are no different to anybody else.

We all have the same opportunities, yet the only difference is not everyone takes them. So people who feel overwhelmed and awestruck by our results would prefer to learn from someone else who's not been doing it quite as long and is nearer their level.

And even better than this is that Progressive will teach you how to do exactly this for a fraction of the cost of becoming a long-term 10,000 hour expert. We all get to serve and give back to our industry and keep the flow of money and success within our field.

And the best way to cement any learnings you get is to teach them immediately. Please don't underestimate the unique talents and skills you have to offer the world and how other people crave them. Don't do them a huge disservice by keeping it all to yourself.

Summary

There are multiple streams of cashflow available through property investing, not just Buy to Let. Over time add additional cashflow strategies to your overall strategy, and think outside buying and renting. Sell to and help other investors, share and sell your knowledge and information, and sweat each asset to its maximum by renting out multiple rooms.

Letting, tenancy & management

Tenant selection can be a minefield. Voids can be a killer. Eviction can be a nightmare. Perhaps that's why amateurs and part-timers don't like renting out properties?

Perhaps one of the most common fears in property investment is the prospect of having properties vacant and not being able to rent them out, thus being stuck with mortgage payments on properties.

This is a sensible concern, as void periods consume the profits.

We've been studying what types of property rent out the fastest, the longest and with the least amount of hassle for many years now.

You have probably realised now what type of property we like and why. One of the biggest reasons for loving [and making money from] the 'lower' end existing [not new] property market, as opposed to new build, overseas and off plan, and high end tenant, is 'rentability.'

For single lets, target the mid to low end or the market: There is an optimum price point for rentals, and it will vary from area to area. Our optimum price point for rentals is £65,000 - £120,000; specifically studio, 1 & 2 bed flats and 2 & 3 bed houses in 6 very focused 'area within area' Goldmine areas. These areas are 'not best not worst' areas which are affordable to the masses.

When you find these areas local to you, with everything you've learned in this book, you'll notice that void periods dramatically reduce to 8 days a year [or less], times to find tenants significantly reduces, duration of tenants staying will increase and the 'pain in the backside' factor will evaporate. We're currently renting out many of our properties within a day after completion, and even have a waiting list on many and our tenants tend to stay for long periods of time.

And the types of tenants and areas that work weren't necessarily the ones we initially would have chosen or assumed.

Never mix tenant types: there are different tenant types in single lets and HMO's, and you should never mix them. Don't put a high end professional in an LHA house, and don't put an LHA tenant up market. Especially don't mix tenant types in Multi-Let HMO's, in the same house. It's like when one infected virus-vampire gets locked in a room full of innocent people, soon enough they're all eating each other and trashing the pace.

Match refurb standard with tenant type: if it's a nicer area, the standard of the refurb will need to suit. If you're going for high end tenants in your 'Boutique HMO's,' then they need to look like 'Boutiques. If you are in the lower, single let LHA areas, clean and tidy is more than enough, you'll be wasting money on fancy fittings and it'll make no difference to the rent.

Letting yourself vs. Letting Agent: when it comes to letting out your properties, there are advantages to letting yourself – you save some money. For HMO's, that can be a reasonable sum, and you may not be able to find good enough Letting Agents to manage HMO's.

But for single let's, it is very counterproductive. It will cause you hassle, grief, pain, multiple hernias and coronaries: all to save 10-15% per property. In the long run it will end up costing you way more; in money and time.

You may like the control of letting and managing yourself [if you have 37 hours in a day to manage it], and you may feel that Letting Agents get a bit heavy on maintenance costs. These can be controlled.

It is definitely NOT an IGA task to manage yourself. You didn't get into this business to manage tenants, and you don't know anywhere near as much about is as a [good] professional Letting Agent.

Not everyone will agree with this, and that is fine. Some people have been Landlords a long time, and know what they are doing, and have learned to systemise the tasks. It is very difficult without a lot of experience and can tarnish your enjoyment of the investment process. It also goes against all the concepts of leverage that we have been discussing so far in the book. And most Landlords who I know who manage their own properties are not rich in time or money.

For those who want, and are still not convinced or are having doubts, read the following mini-section on using a Letting Agent vs DIY. You will be glad you did!

Letting agents offer two levels of service: a 'let only' service a 'full management service'.

Let only: this level of service requires the agent to carry out the following basic steps:

1. **Produce lettings particulars of the Landlord's property for marketing purposes** – This will involve the agent providing a rental assessment which gives the Landlord an idea of the rental value which can be achieved in the 'area within the area' of your chosen investment property.

2. **Marketing the property** – The agent will advertise the lettings particulars on the company's website, with accredited letting sites such as Rightmove. They will also include your property in the weekly local newspaper.

3. **Viewings** – The agent will take the prospective tenants on viewings to your property

4. **Referencing** – The agent will carry out the referencing process of the prospective tenants, and provide the landlord with their assessment so the landlord can then make an informed decision.

5. **Tenancy agreement** – The agent will determine the type of agreement, which will usually be an up to date Assured Shorthold Tenancy Agreement [AST].

6. **Deposits** – The agent will take the first rental and deposit payment and pay it over to the account which is nominated by the landlord.

7. **Check in & handover** – The agent will carry out the necessary 'check in' and 'handover' of the Landlord's property to the tenant.

8. **Inventory** – Although the agent may charge a little extra, they can prepare an inventory for the landlord.

Full Management: the other option is on a full management basis, this is for landlords who do not like dealing with tenant issues and don't want contact with the tenant. If this rings true for you, it will be a good idea to employ Letting Agents who are worth their weight in gold [if they're good – explained later].

Filtering: a good letting agent will filter out some of the poorer quality letting applicants. This is a good process as it means the more financially risky tenants, some on benefits, or ones with a bad history, are less likely to come through to the agent. It is important to note, some agents are specialists in benefit tenants [LHA], and many are NOT. It's your responsibility to find out which.

Cost comparison & opportunity cost: traditionally Letting Agents charge in two ways: a fee relating to a multiple of the weekly rent, two weeks + VAT is typical or a percentage of the rent due of the tenancy contact, typically between 8% and 12% + VAT. This figure is reasonable and only equates to between £30 and £100 per property per month, depending on the value.

One hour of your time is worth more than that.

A number of Letting Agents are also charging on a fixed fee for their service, and can be attractive to a Landlord who has a higher value let, as it can equate to less than 10%.

Most Letting Agents would prefer landlords to use the full management service, as the agent will make a lot more money and get a regular income for doing very little, once all is set up.

That's good, because you also want to do very little.

Cost of DIY: to explore the cost element of managing the let yourself, it is important to compare both assessments like for like, with opportunity cost of time factored in:

Cost comparison between a Letting Agent vs. DIY Landlord

Advertising	Letting Agent	DIY Landlord
Newspaper (4 ads)	INC	£200
To Let Board	INC	£40
Internet add	INC	£30
Notice Board	INC	FREE
Viewings -5 hrs @ £15p/h	INC	£75
Admin – 5hrs @ £15p/h	INC	£75
Cash Cost	**£480***	**£270**
Cash & Time Cost	**£480***	**£420**

Please note the above figures are based on rent at £675 pcm and standard let only fee of 10% on a 6 month rent.

As can be demonstrated Landlords can only make a marginal saving on DIY lets in real cash terms. If the rent were higher, the Letting Agent's fees would increase, but nowhere on here is time factored in for not knowing how to find a tenant/the right tenant in the first place, all the form filling, for visiting the tenant, gas safety checks, cleaning, repairs, renewals, your time and travel costs, phone calls, cost of one bad tenant not properly vetted, eviction time and cost of mistakes.

Tax: Letting Agent's fees are all off-settable against the profits of your property business. That £480 per month can offset £480 net cashflow you bring in. You can show an actual profit but a tax loss, paying little to no tax on your property income.

Sanity: then there's your happiness and calm :-)

Opportunity cost: And then there's the 3-5 hours per month [or more] per tenant time that you can put back into your property business buying deals and generating more cashflow.

Finding a good Letting Agent then, they are worth their weight in gold. It might take a while and you may have to get through a few, kissing a few Frogs. However the good ones are worth every penny of the 8% - 12% % they will charge you. But remember they **must** be good, because you'll be watching over them watching over your properties. It is a good idea to note the following:

Always make sure that your agents are working in your best interests. Check them out. Ask to see details of how they advertise and how [and where] they present the properties that they rent out for you. What papers do they advertise in and how big is the space? How does their website look [do they have one?] and how often is it updated? Compare them with other agents in the area too.

Test: Your job has only just started once you have decided on an agent, because for your next 3 properties you'll want to use 3 different Letting Agents and test them against each other.

The reality is you'll only know the reality when you have had them with an agent for 6 months to a year.

Hunt out other investors locally: which Letting Agents do the top dog investors use? Chances are they've gone through the testing process.

Competition: we like our agents to know, in a subtle way, that they are competing with other agents. It keeps them fresh and doing their job. They stay proactive because they want the business and they don't want to lose out to a competitor.

When they get complacent their work standards will drop. This is something that we have experienced firsthand. They might be a ball of energy to get you, but how do they keep you? If they think they have a monopoly on your business and you get too friendly, things can very quickly go south.

Random spot checks: get your letting agent to list their charges, including finding tenants. Check how many times they do an inspection and ask tenants if they have seen the agents when they last came round. Make sure you keep your eye on them, as some have been known to make large amounts of money out of Landlords and tenants by not doing the services they list, or hiking up the charges.

Rent expectations: Often most agents will give you a figure of what they think they can achieve for rent, and then a few weeks' voids later and you're accepting £50 less. We very often take rental figures with a pinch of salt until we have seen figures and tested them ourselves. In some instances we have had to take £50-£100 off what they say they can get, especially when we were new to them, as they were selling themselves to us.

It is up to you to set the expectations. If you set the expectation of what you want to achieve, then challenge them to get it [with a view that you will not accept lower], then you may achieve more rent. It can be done, but you must be realistic and aware of how they play their game. You are trying to set the expectations for any future dealings, and keep them aware that they're competing for your business.

Increasing rents: your cash flow relies on steady incremental increases in the rent. Good Letting Agents also know this, and want to keep your business, and will do this gradually to keep the tenant happy [better than finding out that the rent has doubled because it has not gone up for 10 years!]. Poor agents may be afraid to ask or not be organised enough to notice it is needed.

Vet your Letting Agents vetting your tenants: always make sure your Letting Agent does a proper credit check on your potential tenant. Any financial grief further down the road will be hugely reduced. Even if you are 'desperate' for a tenant, don't cut corners here. A bad tenant can really upset your investments so selecting a good one is vital.

Always take a deposit: never let a tenant into your property without as big a deposit as you can get. It should be at least one month's rent. The more you can get the less likely your tenant is to trash your place and nick your radiators.

Always have a contract: this seems so obvious, but isn't always to some investors. An AST agreement should be a pre-requisite for a Letting Agent, but you should make sure. It is advisable to get your solicitor to look over one the first time you use an agent.

Make sure you get your monthly statements: you need to keep a close eye on what is going on. We have had months where our rent has not been paid in. The only way to keep a check is to receive [and read] your monthly statements. It will ensure that your agent knows you are keeping an eye on them and you won't miss anything. Remember that one missed rental payment to you could cause a missed mortgage payment. That could cause a black mark against your credit and hinder further borrowing.

And remember this: *your credit score is your holy grail.* It is your little golden cup. Guard it with your life.

Systems: do they have a procedure for everything they do? Are they making sure the gas safety checks are done every year? There is a lot of paperwork around finding and housing tenants. The more disorganised a Letting Agent is, the less they will get done, and the more problems you will ultimately have. Look for those who systemise and log their procedures, use dedicated Landlord software, have tidy organised offices and are attentive to detail.

Changeover: letting is not just about getting a tenant in your property. Make sure you know in advance that everything is done properly when a tenant may leave.

Don't let the agent release the tenant's deposit until you have inspected the property yourself, at least every few properties, randomly, so they know you are watching them. So often have we seen properties not left in the right state afterwards – go round *yourself* and stand firm on the costs to clean and return the property to the standard that it was when they moved in. You are managing the behaviour of the tenant *and* the agent. Video inventories are great for this, and now should be standard practice.

Be proactive and friendly: this goes for you and the Letting Agent. The more proactive you both are, the more you will get done in the shortest possible timeframe. The more your agent looks after your tenant, is likeable, quick and efficient, the more likely they are to both stay and pay your rent on time, every time and treat your place like their own. Despite many myths about tenants, they're human just like us, and respond well to being treated well!

Remember your role in all of this. There is a chain that goes from you to your agent to your tenant. If you bully or complain too often [or even if you are too lenient] then life will be more difficult for you than it should be.

An opportunity: Letting Agents can also be a good source of deals. Make sure you let them know what you want and how you work and open some potential doors for referrals. Try to incentivise them to do this. If it is their own business they could invoice you for a finder's fee. This incentivises them and makes them come to you rather than anyone else.

Always pay them on exchange *immediately*. It will only make them more likely to do it again for you. It is amazing what money does to people's passion and productivity!

Summary

Letting yourself saves a little money but costs a lot more, and takes up your time that could be put to better use. Vet, monitor and test Letting Agents, find the good ones and keep them competitive to free your time to buy more and more.

Protect the Downside

There are risks to property investing, just like any investment. The upsides are so big that the downsides can be bankrupt-inducing if you get it badly wrong.

The R.E.A.S.O.N model will immunise you from most of the mistakes, but there are other factors you need to know to add a dose of protection and commercial reality to your big goals and dreams of financial independence.

Keep your costs down: everything that you spend on your property portfolio eventually comes out of your profit [or your pocket]. You must know exactly where [and where not] to spend money. Keep a hawks-eye on your spreadsheets and numbers like Mark Homer on steroids. Or get someone to do it for you [like Rob has].

Holiday homes will cost you £1,000's. Emotional refurbs will drain years of profit. Overpaying for properties is a waste of cash. Bad mortgage deals can cost you for 25 years. Paying a JV partner too much could eat all of your cashflow and leave you in a legal battle.

If you want to *profit*, then you need to keep the costs as low as you can, and then keep trying to get them lower. Now of course there is a limit, doing things too cheaply so that it ends up being far more expensive in the long run. We are not talking about cutting corners or pulling fast ones.

You will learn the right balance as you go, and it will be specific to your area and the people you use. As a guide, be on the tighter, Mark Homer end of the scale ;-)

Always get at least 3 quotes for any job: in trades where the trades' people hold the knowledge and skills, it is quite easy for them to pull the wool over your eyes. Boiler quotes are the best example of that. Most of the time you will get told you need a whole new boiler system that will cost you £3,000 when perhaps it is just the ignition that needs fixing. Boiler costs can vary by 100%. Refurb costs can too. Scrutinise and itemise every cost, take out everything that is not necessary, and then drive the price down again. People need your business right now, and you're probably having to do the same for your clients in your business or job.

Be cautious and question *all* costs. The compounded effect of saving 10% on all your costs is likely to be thousands a year, and hundreds of thousands, even millions, in your life.

Fundamental tip No.8:
When you make a pound, you can end up paying up to 70% in taxes, but when you save a pound, you save 100% of it!

You set the expectation: most people make the mistake of asking for a quote and accepting a price. This is a big mistake. You should be letting any supplier/retailer or tradesman know what you are willing to pay for a job or service and let them meet your price. If they can't — fine. Find someone who can. There will be people out there who want your business.

Only make basic/light refurbs: when refurbishing a property, you're not looking to make a MTV crib footballers' wives' home. You're looking to make the property clean, rentable and neutral so that any person can quickly and happily move in and make their own mark on it. You may like purple carpet, other people may not. You may like floral curtains, mint green wallpaper and brown bathroom suites [if you're still living in the 1970's], other people may not.

Spend your time and [tight] budget on kitchens and bathrooms and keep them basic, neutral and cost effective. We use Howdens or go through LNPG. This is what most people will notice, and make the biggest difference on the value uplift. Carpets should be neutral but dark enough to hide stains; walls should be eggshell white or magnolia to look clean and open. Perhaps spend on light fittings/lampshades or mirrors to make small rooms look bigger, but remember every penny you spend is money out of your profit.

Match your refurb to the type of property you are renting out — lower end means lower end. No need to spend on white goods, they'll bring their own and only cost you when they break the ones you put in anyway.

At Progressive we look to keep a full redec [redecoration] under £2,500 and a full refurb [redec plus kitchen and bathroom] under £5,000. These prices haven't gone up much since 2006.

The more you get tradesmen fighting for your work and the more you set the expectation, the more you will be able to get them down to a price that you want to pay.

B.O.Q: always produce a Bill of Quantities [a list of what you expect to be done]. Go through it with the tradesmen and get them to check and sign it to agree. *Do*

not pay them all of the money until the job is complete and you have snagged the B.O.Q [check it has been done and make sure you oversee any corrections].

You know what happens if you don't, don't you? Jobs not finished. Jobs not done properly. Once they've been paid you can almost guarantee that unless the work has been done, the motivation to maintain the quality will diminish.

Interest rates: interest rates are a big expense for you. Whether it is linked to your mortgage payments, cash held in the bank, or the returns you pay your JV partners.

Bank of England base rate: since the 1st edition of this book, when rates were 5.5% in 2007 and people were worried about rate rises, the property market, in fact the world, has changed, and rates have been held at 0.5% [at the time of writing]. It is predicted that rates will stay this low until almost 2015.

Whether this is true or not, until the market completely recovers rates are going to have to stay low to protect over geared borrowers and prevent more repossessions. Of course there are many other factors – this is the most relevant to investors. Our crystal ball says rates stay low :-)

Low rates mean low interest for savers. Savers and wealthy people need to get their money out of the banks, it's getting eaten by inflation and it needs to be leveraged. Low rates mean lower cost of finance, which means higher net yield and cashflow. 'Benchmark Cashflow Neutral' in 2006 was a good 2% higher than it is now. On a £100,000 house, it was costing you at least an extra £2,000 a year in finance costs.

Protect against 80's style rate hikes: despite low rates now, they will eventually have to go up, we all know that. People who experienced the rate hikes in the 80's [while we were in nappies] felt how real and painful it was, and don't want to go through it again.

Despite it being very unlikely to happen again, the same results in a different way could occur, and it is smart to protect your downside risk. There are 3 ways you can do this:

1. Get a fixed rate mortgage
2. Get rate rise insurance
3. Save the predicted rate rise as a contingency

No.2. varies from company to company, and day to day, so you'll need to do your own research. It's the more complicated of the 3, and the strategy that is the most out of your hands. We'll focus on no.s 1. & 3.

1. Get a fixed rate mortgage: depending on the market, you can get 5 and 10 year fixed rate mortgages, which cannot go above a set level in the term of the fixed part of the loan. This is a sure fire, guaranteed way of protecting against rate rises, and very secure. You know from day one what you'll be paying. You can work out your figures to cashflow with your fixed rate. Downside protected, and you can sleep easy. But...

You will overpay slightly for a fixed rate vs. a variable [tracker] rate mortgage. You're paying [a little] extra for the security, and the banks want to hedge against future rate rises by charging you more. But if rates don't rise, you could have paid a decent amount more over the term, which could have gone in your pocket [which you can never predict]. So...

3. Save the predicted rate rise contingency: as a tracker rate mortgage [variable with the base rate] will cost less in the short term, you might prefer a tracker to keep the net cashflow as high as possible. But there's a risk – base rates go high, and so do your payments. I [Mark], like to vary the mortgages across the portfolio to mitigate risk, and so don't want too many fixed rates.

To protect against possible [though unlikely] rate rises, I'll get a tracker mortgage, and however much it costs less than the equivalent fixed rate, I save the money in a high interest account. I've been doing this for years and have built a big buffer that I can earn interest on, or lend out to my property company, and it helps me sleep at night. I'm quite risk averse, and I do worry about doomsday scenarios, and want to make sure I'm covered. If you're anything like me, mixing this strategy with some fixed rate mortgages will suit your personality.

Protect with discounts: a double win for you in the crash is to get the biggest discounts that you can. Yes, it's one of the driving factors that make you money, but it's also one of the biggest downside risk protections you can give yourself.

If you get a 30% discount, then you are immunised from a further, bigger crash than we've already had. The bigger the discount, the lower the loan on the property, and the higher the cashflow. The bigger the discount, the more liquid you are because you can exit quickly without taking a hit. Most people only see the one side of getting discounts, we [Mark] think this is the biggest benefit.

Cost of finance: with mortgages getting harder and harder to get, more creative ways of raising finance will help you to property success. Some novice investors assume that the terms will be better because they're not borrowing from a bank, which it can be, but it can also be the reverse if you don't know what you're doing.

Don't over pay on borrowed money from JV partners. Just because a private investor or bridger wants 1.5% per month, and you need money for the deal, does not mean that money is right for you. 1.5% a month, even using the **BRR** strategy, is 17.5% a year! That's 3 times the cost of an expensive mortgage. You'd need a 45% discount to get all that money back out with the deposit to pay off your JV partner! Bad idea, unless it is **very** short term.

Gill Alton, a well respected Progressive VIP member, borrowed from her family at 5% a year. Nick Hague, a fellow Progressive community VIP member JV's on family funds without a repayment [he offered equity share], others have borrowed at 6% - 8% a year. Fran & Jane Dolley borrowed from fellow Progressive VIP members at similar rates. There are many people out there who are looking for better returns than the bank, and that's not hard right now.

Your relationship skills: you are managing these processes and relationships, so think about what you have learned and how good you are with people. Be firm and fair and you will get respect from your powerteam, and **profit** for your portfolio.

Summary

Reduce your downside risk and keep your costs down. Get 3 quotes for any job relating to your portfolio and don't be tempted to spend where you don't need to. Think of property as a business with a tight profit margin and don't make decisions emotionally. Protect against interest rate rises, don't overpay when borrowing money and keep good, firm but fair relationships with everyone in your powerteam you are using for services.

Sales [Without Selling]

We are all 'in sales.' We're all selling something, and the one most important thing you're selling is not a product, service or 'pitch.'

You know what it is, don't you.

Yes, it's yourself.

We know that many people don't like to think of themselves as salespeople. Just the word 'salesman' makes many people in the UK come up in a rash. Strange.

In the US, if you're 'salesperson,' let's say a car salesman; you're in a great, well respected position. Take Joe Girard, for example, in the Guinness book of world records for selling. World record holder for number of cars sold. One of the very best.

But what do we think or car salesmen in the UK! What a slimy, desperate position. Don't approach me, and don't use tactics on me. I don't want to be 'sold to.'

I [Rob], have gone full circle through these beliefs and associations. If you were with me in 2005, on the last legs of struggling as an artist, you'd have seen me do everything right in my art business: paint great, individual, creative works of art, get the pieces in galleries and competitions, build great relationships with people, interpret their exact needs for each commission...

And then fail. Badly.

And it was nothing to do with being a bad at art..

In fact, I was, to my and our schools' knowledge, the top artist in the UK at age 15: the only person in the UK to get 100% at GCSE art in that year. I even won a school prize for it. Paraded like the next Da Vinci. I don't say this to boast, you'll see why in a moment.

It got even better. At A-Level, I got 98%. But in the second year of 6th form college I had a near death motorbike crash and spent most of the year either in hospital or in physio, missing most of that year of college. I simply re-submitted much of my GCSE art, and some drawings I'd done in the summer holidays at 15 years old, and got 98%. Boom.

So when Tiger Woods or Michael Owen were at this level, at that age, they went on to be the best in the world. Why didn't I? Why did I fail so badly?

Not because I couldn't paint or draw, not because I wasn't a good person, not because I didn't deserve success, but because I couldn't **sell**. I couldn't **sell** my work, because I was scared. I was scared that they might not like it, that they might reject me and that they might not think the art was worth the [small] price I was asking.

It wasn't even that I wasn't good at selling; it was worse. I didn't even try to sell. Every time a gallery owner or commissioner would talk about price [they'd have to, because I would avoid it at all costs], I would collapse.

'Er, what do you think it should cost?'

'Um, I don't mind, it's up to you'

I might as well have said pull my pants down and slap me, then take all my work for free because my self worth is zero.

It was the lack of confidence, ability to sell my work, and more importantly my lack of ability to sell myself, that led to me failing as an artist. And the saddest thing about it was that I had real passion and talent [at least that was what Mum told me!].

I don't want to see the same thing happen to you in property, because there's a big risk that it will if you can't get your head around this one. You see, having trained 10,000's of people that we have, we'd have to be idiots not to spot the common things that sabotage people's success. And at first, we thought it would be lack of knowledge, experience or strategies in property. Couldn't have been further from the truth.

So many smart, likeable people with such potential actually have negative associations around salespeople, selling, asking for the money, selling themselves, and closing the deals.

Now we're not saying this is you, but here are some very common and real beliefs that people have around selling, that chains them to a lifetime of underachievement.

"The 'American,' pressurised way of selling is awful."

"People don't want to be sold to."

"People won't like me if I sell to them."

"I'm really bad at selling."

"What if I mess it up, or people say no."

"What if people reject me."

Don't know if you can relate to any of these. But they're all imaginary. Let's look at each one. If you can come out of the right side of all of these, with a new, fresh and self empowering belief, you win immediately. If you hold on to the old ones, everyone loses.

"The 'American,' pressurised way of selling is awful."

We're not in America, we're in the UK. You don't have to sell that way, and it doesn't work as well here anyway. People are smart, they've seen the tricks. Let people know they are smart, don't patronise them; listen to them. Get to know their desires, needs and pains, find out what's important to them, then package what you do and offer around those needs, pains and desires, and you both win.

"People don't want to be sold to."

Correct, much of the time. But they love to buy.

"Don't make them buy, let them buy." - Joe Girard.

You love buying stuff. You love acquiring things and services that improve your life, so don't deny people that enjoyment. Assist them to those outcomes, let them buy, and they'll love you for it. And they'll buy more and more and more of you. Do you think Apple-junkies hate being sold iPhones?!

"People won't like me if I sell to them."

You and selling are not linked. Plus you're making a big judgement here that **everyone** dislikes selling. People don't dislike or reject you, they are rejecting the sale. So even if they say no, they are not blowing you out, they just don't want the thing you are selling. At that time. It is NOT personal. You are *not* the thing you're selling. And if the thing you're selling is great, they might not like you if you don't sell it to them. Sound weird? Well listen to this:

I've [Rob] gone through different stages as I've been a property investor. Totally [annoying] evangelist, pushy gloater, scared timid mouse, quietly confident achiever, you name it. After trying to get every friend and family member involved in property with a hammer and blowtorch, I calmed down and found my own comfortable skin.

Mark advised me, from his experience, that the best thing to do is not to go around shouting about what you do, but go and do it, and then when you get asked in the future about your results, you can calmly drop into conversation that you own 20 properties, and then watch their dribbling jaws drop. So after my initial over excitement, that's exactly what I did. Subtle and cool and collected. Then my Mum found out and exclaimed:

"Rob, why didn't you tell me? Why didn't you involve me, I have some money, you know. I want to be involved!"

"But Mum, I've been draining your financial resources for 26 years, I didn't think you'd want me begging you for money again!"

My Mum was disappointed, almost offended, that I hadn't asked her to be involved. Lesson learned. Tell people about what you're doing, always, in the right way, and the money will find you.

"I'm really bad at selling."

You're probably bad at manipulation, coercion and unethical daylight robbery. But I bet you're great at helping people, leading and guiding people to a better life, and inspiring people. Do that and the money and results will come.

"What if I mess it up, or people say no."

What if you don't? *"You don't score from 100% of the shots you don't take."* The more mistakes you make, the luckier you get. It's a numbers game. Pull out all the clichés because you know this intellectually. You just have to trust yourself to go out and make mistakes and enjoy the process. Sound strange again?

In many of the one to one coaching sessions I take [mark], people are strangely scared of the thing they want or need [to do] the most. A common example of this is buying a property. Everyone I coach without fail wants to buy property, but many people are scared of putting offers in, just in case they get accepted ;-)

They may worry that if they put 10 offers in and they all get accepted, what do they do then? What if they buy a kipper? What if the numbers don't work. What if they can't get the finance and the agents ends up hating them?

I have learned that these issues are not real to the investor. How can they be, they haven't done it yet?! They are merely imagined realities that don't exist and have not happened, but at the time they are real to the individual. So here's the task I set them:

"Go out and view 25 properties in the next month, and offer on at least 20. Just do it"

You can imagine all the 'what if's,' 'buts' and 'maybes' I get. But I explain that they should detach from the outcome, and do it for the process. I'm there to support them, and they won't die in the process [at least no one has yet]. They're still a bit scared, but when they go out and do it, they always get the same lessons:

"I really got to know the Estate Agent well, we have a good relationship. I never got punched putting in an offer, it's actually quite easy, isn't it! I didn't get it right at first, but I got a lot better as the offers went in. I have 4 potential deals!

*"What if people reject **me**."*

What if they do? But they don't. They may reject your proposition, but they rarely reject you. Disassociate with the outcome, and don't take it personally. And if they do reject you, it's their issue, not yours, so let it float over your head. The more people that reject you [not you], the more people accept you.

We are selling ourselves to others every minute of every day. Every time we debate or argue we are selling someone else the idea that we are right or that we are knowledgeable.

In this book, we are selling to you that we have experience and knowledge in property. If we are not as good salesmen as those new build off-plan property companies or your career advisors, then we'll all be worse off [except them].

We are selling to our friends, our customers, our colleagues, our boss, our partners and our children. If a child turns to drugs who do you think is the better salesperson, the parent or the drug-dealer?

If you ever want to borrow money from the bank then you need to sell them on **you** and your ability to pay them back. Even more in today's world, people are buying relationships. Trust for big faceless corporates has gone. People want to 'buy' real, honest, credible people and relationships with them. Now, more than ever, these skills are essential. It's not enough to just learn about property investing.

If you want to convince someone to sell you their property for less than it is worth, then the best 'sales person,' you or your competitors, win, and the rest lose. Its dog eat dog out there, and you need to be the best. The good news is it's easier than you think.

If you want someone to come on a date with you then don't you think your ability to 'sell' them that you're good dating material is important? If not tie them up and put them in the boot of your car – no really, *I do not* mean that, it does not work. Mark keeps trying it and I keep trying to tell him there are more subtle methods!

You get the message, right?

If you have a preconceived notion about a salesman being the stereotypically suited person who struggles from month to month [mouth] and harasses people, then that will be your reality, and you'll either live it, or rebel against it. Neither suit your desired outcome.

The 80's 'Glengarry Glenross' stereotypical salesperson is a thing for museums now; it's not about Eldorado's or steak knives anymore. If you've seen it, you'll know what we mean.

Selling is the process of finding people's needs and giving them what they want. The best salespeople in the property world are the most ethical, best listening, most conscientious and empathetic people you will meet. They understand totally the desires, beliefs and needs of other people. They solve their problems and alleviate their pains, and the 'buyers' love them for it.

You are the same, and you will always see sales that way.

This book is not a 'sales' book, so it's time to move on. But if this subject interests you, or rather if you want to be successful, here are just 3 of many great people we have learned from. In today's world, 'selling without selling' works the best, especially in the UK.

Joe Girard – "How to sell anything to anybody" – a great relationship based sales book.

Johnnie Cass – "Under the Radar influence." A great CD package about how to sell to people without being pushy or salesy, and leading them [sometimes unconsciously] to buy you, your ideas and your products. You'll recognise someone on it too.

Jeffery Gitomer – "The little red book of sales." A quirky, no BS way to sell on fundamentals and not gimmicks.

Go buy them all when you've read this book.

Summary

Being a successful, non gimmicky 'salesperson' will lead you to great wealth in your property portfolio, and in life in general. If you're not convincing people to work with you, believe in you, to sell their property to you and to like you; then someone else will. They'll win, and everyone else will lose. Selling is not a hard pressurised business, but an influential, ethical method to help solve people's problems.

Dealmaking & negotiation

It goes without saying [so why are we saying it?], that there are certain skills that are essential in attaining long term wealth and success in property. Sales and marketing are essential. A part of any sales or property marketing process is being able to negotiate a deal.

Dealmaking and negotiation are where you make most of your money in property investing, and the biggest 'chunks' of cash too. Like sales, if you have fears or limitations around this, you'll be fighting for the scraps with everyone else.

Firstly, let us talk about what dealmaking and negotiation is *not*:

Gazumping, ripping people off, lying, pulling out of deals at the 11th hour, reducing your price at the 11th hour [gazundering], one upmanship, conning, cheating, bullying or a big ego tripping and power.

You probably don't believe these either, but imagine if you held just one of these beliefs around dealmaking – you'd never want to do it, because you wouldn't want to do or be any of these things.

These are sure fire ways of ruining your investment career [and losing all of your friends]. We've seen it happen, we've even worked for people just like this in the past. It's not pretty and it doesn't work. You might get a biceps flexing short term power victory, but you'll create so much long term collateral damage that you won't be in the game long enough to take all the money.

If the vendor feels pressure or thinks you've railroaded them with NLP and hypnosis, you'll get a phone call a day later from the vendor or message from the agent giving you excuses as to why they won't sell to you. Even if your price was the highest. Buyer's remorse almost always happens, and sometimes, right at the death when you've paid all your valuation fees.

This is what good and great dealmaking and negotiation is:

Helping people. Solving their problems. Listening. Finding out what is most important to them and giving it to them. Being flexible with multiple solutions. Genuinely caring about them and doing the right thing in their best interests, even if it doesn't benefit you [directly]. Creating win-win deals for vendor, agent and yourself. The good news is anyone can do these, they are easy and they build the best relationships with the least resistance.

Yes, you are influencing people, make no mistake about it. Don't you think we are all influencing each other all the time. Go to the bank and get me money. If you think about it, you're either [ethically] influencing someone to do what you want them to do, go to the bank and get me money, or you're being influenced by them to do what they want you to do. Go to the bank and get me money.

Fundamental tip No.9:
Go to the bank and get me money.

"You're either influencing people to help you to your vision, or you're helping others to their vision" – Rob Moore

There is no middle ground. There is no standing still. It's your choice: influence or be influenced.

Did you get me that money yet?!

So clearly, there is a subtle, smart and ethical way to influence for dealmaking. Here's our definition, thanks to many mentors far smarter than us for helping us develop this over the years. Influence:

"Getting people ethically to do what you want them to do, that they thought was their decision, and have them thank you for it" – Rob Moore

Imagine that. People helping you to your vision, doing what you want them to do, buying into it, enjoying it, loving it, and thanking you for doing what you want them to do. Sound hocus pocus?

Well if a vendor doesn't thank you for buying their property, helping them out of pain and debt [despite the low price], then something has gone wrong. You solved their pain [money wasn't the biggest one], you helped them, you did things they couldn't do, sometimes you even save them. They'll thank you, and you won't know why. That's when you know you've got it spot on.

Negotiation: is agreeing on the terms of the sale. The 'selling' and dealmaking is done, now it's time to get agreement. It is all about coming to an end result that is beneficial to both parties; the vendor and the buyer [and not just yourself]. If the price is too low, no matter how many tricks you use, you'll get remorse. If it's too high it will never sell. There has to be something in it for each party, but the primary driver isn't necessarily price.

Professional investors know this better than anyone, and are smart with their time. At least 90% of standard property sales on the open market don't have a high enough 'motivation' behind them – the vendors don't want or need to sell it badly enough, and so the kind of price you want is unlikely to materialise.

Novice investors chase these, because it's all they can find, and try to 'negotiate' [they even tell the agent and vendor they want to 'negotiate' – schoolboy error] with sellers who don't want to sell.

Professionals let everyone else argue over the over priced deal, and know how to find, or get tipped off on, the best deals, where the vendor wants and needs to sell, where **price is not** their highest motivator. If the pain of debt or divorce, or an imminent relocation or a tenant from hell is big enough, it will be more important to get rid of this than achieving a maximum price. These deals, around 7% - 10% of total sales [but still a huge number], are the deals you want to focus all your time on. Huge leverage. Contrarian thinking.

The 3 stages of motivation: there are 3 stages of vendor motivation. Walk away if the vendor is not at least at stage one. Let the market reset their expectations, put them in your follow up pipeline, and check in later when the motivation has grown. And if the property sold, it wasn't right for you, as it would have been too expensive.

Stage 1. Motivated seller
Stage 2. Distressed seller
Stage 3. Desperate seller

Stage 1. Motivated seller: there's a motivation, a pressing need and reason to sell. One of the 7 of the D.I.S.R.U.P.T model

Stage 2. Distressed seller: the motivation is causing distress. The pain is high and a fast solution is needed. Price is less important than speed and the specific motivation.

Stage 3. Desperate seller: the need is as painful as it gets and immediate. If the sale does not happen fast, the pain gets to breaking point, and at worst the house can be repossessed. It's far too late to be able to negotiate, and the best offer is sacrificed for the quickest, and best alternative solutions.

The best negotiators hunt out the deals with these motivations, where the pain already exists, and highlight perceived benefits to the other party, and quick solutions to the pains and problems. They do everything they can to help the vendor, making the transaction as easy and quick as possible, letting them feel like they have benefitted from the transaction. They have to win, for you to win.

Let them 'win:' if you are negotiating a discount, always let the negotiation end on a price that the other party offered, so that they feel like they have controlled the deal and won. Sounds a little silly but if you play your tactics right you will still end on the price you desire. You will also hugely reduce the risk of buyers' remorse or the buyer pulling out of a deal, which can be expensive and annoying.

"Let them win, you take the money"

Seeing the negotiation from the vendors point of view: this was such an epiphany for us, in life and in business as well as in property negotiation. It seems ridiculous, looking back, that we only saw the world through our own eyes, but then that's what we all do, don't we? How can we view life in any other way?!

Get right in the mind of the vendor, wearing their skin, in anticipation of what they might think, how they might feel, how they may react and the result they will want to achieve.

Let's be honest, they don't really want to sell their house for 70% of what it's worth. But what they might want is a fast sale, a discreet sale, a hassle free sale, to someone they want to sell to, someone they quite like [no one is ever very likely to sell something to someone they don't like].

Never buy/sell on price: finding those 20-35% BMV deals is all about finding those buyers whose prime motivation for selling is not driven by price. [You'll spot those that are; very often a little stubborn, won't budge on price, often in no hurry, sometimes have an unrealistic perception of the market]. This is totally pivotal, and the more you view, the more agents you use and the more vendors you speak to, the more intuitive you'll become.

You are looking for the people whose prime motivation for selling might be speed or security or discretion. Remember that selling a house can be one of the biggest and most stressful events in a vendor's life, and with big pain comes the need for a fast solution.

Fundamental tip No.10:
"If you can take people's pain away, you'll go a long way" – Rob Moore

Think co-operation not competition: think partnership and long term benefits to building a great relationship. Always remember the following when entering negotiations:

Know the maximum you are prepared to pay and do not go over it: don't get the eBay bidding syndrome; walk away if the price is not right. There will always be other deals and the chances are at about 30% that you might be re-contacted. Be patient as many deals will come back to you that you didn't expect, sometimes one or 2 years later, at a much cheaper price.

The numbers game: if you are putting enough offers in on properties then you will get some. Many vendors wait for months and their expectations change. People's expectation of what they can sell their property for is nearly always too high, so let the market 'chisel' them down [Mark likes that phrase].

Know your end goal and what you want out of the deal: this must be planned in advance [remember e-Bay syndrome]. Know your numbers. Find out what they want. Be cool. Be patient. Stick to your rules and don't get emotional.

Understand the emotions involved in negotiation: don't wind people up or get angry. Easy to say, but keep calm. Be diligent and educated about the deal. Be flexible: offer other benefits. Be strong and fair and don't give anything away; offer exchange. Let them feel good about the negotiation; it is not a fight or a testosterone kick. Do you know what motivates them? If so, use it.

Once you have mastered the Art of negotiation you will be halfway there to being a great dealmaker. Being a great deal maker requires the following traits:

Being a good negotiator!

Knowing what value and price the property is worth: know what the equivalent properties are worth on the same street and of the same type. This is known as 'information power' and is vital in your negotiations. If it is clear to people that you know your stuff then a) you'll command respect and b) no-one will pull the wool over your eyes.

If you don't know your stuff you will end up paying too much. Estate Agents can be good at setting your expectations too high [or too low in some cases] so you need to know what the real value is. What might seem like a good deal in isolation might be expensive when compared to the market.

Understand the definition[s] of value: if you want to achieve real discounts, release deposits, or put none of your own money into a deal, then an acute awareness of value is vital.

What an Estate Agent values a property at will likely be different from your interpretation, which will be different the perception held by the vendor, which again could be different in the OPINION of the surveyor [Valuer].

All these variables can play into your favour, when understood properly. Armed with this knowledge, you know that there is a fair 'spread' of value, where opinion may vary, and this can be up to 20% of the value in many cases. An Independent Estate agent who wants to buy the deal himself [naughty, but rife] will value a property very low. A 'Lister' who works for the Estate Agency, who wants to win the property onto their books, may value it very high to lead the vendor to believe they can get a top price for the property. The vendor is likely to have an unrealistically high perception of the value. You, as the investor, may have a lower expectation of the true value, such as the average of comparable sale prices shown historically on Land Reg. These will definitely vary compared to a surveyor's opinion of value.

All of the above can be influenced by you, but must first be understood. Information is power, my friend.

Don't show your hand: a big mistake many 'dealmakers' make is that they always state from the outset that they want something cheap or at discount. Do they think that is what the seller wants; to give his property away for less than he sees it is worth?

Do you think the Estate Agents are sitting just waiting for them to come in and ask for a huge discount so that they can get lower fees?

Be opportunistic. know that you have things, products, services and knowledge that other people need and offer these in return. Be diligent and educated about the deal. Know other people that can help. Be flexible, professional and personable, and always find ways to help the other party.

"100% of the shots you don't take don't go in." Wayne Gretzky put it very well.

Opportunity is the same.

The perception of price and percentage: when working on negotiation, in our experience in viewing 1000's of properties, you have more chance in getting a higher percentage discount on a lower priced property. Here's why:

When using our spreadsheets, the deals are mostly about percentages, with only a few absolute numbers. A 25% [on the current 75% LTV] discount can give you a no deposit deal, at 30% can mean you can get your deposit as well as cash back to cover your fees.

Vendors [sellers] almost always see price in absolute terms rather than percentage terms.

For example, we recently bought a flat for one of our investors for £50,000, which was on the market for £75,000 and worth £70,000 through comparables. This is a massive discount, but in absolute terms is only £20,000 off market value. It is generally as hard for us to get £20,000 off a house that is on the market for £120,000, despite the fact that the percentage discount is much less; only 17% as opposed to 29%!

Fundamental tip No.11:
Percentage vs. absolute terms. You get bigger percentage discounts on cheaper units.

Summary

Be great at dealmaking and negotiation and you will attract wealth in your ever growing portfolio. Always be thinking in terms of the other person's wants and needs and aim to present 'win-win' negotiations. Help the other party get what they want ethically, and have them thank you for it. Knowledge and information are power, so get a true understanding of value variations. Know the 3 types of motivations and ONLY deal with sellers who have one of the 3 motivations. Don't buy from people who are fixated on price and keep track of every offer, even a rejected deal, as it will stay in the pipeline and there's a 30% chance it will come back to you, only much cheaper.

Finding the Deals [Marketing]

Without deals, the discounted, cashflowing properties that build your portfolio and lifestyle, this business doesn't even get you off the ground.

Your success in property is measured against the strength and volume of deals, so this section is very important.

And marketing is how you get to communicate with the world, and how you attract, find and purchase those deals.

The very 1st step in 'marketing' to find your deals, is to tell everyone that you meet about what you do. Tell everyone that you are a property investor, and that you buy properties and help people out of debt or sensitive personal difficulties.

If you don't tell people about what you do [and more importantly how you can help them] then no-one will ever know, will they? It sounds so obvious, but you can be the most skilled buyer in the world that no one knows, and you'll be the poorest most skilled buyer in the world. The sad fact is that there are many skilled, knowledgeable people out there who don't really understand how to market themselves, their products, their brand or their services.

When I [Rob] used to paint, in my harder days as an artist, I totally knew nothing about marketing, so little that's it's almost embarrassing. I couldn't sell because I was scared of rejection. No one knew about my work other than through recommendation, and the little talent that I had was totally wasted and slowly driving me insane because I couldn't get any of my work seen, let alone sold.

In building your portfolio and finding the deals that you want, you need to think of marketing as a two way process:

1. How you market yourself.
2. How you appeal to the needs of others.
3. How you're remembered [mindspace]

1. How you conduct yourself, your image, your brand [because everything that says anything about you is your brand] is of vital importance.

What are your personal values? The most important things to you in your life? From your personal values should come 3 to 5 'brand' values – what you are all about, and how the world sees you. These must be clear, and must be inherent in everything you do and the way you communicate.

You should really take the time to think about this, as it drives everything you communicate. To help you, here's a reminder of the Progressive values:

Progressive | Innovative | Personal | Prepared

These aren't right or wrong, they are us. That's why you don't get dull and boring from Progressive. That's why you get the newest, most up to date strategies. That's why you can talk to us personally. If our brand values were:

Professional | Consistent | Intelligent | Efficient

You'd get an entirely different message from us, more like a German car manufacturer or something. Ja, guuuuut.

Perhaps you are organised, friendly, efficient, consistent and trustworthy? If you are, sellers, agents and contacts will be happy to do business with you. They may even go above what's expected of them and surprise you because of how you have treated them.

Just look at how Richard Branson manages to instil brand values within his organisation. He gets passionate people [not monkeys] working for peanuts. He conducts himself in such a way [passionate, committed, fun-loving] and people are attracted to that.

He instils 'sex appeal' in his brand and does anything however outlandish which will generate media coverage for Virgin. Now we are not talking about dangling yourself in the buff over Times Square or bungee-jumping 100 feet below a helicopter to be landed among 100 beautiful female lifeguards on Bondi Beach [although this would be nice :-)] but getting out there and using yourself to get other people to believe in your brand.

Take your time to brainstorm your values, then live by them and push them through all your communication.

There's a section in the back of the book for you to brainstorm your values. Come up with 25, then chop them down to 10-15, then ask as many people as you know to pick 4 that say the most about who you are – it'll soon become clear.

Turn to page 298

2. How to appeal to the needs of other people.

We are not really talking about the traditional definition here; something like:

'The total of activities involved in the transfer of goods from the producer or seller to the consumer or buyer, including advertising, shipping, storing, and selling.'

Thanks to dictionary.com, though it doesn't really help us to make profit in property. Every great marketer we've studied will say that marketing is about how you deliver a message that triggers a desired decision in someone's mind. It's about cutting through the noise, getting positive mindspace and turning that into your desired action.

That could be a buying decision [action] or a selling decision [action]. What is important is that you understand the ways in which you communicate, and how they can trigger [or turn off] the outcomes you desire. If you can occupy space in the mind of someone you want to make a buying decision in a positive way, you have nailed marketing.

OK, so here are the fundamental things in marketing that you must remember, and then we'll move on to the best marketing strategies to help you find the best deals:

Trust: people will only buy from or sell to people they trust. Remember that in some instances you are buying property from people under very sensitive circumstances, so they absolutely must be able to trust you.

Trust and permission based marketing works. Pushy, spammy marketing does not. And the same principles always apply in person, in print or on screen.

Anything that you can do to increase trust comes off the asking price and you get more properties, faster and cheaper, with less buyer's remorse.

Putting a woman's name instead of a man's name on a leaflet to receive a call increases conversion, because of a perceived increase in trust.

Real pictures of you and a friendly, up to date website with full contact information increases conversion because of a perceived increase in trust.

Handwritten leaflets increase conversion because of a perceived increase in trust.

Testimonials and how others have benefitted increases conversion because of a perceived increase in trust.

Go to all lengths to gain the trust of your vendor. In an increasingly untrusting world, you stand head and shoulders above your competition, without having to be all sales-y and spammy.

Understanding your target market: the vendors and agents you work with all have wants, needs, pains and importance drivers that are most important to them, in their life.

If you're running newspaper ads, what publications would your target demographic audience read, what is the common age group, what are the pains they want alleviating? The more of this information you have, the more targeted and specific your marketing is to your target customer.

Put yourself in their shoes, in their skin; see the world through their eyes. Work out what motivates them and leverage it. What makes them take action?

Even easier still: ask them!

WIFM? What's in it for me? This is all that people are interested in: period. They don't care about you [honestly, they don't]; they just care about how you can help them [in the case of buying repossessions, for example] or how your product or service can benefit them, and ease their pain, and make their life better.

The more you understand the people you are communicating to, their behaviours, decisions, interests, places they go, films they like, the more you can communicate to their model of the world, tap into their wants, give them those things, and profit too.

We all like to be around, buy from and sell to people we like and share common interests.

"No one likes being sold to, but everyone likes to buy."

Communication: Whether it is how you speak to an estate agent or how you write your website/leaflets, how you communicate is how you 'sell,' or buy. Understanding your market is not enough. You need to know how to communicate with them effectively so that they get it; so that you trigger that desired decision.

The art of the spoken and written word is simple. Be clear and concise. Use plain and simple English that everyone can understand [no one likes a smart-ass self professed Guru do they?]. Talk in terms of other peoples and get them saying **Yes**. Think **WIFM** and benefits. Use the word *'You'* at least 3 times as much as you use the word 'I.' Listen at least twice as much as you talk. Then ask nicely for the money :-)

Testing and measuring: This is quite possibly the most important aspect to marketing, and one that most people overlook completely. Don't shortcut this.

The best 'marketers,' in the property world; the ones who get consistent deals of 25%+ evidenced discount, do so because they continually improve and tweak what they do, constantly moving towards the best practice method.

In order to be able to continually improve, you need to measure each marketing tactic that you use, knowing all the numbers [offers, leaflets delivered, calls, offers, purchases], and always trying to beat your best marketing strategy.

Most people guess. Which means they lose money.

It takes the guessing out of everything, and creates predictable, scientific, scale-able results.

Use different phone numbers on leaflets. Use Google analytics on your website. Split test ads on Google Adwords to keep improving them. Split test ads in print media. You should always AB test [split test] one thing at a time [headline, text font, pictures etc] and continually try to beat your best performing ad.

"Investing is all about testing. Test. Test. Test. Protect, replicate then aggressively scale up" – Mark Homer

The 'cost' of marketing: Everything in life comes at a cost, even 'free' marketing such as Estate Agent sourcing, and it is important that you know what your cost is.

And that cost is not just financial.

How much time out of your life does your marketing take? Is that time replacing other tasks that make you money or give you enjoyment? Are you delivering all of those leaflets yourself? Are you paying someone else to do it [who might deliver 30 then throw the other 9,970 in a skip?].

Property can be a very time intensive career if you don't monitor the time, and that needs to be measured [against financial cost] so that you can get the right balance for you (or get someone else to do it for you) so that you can take the benefits without the time cost].

Your website marketing may cost 10 times as much as your leaflet marketing. We don't know. It will be up to you to test, but don't you think that is useful information for you to have?

If it takes you 35 offers to get a deal with your local Estate Agent, but that takes up 55 hours of your time at £20 per hour value, could you source more deals investing £20 × 55 in other marketing strategies?

Testing will give you the answers.

3. How you're remembered [mindspace]

Unless you and your marketing are memorable, everything to this point means nothing.

"Visibility is credibility"

The best isn't necessarily the most credible. Nor the most diligent. Nor the most honest. But the most remembered often is. Even better, be memorable with great values, and you win big by helping others.

What makes you unique? What stands you out from the rest? What brings you to the top of the Estate Agent's mind when they get a call from a Lister with a really cheap deal, such that the first person they think to call is you, regardless of experience?

Marketing vehicles part 1: at Progressive we use many forms [vehicles] of marketing, and you may well have been exposed to one or more of these media. Better to have multiple marketing channels than one, because the effectiveness of each is always changing.

These can be for sourcing properties or customers, and include direct mail, e-mail marketing, Joint Ventures, affiliate marketing, leafleting, business directories, forums, CPA/CPL, social media, Estate Agents, SEO, Google Adwords & Facebook PPC, viral and article marketing, Youtube, banner advertising, commission incentives, 'birddogs,' word of mouth referrals, and so on.

Here are the first and most important few to get you started sourcing the best deals locally to you. There are more advanced marketing strategies in "Make Cash in a Property Market Crash" for when the time is right for you.

Estate Agents: Estate Agents could be vital to your negotiation and dealmaking success. The great thing about sourcing through Estate Agents is you don't have to pay for entry into the agency, you don't have to pay the 'consultant' for his time, and you don't even have to pay the vendor to buy their property, or the agency.

Free [financially] deals, my friend.

And the place where virtually all properties are sold. And mostly a 'done for you' service.

It doesn't matter what you think of Estate Agents (and any, often false, preconceptions) you need to make these guys your friends. We've bought over 220 deals through Estate Agents alone, and in the early days when we didn't know how to market in different ways, it was our Golden Goose. Still is.

You must deal with each agent differently depending on their character, age, sex [Wheeler Dealers vs. Aunt Mary]. The end goal will be to have a relationship with the agent that is more similar to friendship as opposed to a business relationship. Contrary to what many people believe, most are honest and hard working with a load of knowledge which you can leverage.

Despite working on behalf of the vendor, Estate Agents can be very helpful to you. Their job is to sell properties and meet targets, and for that they need buyers, not just sellers. Their ideal buyer would be fast, efficient, friendly and trustworthy, and someone who is going to buy over and over. Does that sound like someone you know?!

Despite the increase in direct marketing methods, 90% of houses are still sold through Estate Agents. There is a far lower financial acquisition cost through agents and there is better leverage in getting someone else [or many agents] doing the groundwork for you.

Estate Agents need good buyers like us, like you, as much as we need them. Not only do they have sales targets, they also have heavy competition from other agents to be proactive so that they don't lose their listings to other agencies. This would be a disaster to an Estate Agent, not so much because of the loss of a couple of grand commission, but more for reasons of competition and reputation.

Just viewing properties and making offers will build rapport and gain the trust of agents, getting you closer to your first deal, or your pipeline of many future ones. This will be your 'alone time' with the agent out of the office where you can 'test' some information about the vendors motivation, who else gets the best deals, if they understand 'no money down,' if they are proactive, hungry, motivated, what drives them and so on.

Viewings not only enable you to build out of office, honest rapport with an Estate Agent, it goes without saying that without viewings you can't offer, and without offers you can't buy. You also help Estate Agents hit viewings targets, which many of them are measured by, with their bosses [Godfathers], and vendors.

This knowledge is also vital, because you are much more able to help them get what they want, as you get to know them better. And it aligns perfectly with your goals; view 20, offer on 12, get at least 1. Your low offers may at first start as favours to agents for perceived activity, but some will turn into deals.

It's a numbers game. And your numbers will get better the more you view and make offers. And all those things you might be worried about [low offers offending, too many offers might get you more deals than you can finance] will disappear with the real experience.

Fundamental tip No.12:
Revelation alert: The more properties you offer on, the more you will get.

The more you offer on at the price you want to pay, the more you will get at the price you want to pay.

If you want 10% BMV [Below Market Value] deals, you probably won't have to view that many to get one. If you want 35% BMV deals [which are out there] then you'll have to view more and offer lower.

We have built up a network of Estate Agents in our local area, many of whom have become genuine friends. It is essential to strike up a good rapport with your agents and become someone who they will call ahead of the rest of the pack. Trust and friendship: 'people buy people.'

It is also very important to build rapport with everyone in the Estate Agency, not just the boss or decision maker. We see so many people bound in and go straight for the kill, crushing the admin staff in the process. This is a big mistake because a) they could have a good relationship with everyone in the office b) they could be the boss's daughter, spouse or lover and c) they want respect and importance just like everyone else and could be your best route in.

A great way to become close to agents is to go out socially with them; go above what they would expect of you. Perhaps take them out for lunch. Think about what it is that they want. Maybe they have specific interests that you can relate to. Use your creative imagination to add value. Find out what it is that gives the agents their importance and significance. It might be success, power, respect, recognition, tanning vouchers, track days, dental work [all real examples] or simply someone who is nice to them.

Ensure you have done all your number crunching before you view, or on the Deal Analyser App while you are viewing, so that once you have viewed a property get back to them immediately with your thoughts and an offer if necessary. Commit to calling the agent back in the morning ["I just need to run over the figures overnight"]. Tell them you will call them tomorrow and make sure you call them before they call you – the next day. Offer if the deal is right for you, and don't waste time. And if the deal isn't right, either offer very low so that it is likely to get rejected [or if you got the deal the numbers would work], or give them genuine, honest feedback as to why. That way you teach them gradually what you would buy.

This will let them understand in a more specific way what you are looking for and will keep you in their mind for when the next deal comes along if the offer does not get accepted.

Mindspace: you need to "occupy a space" in the Estate Agents mind, especially if you are just starting out. You'll only have a split second when the agent gets the call to pop into their mind. Be memorable by complimenting the agents tie, shoes or necklace. Talk about the market. Joke about other investors. Have fun. Smile. Be quirky. Talk about football- anything to differentiate yourself and be remembered. Make an impression.

Estate agents get people all the time who are 'investors' and who walk in asking for the 'deals' and they get pretty sick of it. Do not be another number; these are called 'binners.'

Always be honest with them. If you don't want a property tell them immediately and why, but be very short with the dislikes. If you do, try to gauge where the vendor is [what is their expectation and motivation?] on price. The agent is likely to know this, so if you get on the right side of them they are likely to tell you.

Although they 'can't tell you' exactly what offers they have had for a property, they will be able to give you a 'good idea.' This can be really helpful for you [for obvious reasons].

You may not get the property the first time as the vendor's expectations may be too high [in terms of price]. It may work later for the vendor though, and you may get the property for a reduced amount, when the market has reduced their expectation.

The mindspace you create keeps you in the game a few months down the line, when the deal will be cheaper anyway. It's often best not to negotiate too hard, let the market 'chip away' at their expectations and buy it in your 'pipeline' many months later, even cheaper.

Never but never pull out of deals— this is *so* important. You will shatter any trust you have with the agent and make it very unlikely that they will give you any deals again. Your reputation, credibility, and professionalism [what others say about you] is your brand, and you're only as good as your last deal.

The whole idea of them coming to you with property is that you are a fast purchaser who is not in a chain. You guarantee to buy and they will have a hassle free sale [and earn their commission quickly].

They can then 'sell' this to the owner of the property who actually needs a purchaser like *you*. It gives you advantage over other buyers who might even offer higher, but be less likely to complete.

They may be in financial difficulty and facing repossession of their home, which you will stop if you purchase their home [quickly]. They may be going through a divorce or the property may be part of an estate of a deceased person and the executors may be trying to sell it quickly to pay the inheritance tax.

The point is that all of these situations require a fast guaranteed sale and in return these vendors [or sellers] are willing to accept a reduced under market value [BMV] price for the property. In these circumstances price is not the most critical factor. The agent is looking for a purchaser like you to take the property; someone who can offer a sure, fast sale.

And then do it over and over on the next deals.

Fundamental tip No.13:
To get great BMV Property, you need to find vendors whose primary motivation for selling is **not** price.

So even if you realise that you have paid more than you wanted to, or that the refurbishment work may cost more than you thought, go through with the sale. Your word is your bond. Commit and go through with your promise and trust will be given. This will earn you future deals. It will cost you a lot less in the long run. Agents [like everyone] talk, this is what they do for a living, and you want them to be talking about you in the right way: positive mindspace.

You may also find that you are competing with the owner/manager of an Estate Agency [the Godfather] for deals, as they are in a perfect position to take advantage of them. They see deals everyday because that is what they do.

It is a good idea to try and get on the right side of the owner or manager if they are taking deals themselves. I [Mark] can think of one particular owner of an Estate Agency in our town who has bid on the same properties as me. This has happened for sale both through his agency and through others. This has not always created a great situation and I wish I had managed to form a relationship with him beforehand.

Buying and selling houses, whilst popular on TV, costs a lot more than people think. On average it costs about 10% of the sale price to buy, pay the mortgage and sell a property in 6 months. On top of this you a have the refurb or renovation costs, your time and tax. Re-read the section on 'flipping' deals in this book if you want to use this strategy.

And drop us a line if you're interested in us helping you further to become the 'banker' with the Estate Agencies in your local area, beat your competition hands down and get the first pick of the best, biggest discount, highest cashflowing deals.

www.progressiveproperty.co.uk/events

rob.moore@progressiveproperty.co.uk

Leafleting: leafleting has provided us with 4 of the top 6 best ever deals we have attracted in discount terms, the best of which was 70% discount from sale price with a corner plot piece of land that we sold off too, and kept the house.

If you get leafleting right, it can pay you handsomely.

When you advertise 'direct to vendor' [D2V], you bypass the Estate Agent, and also you find vendors that would rather sell directly to someone they trust, because some vendors don't like or don't want to deal with agents.

You also often find them at the 3rd stage of motivation: desperation. You'd probably need to be quite desperate to pick up a leaflet off the front door mat of your house to sell your property, and this is a big reason for the very cheapest deals to come from leafleting and D2V strategies.

The important concepts about leafleting are:

Targeting: only drop leaflets in your 'Goldmine,' area within areas. There's millions of houses you don't want, so why waste your time and money delivering leaflets to the houses you'd never buy anyway?

Reduce volume, increase frequency: far better to deliver one leaflet a month for 6 months to the same property, than one to 6 different houses. It takes time to build trust and visibility, so reduce the volume, target the area, and deliver every month for 6 months at least.

Make the leaflets personal: the more personal the leaflet, the more leads and deals you'll get. Personal handwriting, women's names, home/mobile phone numbers, and pictures all give a more personal feel to the leaflet, and higher response rates.

Split test: Always test one thing for every leaflet drop. Test the paper, the colour, the headline, the font, the name, the phone number, the wording. On EVERY drop, just test one of these variables, keep a note, and after 10 or 20 tests, a 1% improvement on each variable compounds to a lot more leads and deals.

The easiest way to test a leaflet drop is to have a different person's name on the leaflets being tested. When the leads calls, notice who they ask for, and you know which of the 2 leaflets it is.

Strategy: personal or leveraged? Decide from the outset if you are going to be personally involved in the leafleting/buying process. If you want to view and visit the vendor and help them personally, you'll probably get the best conversion. If you like helping people, this will align with your values too.

If you're busy or want to grow a business, setting up a virtual assistant [VA] to take all the calls, manage the messages, pass the leads through, even visiting the vendor and doing the deals, will be important to you. This takes some training, and isn't always as highly converting, but leverages your time.

Monitor delivery: people often think their leaflets are failing, when in fact they're not even getting through the door. It is NOT a given that the first person or delivery vehicle will get all your leaflets through every letterbox.

Test local paperboys vs. local delivery companies who attend your local business clubs/BNI's, vs. Royal Mail door to door. Each delivery 'vehicle' will vary in your local area, and testing these is as important as testing the leaflets themselves.

You should expect 5-10 calls per 15,000 leaflets, and one deal every 25,000 leaflets. Of course this varies area to area and market to market, but we thought you might ask :-)

Newspaper ads: we turn Newspaper ads off and on as we need to scale up or back our buying volume, depending on how many deals we want to buy. Our volumes are 5-15 deals per month. If we want more volume, we'll put some Newspaper ads in, negotiate an 80% discount from rate card price, and will usually get a deal within the first 2 months, putting in 4 ads per month.

When we switched on our newspaper ad campaigns recently we got 2 better than 30% BMV deals within the first 4 ads [the first month]. Job done.

There are many different types of Newspaper ads you can run, in different publications and different placements of those publications.

We suggest you read your local papers daily and look for the ads, their placement, how they engage you, and 'model' and test them. Don't re-invent the wheel.

All of the rules for leaflets apply for Newspaper ads, with the following additions:

Test ad placement: it's often best to put your ad in a different place to all the property ads, as there is less competition for the eyes. But you'll need to test sections, pages, sizes and so on.

Negotiate hard: but fair. You should find out the print deadline and tie up your deals at the latest possible time. There is always ad space, and publications really need advertising business now, so you should be getting 50% to 80% off the rate card price.

Test publications: free publications often work best for LHA type housing, and higher end paid publications for 'Boutique' HMO's. Match publication to strategy, but always test first.

You should expect 7-15 calls per ad, and one deal every 4 ad placements. Of course this varies area to area and market to market, but we thought you might ask :-)

Social Media: the power of social media needs no introduction, but how to monetise it and use the time effectively does. No one wants to get sucked in hours on end in mindless conversations taking you away from your real income generating activities, and if you're not careful that's exactly what social media does.

So let's be careful. And smart.

The great thing about social media, especially sites like Twitter, Facebook, LinkedIn and YouTube, is the access to many millions of people from your home computer. You literally have access to half the population at your fingertips, without having to leave the house. This includes sellers of properties, Estate Agents, customers for your packaged deals, JV partners.

And even better is that it's totally free.

Using the search facility on Facebook and LinkedIn, you can search for any group that you want to be a part of. It's just like having Google within social media sites and you can quickly find all groups and communities for your specific target audience[s].

For example, if you type in 'property' in Facebook, a drop-down bar will appear with all of the property and property related groups. Simply add yourselves into all these groups [assuming you have a Facebook account] by clicking on them, and over a period of a few weeks have a look in each one to see how active these groups are. Where there are active discussions between people, and genuine value and sharing, become active in the group. Where there are just spammers and people selling trainers and people wanting to love you long time, remove yourself from these groups.

In the property groups alone you'll probably connect with up to 50,000 unique people in 20 to 25 active groups within the Facebook and LinkedIn communities.

Oh and did we say this is all completely free?

You can do the same thing for 'joint ventures,' local town or city groups to find vendors, 'business' and 'Entrepreneur' groups, 'sell your house,' groups. You can even target specific motivations such as 'divorce,' groups and people moving abroad.

Through all these social media channels you'll be able to find all your local networking groups for property and business, and meet local investors JV partners and vendors.

And the great thing about Facebook and LinkedIn, is that if you use it properly you will get instant connection and trust much faster than having to meet face-to-face, or not being able to find the target group so quickly.

You also get quicker access into other people's very valuable networks that they have taken years to build and nurture

Did we say it's free?

Add us on Facebook and you have immediate access to a very well-connected Progressive community: **www.facebook.com/progressiveproperty**

JV's: There are some really smart, leveraged ways to JV with people in the property business to get cheaper deals before anyone else. Here are the ones we've done, though you can get as creative as you like and work with anyone who you think could get access to the types of properties in your local area that you want to own.

Window cleaners: we have to confess that we didn't design this strategy, we borrowed it from a Progressive Community member, Andy Watkiss. Andy bought the best part of 40 deals in a very short space of time, half through leaflets, and half JV'ing with a window cleaner, all whilst still working as a full time Lorry driver.

He approached a window cleaner who was cleaning the windows on his local patch [not to demand Mafia money], and asked him if he'd consider putting some signage on his van advertising to buy houses.

Here's the deal they cut: in exchange for double sided signage on the window cleaners van, Andy paid his tax and insurance on his van for one year – around £200.

That's £200 for a constant advert that drives all day every day around his local area, stopping outside each house for 40 minutes a time and waits for him to complete his job, until he's onto the next, like postman Pat.

This single strategy produced 20 discount 'BMV' deals. Clever right?

If you want to watch the interview, you can see it on the Progressive YouTube channel, simply visit the page below and search 'Andy Watkiss.'

www.YouTube.com/progressiveproperty

Take-aways: another smart, creative, competition baffling JV is with local take-aways. Visit the local take-aways on your patch [don't demand Mafia money], order a big order from them, the biggest they've had, and while you're waiting ask conversationally who owns the place while looking at their leaflets. When you find out who the owner is, ask them if they'd like help paying for and/or delivering their leaflets, and you're in.

Once you get agreement on this, share the cost or the delivery with them, in exchange for an ad on the back of the leaflet, about 1/3 of the size of the back page. No bother to them, perfect ad space for you.

This might not yet sound as smart as it really is, but ask yourself this: if you get a leaflet through your door, do you chuck it away? Yes, we thought so. But...

If you get a take-away menu through your door, what do you do with it? That's right, you put it in your drawer or better stick it on your fridge for when you get dumped or have a lonely night in, right?

It just sits and waits patiently until the vendor is ready to sell, and generates far more 'calls per menu' than a leaflet ever will.

And when you have 2-3 window cleaner or local tradesmen with ads on their vans for you, and 2-3 local take-aways with your ads on, your advertising owns the local patch and the deals flow.

Postcards: have a drive around your local area, and make a note [Mark: on a spreadsheet] of all the shops, take-aways, news agencies, post offices, pubs, doctors surgeries, pound shops, supermarkets; all retail.

Then buy a batch of 5x7 postcards, and hand write a simple advert about buying houses in the local area, paying all fees, helping people out of debt and making a fast, easy, discreet offer and purchase.

Then each time you go on a viewing [to leverage your time], drop in to a few of these places and ask if you can stick your postcard up. A few may say no, most will say yes, some will charge a nominal fee.

With each viewing you 'own' more of the advertising in your local patch, and you have more chances of getting in front of the right eyeballs to get more deals.

A nifty trick Alan Graham did, as a headmaster at his school [you'll remember him: he's one pair of the 'Buy to Let Doctors'] was to issue out more detentions so that whilst supervising his [now full] detentions he could get all the kids handwriting his postcards for him as 'punishment.' Thought you'd like that one, but we're not recommending it! You could handwrite them in nice bright colours and then colour photocopy them though, and always have a stash in your glove box on the ready.

Forums [paid & free]: forums are a fantastic source of low cost or free leads for almost anything you can think of in your property business. In fact, you can decide exactly what type of lead you want, and then find a forum that will have those kinds of leads.

Let us give you an example. There are 7 motivations for someone selling BMV:

D.ivorce
I.n debt
S.caling back
R.elocation
U.psizing
P.robate
T.enant issues

If you want to specifically help people who are getting divorced [and make a handsome profit in the process buying their property], simply type 'debt forum [insert your local area],' into Google. If your local area is Plymouth, type in 'debt forum Plymouth' and you will have access to forums filled with your potential customers/vendors. Some forums/groups will be local, some national, and some linked to 'real life,' events and groups, not just online.

IMPORTANT:
You must make sure that you have the vendors' best interests at heart. Fishing on divorce forums and breaking up relationships just to buy BMV property ain't

gonna send you to heaven ;-)

The great thing about the property industry is that you have the power to really change people's lives. When a film company on behalf of Channel 4 came to us to film our 'property business' [that's what they told us] the camera crew were blown away that vendors actually thanked us, were hugely grateful, many of them breaking down in tears, because of how much we had helped them and eased their financial pain – and every time we are buying houses at 30% plus BMV. We think they we're expecting us to be taking advantage of people: they were genuinely surprised [and the show never got aired].

So if you want to find people with financial based motivations, simply type in 'debt forum [insert your local area here].' Keep doing it for all the motivations, add value to people who have problems through time, knowledge, understanding and offering solutions to problems, and you will find an abundance of free 'motivated seller' leads.

Because you are finding people with the specific motivation, you are much closer to the sale of the deal that if you just find 'property people.'

Free forums are fantastic for finding motivated sellers, but if you want to find 'leads' for deals you want to sell, Lease Options and so on, then the low cost paid forums are better.

Paid forums will provide you with a highly qualified, serious 'customer' for your deal packages and Lease Option deals you have, because they have qualified themselves more by paying a recurring amount to be on the site. The best site for finding all kinds of leads is the one below:

www.progressivepropertyforum.co.uk

When you spend a small amount of time on sites where serious property investors network and do deals, you will be able to monetise the deals you find by building relationships with people there, and helping them to solve their problems.

You'd be very surprised how many people need your help, want your deals, have been in property but can't get the results you have, don't have the time to source the deals themselves and so on.

You can also find people in different industries. You can network online at business networks, business angel networks, other wealth creation industries, and of course you can do the same offline – go to charity balls, rotary clubs, business angel events, parties, social events, launches and so on and you will meet the people who want the returns you are getting, want the knowledge you have, but don't have the time, belief or desire.

Summary

Marketing is not just about vehicles to find the deals, but understanding what people want: their hopes, dreams, desires, fears and pains, and offering them solutions and hope. You must be memorable to even exist in the property world, and then use multiple marketing vehicles to communicate to your vendors, customers and JV partners. Use Estate Agents, postcards, leaflets, Newspaper ads, forums [paid and free], window cleaner and take-away JV's and social media, and watch your deal volume multiply.

Joint Ventures

If you have a preconceived notion about a salesman being the stereotypically suited person who struggles from month to month [mouth] and harasses people, then that will be your reality, and you'll either live it, or rebel against it. Neither suits your desired outcome.

A Joint Venture [JV] is a venture between two or more people. In property investing, the joint venture is usually based around an individual who has time or experience, working with someone who has little time but has funds. JV's also occur when the following exist:

Complementary or opposing skill sets: one partner is an expert marketer or negotiator in trade for the partners' mortgage-ability, mortgage hosting, refurb or management skills.

Cash & time: One partner is cash-rich, but time-poor; the other is time-rich, but cash-poor.

Time & experience: one partner has lots of experience, but little time; the other has lots of time, but little experience.

Experience & cash: one partner has lots of experience but no cash; the other has lots of cash but no experience.

Why Use a JV Partner? using a Joint Venture [JV] partner is one of the most efficient ways to build up your property business in a shorter period of time with minimal risk and capital from you. This will increase your buying power, reduce the time it takes to build your portfolio and wealth and significantly reduce your risks in many cases.

It can also make every deal NMD. Here are other great benefits:

Business experience: a lot of private investors will have business experience that they can bring to the table. This could be very beneficial especially when analysing new deals, legals, negotiations, contracts, profit and loss, managing teams, etc.

Rewards: 50% of a deal financed by a JV partner is better than 100% of nothing.

Contacts: your network is your 'net-worth.' Your JV partner will have a contact base of extremely useful people that can be called upon, which otherwise would have taken you years to find and build a trusting relationship with on your own. This can be as valuable as their cash.

Multiple deals: You will be able to develop your portfolio quicker, take on more deals and increase your credibility with agents, attracting better quality deals as the volume increases.

Why would they invest in you?

In the current market, with cash savers getting negative growth in the bank [0.5% plus or minus inflation], many asset vehicles risky and unstable [stock market hardly any higher than it was 10 years ago] and people busier than ever and little time to research investments themselves, many private investors are flocking to property and people like you in property for a better return on their money.

People trust banks, corporations and pensions way less than ever before, and business is once again becoming more about people and trust, like it used to be.

They are the new motivated sellers, because the money they have been used to receiving has disappeared and the lifestyle they had built on that passive income can no longer be maintained. This gives you great power and far easier access to private investor [JV] finds than in previous markets.

And if you still can't convince them, buy them a copy of this book.

How will the JV Partner make their Money?

Split of the profits: when the property is sold or remortgaged, they will have a percentage stake in the property, and ongoing profit. You can own the property together, or use a DoT [Deed of Trust] and they could hold or host the mortgage, for security if necessary, or you could hold the mortgage and they have a restriction, charge or DoT with you.

Monthly interest charge: the private investor lends you the money directly [i.e. pays it to you or into the property, as opposed to buying the property]. You will pay the agreed interest per month until the full loan is paid back. As soon as the property is sold or refinanced you will be able to pay off the loan. The likely interest rate you will pay is 1% - 3% per month for short term finance and 0.75% - 1.5% for longer term [more than 6 months].

A mixture of the two above

A share of your business: a JV partner can act as an Angel/Dragon investor and invest in you/your business. They have a partnership or share of the company not the properties directly

Security – Whose Name to Use?

Option 1. The property is under the name of the private investor: This is the most likely way an investor would want security to use his/her money. Hence if the worst would happen, the investor could easily dispose of the property on the market. The partner could have an agreement in place when the investor sells the property the partner could be paid his share of the profit. This reduces the risk to a JV partner working with you, and also allows you to own assets if you can't get a mortgage or have bad credit.

Option 2. You own the property under your name [your own personal property or the property bought for the JV] and the private investor takes a charge or restriction over it. The property is now security for the debt for the monies borrowed. If the property is sold or refinanced the investor will be notified and or paid before you run off with the money! If they put up all the cash they may expect 1st charge, if they put up the deposit then 2nd charge or restriction.

Option 3. A DoT legal agreement. There will be no charges in this example placed on any property: you promise to repay the money back to the private investor when the property has been sold or refinanced. The investor will instruct his solicitor to take an undertaking agreement with your solicitor to ensure he will get paid first upon the sale or refinance of the property.

Option 4. A handshake – not recommended, even with family & friends, but surprisingly frequently done

The Progressive community power team: the only thing left is for us to tell you where to find these cash rich, open minded JV partners.

Local property events, business networking events, business angel events, charity balls, flying clubs, rotary clubs, functions and openings, online forums, property portals, private member clubs, personal concierge and Mark Homer's birthday party to name just a few.

The Progressive community is also a great place to meet JV partners, both online and off-line and on Facebook. There are thousands of active investors looking for partners just like you, many with cash. You can find them here:

www.facebook.com/progressiveproperty

If you get the chance to meet us personally at a local or national Progressive property event, you will meet and network with many of these partners yourself in a safe, comfortable and like minded environment:

www.progressiveproperty.co.uk/events

Your network: the more like-minded people you know will have a direct impact on your net-worth. It is said that you are the sum of the 5 people you spend the most time with. Observe the people you spend the most time with, it will have a strong bearing on your results.

We all know when starting out in property that it can be lonely or challenging without support or guidance. Your network will guide you or pull you down. The upside of your readymade network is the virtually leveraged building of your property portfolio and business.

The great thing about property investing is the experts who are willing to share their knowledge openly and freely with you. You would not experience this in most professions or corporations, but because property is a local business, people are happy to share their ideas and strategies with you because you will not be in competition with them.

Imagine in the corporate world going up to your boss, sitting him down, buying him a drink and asking him to share with you exactly how to do his job. No chance. You'd get fired for your audacity. But most professional investors love to share; it's a great industry to be in.

Networking and working in partnerships never ends. You can continually grow and network into ever increasing circles of wealth and influence. One person you meet could open the door for you and introduce you into a seriously wealthy and powerful network.

The Progressive community does exactly that, with a £65million joint venture network already in place, and with the six degrees of separation theory, You're only six steps or six people away from any contact you need, in any industry, on any part of the planet

Summary

Joint ventures enable you to leverage all aspects of your property business to make more money in less time. Joint ventures can make every deal a no money down deal, provide infinite returns on investment and cash flow from no capital outlay. Your network is your net worth; continually build it and open doors to higher circles of wealth and influence.

Become an Expert

Only listen to those who *really know* and have done what it is that you want to do.

You'll get every 'expert's' opinion on how to be a property investor, all day every day, without asking for it. This is just fine; we are all entitled to that, but the big questions is:

Have they done it themselves?

The only way we are going to become an expert is to listen to the experts [rather than newspapers and pub talk], do what they do, and then physically go out and get the necessary education, experience and action to get the same results.

It's actually not complicated at all, and easier than most people think.

Actively seek out people with a portfolio of 20+ properties or more, especially locally, and see how you can help them, so that in turn you can learn from them. Find out what kind of properties they are buying, on what streets, using which agents, and their preferred strategies. Who are their friends and where do they spend a lot of their time.

Actively seek out multi millionaires. Ask the same questions above. Observe their behaviours, attitudes and beliefs, especially around money. Rob even copied James Caan's walk at the 2010 Property SuperConference [don't tell James]. He even walks like a multi millionaire ;-)

Success and wealth leave tracks: the good news is that there are learned systems, strategies, mindsets and behaviours that lead to great wealth. Your mission: find them and replicate them. Then turn that knowledge into cash.

Don't be scared of them. Don't be envious of them. Don't be awestruck by them. Just find them, offer them value, and spend time with them. They're real people just like you, most love to share their time and knowledge, and almost all love having a chat about themselves :-)

We used to be too proud in our youth to learn from those who were good. We were always either a tad jealous or thought they were just plain lucky. The best thing we ever did was grow out of our ego, and get out of our own way. OK so this is more Rob than Mark. No one knows it all; we can all learn so much from eachother if we just ask, listen and stay open minded.

We now regularly pay £1,000's per session for people who are experts in their respective fields and can teach us things that we don't know and need to learn, and not just in property. In fact, it's often better to find niche experts who know the most about their specialised fields such as employment law, selling to the affluent, online marketing, people and communication skills and so on.

The £600,000 we have spent on this education has brought in many millions of pounds we'd have never seen if we thought we knew it all, could do it ourselves and 'save' the money, or were too proud or nervous to simply 'ask.'

Wealthy and successful property investors are such for a reason. It's a culmination of everything they have learned, tested, failed at and people they have learned from along the way, and you can fast-track and leverage all of that. Most of the time it is nothing to do with luck. Most of the time you can find out their exact strategies, and most of the time they will be happy to share their knowledge with you.

Then you copy it, and you get the same results.

You've probably heard of the 10,000 hour rule to becoming an expert. You need to spend 10,000 hours or more to become the very best at something. It certainly takes time, and you have to earn and invest your entrance fee, but there is a way to accelerate that:

Hunt out as many experts as you can who've already spent 10,000 hours in their chosen field, and model exactly what they have done.

"It's not what you know, it's how many millionaires you know" – Rob Moore

Make it a lifelong mission of yours to seek out those who have what you want and to learn from them. Read books about wealthy and successful people you admire. Subscribe to their newsletters and read their blog entries. Hunt them down and buy them lunch. Take them out and ask them how they did it. Sleep with them if you have to ;-) Believe me they'll be happy to share their stories with you.

Learn from their mistakes as well as their successes. Save yourself years of time, energy, trial and error. Become the one who is writing the book and teaching other people how to do it.

Try and get as much coverage for what you are doing as you can. As you build your portfolio contact editors of relevant local and property publications and let them know what you are up to. If you publish on a website contact them with your entries. They will not always respond to you right away, but just keep letting everyone know of your successes and they will want a piece of you.

Before you know it, you are perceived as the expert, and rather than pushing hard for business and income, you pull it in with less energy and more speed.

Knowledge and action are power. Do you have contacts that can help you reach more people? Do you have a story to tell that radio or TV might be interested in? We all have something to tell:

"Don't get ready, be ready" – Craig Valentine

Can you mentor other people and teach them what you know. We know that you are an expert in one area, we all are uniquely talented, even Rob. Transfer what worked in that strategy to your property portfolio through transmutation.

Success leaves tracks. Use other people successes and expertise to help you to become a wealthy and successful Property investor.

Whose success clues are you studying? And whose model are you duplicating? If they've got what you want then you're doing it right If they have never done it, put on your headphones and mime with a smile.

Summary

Become an expert in property and you will be successful. Your strategy will work for you and others will want to learn from you. Alternatively find an expert and leverage their skills and experience and you will fast track your expertise. Only listen to those who've done it and actively hunt them down and suck them dry for their experience. Buy them lunch or sleep with them; whatever it takes my friend ;-)

Exit Strategies & Tax [how to pay less or none]

"Start with the end in mind" – Stephen Covey [RIP]

"Smart investors know how they'll get out before they get in" – Rob Moore

Knowing how you'll 'cash out' is important because it dictates your tax strategy and also protects against downside risk. If you have children your exit will be impacted, and variables such as your current income level and company structures will also impact your strategy.

We'll be introducing you to a property tax expert from within the Progressive community to give you the up to date details and strategies far better than we could, in a moment.

The most tax efficient way to 'exit' is never to exit. When you sell, you will incur a capital gain, details later in this section. This can be a considerable amount. But more problematic is that you've disposed of the asset, you no longer own it, and someone else earns on it.

Most people don't realise they can continue to take income and cash chunks without selling, and not pay tax on the 'capital.' Instead of selling to gain access to your cash equity, you can simply refinance [remortgage] and access it that way. You won't pay tax on it because it's a loan, and you haven't officially disposed of the asset.

In this instance you have raised more finance [debt] against your property, you have legally avoided paying tax on that extra cash, and you still own the property, which will continue to rise in value over time and pay you again and again.

The **Progressive perpetual finance model** is as follows:

Buy at the highest and safest LTV ratio, to enable you to get all your cash back out without being over exposed. This recommended LTV is around 70% to 75%. Much higher and you're exposed to a fall in values and high debt costs that can't be sufficiently covered by the rental income. Lower and you're leaving cash in, unleveraged, that could be working for you in other assets.

Over time your rents will increase, and you'll have a greater margin that will allow you to increase your debt against it without sacrificing too much income. Your LTV will decrease in that same timeframe, giving you more equity that you can leverage against other assets.

We like to keep our LTV/debt ratio at around 50% - 65% perpetually. We 'buy in' at around 75% LTV, and as time goes on and values increase, when the LTV's drop under 65%, we remortgage back up to between 50% and 65%.

That extra cash is paid out in lumps over time, and compounds and becomes more frequent the more properties you have. And the more you do it, the more properties you can buy.

At this LTV/debt ratio you are protected against dramatic falls in prices, and you'll still have enough margin that the debt will be covered by the rental income at around 250% [rent should be around 250% of the mortgage]. This gives you enough income to live off and reinvest, but not too much that you're paying loads of tax on it. This also gives you a constant stream of cash free tax to re invest/spend, without unnecessary risk, and will dramatically reduce IHT when your time comes.

Please welcome Iain Wallis. Iain first joined the Progressive Community in 2010 and having gone through all the training is now a mentor on the VIP programme. Having learnt and applied his knowledge Iain has now bought over 25 properties for himself and other investors generating £1,000's of per month net cashflow. A Chartered Accountant, see more at **www.iainwallis.com**, he also owns a niche property tax business, so who better to detail some important tax saving strategies?

In the world of property taxation the big five are Income Tax (IT) Capital Gains Tax (CGT) Inheritance Tax (IHT) Corporation Tax (CT) and Stamp Duty Land Tax (SDLT).

Do not be afraid of tax (and I would say this wouldn't I?) but learn to love tax and know how knowing the rules can save you thousands of pounds worth of tax. Start by knowing the rules and then appoint a property tax specialist. You wouldn't go to a dentist to get your heart looked at so don't go to a general accountant who won't know what you can and can't claim for.

As always don't let the tax tail wag the dog. There is no point in doing something if it saves you tax but actually costs you money! That's plain dumb but believe me people do it.

So let's look at each of these taxes and see what we can do to avoid tax.

First of all remember that there is nothing, I repeat nothing, wrong in arranging your tax affairs to legally pay the least amount of tax.

Stamp duty: when you buy a Property you will have to pay stamp duty. If you notice throughout this book, we mention that we are buying Property under £125,000; well that is because we are saving a 1% stamp.

Stamp duty is currently set out as follows:
Up to £125,000: 0%
£125,001 - £250,000: 1%
£250,001 - £500,000: 3%
£500,001 to £1,000,000: 4%
£1,000,001 to £2,000,000: 5%
£2,000,001 : 6%

This is important information for your strategy. You should be able to negotiate prices around the stamp duty thresholds. Very often little 'vacuums' in the market are caused around this. You may get a Property that is really worth £130,000 - £135,000 for £125,000 because of the 'sticking point' around the stamp duty threshold.

A sharp Property investor will always be on the lookout for these 'vacuums.'

Conversely, if you don't stick to the strategy and you buy a Property for say, £255,000, it will actually cost you £262,750. That is an additional £7,650 you have paid in tax. That could be nearly a year's growth [profit] on a small Property down the swanny!

Capital Gains tax is the most significant tax for any property investor.

Be very aware of the distinction between investing and trading in property. If you buy to hold, you're an investor and any sale will attract capital gains tax. If you buy to flip then you are a trader, and any profit will attract income tax or corporation tax if you buy through a limited company.

When property investors come to sell an investment property the sale **may** lead to a CGT liability.

Any tax liability will naturally reduce the overall proceeds and thus the gain. **Why may?** Well there are numerous reliefs and exemptions available and also planning opportunities too complex to explore in this chapter but used correctly they can lead to significant tax free gains. And you'd all like some of that wouldn't you?

Who pays CGT?

Capital gains tax is payable in the UK by:

1. Individuals who are UK resident or UK ordinarily resident
2. UK resident trusts
3. Non-resident persons trading in the UK through a branch or agency.

So what is a Capital gain?

A capital gain arises on the disposal or part disposal of an asset or part of an asset.

A disposal is deemed to take place as soon as there is an unconditional contract for the sale of an asset. This is not the same as the completion date so beware if you are disposing of an asset around the end of the tax year 5 April!

An exchange on April 4 2013 with completion 10 days later would put the sale into 2012-13 with the tax due 31 January 2014 and so bring forward the tax liability by 12 months. A simple delay to put exchange on 6 April just two days later would push the tax bill back to 31 January 2015.

A capital gain is the difference between the net sale proceeds on sale of the asset (sale proceeds less disposal costs) and the cost (cost of asset plus acquisition costs).

Be aware that in certain circumstances on disposal there is deemed to be no gain nor loss on disposal. So transfers between husband and wife or registered civil partners will be totally exempt from capital gains tax.

Net Sale Proceeds

This will usually be the actual sum paid to the vendor from which may be deducted the costs of disposal. These costs need to be spent wholly exclusively for the purpose of the sale and typically would include, agents' fees, advertising, legal fees.

I sell my house for £400,000

Proceeds	400,000
Agents Fees	9,600
Sunday Times Advert	2,400
Legal fees	1,000
Total Costs	13,000
Net Proceeds	**387,000**

Rates & Allowances

Each tax year nearly everyone who is liable to Capital Gains Tax gets an annual tax-free allowance - known as the 'Annual Exempt Amount'. You only pay Capital Gains Tax if your overall gains for the tax year (after deducting any losses and applying any reliefs) are above this amount.

The annual tax-free allowance (known as the Annual Exempt Amount) allows you to make a certain amount of gains each year before you have to pay tax.

Nearly everyone who is liable to Capital Gains Tax gets this tax-free allowance

2012-13

In 2012-13 the Annual Exempt amount was £10,600.

The following Capital Gains Tax rates apply:

* 18 per cent for basic rate tax payers and 28 per cent tax rates for higher rate payers

So work out your total taxable income before working out which Capital Gains Tax rate to use.

1. First work out your taxable income by deducting any tax-free allowances and reliefs that you are entitled to.

2. Next see how much of your basic rate band is already being used against your taxable income. The basic rate band for 2012-13 is £34,370.

3. Allocate any remaining basic rate band first against gains that qualify for Entrepreneurs' Relief – these are charged at 10 per cent.

4. Next allocate any remaining basic rate band against your other gains, these are charged at 18 per cent.

5. Any remaining gains above the basic rate band are charged at 28 per cent.

Simples!

So did all of that confuse the hell out of you? If not, then you should be working for the Inland Revenue! However, if that sends you into a bit of a spin then, don't worry. The whole point of this is that you can avoid all of the messing around, calculating and analysing by holding your properties and never selling them!

You should know this by now! And at least you can't say that we didn't tell you.

Now we don't know about you, but we want to do as much as we can to reduce our tax bill. The simplest way in Property terms is, and we'll say it again: **to never sell your Property.**

2013-14

In 2013-14 the Annual Exempt amount will remain at £10,600 and again there will be a two tier rate of 18 and 28 per cent.

Separated couples will still be considered as connected persons and divorced couples only become unconnected for tax purposes once the decree absolute has been granted.

Tax is always paid on the 31 January following the year of assessment. So if a gain is made during the tax year 2012-13 then the tax will be due 31/01/2014.

If you hold your properties and access your gains through remortgage, then you are effectively accessing your gain by borrowing it against the value of your Property. You do not have to pay tax against a loan [mortgage]. The great thing about this system is that most people remortgage every three years or so anyway and actually never pay off their mortgage. They can apply this strategy without changing anything they do. All we need to do is buy more Property and compound the gains and keep accessing them this way.

This enables you to access your money incrementally rather than having to wait 25 years for it. This also saves you shed loads of tax! In addition, this reduces your inheritance tax bill because you have less profit in your asset when it comes time to pass it on.

Inheritance tax: can be just as nasty. The more assets you own when it comes to passing them on, the more tax the recipients will have to pay. So if you have been following the strategy of borrowing and taking equity from your portfolio as you earn it, your IHT bill will be greatly reduced.

If your portfolio has grown to £5million and throughout your life you have used the equity to live, buy more assets and enjoy your life, then your children or other recipients will have a much reduced tax bill.

The first £325,000 is allowed to be transferred free of Inheritance Tax so a married couple ignoring all other allowances for this example can pass £650,000 worth of assets to their children completely tax free.

Some figures for you:

Traditional thinking: own one Property outright. Bought for £50,000 in 1985, worth £800,000 in 2025 [generic example based on historical growth]. Mortgage fully paid off:

Initial taxable profit: £750,000 on death. For this example I've assumed one partner dies, then passes to surviving spouse with full nil tare band transferred.

£750,000 less tax free amount of £650,000 will leave £100,000 taxed at 40%. So £40,000 of your wealth goes straight to HMRC and your estate will probably need to sell the house to pay the tax.

Progressive thinking: own 11 properties using equity from your first home. Total portfolio value in 2025: £4million [conservative estimate of only 5% growth]:

Taxable equity of 15%: £600,000.

Using traditional thinking, you have paid off your own Property by 2025. Your asset has grown to £800,000 in 40 years and you have not remortgaged it. You have not been able to use, invest, spend or enjoy any of that money and your next of kin are lumbered with a big tax bill; £40,000 in the example above.

Using **Progressive thinking,** you have used equity in your own home to buy more Property. Perhaps you bought the next 10 from that one remortgage or you kept remortgaging over the next 20 years and re-investing. You have taken your money as your Property has grown in value and you have enjoyed at least £1.25milllion in that time. Your asset base only has equity in it of £600,000 [less than with traditional thinking] and below the nil rate exemption of £650,000 and the tax bill you are leaving is NIL (yes NOTHING) on a considerably larger asset base.

In all the years of investing, studying, testing, trailblazing and meeting the richest investors, we have not yet found a better strategy than this.

So die in debt and pass assets to your children tax free with the right strategies in place.

Companies

The Million $ question I always get asked is should I use a Limited Company and the Million $ answer every time is it depends! For there really is no one size fits all solution.

- It Depends

On the Type of Property Income you have and what you are doing. All will spit out different levels of profit.

- Buy & Flip
- Buy & Hold
- Deal Packaging
- Lease Options
- MLTWTS
- HMO

- **It Depends**
  On your other sources of Income

  - Are you a basic rate tax payer (up to £32,010)
  - Higher rate (40% up to £150K then 45%)

Do you need income now or later?

  - You can leave the post tax profit in a company until you need the income having quit your job

Is this part time or full time?

Who are you buying for?

  - Yourself, to build up something for the kids or grandchildren

I recommend that you forget trying to buy and hold properties in companies because companies don't get the annual capital gains tax exemption though as indicated above it really is dependent upon your own personal situation so as always seek professional advice before you act.

I would certainly avoid anything 'off-shore'. Nor would I be buying property in other people's names for the purposes of saving tax. It might save you a little tax in the long run, but it will require expertise, can end up costing and taking up a lot of your time, and may give you a long term headache.

Income tax is the tax most likely to impact on the profit that you make from your property investment. Yes, there are many expenses that can be claimed against your income but at the end of the day the intention is to make a profit; so yes, you will pay income tax if you hold the properties in your own name.

A relevant point to note here is your loss on any property is carried forward. If you register a loss on your income tax for the year, you can carry that forward and it can be offset against the future years that you may make profit.

Even though your property does not yet make a profit you will need to tell HMRC and file a self assessment return. You will need to make up accounts to 31 March each year and file your return in the following tax year. So income earned up to 5 April 2013 will go on the 2012/13 Self Assessment Return. At present this return can be filed by paper by 31 October 2013 or online by 31 January 2014. Any tax due will be payable by 31 January 2014.

So what can you claim against your rental profits?

In a nutshell any expenditure incurred from a simple stamp sending back the paperwork to the lawyers through to expenditure on refurbishing your property.

This is a book about property not tax so space dictates that we concentrate on a few of the key areas.

Repairs and renewals; never has so much been written or discussed about the treatment of repairs. The simple reason is that repair expenditure will be deducted as an expense whereas capital items you will only get tax relief when you sell a property so over time with inflation the real value of that money diminishes.

The HMRC gives clear guidance on the fundamentals:

- **When first brought into rental market (usually purchase) expenditure to make it fit for purpose is CAPITAL expenditure.**

    - So if you buy a property then redecorate and repaint to make it habitable (fit for purpose) then you have capital expenditure

- **Restoring a property to its previous condition is REVENUE expenditure**

- So if you've let out a property and then redecorate and then replace carpets then that is revenue expenditure

- Same expenditure but completely different tax treatment, so the key is to get the property tenanted, even for a short period, before any significant work is undertaken

- **Enhancement expenditure will be CAPITAL expenditure**

  - So if you add a conservatory then that will be capital expenditure

If expenditure is of a capital nature however all is not lost. Certain items of expenditure will qualify for what HMRC call "capital allowances" and particularly useful is the Annual Investment Allowance. This has recently been increased to £250,000 so expenditure that falls into this category can generate a tax refund against your PAYE Income. Capital allowances is a very niche and specialised area, so yes you will need specialist advice but the tax savings could be quite significant.

Mileage: You would be amazed how many miles you travel as a property investor so it's essential that you make a claim for all those miles travelled. Some of you may invest in areas well away from where you live as the yields in your area don't stack up. So if you find yourself hurtling down the M4 to Wales or heading up the M1 to the frozen north (it's not really it's just wonderful) to undertake viewings then be sure to keep a record of the mileage undertaken. Just think how many times you will clock up mileage: attending viewings, a trip to the auction house, a visit to your IFA, a visit to your solicitor, your friendly accountant, networking events, training events. Keep a diary for a month and you would be amazed at the miles undertaken.

A simple multiplication times 12 would give you a typical property mileage on which to make a claim. If you have an anorak or maybe work for HMRC then you would dutifully record every trip 365 days of the year. Yes the second method will be 100% correct the former there or thereabouts and a quicker more commercial approach.

Those wonderful miles can then be claimed @ 45p for the first 10,000 and 25p thereafter though these rates do change.

Legal fees: Your first encounter will be when you buy the property. Legal costs in acquiring the property cannot be claimed against your rental income and will be treated as a capital expense. You will get tax relief when you sell the property. All is not lost, however. Within the conveyancing process part of the legal work will relate to the raising of the finance and them helpfully telling you that you are borrowing @ x% and that your home will be repossessed etc etc (stuff that as a wise property investor you already knew). So ask your solicitor how much of the bill related to raising finance and then claim that part. If needs be, arrange for a separate bill and claim that deduction.

Somebody came to me and asked about this. He was appalled to learn that his accountant had not done this and he had over fifty properties. Fifty properties at say £150 per property amounts to £7,500 expenditure left and @ 50% that £3,750 more tax paid that necessary. Ouch!

Where tenants fall behind and you have to bring in the strong arm of the law then those costs will always be allowable.

Section 5: What Are You Going to Do Now?

A quick breath: that's nearly all the information you need. Now it's time to turn your knowledge into cash [only if that is Ok with you of course]…

Time: Your most precious commodity

Money – we can get back. Invest it – you'll lose some, get modest returns on some, and win big on some. Trust, love, property, fitness – we can get back.

Time – you can't. Once you've used it, invested it or wasted it, it's gone. And if you're not careful, your whole life can catch right up with you and you may have little to show for it. You may regret how you invested your time as it begins to run out.

You know it's the one thing that is most valuable to you. So with that in mind we're going to share with you some Progressive time 'models,' – ways to monitor and invest your time, for the maximum return.

But beware – if [when] you use these proven systems for time and life management, all other parts of your life, especially your free time, will dramatically improve.

Fair warning – there's a price to pay. That price is discipline.

"It's easy to do, but it's just as easy not to do." – Jeff Olsen

You choose which price you will pay – the short term delayed gratification or the long term regret.

And just before we share Progressive time freedom models, this is one of the very latest additions in the 3rd edition of the book. We've been developing these models for many years, whilst running a 7 figure property business, buying over 350 properties, setting up another 4 businesses, having babies, getting pilot's licences, travelling around the world, racing cars, trying to be good partners to each other and our 'bosses,' raising 6 figures for charity, spending meaningful family time and doing our best to really contribute to the property and entrepreneurial world.

And trying to stay humble :-)

These are certainly not said to blow trumpets, but to share that without these models learned the hard way [burnout, lost money, failed JV's], it would have been impossible to do and achieve all these things. We have many people far smarter and richer than us to thank for guiding us through and helping us refine these systems we are about to share with you...

And having delivered these models to many of the Progressive community now, this generates much of the meaningful, life changing feedback we get – and it's often not what property investors thought they needed.

L1. M2. DL: Leverage 1st. Manage 2nd. Do LAST! When you're busy, perhaps the first thing you think is 'what do I need to do? Or 'I've got so much to do, where do I start? Or 'when can I get this done?'

Well try this: next time you start your task or to do list, instead of starting with a task, start with what you can leverage or outsource. Who can you get to do the first task you were going to do?

And the second, and third. Out of 7 tasks for the day, if you've leveraged 4 of them, and you do 3 of them, you'll achieve more than double the results in less than half of the [your personal] time.

But unfortunately, once you've leveraged out tasks you would ordinarily have done yourself, they don't just magically arrive on your desk the next day in shiny wrapping paper. Any task 'leveraged,' needs managing through to completion [time invested].

Check through your leveraged tasks and manage them accordingly, and only once you have gone through these 2 steps should you consider 'doing' a task [time spent]. A few small hours moved from doing to leveraging, from time spent to time invested, has huge compounded benefits. And if you're too busy to invest time, that's probably the very reason you need to do it. And if no one can do that task or job as well as you, that's probably the very reason you need to do it too.

Ti vs. Ts: Time invested vs. Time spent. Working for an hourly rate, doing a task, or exchanging your time for money, is time spent [Ti]. You can never get it back. Unsuccessful people 'spend' most, if not all of their time.

Leveraging, leading, inspiring, influencing, managing, outsourcing, networking, training and building systems are all examples of time 'invested' [Ti].

Time invested continues to earn or leverage long after that task was completed. Buying a property in time invested [and money invested], building your team and training them is time invested. Become aware of where you are spending all of your time in one of the 2 areas above, spend less time, and invest more of it. Passive income comes from time invested.

Dividends come from time invested. Salaries come from time spent. There's nothing wrong with exchanging time for money, as long as there is a vision to invest it. When you package deals, you can earn a lot of money per deal or per hour. That can get you on the road to being wealthy, and investing time. It serves its purpose. But you'll never be time wealthy unless you invest time for residual returns.

So be *very* selective in how you use your time. Measure it, monitor it and be strict and disciplined with where you invest it. Lead, manage and leverage. It's not about how much you do, but how much the world is doing for you and for your vision. Then you have more time to **do things you love**. To do things that build you a future. To do things that make you money. To do things that build your property portfolio and to do things that help others and contribute to the great world we live in.

Don't waste your time with anything else. Don't waste your time doing things you don't want to do and don't have to do. You have ultimate choice. That's the great thing about the free information world we live in. It's so easy to get someone else to do all the things you hate, or you're terrible at. And they probably love it! Freaks ;-)

[For the avoidance of doubt – doing things that you don't particularly like, but you know, being honest with yourself, are IGT, Ti & Leverage, show true discipline that will lead you to great success and riches. There's a world of difference between doing these important 'tasks' and everything else that you don't like that is useless to your life – or you do like but is useless to your life].

Throughout the years that we've been building our portfolio and businesses, we've always striven to become more efficient. That was harder for me [Rob] than it was for me [Mark] because I'm a 'fire, ready, aim' and 'get perfect later,' kind of person. Mark taught me systems, and constantly duplicating work and time taught me systems. We now consistently and painstakingly look at how we can get better and do things quicker without duplication of time, resource or personnel, and you should too.

We've built systems and checklists to control property viewings, automatically evaluate deals, monitor and control refurbs, manuals to manage the people managing the systems, people to manage the people managing the systems, and systems to manage the people that manage the people that manage the systems. James Caan really helped us with this, he's smart when it comes to systems – thank you James.

One of our best systems is Mark's 'Deal Scrutiniser™'' – and as a thank you for getting this far, and because those who keep going get rewarded, you can download the iPhone App version here, unlocked and free on the App store when you type in 'Property App.'

You can choose that you are only going to do what you love, what you want, and what makes you money, and the rest can be delegated, leveraged and you can lead all that serve your vision.

And when you've 'bought back' and leveraged all this time, you can either fill it doing more of the above, as we did in the first few years, to get compounded results quicker, or simply spend more time doing the things you love the most, with the people you love the most, when you want, where you want, whenever you want.

Summary

Use your time wisely, efficiently and systematically, because it flies by. Don't waste a minute. Make your decisions quickly; use L1. M2. DL. & Ti vs.Ts time freedom models and be disciplined to follow through. Either you're using your time to serve someone else's vision, or the world is serving your vision – you choose my friend.

To know and not to do...

So now you have all the tools, you really do.

But of course you know that this is not the end of the road. The rest is up to you and the action you take from here on.

I hope that we will talk in the future and you will be telling us your stories of action and success, and hopefully some of those will be down to what you have read here in this book.

"It's easy to do, but also easy not to do"

We hope you choose the easy part :-)

Get perfect later. Fail forward fast. Decide forward.

Education. Decision. Action

Decide on Your strategy

Unfortunately, we know that a large percentage of people who read this book will now go and do nothing. Statistically the sofa, the PlayStation, the Pub, the bingo hall and the bookies are all far more appealing than getting up, going out and making cash.

Now we know that is not you, but that fact still remains.

Knowing that you want to do something about it; you have 2 choices [you have dismissed the watch TV and do nothing strategy, haven't you?]:

Strategy 1: Take everything that you have learned here and go out and get your 5 properties. Then buy 5 more and 5 more and keep going as long as you desire. You really can do it. It won't always be easy, but nothing that ever meant anything was. It will take time, effort, dedication, money and hard work; but you really can do it, and remember:

"You have to work hard enough not to have to work hard"

It can be done part time to start with, but once you get going, break through a barrier or two and start to see the results, it will likely become a full time career, so you need to think about that and if you want it to be that way for you.

If you follow the principles and 'secret' tips in this book, and the sister book "Make Cash in a Property Market Crash," and if you use them as a manual then you will succeed; guaranteed. So many people before you have done exactly that using exactly the same tools and tricks, and most of them started from a similar position as you, if not further back.

Rob started with £30,000 worth of debt in interest payments on loans and credit cards. Mark started at 15 years old as an 'Entrepreneur,' with a very small amount of business knowledge.

You know you can raise finance as we have discussed earlier, no matter where you are in your life, and no matter what your financial position. You can get started right away by setting your strategy and making it happen.

You can become a full-time property investor and you can make whatever wealth you want to make and beyond. Please just make sure you tell us all about your successes, we would love to know and be a part of it in some way.

Strategy 2: perhaps you don't have the time that others have to become a full time investor. Perhaps you don't have the inclination. Perhaps you want all the benefits with none of the drawbacks: you want the baby without the labour pains?

Perhaps you already love what you do and you just want to take the money and run? Perhaps you want to accelerate your earning time by not having to go through the experience process [because you want to earn on your portfolio in the meantime]? Perhaps you want to utilise [leverage] the knowledge and experience of the experts who are already doing it for themselves?

If this is the case then we can help you, and would love to help you.

We can save you time and make you money by building and managing a hands-free Property portfolio that you can retire on; enjoying financial independence.

We can help you if you are young or not so young. If you have savings or equity in your property then we can build you a portfolio that at current rates will comfortably earn a potentially job replacing income. All you will have to do is sign papers. You can have an asset base that has cost you nothing in time but given you choice, freedom, passive income and something to pass on to your children [if you have/plan to have any].

Perhaps you want to do both. Perhaps you would like to earn while you are learning and you would like to learn from us. The point is you can and you have the choice now.

If you would like us to help you it couldn't be simpler. You can reach either or both of us at the following now:

Call us: **0845 1309505**

Email us: **rob.moore@progressiveproperty.co.uk**

Enquire on our website: **www.progressiveportfoliobuilder.co.uk**

We would love to chat to you; or even better, meet you personally.

As you know, life rewards people who take action. Education. Decision. Action. Everything in this book is about becoming informed and then making a commitment to taking immediate and decisive action now to create the life that you want and deserve.

Procrastination is a disease and life rewards momentum.

Your Next Steps...

Is this the end, my friend, or is this just the beginning?

"When all is said and done, more is said than done"

But the reality is that you have gotten this far, and the statistics are terrible – most people fell off the boat hundreds of pages ago.

So you've proven that you can go the distance, and you clearly want something more. You must be ready, and for that we want to thank you. Without you we'd be a couple of six-toed geeks [we're from that part of the world] who would have a decent portfolio, reasonable cashflow, but not many friends and no greater purpose for life.

Thanks to you, and hundreds of thousands of others just like you, we get to live a far greater purpose. We don't have to buy our friends [any more] ;-) The Progressive community has something so special about it that just can't be put into words, and it's all about the great people in it.

People from all walks of life – man, woman, 17 years old, 85 years old, billionaires and zero-aires, people in terrible debt a year or two ago, highly educated people and others like Rob ;-) From 32 countries across the world and counting. Everyone with totally different backgrounds, cultures, experiences and beliefs, but with couple of key distinctions and common goals – to do better, be better, have a little more and give more.

And when Mark was a glorified butcher and Rob a struggling artist, we never got to be in a community like that.

Where else do you get so much shared information, resources, contacts and experience? Imagine asking your boss for all his secrets – he'd tell you go and do a little dance for it or give you the 'bird.'

So if you'd like a little help where to go to continue your journey, here's a little help:

Have you read any other Progressive property books? Did you know we have others? Yes, more of the same!

"Make Cash in a Property Market Crash" [3rd Edition] – does what it says on the tin. Either search on Amazon or go here: **www.progressiveproperty.co.uk**

Or for a heart warming, inspirational series of stories and proof of Progressive community members sharing their secrets, results and breaking it down into 'how-to' steps, with a huge dose of inspiration, you might want to read "Progressive in Property – from Beginners to Winners."

"Progressive in Property – from Beginners to Winners," got to UK's 5th bestselling book on launch behind 50 shades of grey, 50 shades of grey 2, 50 shades of grey 3, and the 50 shades of grey trilogy box set! A nice claim to fame :-)

Either search on Amazon or go here: **www.progressiveproperty.co.uk**

To meet us and the Progressive community personally, you can join us at a Progressive Property Networking event [PPN] near you: **www.progressivepropertynetwork.co.uk**

Or for more information on our more detailed, specific events, training programmes and higher education for accelerated property success, go here: **www.progressiveproperty.co.uk/events**

Summary

You've got this far; congratulations because you are one of the few. "To know and not to do is not to know – just go." What is your next step? What action will you take now to get you one step closer to your goal? We'd love to help. We'd love to be a continued part of your successful journey, and above all else we'd like to thank you for putting your faith in us. So thank you.

Are You sitting on an asset

If we were to tell you the single most common reason, or [translated] excuse for not getting into property, or buying enough once you're educated, or scaling up once you've bought a few, or moving up to your next level, we'd bet a few of our houses that you could guess it.

It's the thing that stopped us for many years. Maybe it's the thing that has taken you this long to get to this point...

You guessed it – finance.

'I don't have the money to invest in property.'

'I can't afford the deposit.'

'I'm worried about voids, mortgage payments and debt.'

I [Rob] started with more than £30,000 of *credit card and car loan debt* [but had sold the car – still paying off the loan]. You didn't pop out of your Mum with a briefcase full of money, and nor did anyone else. Very few start life with enough money to live forever, and the very few that do mostly squander it, right?

You know this to be true, so the big question is 'what's been stopping you?'

Well every penny you've ever *attracted* into your life to buy or investing in anything, or donate, gift or waste, has literally, in your material world, come out of 'thin air.' If you total it all, you've probably *magnetised* millions in your life, right?

OK, so you probably want to be able to do it quicker this time round, but now we know that you can do it, let's just work on doing it a little quicker, together, shall we? Some facts about money:

At the time of writing, depending on the source, there seems to be between $40 trillion and $53 trillion circulating around the world. So let's get rid of 'I don't have any money,' 'I can't afford it.' 'There's not a lot of money around at the moment,' 'No one's spending/got any money.'

B.S. [Belief systems].

Those ridiculous statements aren't just damaging to your wealth, they are magnificently untrue!

Next.

'I don't have the money.'

You never did. You never do. You borrow it from the 'world.' You weren't born with a bank account, you don't get given a limited share, it's not scarce [QE - more and more is being printed], and you 'attract,' or 'repel,' it according not to what is fair, but what you believe, do and give.

Believe more, do more and give more, and you'll get more.

Your bank account is not held with Barclays or HSBC, your bank account is held in the 'world.' It's all there, waiting for any deposit or withdrawal, at any time, with no daily limits or restrictions, with unlimited overdrafts and infinite repayment terms.

All the money you need for anything is moving constantly around the contacts you know. How many people do you know who are good at 'attracting,' money? How many wealthy people do you have in your extended bank account? How far does it reach?

In the "Joint Venture – Be Your Own Bank™" audio programme, there's a whole disc dedicated to your money beliefs. That's one-eighth of the entire programme. Most property people don't get into property thinking they need to learn about beliefs. They want strategies, tools, tactics and information.

"The skillset without the mindset will leave you upset"

Well what's the difference between giving a Michelin star chef a knife, and a murderer? Do you think their beliefs may impact how they use the 'tool.'

What about alcohol? Give it to a doctor and it can heal, give it to someone depressed and it can kill. Your beliefs totally dictate what you do with the tools and opportunities that are passed your way by the world every minute of every day [notice your beliefs about that statement too]. So how about we share a detailed list of from where you can attract money. If we give you a dozen or more proven places to raise finance, then your excuses for not having any of it dissolve to non- existent, right? So here we go:

- Crowd funding sites
- Peer to peer lending sites
- Market invoice sites

- Asset based lending sites
- CDFI's
- EFG's
- Venture Giant
- Business Angel events
- Property portals & membership sites
- Personal concierge
- Flying clubs
- Charity balls
- Friends & family
- Early inheritance
- Pension redemption
- Dating websites [we have a great story about that]
- Social media groups
- Business networking events
- Property networking events
- Progressive events
- Pay per click
- Private members clubs
- List rental/CPA/CPL
- Affiliate and Joint Ventures

How would you like to be financially independent, living your life of choice, with no loss of your time, all from the equity you have in your house, right now?

And you don't even have to sell your house or pay anything out of your own pocket or earnings.

Imagine creating your dream life from an asset that you already have now...

It is simple, easy to follow, will take you very little time and you can start right away without any knowledge of Property.

So many people who have become financially independent have accessed their money through remortgage of their existing home. Many of them have gone on to become multi-millionaires. You can do the same now.

Many people didn't even realise the asset they were literally sitting on. Do you remember earlier in the book we asked you to think about your home: what you bought it for and what it is now worth? Or if you have a family member who has a house and you can ask them the same question…

The major benefit of this strategy is that your income and savings are not impacted in any way. If you have a property with sufficient equity in it, or you can access funds from any of the vehicles/places/sites above, you can get started right away.

And even if you can't, you can!

About Mark & Rob

This seems like the right place to tell you a little more about us. If you're already in the Progressive community, you've heard this all before [from Rob!]. If not, it's a pleasure to be on a similar journey with you.

This book is not about us, it is about what you can do with your financial future and how you can have security and wealth through property. And all those other things you want too. However you could, no should, be asking this important question:

"Who are these guys and why should I trust them?"

OK. We absolutely regard ourselves as 2 'normal' guys. In fact Mark is very boring! We're not 'Gurus' or self proclaimed cult leaders or evangelists. We don't have a long CV of master degrees and diplomas. In fact there are no such qualifications in the property 'industry.'

Even if there were, they would probably mean very little to us, because we like to be able to give real life evidence and experience.

Rob scraped a degree in Architecture that he's done nothing with, and Mark's degree in Economics, though a useful stepping stone, never prepared him for the real world of business and investing. I guess we went down the 'traditional' education path initially, because that what you're supposed to do if you can.

We certainly won't be teaching our children the 'traditional' way.

Funny how we both sunk around £50,000 a piece into 'traditional' education [University], much of that from our parents, and that has yielded virtually no return. Yet from minus £30K [Rob], self education, real life investing and business has returned infinitely – the £26M JV mini-empire we have all came from starting in debt.

And funny how most people do the same with blind faith, yet baulk when it comes to investing in themselves. Funny how they'll pay £60 per month for Sky and £300 per month for a car lease, but spit at investing in the very thing that will make them rich – their own education.

So we both started from relatively humble beginnings. Mark is obsessed with figures, details, economics, business and investing; and has been since a teenager. He'll explain in a moment.

Rob is a disruptive, impatient, never-satisfied Entrepreneur who gets perfect later, decides forward and strives to continually improve. He needed to between the age of 18 and 27, because he kept failing in strange ways that he will reveal in a moment too.

It was an unlikely partnership. We met at a dingy property networking meeting – you know the ones where you were told there would be 50 people there and there are 9, everyone is a bit coy, it's all a bit tin-pot, the speaker is dull and stands in front of the screen so that his presentation that he is reading like a script is actually projecting on his penis area. I forget what it/he said.

I [Rob] must have thought to leave half a dozen times. The last time was as I walked past the bar towards the exit, but something made me stay for one drink [water of course].

So after 'strategically' networking with everyone, sharing cards and talking shop [which I had to fake at the time as I didn't know anything about 'shop'] the last person I met at the bar was a bit rigid. His shirt was even tucked in and his jeans had creases in them, pulled up near his armpits.

After 15 minutes of trying to drop words that made me sound like I knew what I was talking about, I swapped cards with Mark and our partnership started. We thought we had everything in common, because we both talked property and we had both been recently 'evicted' by our respective girlfriends. Grounds to start a lifelong partnership right?

Well that is where the similarities ended. And lucky too. The best JV's and partnerships are built on polarised skillsets, and we were lucky enough to be virtually opposite.

But with a shared vision.

Fast forward to now and Progressive has become a £multi-million business, with spin off businesses in personal development, letting, bridging/finance, networking and portfolio building.

Who'd have ever thought we'd build a business 'mini-empire.' Being honest, we never looked beyond buying single let 'grot-boxes' in Peterborough over and over. It just didn't seem possible or realistic.

Over 350 properties bought and sold in a few short years, including larger scale HMO's, offices, training suites, flat and title splitting and conversions/developments, and we're literally pinching ourselves.

4 best-selling property books, including "Progressive in Property – from Beginners to Winners," which, on launch, was the best selling property book in the UK and the 5th best-selling book of any genre. The 4 that beat it were "50 shades of grey," "50 shades of grey 2," 50 shades of grey 3," and "50 shades of grey – the trilogy box set."

Who'd have dreamed we would come so close to out selling the worldwide 'Mummy-porn,' phenomenon?! 2 chaps from Peterborough; a place most people either don't know or travel through to get somewhere decent? No chance!

So imagine what our old friends thought when we bought our first Ferrari [for those that care, and since we get asked all the time by fellow boy racers; an f430 Spider, bought with cash because apparently anyone can rent one, and it spends most of its life in the Garage]?

Correct, they all thought we had set up a local drugs ring. Of course they had no idea we had a £140,000 car paid in cash 100% funded by profits from property.

Someone did actually comment on YouTube that we didn't own it. In fact, we had stolen it and got the bus to work every day ;-) You might find that comment on our YouTube Channel to this day [with 100's of Progressive case studies of success & cashfllow], as it was too funny to delete.

Imagine what our old friends thought when we had a fleet of sports cars, and when we gained our pilot's licence and started flying to places in Helicopters, and when we bought offices and training suites and commercial buildings for cash. All funded by income from our property portfolio and business that started as a 'Net £3K per month' 3 year goal.

And all learned from the *systems* of property investing that you've learned here, and that Progressive have the great privilege to pass down.

Imagine what Mark's friends thought when he finally threw away his 12 year old M&S suit and started wearing good clothes, and when he sold his £47 Nova that he'd been driving for over 150,000 miles and changing the oil himself.

That was the final straw, we were officially evil, money grabbing, had-to-be-screwing-people b*stards, and of course they were all waiting like a pack of wolves for us to fail to tell the world "we told you so."

And for those non-materialistic types, forget the possessions and money and negative reactions from friends. Just think about the freedom, autonomy and choice. Never again having to answer to anyone but yourself, knowing that everything you wake up to is your choice, not an obligation. Going on more holidays and doing more of the things you love, funded entirely by property.

Imagine cleaning your friendships and moving away from the 'Crabs' to amazing, inspiring, big thinking, fight-your-corner people. And not just Lord Sugar, James Caan, Frank Bruno, Bob Geldof, Karren Brady, Neville Wright [Kiddicare] and a whole list of inspirational and wealthy people, but a whole Progressive community, literally thousands of people, all of like mind, supportive and genuine.

That's the part we n e v e r dreamed we'd have. We thought it would be years of struggle. We were wrong.

And do you know the best part [parts]? Better than the TV shows and media coverage and money and 'stuff?' The best parts are that we succeeded totally despite ourselves. We made so many mistakes. We bought some total kippers. Eeek. Cringe.

If we'd have made so many mistakes in a n y other business we'd have got wiped out 17 times over. But we succeeded not because of our superior greatness, we succeeded because of the vehicle and *system* of property investing. The leverage-able, forgiving and limitless investment vehicle of property.

And you can too.

All we did was take what people far smarter than us had learned, add our own special sauce over the years as we 'failed-forward,' and refined a system that we've taught you in this book, and is on our other books and programmes too.

And Progressive has grown into a force of inspiration, action and success because of this *system.*

The other 'best part,' is the people we get to touch. In no other business that we've ever been in can we make such a difference and contribution. It's impossible.

For those who think property is all about money [like we probably did when we started – nowt wrong with that], imagine how great it feels to build the UK's largest property community with over 100,000 people online and live all on the same mission.

Imagine having thousands of people who've gone out, followed the simple system, kept going, and bought cashflowing properties, built property businesses, housed tenants, saved people from repossession, and contributed to the community so positively.

Imagine as a community raising £100,000's to charities and openly sharing ideas and successes. Not that I'm sad, but I've counted over 7,000 emails to my personal address all feeding back this gratitude and these results.

I've seen a lady six figures in debt and painfully shy raise £500K of JV finance within six months. I've seen a young man be a victim of a £20M VAT fraud in his name, with family death threats, create a cashflowing portfolio of many thousands in just a few short months. I've seen people of 17 years old build a property business before they can even get a mortgage, people who can't see or have cerebral palsy buy cashflowing properties, all with zero previous experience.

You can find all the proof on our Progressive Property YouTube channel. And honestly, that means so much more than the money. Don't get me wrong, the money is up there with oxygen, but the freedom and the feeling and the community – yeah baby that's what it's all about.

Over the years, going through our 20's and into our 30's, it's been a continual path of education.

"If you're green you grow, if you're ripe you rot."

The £50K that got us degrees came to virtually nothing of financial note, but the continual, Entrepreneurial, self education has paid huge dividends.

Our budget for personal education in each year is £140,000 – four courses, trainings, CD programmes, flying all around the world doing the best business, marketing, sales, leadership…

Whatever training we can get our hands on that we can apply in our property business. There are many peripheral industry experts that have had £10,000's from us, and we're so grateful what that training has done.

But we had to actually do it.

When you do a degree, let's say to be a Doctor, you don't get to pick and choose the modules and when you apply them. You don't get a knife to go 'cutting' after your first semester. You don't move up the ladder for decades, and you'll be six figures down before you're earning. You have to take the long slow path that everyone else does. You have to follow the system.

When you're an Entrepreneur, you're on your own. There are no agenda-ised modules or lectures. There's no 'path.' So it's not for the faint hearted.

But…

You can pick and choose what you learn and when. You can start now and succeed [or fail] fast. You can go straight for the jugular and learn the most income generating, business building strategies, now.

And you can access that information fast and at low cost. When we got into property we paid £4,997 for a property pack [an Arch Lever file with one property strategy in it]. Now that money will get you a whole year with Progressive. That is one twentieth the cost of a degree, and you can start earning now. Not in 7 years time.

The best of the best in the field of property and other related businesses are teaching too. Just like us. And they love it. They'll talk to you for free at networking events, they'll share all their secrets in a book, or CD or DVD set, or a course. They can tell you the truth from the ground, on the front line, warts and all. And it's in their best interests to do so.

Imagine going to your boss in a bog-standard job and saying to him "Can we have lunch as I'd like you to teach me how to do your job please. I fancy having your job and you're going to teach me?"

She'd ask you politely to smoke it in your pipe.

The property industry works in just the opposite way to the *system.* The *system* produces sausage-machine clones to fill the public sector. Entrepreneurs fund the public sector.

And you don't have to train with Progressive. We've learned so much from so many great Entrepreneurs and business people. Go dine with as many millionaires and billionaires as you can find. Be a networking pimp.

"It's not what you know, it's how many millionaires you know."

Just the talk of property, business, investing, money, finding deals, the entrepreneurial spirit, turns us both on big time!

And if you can't get yourself juiced up knowing you have full and limitless control, then you should get a job at Greggs.

We started Progressive Property on £300 each. Mark had the cash, Rob had to put it on a credit card. We are proud of what Progressive has become, and it's just at the start.

And we want you my friend to grab on, hold tight and fulfil your goals, plans and dreams through our community.

Mark about Mark

I had dreams of becoming an investment banker because it seemed like they earned the most money, had the most glamorous lifestyle and the most *fun*.

I soon realised that the competition was intense and I would not even be considered with my grades [although I enjoyed university very much]. I hit a wall because I had been working to this point for many years of my life.

I made money in the interim in true Entrepreneurial fashion selling various products; importing and exporting and such, and raised enough capital to be able to start investing.

Following University I went on to work for a multinational company on a graduate scheme. I thought I would be an integral part of a big company with great prospects.

As it turns out I was a glorified butcher earning average money with little future. I didn't like the corporate 'way' and the hierarchy. Looking up at someone's ass on a ladder I was at the bottom of was not my idea of happiness and freedom; having to wait in line for mediocre 'success' and 'status.'

I looked at the guys 20 years ahead of me and I didn't like what I saw. They were wrinkled, tired, financially stretched and they never looked happy. I thought to myself; all that work [weekends as well], and this is where I will be heading in 20 years?

Who wants to be like that?

Not me. I wasn't that happy. My zest, enjoyment and passion had been sapped.

I joined a property investment company thinking that I could change my life by becoming a business owner. I was made a director for impressive property sales, however the reality was that I was a glorified employee. My boss certainly didn't look happy or live the kind of life which I aspired to, even though he 'read all of the books' and 'did not deal with negativity.' I didn't want to model him.

I was genuinely down at this point; nothing seemed to be going right. I wasn't sleeping for months on end because of the worry of work, and it began to affect my personal and working life.

Yeah on the outside I had the job title, yeah I was investing, and yes I was making money. But I wasn't happy.

And that is what is most important for me. For all of us, I think.

Then I met Rob. He joined the company I was at and we hit it off immediately. He was [and still is] a qualified coach.

We struck up a gentleman's deal that he would coach me in areas like relationships, health/body, work, mindset and I would teach him how to invest and make money.

This is where my whole life changed. We got on so well and our skills seemed to dovetail. Whatever Rob was weak at I could help him with and vice versa.

Over a period of months I learned how to develop every area of my life to become the best that I could be. I started to run faster and longer than I had ever before [I now go almost everyday and for 2 months I ran every single day]. I ran a half marathon after 4 months of training and have lost a lot of weight to become fit and healthy.

We've since run 2 marathons for Sense. This was a huge add-on benefit from wanting to be better at investing.

I became so much better at building relationships with people and I started to feel great and love every day of my life. Now I sleep like a baby and have massive energy all day long [as long as I have been for my run].

And you know the best bit?

My property investment ability rocketed! We bought around 20 properties in 2006 with a relatively small amount of money and refined a property buying system so much that we now have over 350 for ourselves and in JV's with other investors.

As we've gained more experience in property I spend a lot of my time now on commercial investing, developments and high end 'Boutique' Multi-Lets. I'm totally hands off from buying single lets, as the Deal Analyser [Rob calls it a Deal Scrutiniser] I developed buying all the properties now runs as an automated system. It buys us 7-15 single let properties a month.

Pretty much every deal we've done since 2006 has been without money, or has recycled money back that we made from a previous deal [that required no money]. Although I started with money from previous small ventures I did since the age of 15, I've been careful not to use it. I've always believed that knowledge reduces risk and learning h o w to invest like the best negates the need for any money in any deal.

If a n y o n e ever tells you, you can't, or that you can't because you have no money, or you tell yourself that, you and they simply don't know how. Learn how, and everything will come to you, starting without money.

I am now happier than I have ever been in my life. Don't get me wrong, I am not a happy clappy faux positive personal development junkie. I have my moments, but I know that I am in control of my feelings, my decisions, my actions and my future, which has been a huge development in my life, and something I never truly understood before.

I enjoy spending time with Gemma [my Gemma, not Rob's Gemma], dining with inspirational people, travelling to great destinations around the world, running, flying and anything to do with property and business. I'm crap at sport and my hobbies and 'work' are the same things, which is lucky for me, I guess.

Rob about Mark

Mark is a dealmaker. He is highly anal-ytical, quite risk-averse, semi paranoid and very detailed. He has a sixth sense for property investment deals in my opinion, researches thoroughly, protects the down-side, and is definitely one of the most [if not the most] knowledgeable investors in the UK.

He's also semi-autistic, and is the property equivalent of the rain man. He sees everything in numbers and figures, and constantly thinks and evaluates everything in his life like a property deal.

And doesn't sleep much because of it.

He bought some quite amazing deals in 2004/2005 when he was relatively new to the market and it was clear to me that I had to learn what he knew. He had a talent and was only going to get better. I wanted in on those kinds of deals.

He has helped me immensely with my property knowledge and just being around him helps me grow immeasurably every single day.

His attention to detail is scary. To be honest sometimes he bores the pants off me with the amount of detail he goes into, and how many times he tells me the same thing like I've never heard it; but it's all good. I am one of these kinds of people who likes the baby and not the labour pains. I like to leverage and maximise my own time by positioning myself with people who are better than me in specialised areas. I've done many silly things, but JV'ing with Mark was the smartest one.

Rob about Rob

Ever since I was 17 my life seemed to go steadily downhill.

I was a half-talented sportsman and got mostly A's at my GCSE's [through hard work, the fear of failure, and a £200 bet with my Dad, rather than talent]. I was accepted to one of the best Universities in the country and felt I had a good future ahead of me [or so I thought]…

Then in 1996 I had 2 serious injuries within the space of 6 months. I crashed my motorbike [and not by half]. It was my pride and joy at the time because I no longer looked the pillock that I did on the provisional-licence moped I had previously. It took me one year of begging my parents to let me get me one. I spent 6 months in rehabilitation from multiple breaks. [If you are considering getting a motorbike: DON'T! My son Bobby certainly won't].

That ruined any prospect of me becoming a professional Golfer or Cricketer, which I had genuine aspirations for. I held much resentment and never really recovered from that. Six months later my appendix burst [a close run in with the big man upstairs] whilst in a nightclub. The whole second year of my A-Levels was written off.

I spent the next 7 years always living in the shadow of myself and what I could have become, bitter, resentful and a feeling that everything had been taken away from me. I lost my ability to dream and believe in myself.

I managed to scrape into a University and pulled off a good degree in Architecture [fear of failure again]. As soon as I graduated all I wanted to do was anything else other than Architecture. The only reason I didn't quit the course after 2 months was my pride [ego] as I did not want anyone to think that I gave up on things.

I came back home to help my family in their pub as my Dad was very ill. What was essentially a 3 month plan ended up being nearly 3 years.

I tell the full story at our events and the feedback is that it is the single biggest thing that gets people into property. If we get to meet personally I'll share it with you too.

All the while I knew that working in Mum and Dad's pub was not what I ultimately wanted to do. But it is hard to break away when you think you are letting your family down. I'm sure you may have felt the same. I finally broke away in 2003 and set out to make a living in my real true passion: Art.

I have loved Art since before I could talk and that is something that I did actually have some kind of talent for. I believed that talent was enough to bring me the success, wealth and happiness that I desired.

As it turns out talent was not enough. I struggled for 2 years working 16 hours a day and failing to pay my debts of over £30,000 that I amassed at [and since] University.

I felt pretty low at this point. It was impacting other areas of my life such as my relationships with friends and family and my ability to socialise and enjoy life. I had completely lost my drive and enthusiasm.

I was constantly looking back at what I should have been and that, 7 years on, I had still achieved nothing in my life that I wanted.

I realised that I had no savings, no future, and that if something happened to me I would be in big trouble. I was literally less than a month, every month, away from having nothing. I was not looking forward to working 16 hours a day for the rest of my life. I mean, who wants that?

My Dad worked for 15 years in the RAF serving his country to receive a pension of £19 per week. £19 per week. What an absolute joke. I did not want the same fate, and I wanted to be able to help him having sponged off him for the best part of 27 years.

I knew that I was missing something and in 2005 I met Mark, my business partner, great friend and investment partner. And co-author of this book, of course.

Those 2 months were the best, most exciting turning points in my life. If this is the beginning for you, despite all the things you want; the things you don't have yet, revel in this time of excitement and change and mystery and the opportunity for something new and better.

Since then, since finding what I consider to be my purpose and what I am meant to do, everything has accelerated so fast and I have learned so much that sometimes I wonder what on earth I was doing for 27 years.

And not a day of it since then has been work.

Mark and I really have had the most amazing journey and I feel very fortunate to have forged such a relationship with such a great guy, and someone with such vast knowledge.

I was out of debt by April and in the same year I partnered with Mark [my interest payments alone were over £2,000 per month - more than I was earning], we reached a £1million Property portfolio [most of which was gained through one simple remortgage of my existing house] and job replacing income by the end of that year, and Progressive started to grow into a £Multi-million business.

Since then we've used the life coaching training to rescue a personal development company. We invested 6 figures into delivering courses for many people, and have grown that business to help people with their mindset, beliefs and results. "The mindset without the skillset will leave you upset." Once we hit the 300 property mark we set up a Lettings Agency with an expert in the field. Progressive Lets has become one of the largest Letting Agencies in the area, and is another income vehicle we didn't plan or dream of when we started buying our little single let 'grot-boxes.'

I really don't consider this to be 'impressive.' Being in our early 30's, we still have so much to learn and experience. I plan to be alive until I'm at least 85, and my exit strategy out of business and property is death.

This business actually isn't difficult. It's not easy, but it is just as easy to do it as it is not to do it. Follow the system, tap into passion and enjoyment, and go and get all the things you deserve. Property saved my life in spite of all my mistakes, and you've likely got a much better grounding and life experience than I had when I started, so you'll get success even quicker.

If only I had started sooner, but then I guess we all say that, don't we? And I now know that **Now** is always the best time.

It's funny because so many people think they have missed the boat with property. I thought that myself for about 4 years. I was looking at 3 bed houses for £70,000 in 2003. And I did nothing [but watch them go up and up and up and tell people stories about why I didn't-couldn't-wouldn't-shouldn't buy them]. These are worth over £150,000 now, even after the crash. I am just so glad that I know what I know now. Now is always the best time.

Things just keep moving for Mark and I now and we have newer, bigger goals. We have finished writing our fourth book and building our portfolio both for us and our investors daily. We've had offers to do TV shows, invited to appear on the 'Secret Millionaire,' endless Joint Ventures and business partner alliances, and met some really great people. It is amazing what a bit of momentum can do. It is the security that I feel from having a property portfolio that will look after me for the rest of my life that enables me to really go for it in other areas too.

Mark about Rob

It's Rob's drive and focus that inspire me the most. When I first met him he knew only the basics about property, but within his first 9 months his portfolio was up over £1 million [and he was £30,000 in debt at the time].

I have not met many people who have the ability to do this and the fact that he has done it in a very short space of time gives me the evidence I need to know that you can do the same.

Rob encouraged me to start out on our own and we haven't looked back since. I think it is his ability to just go for it and make things work regardless of what people say that keeps us going when many people have been saying [through the last 5 years] that the property market is dead. If we believed them we would still be employed and not have the freedom or the results.

He learns very quickly and has seriously added to his skills since I have known him. Sometimes he thinks so much to the future that he forgets about detail, and I have had to help him with his driving licence, a couple of parking tickets, the odd speeding fine and some household insurance. I feel like his PA sometimes and wonder if he could manage his way out of a paper bag.

If it wasn't for him we'd probably just be buying properties. That would of course be fine, but we wouldn't have the businesses that support it and create more income. I'm sure when you meet Rob he'll share just how many opportunities and income strategies there are to 'bolt-on' to 'Buy to Let' that will turn a few grand to many millions, with proper application and planning.

Your figures & projections

Your rules

Pages 74/5, 96/7 and 102

Enjoy filling in the questions below, they are tested and just writing them down will increase your chances 10 fold of achieving them.

Remember; be as specific as You can:

Your Vision, Big picture & Purpose:

[Wealth to change the world? A higher standard of living for you and the ones you love? Shelter or charity? Freedom? Financial Independence? A collection of supercars?]

_____

_____

_____

_____

_____

_____

_____

_____

_____

_____

Where are You Now?

Your Equity statement: pages 68, 79/80, 102/103

[State exactly where you are. Subtract your total debt from the equity in your assets and your savings. It's great to go back to this year after year to see your progress]:

Equity in assets:

_____

_____

Cash & savings:

_____

_____

Fixed expenses [pcm or pa]:

_____

_____

Estimated variable expenses [pcm or pa]:

_____

_____

Value of Possessions:

_____

_____

All debt ex. mortgages [loans, credit cards, hp etc]

_____

_____

Total personal equity [equity in assets + cash – debt]:

_____

_____

What specifically do you want to enable you to achieve Your goals?

[How many properties do you want in your portfolio. How much cash do you want per year? Is it passive? Do you want to work or retire, and by what date? Property full time, part time or leveraged? This is your means of getting your goals]:

_____

_____

_____

_____

_____

_____

_____

_____

_____

_____

_____

_____

_____

_____

_____

Your goals:

[Best selling author? Property expert status? A self built mansion? A collection of supercars? 10 properties? 100 properties? Body building world champion? Pro golfer? Lady of leisure married to James Bond? Go for it; everything that you want]

_____

_____

_____

_____

_____

_____

_____

_____

Your unique talents, skills, expertise and qualities:

Pages 75/6, 98/99, 104

[Don't be shy, we all have them. Anything at all, you might be surprised]

_____

_____

_____

_____

_____

_____

and a few more lines, because there is always more!

_____

_____

_____

_____

_____

_____

— _____

_____

_____

Your values:

Pages 75/6, 98/9

[What are the core values you'd like the world to recognise about you and your property business]

_____

_____

_____

_____

_____

_____

_____

_____

_____

_____

The Law of compounding: Page 38 & 59

On Page 38 we were discussing the figures using the Rule of 72 and the Laws of compounding and leverage.

Here are the calculations behind the figures shown on Page 58

The Rule of 72:
5% growth: 72/5 = 14.4 years to turn £5,000 into £10,000
8% growth: 72/8 = 9 years to turn £5,000 into £10,000
11.74% growth: 72/11.74 = 6 years 48 days to turn £5,000 into £10,000

Property growth on the example £100,000 Property in 10 years:
5% growth: £100,000 becomes £162,889
8% growth: £100,000 becomes £215,892
11.74% growth: £100,000 becomes £303,450

Example capital employed [spent] to purchase a Property worth £100,000 for £85,000: £5,00

[This example takes into account all fees of buying a Property such as valuations, conveyancing, solicitors fees and legal work, Land registry and transfer fees, office copy and disbursements, broker fees and so on. Using our suggested investment model, you would get your £15,000 deposit back, therefore it is not employed or spent capital].

Therefore, using the example of 11.74% growth every year for 10 years, your growth would be:

Total Property value: £303,450
minus existing mortgage: £85,000 = £218,450

£218,450/5000 = 4369% return on your capital spent [ROCE]

Interest only vs. repayment: Page 79

Option 1: You invest the £20,000 and with it, using your increasing knowledge, you can plausibly buy one property per year with the same capital. For ease of figures; these properties are worth £100,000 based on today's figures.

Compounded equity at end of yr 5 [based on 5% growth]: £168,461

Property 1: Value after year 5: £127,628
Property 2: Value after year 5: £127,628
Property 3: Value after year 5: £127,628
Property 4: Value after year 5: £127,628
Property 5: Value after year 5: £127,628

Total value: £638,140

Less 5 mortgages of £469,679

£638,140 - £469,679 = £168,461

"Multiple Streams of Property Income"

Simply relying on buy to let to fund your retirement or get out of your job is not enough in this fast changing economy:

"Never depend on a single income" – Warren Buffett

Multiple Streams of Property Income takes you through UK Property Multi-Millionaire Rob Moore's 6 Stage Investor System, taking you on a proven journey from new investor to £Multi-Million property business owner, revealing and detailing multiple income strategies through property investing for long term and more short term, immediate cashflow.

Find on Amazon or at: **www.progressiveproperty.co.uk**

"Make Cash in a Property Market Crash"

If you'd like to cash in on the crash like almost all millionaires and billionaires do, create more Cashflow, buy assets at rock bottom prices, replace your pension quicker than previously possible, and have much less competition, then this book is for you.

Read this book and you will discover how to:

- Make cashflow faster in the crash
- Spot market trends and cash in for life
- Buy property with bigger cashflow and even bigger discounts now
- Observe the masses, do the opposite and profit with less competition
- Create a property buying system that removes your personal input
- Where to buy, when to buy, what to buy and how to buy, now

Find on Amazon or at: **www.progressiveproperty.co.uk**

"Progressive in Property: Beginners to Winners"

If you want to make more money using the most proven asset for wealth creation, property investment, and be inspired to financial success, then the UK's best selling property investment book on launch, is for you

"Progressive in Property: Beginners to Winners" reveals multiple property income strategies through the stories of beginner investors who joined the Progressive Property Community and succeeded big. Many transformed their lives and income [up to £10,000 NET cashflow per month] within 12-24 months, and you can too, because they show you how.

Find on Amazon or at: **www.progressiveproperty.co.uk**

"Be Your Own Bank – the Joint Venture Blueprint"

2nd Edition 8 CD Audio Programme plus Loaded Bonus CD ROM

The No Money Down, Joint Venture Blueprint for Property Investment & business with other people's money, time and experience.

Learn how to raise finance for business & investing without banks or mortgages, and create bigger cashflowing portfolios & businesses in turbulent times.

Includes legal agreements, contracts, templates, scripts, JV checklists, personality profiling, influence strategies to close the deals and bank the money, plus 21 places to meet Multi-Millionaires and 12 ways to structure the finance/partnerships detailed.

"Through Progressive I have raised around £600 of JV Finance" – Nick Hague

www.progressiveproperty.co.uk/eshop

"Advanced Bareknuckle Negotiation"

8 DVD's , 5 Bonus CD's & Lifetime online membership community

"Get MORE deals, MORE often, with Bigger Discounts, in less time"

Learn how to negotiate powerfully, confidently and influence anyone in any situation to get what you want, ethically. Persuade and negotiate so powerfully that the other party think it was their decision and thank you for it.

13 discs and over 15 hours of underground strategies and tactics that you wouldn't want any vendor or seller to know, from 2 of the best negotiators in the UK, and one internationally acclaimed.

www.progressiveproperty.co.uk/eshop

"Progressive Property Super Conference DVD sets from 2010, 2011, 2012 & 2013

Entire Bundle of 42 Discs including all keynote speeches

The *Largest UK Specific Property Event* of the year, every year since 2010, headlined by some of the biggest names in business such as James Caan, Lord Sugar, Bob Geldof, Karren Brady & Frank Bruno

PLUS: All the DVD sets include ALL the 2nd & 3rd stage talks so if you missed any at the event you will be able to watch *all 42 keynote speeches* at your own leisure

"It all started at the Property SuperConference – since then I have bought 21 properties and it's all thanks to you guys " – Iain Wallis

www.progressiveproperty.co.uk/eshop

"Property Auction Profits - How to Gain an Unfair Advantage at Property Auctions"

6 DVD's , 6 Bonus CD's, FREE Auction Tour, Bonus Recorded Trainings, P.A.P Community & more

For any existing property investor who wants to buy more discounted cashflowing properties, Property Auction Profits offers a timeless and very effective strategy. Especially powerful in the current economic climate where asset gain is limited and cashflow is paramount. Also highly recommended for novices who want to find a niche strategy, get started, avoid costly mistakes & create quicker income.

Would you like to buy auction bargains with massive uplift potential and higher than average cash return on your or other people's money? Auctions have been and continue to be the serious investors' playground. If you want to join the elite, this is the place to start.

Bonuses included in the pack:

- Huge Value – Free Auction day tour with Mark Homer at Live Auction
- Private invitation to 2 Live Bonus Webinars with Mark Homer and Daniel Wagner
- The Complete 6 CD Set course Manual
- Access to the Private Property Auction Profits Community group
- Special Unlimited Access to the Online Resource Centre

"We flipped a property and made £23K NET – thanks guys" – Francis [& Jane] Dolley

www.progressiveproperty.co.uk/eshop

Call us: **0845 1309505**

Email us: **rob.moore@progressiveproperty.co.uk**

"The Progressive Insider Secrets Property Investing Masterclass" 3 Day Training

The UK's Flagship, all encompassing Property Investing Training Programme.

The flagship Progressive Event & the course that many of the well known professionals are attending. Designed to take you from where you are [Beginner or Intermediate] to Professional Property Investor.

Uniquely; with 1 year's full follow up support & Community membership for FREE.

Attending this Essential Masterclass you will get:

- 7 Low or No Money Down Creative Financing Techniques SS/FL, LO/JV, IR, CP, MH & DoT [what all these stand for & how to use them for cashflow]
- 32 Advanced Negotiation Strategies & 7 Low Cost Deal Marketing Strategies
- How to go from small-time Investor to Property professional in 12-24 Months
- How to Leverage & realistically Quit Your Job & go part time within 30-90 days
- The Progressive Property Multi £M Deal Scrutiniser™ - Value £1000
- Your local Goldmine area Training: Find Deals Right Under Your Nose [Record: 6mins 17secs]
- 21 Personal Strategy with an Expert Property Mentor – Personal & Bespoke to You
- The latest Tax, Marketing, Refurb, Valuation, Cash Recycling & Deal Sourcing Strategies

"We decided to call an estate agent and he has offered us a 15 property deal. All 15 are cash flowing. Wow! Take action and look what happens. Once again thank you for a fantastic and illuminating weekend" - Alan and David

www.progressiveproperty.co.uk/eshop

Call us: **0845 1309505**

Email us: **rob.moore@progressiveproperty.co.uk**

"SuperHMO Masterclass" 3 Day Training

The UK'S only fully comprehensive Multi-Let/HMO Cashflow course. All 5 HMO/ Multi-Let models Detailed in one 3 day 'Super Course' – including 'No Deposit Down' HMO's

Uniquely; with I year's full follow up support & Community membership for FREE.

On this all encompassing 3 day training you will learn in detail:

- The 5 proven HMO/Multi-Let Cashflow models revealed, & detailed – "Boutique," "Blue collar," "Post grad," "Student," & "LHA/DSS."
- Realistically make between £300-£900 per property, per month, NET income after all costs
- Learn multiple low/no money down HMO/Multi-Let finance techniques in detail – JV, MLWTS, Commercial finance & options/IC's
- Every script, system, checklist, spreadsheet & time saving model Included FREE, to make this an *HMO/Multi-Let Cashflow business in a box*

Never before in the property industry have ALL HMO models been brought together in ONE training. You are investing in 5 £1,000 courses in ONE*

"This course has given me new insight in how I can still continue with a multi-let strategy but with little initial outlay" - Jane Beard

"We make £4,900 NET Cashflow from our Multi-Let Without the Sweat Properties, and we did it in 5 months!" Francis & Jane Dolley

www.progressiveproperty.co.uk/eshop

Call us: **0845 1309505**

Email us: **rob.moore@progressiveproperty.co.uk**

"No Money Down Cashflow Control" 2 Day Training

No Deposit No Mortgage Property Control for £400 - £2000 Per Month Per Property Cashflow

The NMDCC Training is for you if you would like to build a future portfolio but don't have a deposit, can't get a mortgage, don't want a mortgage or want to use other people s money.

This 2 Day Intensive NMDCC Training [including Lease Options, EDC's, Instalment Contracts, Assisted Sales] will teach you how to:

- Make £400 - £2,000 pcm net Cashflow from each Deal Plus minimum £3K in fees
- Control Property with No Deposit or Mortgage, Even if You have Poor Credit
- Build a faster Portfolio, get Gazumped Less & Reduce Your Financial Risk
- Convert Leads Yourself: *Live Deals* Converted on the day from Your Local Newspapers

"It was a fantastic course and fits nicely with our strategy. We have taken action and had success and we approached a tame EA and when we were viewing an apartment block with her I just dived in using the scripts and approaches Trevor had given us and discussed creative ways of moving those deals she can't because of negative equity or no equity, and also unrealistic expectations on price." - Paul Crain

"I've done over 20 deals with other people's money, and have over £35,000 per year net cashflow, and it's all thanks to Progressive" – Trevor Cutmore

www.progressiveproperty.co.uk/eshop

Call us: **0845 1309505**

Email us: **rob.moore@progressiveproperty.co.uk**

"Deal Packaging for Cashflow: Intensive" 2 Day Training

Make £3K - £8K per Month as a Property 'Deal Packager + Trader'

Monetising 'Reject' Deals You Don't Keep in Your Portfolio

It is THE Property Cashflow course in the UK: This course will help you turn your deals into cash [even deals you don't want for yourself] and help YOU with more immediate Cashflow.

The Benefits of Attending this Essential Deal Packaging Course & What you will learn:

- 11 Ways to package and sell on almost ANY deal for Positive Cashflow
- How to 'Package' the Deals to make them Irresistible to Investors
- How & where to find JV Partners & Investors who will Fund you and Buy your Deals
- How to Create Magnetic Marketing Packs that Attract Clients to You
- How to Monetise almost Every Deal: From 30% BMV Discounts to Negative Equity: & where to Find Each 'Level' of Investor'
- No ongoing management or tenant hassles to deal with – once the deal is sold it's sold! You just move on to the next deal.

A great strategy for cashflow because just one deal traded per month = £3k - £8k income that month. Get the money in your bank account TODAY instead of having all your funds locked up in property for the long term! No mortgage, debt, loans or any kind of borrowing required.

You can package and sell deals using just a mobile phone and computer – you could literally trade deals from the beach if you wanted to.

"I've made £58,000 Cash Income in 9 months Selling Deals thanks to Rob, Mark & the Progressive trainings. These guys talk real sense and no BS" Geoff Whittaker

www.progressiveproperty.co.uk/eshop

Call us: **0845 1309505**

Email us: **rob.moore@progressiveproperty.co.uk**

"Estate Agents Secrets" Sourcing Free Deals | Day Training

The Shocking Secrets Only Ex-Estate Agents Will Tell You About Sourcing 28% - 62% BMV Discounted BMV Property From Agents For Free.

I Day Intensive Course PLUS I Year Full Continued Support.

In the Recession & Crash, getting Deals through Estate Agents has become easier than ever, but ONLY if you know how.

Get in with the Agents, become the 'Banker' rather than the 'Binner', & use little known strategies including "The Long Game" & "Time Bridging," as well as 21 Advanced Negotiation strategies that have made us £5,000 to £10,000 extra per deal across more than 350 properties.

And in being at this Course, you will learn:

"I've had an offer accepted on a one bed flat in Swindon that we identified was initially on at £70,000 when we saw it. It was [then] on for £53,000 and our offer was accepted at £40,500" - Sebastian Brown

www.progressiveproperty.co.uk/eshop

Call us: **0845 1309505**

Email us: rob.moore@progressiveproperty.co.uk

"The Progressive VIP Property Millionaires Club"
12 Month Accountability Programme

By Application only & strictly limited availability

On the 12 Month VIP Programmes you get:

- 12 Months of training, hand holding support, mentorship & accountability
- The UK's Largest Professional Property Community with over £65M of JV's in 3 years!
- Ongoing Investing, Cashflow & Public Speaking Training, & possible JV's with Progressive
- The Best & Biggest Discounts to all other Progressive Trainings

A close knit, lifelong social community of holidays, competitions, field trips, tours, training to be a mentor and trainer yourself, VIP only events and so much more...

www.progressiveproperty.co.uk/eshop

Call us: **0845 1309505**

Email us: **rob.moore@progressiveproperty.co.uk**

Remember that You can be, do and have anything you want. Never let the others and the voices tell you otherwise. We believe in you... ☺